Who Is a Muslim?

Who Is a Muslim?

Orientalism and Literary Populisms

MARYAM WASIF KHAN

Fordham University Press

NEW YORK   2021

Fordham University Press gratefully acknowledges financial assistance and support provided for the publication of this book by the Mushtaq Gurmani School of Humanities and Social Sciences, LUMS University, Lahore.

Copyright © 2021 Fordham University Press

All rights reserved. No part of this publication may be reproduced, stored in a retrieval system, or transmitted in any form or by any means—electronic, mechanical, photocopy, recording, or any other—except for brief quotations in printed reviews, without the prior permission of the publisher.

Fordham University Press has no responsibility for the persistence or accuracy of URLs for external or third-party Internet websites referred to in this publication and does not guarantee that any content on such websites is, or will remain, accurate or appropriate.

Fordham University Press also publishes its books in a variety of electronic formats. Some content that appears in print may not be available in electronic books.

Visit us online at www.fordhampress.com.

Library of Congress Cataloging-in-Publication Data available online at https://catalog.loc.gov.

Printed in the United States of America

23 22 21   5 4 3 2 1

First edition

For my Nano, Soheila Khalid; my Dado, Shaukat Mumtaz Khan;
and my Papa, Mumtaz Ahmad Khan (1920–2014),
who raised me as all kinds of Muslim

and

for my Amma, Zeba Aziz; and my Abu, Wasif M. Khan,
who love me in the bravest and best of ways.

Note on Transliteration

For all transliterations from Urdu, I have followed the *Annual of Urdu Studies* guide (2007) with some variations that are available as follows. I have not transliterated each and every passage but rather privileged words and phrases that are critical for those readers of Urdu looking to trace particular concepts and meanings as they emerge in the modern vocabulary.

Vowels

a, ā, e, ē, i, ī, o, ō, u, ū, ai, au

Consonant

bē	b
pē	p
tē	t
ṭē	ṭ
s̱ē	s̱
jīm	j
čē	č
ḥē	ḥ
k̲ē	k̲
dāl	d
ḍāl	ḍ
zāl	ž

NOTE ON TRANSLITERATION

rē	r
ṛē	ṛ
zē	z
sīn	s
shīn	sh
ṣuād	ṣ
źuād	ź
ṭō'ē	ṭ
żō'ē	ż
'ain	'
ġain	ġh
fē	f
qāf	q
kāf	k
gāf	g
lām	l
mīm	m
nūn	n/ñ
vā'ō	v
hē	h
dō čāshmī hē	ħ
yē	y
hamzā	'

Who Is a Muslim?

Introduction

Who Is a Muslim?

> Much of the personal investment in this study derives from my awareness of being an "Oriental" as a child growing up in two British colonies. All of my education, in those colonies (Palestine and Egypt) and in the United States, has been Western, and yet that deep early awareness has persisted. In many ways my study of Orientalism has been an attempt to inventory the traces upon me, the Oriental subject, of the culture whose domination has been so powerful a factor in the life of all Orientals.
> —EDWARD SAID, *ORIENTALISM*

> Unlike many Muslims of today, the Muslims of the Balkan-to-Bengal complex did not feel the need to articulate or legitimate their Muslim ness / their Islam by mimesis of a pristine time of the earliest generations of the community (the *salaf*). Rather they felt able to be Muslim in explorative, creative, and contrary trajectories . . .
> —SHAHAB AHMED, *WHAT IS ISLAM: THE IMPORTANCE OF BEING ISLAMIC*

This book argues that a modern Muslim identity, one that has taken on dangerously orthodox, populist dimensions in contemporary Pakistani culture, has evolved from what was essentially a moment of orientalist literary invention in the late eighteenth and early nineteenth centuries. It is informed by a single question—*who is a Muslim?*—one that is and has historically remained at the core of early modern and modern Western literariness, but that in the past century or so has taken on precarious significance in postcolonial Muslim societies and nation states as well. It shows how modern Urdu prose fiction, from the moment of its inception at Fort William College in colonial North India, becomes inextricably bound with the task of defining *who is a Muslim*. Over the course of some three centuries, this question and its answers, originally posed within a series of British orientalist fictions and treatises, become recurrent staples of prose texts that range from the literary or canonical to the popular, first in the colonial North India and subsequently in the postcolonial state of Pakistan.

The epigraphs that frame this introductory section are central to the methodological and ethical directions that this book takes, asking us to consider two aspects of postcolonial Muslim identity. The first, a digression of sorts by Edward Said, offers *Orientalism*, that sweeping history of the socio-cultural politics and intellectual disciplines that undergirded the Western imperial project of the post-Industrial era, as a personal endeavor of sorts, an attempt to read oneself, the individual subject, as indelibly marked by the centuries-long cultural transformation of colonized societies. The second, borrowed from Shahab Ahmed's magisterial study, *What is Islam?* directs us further into orientalized spaces and territories and asks us to confront the problem of how and when modern Muslim subjects in societies ranging from Egypt to Indonesia came to measure themselves, albeit to different degrees, against the classical period of Islam, one that is distinguished by the life of the Prophet Muhammad and his companions and the generation that followed. By imagining this moment as original and therefore authentic, exemplifying a "model Islamic disciplinary arrangement," modern Muslims cast off "subsequent developments as pale reflections or decadent versions" of an incontrovertible truth, thus disassociating themselves from half a millennium or so of their own continuous formation.[1]

Despite the ostensible distance of the intellectual motives, disciplinary underpinnings and historical archives that inform each work, they bear witness to a singular concern. How do we understand, in our various presents, the widescale transformations of peoples, practices, and traditions forced by European imperialisms of the modern era? In this book, I attempt to grapple with this question by focusing on the extended legacies of eighteenth-century British orientalism in the Indian subcontinent—in particular, the orientalist construction of the category of "literature" in the language we have come to know today as Urdu. More specifically, I examine the orientalist reinvention of the Mahometan—a longstanding and variously purposed figure in European literature—and the historical processes by which he traverses the realm of the literary to reappear in the colony as Muslim, a religio-political subject of the modern colony.

In the past five or so years that I have spent teaching and writing in Lahore, Pakistan, a city I imagine as home, I have had to reconsider what it means to be an intellectual in our times. I had imagined, for much of my scholarly career, that the study of Western literature, world literature, or even the history of orientalism had little to do with the oppressive religio-nationalist discourse that appears to dominate every aspect of life in contemporary Pakistan. The simultaneous acts of studying eighteenth-century English fantasies of the Muslim world and teaching Pakistani undergraduates the enduring relevance of Western culture to the postcolonial humanistic project forced me to "inventory" the *many* traces of orientalism, to use Said's words, upon myself as a historical subject.[2] I have had to understand that the "traces" of orientalism are legion, as much a part of my journey as a secular humanist educated at elite North American institutions, as they are of the powerful, orthodox narratives of religious supremacy and nationalism whose intertwined interests have forced ordinary Pakistani citizens—poets, intellectuals, leftist workers, anti-nationalists, feminists, and both ethnic and religious minorities—into positions of physical and attitudinal exile.

Thus, I attempt to understand a postcolonial present that is rife with religio-nationalist populisms, and to historicize the increasingly dangerous inseparability of the supposedly distinct realms of the literary, the political, and religious. I hope to elaborate the processes and mechanisms through which British orientalism—from its popular incarnations in eighteenth-century oriental tales to its more conclusive scholarly endeavors—sets into motion a powerful and irreversible religio-cultural transformation in the North Indian colony. This book, then, is as much a literary history of the ideas and institutions that made up "that formidable structure of cultural domination" as it is an exercise in confronting the cultural ideals that make up modern identity for a postcolonial citizen.[3]

Orientalism and Secular Critique

Since the publication of Said's *Orientalism* (1978) some forty odd years ago, both the work and the eponymous structure that it refers to have become contested categories. While it is difficult to reiterate all of the resulting scholarly engagements with Said's arguments and archive, Aamir Mufti's *Forget English! Orientalism and World Literatures* (2016),

Srinivas Aravamudan's *Enlightenment Orientalism: Resisting the Rise of the Novel* (2012), Urs App's *The Birth of Orientalism* (2011), Suzanne Marchand's *German Orientalism in the Age of Empire* (2009), and Carol Breckenridge and Peter van der Veer's *Orientalism and the Postcolonial Predicament: Perspectives on South Asia* (1993) can be counted among some of the more compelling volumes on this question. Almost all of these works explore the contours and possibilities opened up by *Orientalism* for disciplines such as comparative literature, English, religious studies, and history.

In a partial departure from the broad concerns that inform the abovementioned works, I argue that eighteenth-century Anglo-French orientalist fictions, heralded by works such as Antoine Galland's *Mille et Une Nuits* (~1703), and the scholarly orientalism pioneered by figures such as William Jones quite literally invent, and subsequently import, the idea of a modern, religio-political Muslim identity to the North Indian colony. Less an explication of Said's argument and more an elaboration of his method and ostensibly contentious claims, I show how what can only be termed a crisis of religio-populism in a postcolonial site such as Pakistan has its antecedents in a seemingly obscure moment in the history of British orientalism.

In my use of the term "British orientalism," I gesture toward the massive eighteenth- and nineteenth-century intellectual project, engineered by scholars, travelers, writers, artists, and bureaucrats, whose specific task was to amass knowledge and expand the imaginative possibilities around the territory that was then loosely known as "the Orient." British orientalism, to be clear, was one part of a much larger European complex, whose major players, France and Britain, were joined in the nineteenth century by a number of German orientalists. While German orientalism has been defended in part by Marchand as a scholarly practice that was not "primordially or perpetually defined by imperialist relationships," it remained crucial, as Mufti argues, to the broader imperial effort that defined Europe's relations with South Asia and North Africa in the late eighteenth and nineteenth centuries.[4] Described by the latter in *Forget English!*, eighteenth- and nineteenth-century orientalisms were "simultaneously singular and pan-European" hydra-like systems of knowledge about the orient.[5] In my use of the term "British orientalism," I invoke both the discipline as it was broadly developed and expanded in modern Europe, but also the specific fashion in which it emerged given British imperial interests and expansion in South Asia, Egypt, and adjoining Arab territories.

That is to say, after Said's searing exposition, orientalism, long considered an academic discipline of philological bearings in Europe, could no longer be treated as an apolitical or hermetic intellectual exercise. Neither could Western humanists defend its practices—literary, visual, and scholarly—as benign representations, for as Said argued, orientalism did not merely represent; it, quite literally, *invented* the orients and oriental identities it imagined.[6] While the latter claim has been hotly critiqued by self-described Marxist scholars in particular, their accounts emerge from narrow disciplinary grounds that fail to consider the powerful role the idea and construction of literature has played in shaping colonial and later postcolonial cultures. To phrase the matter more succinctly, we can turn to Mufti's unequivocal definition of orientalism as "the *cultural logic of colonial rule* in the post-Industrial revolution era," or what he calls the "cultural logic of the bourgeois order in its outward or non-domestic orientation."[7] Orientalism, thus considered, is the literal export of structures of knowledge and knowing from the metropolis to the colony, imposed upon peoples and practices designated as "oriental." Literature, a category that is conceived and constructed first in eighteenth-century England and then in colonial India within orientalist institutions such as the Royal Asiatic Society and Fort William College, is instrumental for both the colonial, and subsequently, the national project of the postcolonial state. The newly invented "literature" of an equally newly invented language, in this case, modern Urdu, I argue, is not merely the literal realization of a moment in eighteenth-century British orientalism but becomes foundational for the formation of a modern Muslim identity in North India, one that persists and evolves in accordance with its orientalist ideals well into the present moment.

There remain some misconceptions regarding orientalism, which are worthy of mention given the scope of this project. One of the more elementary of these is the trend in eighteenth-century English literary studies, where a number of scholars, including the late Srinivas Aravamudan and Felicity Nussbaum, have argued for the rehabilitation of forms of "Enlightenment orientalism," which Aravamudan, in particular, described as self-critical, intended to encourage "mutual understanding" across cultures of East and West.[8] Aravamudan, Nussbaum, and Ros Ballaster, among others, invoke the eighteenth-century English oriental tale as an example of Enlightenment orientalism, reading the genre's critique of a rising English identity as a kind of productive or positivist orientalism. This position, as I show over the course of this book, is only tenable if our understanding of orientalism remains restricted to the metropolis. While Aravamudan's or Ballaster's insightful readings into the political and social positions taken up by the oriental tale remain invaluable to eighteenth-century studies, they fail to consider that the oriental tale continued its career beyond the metropolis. Traveling from the European Republic of Letters to a colonial city such as Calcutta, the oriental tale became a prototype of sorts for the invention of new and useful literature for Indian natives, transforming aesthetic traditions and extant textual practices for perpetuity.[9]

On a slightly divergent note, it is also worth briefly clarifying Said's idea of the secular, a critical element of his method that has serious relevance to the arguments and ethical positions that move this book. Emerging out of the premise visible in *Orientalism* as well—that all texts, literary and other, are essentially "worldly," historical events—Said's essay argues for a new critical practice in the academy and beyond, one that he describes as "secular."[10] Described with startling clarity, secular criticism is a practice premised on a "suspicion" of "totalizing concepts," "reified objects," "guilds," and other religio-nationalist orthodoxies that seem all too familiar in our present moment.[11] At the heart of this concept, however, are not religion or ethnic politics, but nationalism and the nation-state, for it is within the latter that the falsely organic ideals of belonging and kinship are reinvigorated to create socio-political *and* religious structures of majority and exclusion. This does not mean, however, that we limit the possibilities Said's conception of the secular offers. His powerful reimagining is one that is oppositional to *any* form of hegemony that seeks to exclude, be it ethno-nationalism, religious orthodoxy, or other. The task of a secular critic, as Said saw it, was to function as "life-enhancing, and constitutively opposed to every form of tyranny, domination, and abuse."[12] In other words, the secular critic resists *any* form of coercive authority, religiously deployed or other. As Bruce Robbins reminds us, Said's method—exemplified in *Orientalism* as an elaboration of what a secular scholarship could look like—offered a new humanism, one that existed in a critical, paradoxical continuity with its predecessor. This last point marks also what I can only describe as an ethics of generosity that Said brought to the field of postcolonial studies, one that is increasingly marked by scholars whose rigid positions against modernity and strident calls to recover an idyllic precolonial past only obfuscate the potential of a meaningful postcolonial engagement.

It is with this concept of critique at the forefront, then, that this book traces the powerful influence British orientalism and its attendant institutions exercised on the invention and subsequent canonization of a modern Urdu prose literature in North India. It offers, therefore, a historical elaboration of how a series of writers, scholars, and entrepreneurs, as well as research institutions and educational networks, were able to produce a literary corpus that accorded with orientalist conceptions of the forms that a "Mahometan" literature could take. But the process by which the Mahometan of the eighteenth-century Anglo-French oriental tale becomes the Muslim of North Indian colony—the latter, at once a religio-political and aesthetic category—is by no means a dormant legacy of empire and orientalism, nor can it be divided along the overt lines of "secular" (here: a- or non-religious) and "religious." In our present, the powerful traces of the British orientalist project in North India exhibit themselves in the affiliation of Urdu—today Pakistan's declared national language—with Sunni Islam. This is a symbiotic partnership that over the course of a century and by way of a wide range of aesthetic forms—novels, stories, and television serials—has subsumed the national into the religious, the vernacular into the sacred, the state into a living Mecca, in short, the Pakistani into a Salafi Muslim (a term reserved for the first followers of Muhammad and his call to Islam in 610 A.D.). This impulse, which in our times is nothing short of religio-populist in its bearings, is gradually suffocating regional vernaculars such as Pashto and Sindhi, a diversity of folk practices, lived Islams, and above all, the claims of women and religious and ethnic minorities to dignified citizenship.

This is not a study of theology or law. Nor does it intend to essay a suitable, alternative response to the question that it argues has been coded into the canon of modern Urdu. This is a study of how a systematic series of answers to the question *"Who is a Muslim"* is disseminated predominantly through the imperially invented domain of literature, first in eighteenth-century England, subsequently in colonial India, and in its most alarming iteration, in present-day Pakistan. In answering this central question, I am not, either by training or by interest, attempting to solicit a pure Islam or a better way of being Muslim, or reclaiming an idyllic Muslim past in precolonial India. My concern arrives out of the danger and political isolation that populist responses to this question pose to so many individuals and communities in a postcolonial Muslim state such as Pakistan. My task, as a secular critic, is to understand how, and through what historical institutions and ideas, has the present moment been brought to its crisis. The various literary members of a modern, colonial vernacular, such as Urdu, I argue, have been and continue to be instrumental in the creation and perpetuation of a narrative that overwhelmingly defines the exclusionary and evangelical realms of culture and politics in contemporary Pakistan.

Confronting the Literary Canon

In recruiting literary texts, particularly those intended for broad, almost mass consumption as historical sources on the way Muslims are defined by eighteenth- and nineteenth-century orientalists, colonial administrators, and North Indian, later Pakistani readers and writers, I am arguing that we ethically scrutinize the domain of literature for its complicity in the violence and exclusions enacted by religio-nationalist politics. The idea of literature, as it is understood first in colonial North India and in the postcolonial state, develops in the late eighteenth and early nineteenth centuries under the aegis of British orientalists and supporting institutions at home and in the colony. I show how a number of fictions—including the canonical *Bāġh-o Bahār* (1803) of Fort William College—that are initially developed as a *literature* for Urdu under colonial patronage form the ideological basis for a modern Muslim imaginary. While this impulse manifests itself in the form of numerous novels and short stories that critics and scholars dismiss or discount as prototypes (Nazir Ahmad's *Mirāt al-'Arūs* [1862]) or bestsellers (Hijazi's *Muhammad bin Qāsim* [1945] or Umera Ahmad's *Pīr-e Kāmil* [2004]) the imbrication of the popular or the low-brow with the scholarly and the empirical is, in fact, essential to the totalizing discourse of orientalism and to its legacies in the colony. This book, then, asks for a radical reconsideration of what constitutes the "canon" of Urdu prose fiction by suggesting that this entire body of works evolves in accordance with, rather than in contradiction to, its orientalist origins.

The troubled coming-of-age of the English term "literature" has been explored from various ends by Marxist critics and postcolonial scholars, including Terry Eagleton and Gauri Viswanathan, both of whom have variously argued that the idea of English literature as a discipline and body of canonical works emerged in nineteenth-century England as a means of containing a burgeoning middle-class.[13] Offering a nuanced examination of the term, its transformations in Enlightenment Europe and then the colonies, Vinay Dharwadker reminds us that literature evolved from suggesting letteredness and knowledge to a broader ideal of an aesthetically refined textual body suggestive of a certain national character or spirit during the latter half of the eighteenth century.[14] Dharwadker, of course, draws on the detailed account offered by René Wellek in his essay "Literature and its Cognates," as well in his opus, *The Theory of Literature*, from which it becomes clear that while in early eighteenth-century usage "literature" implied a grounding in the knowledge of ancient Greek and Latin languages and works, by the second half of the century it had come to connote a body of writing. In Voltaire's 1751 use, "literature" refers to the genres of Italy, while L'Abbe Sabatier de Castes titled his 1772 book *Les Siècles de littérature francaise*, or The ages of

French literature, both inadvertently imbuing the notion of a collective body of works with a tentative sense of having to do with or belonging to a nation or a people.[15]

For an orientalist such as William Jones, then, the self-proclaimed "discoverer" of Sanskrit, the entire body of writing in that ancient language naturally came to constitute the basis of "Indian" *literature*. Somewhat differently, his successor, John Gilchrist, who took it upon himself to *invent* a new Indian vernacular, did so through the synchronized production of a body of largely fictional works, believing that the latter could revive Indian culture to the lost eminence of classical Europe itself. In other words, both Jones and Gilchrist, orientalists whose legacies I discuss at length in this project, rewrite entire traditions and aesthetic practices in both premodern and colonial North India as "literature," whether Indian, Urdu, Hindi, or vernacular. Because Jones, as M. H. Abrams reminds us, in the spirit of Longinus, the ancient rhetorician, had already defined and thus sequestered lyric poetry as the unique expression of a nation's character, the quest of invention focused largely on prose forms, which then bore the onus of functioning as both entertaining and useful.[16]

The English ideal of the term "literature," Michael Allen has argued, is at its heart a "disciplined reading practice," or more broadly, "a cultivated sensibility linked to civil norms of what it means to be educated," which by the eighteenth century becomes attached with markers of nation—whether these be origin, language, character, or domesticity.[17] When we turn to colonies such as Egypt or India, this distinctly English and orientalist ideal of literature comes to be erroneously conflated with the idea of *adab*, the untranslatable Arab, Turko-Indo-Persian concept of being mannered: cultivated in knowledge, the arts, and etiquette, a premodern practice distinctly removed from conceptions of modern nation-thinking.[18] That is to say, as colonial administrators undertook the task of producing the fictional works that would become the earliest examples of a *literature* of modern vernaculars such as Urdu and Hindi, the terms *adab* and *sahitya* are relieved of their broader implications and slowly designated as Urdu or Hindi equivalents of literature.[19]

Thus, a term such as *adab*, with all of its diverse implications (in North India *adab* privileged oral recitation, performance, etiquette, attention to linguistic register, above all else) is reduced to the realm of the textual by the late nineteenth century and begins to imitate European modes of self-historicization and progression. Urdu *literature*, in the then-orientalist (and now universally accepted) sense of the term, therefore, *begins* at Fort William College, Calcutta, a language school for young English officers founded by John Gilchrist in 1800. Mostly in the form of simple, moral stories, this orientalist inauguration of Urdu literature obscures several centuries of Indo-Persian oral fiction and lyric practices, including the widespread presence of the *dāstān*, that grand, morally disinclined fictional telling of alternative magical worlds navigated by great heroes and their companion tricksters. Though the College initially published the *ghazals* of then-revered court poets such as Mir Taqi Mir, by the mid–nineteenth century even that seemingly abstract, Arab-Persianate form of poetry was dismissed by colonial administrators as inappropriate and immoral. What I am briefly describing here, and what the first part of this book explores in some detail, is how an entirely *modern* European ideal of literature is imposed in the North Indian colony through orientalist institutions and individuals.

I argue, therefore, that the body of textual works we refer to as *literature* in Urdu is invented and organized for the particular purpose of moral, and subsequently, religious reform over the course of the nineteenth century. That is to say, prose literature in Urdu, from the moment of its inception in colonial Calcutta, is invested with the *authority* to designate and endorse certain ideals of Muslim practice, while excluding, even condemning, others, a practice entirely at odds with premodern Indo-Persian aesthetic practices. While in its early stages the Muslim of Urdu prose fictions is modeled on the Mahometan of the eighteenth-century English oriental tale, by the second half of the nineteenth century this same Muslim has to be refashioned to accord with colonial culture. The Mahometan, a staple protagonist of the oriental tale, is a refinement upon earlier European emblems of Islam, including the Shakespearean "Turk" or Moor, and or the medieval, all-purpose pagan. His figure precedes the more scientific religio-racial theorization of Arabs and Jews as Semites that orientalists such as Ernest Renan popularized in the nineteenth century. In the latter half of this book, I show how a rising Muslim nationalism in North India fashions itself on and against these early conceptions of the literary Mahometan, giving way in the present to an increasingly insular religio-nationalist definition of the Muslim self.

Literary histories for the most part tend to end on triumphant notes, their undertones often nationalist in nature. In the case of English, world anglophone and postcolonial literatures represent reparations for three centuries of imperialism. In the case of Egypt, the *nahdāh* is celebrated as a moment of literary and cultural awakening for a colonized people, a literary historicization that Allen has argued against in *In the Shadow of World Literature: Sites of Reading in Colonial Egypt*. Likewise, Hindi literature or a modern Hindi canon is directed by "standards proposed by early Western critics and the succeeding generation of Indian critics writing on canon formation."[20] American literature in the twentieth century, Juliana Spahr shows in her recent book, *Du Bois' Telegram: Literary Resistance and State Containment*, is curated as a set of liberal, state-friendly literary texts that celebrate the national mantra of diversity and assimilation, while anti-colonial voices remain suppressed by political and state actors. In the case of Urdu, the Euro-American academy and affiliate liberal scholars celebrate the Progressive Writer's Movement as marking Urdu's embrace of secularity.[21] Valuable contributions, including Jennifer Dubrow's *Cosmopolitan Dreams: The Making of Modern Urdu Literary Culture in Colonial South Asia* and the late Kavita Datla's nuanced study on the Osmania University at Hyderabad, *The Language of Secular Islam: Urdu Nationalism and Colonial India*, have attempted to open up the world of nineteenth- and early twentieth-century Urdu literary production as cosmopolitan and secular, that is non-religiously, or at the very least, syncretic.

What literary histories and, more recently, *world* literary histories, tend to obfuscate in their rush to celebrate a literature or even a particular literary text as worldly or diverse are the broader contexts of its production.[22] The literary histories of modern Urdu prose, both in Urdu and in Euro-American academy, trace a progression that roughly mimics that of literature in English, and subsequently dismisses several hundreds of influential novels and stories as merely pulp or popular fiction. The broad set of works we traditionally know as constitutive of Urdu literature roughly accords with Western norms of canonicity and genre: romance, novel, modernism, postmodernism, and so on. In other words, the nineteenth century is traditionally seen as the moment when Urdu prose fiction matures from its propensity for the romance and other fantastic forms toward the realist novel, while the twentieth century is a moment marked by the modernist works of the All-India Progressive Writers, as well as a number of other experimental, subversive fictions.

While this narrative is a satisfactory one, allowing us the comfort of enjoying literature and literary writing as generally isolated from or occupying a higher moral ground than that of quotidian history, parochial religiosity, politics, and culture in general, it offers only a cosmetic view of a literary canon, or even an individual text. For modern Urdu (though there are several approximate examples), the canon of prose works is the love-child of an uncomfortable union between low-brow English orientalist fictions and the colonial effort to inculcate a subservient, mostly religiously derived morality in native subjects through simple, textbook-like stories produced for the purposes of widespread vernacularization in North India. Only in the past decade or so have we begun to question the so-called origins of what many histories have celebrated as a modern literature, but we have yet to question the various, often futile omissions that are so essential to the making of literary canons.

In an *oppositional* gesture to the fashion in which literary histories are written—celebratory from a national perspective, philanthropic or positivist from a transnational or world literature lens—this project confronts both the canon of Urdu literature and the limits within which this literature continues to be studied and circulated in critical histories, the Euro-American academy, and more recently, literary festivals and related media of a globalized age.[23] In asking that we, particularly humanists from postcolonial states, reconsider or interrogate national canons or accepted literary ideals, I am not undermining the haunting, politically resistant voices of writers such as Saʻadat Hasan Manto and Faiz Ahmad Faiz, the defiant feminisms of Fahmida Riaz and Ismat Chugtai, or even the older, incorrigible notes on exile by nineteenth-century aesthetes Mirza Hadi Rusva and Mirza Asadullah Ghalib. I also acknowledge that the trajectory of literary writing in Urdu in post-1947 India, where the language is now associated largely with the sizeable Muslim minority, has taken diverse directions, evidenced in the evocative magnificence of Shamsur Rehman Faruqi's fictions and the subversive bent of S. M. Ashraf's writings. I am, however, arguing that these authors, whether Indian or Pakistani, and the aesthetic and ethical positions they espouse are *peripheral, minor*, at times even *exilic*, when held up against what is a continuous, cohesive, and fecund body of works, constructed on the orientalist premise of Urdu as an essentially "Muslim" language. Dominant, enduring, and omnipresent in the contemporary Pakistani imagination are writers who have conformed around the task of defining the Muslim. Their contributions, works whose concerns range from the political to the domestic, present the recent religio-populist impulse in contemporary Urdu as continuous with its past, rather than as an anomaly that needs to be explained away.

An honest acknowledgment of the fact that it is this latter set of works that commands the national imagination lays bare the historical processes through which modern literatures in colonized territories first took shape. It directs us to think critically about the fast-shrinking space that progressive or humanist writings occupy in the national narrative of a postcolonial state such as Pakistan. The question I was forced to ask and answer as this project unfolded was simply: What works, ideas, and arguments about Pakistan and Pakistani identity dominate across the literary and broader socio-political and cultural landscapes of the country? In a moment marked by the self-righteous rise of a religious populism whose single-point agenda—one that extends beyond the realm of politics—is to protect the sanctity of Islam and Muhammad as its last prophet, secularity, reflections on exile, doubt, other faiths, and alternative expressions of sexuality present nothing less than a dire threat to Pakistan's *raison d'etre*.

What literature, canon, or textual tradition, then, is complicit in propagating these insularly populist ideals, and what are its historic antecedents? Alternatively, who are the writers we dismiss as nationalist, popular, or one-dimensional, but who, nevertheless, are ubiquitous, their stories, characters, and moral universes affirming the rigid bounds of nation and state? Do they force us to reexamine the generally exclusive, even lofty fashion in which we have so far employed the term "literature"? Or should we perhaps rethink our currently perforated use of the term, which often differentiates high-brow from low-brow, women's literature from that designated for men, world literature from all others? The terms of this continuously self-affirming body of fictional works in Urdu range from colonial language primers inspired by the English oriental tale to longer, complex contemplations on the idea of the Muslims of North India as constituting a distinct "nation," in the modern sense of the word, to bestselling novels that sacralize Muslim pasts in medieval Islamic empires and tout an idyllic future where Muslims, saved from the evil seductions of the West, practice the pure Islam of the Prophet Muhammad and his companions. The production of a consistent and systematically developing canon in modern Urdu is undertaken by a varied cast of authors who begin with Mir Amman, a scribe in the colonial language school, Fort William College, and extend from nationally revered figures such as Syed Ahmad Khan, the leader of the Aligarh Movement; his followers, Nazir Ahmad, an education inspector, Altaf Hussain Hali, deemed one of the greatest Urdu poets in Urdu; to journalists-turned-novelists in the twentieth century, Nasim Hijazi prominent among them; and finally to bestselling women novelists such as Umera Ahmad and Farhat Ishtiaq.

The Postsecularist Politics of Populism

The central argument of this book—an interrogation of the process by which the domain of the literary assumes the authority to determine religious belonging—subverts the claims of postsecularist members of the North American academy who have, in the years following 9/11, argued against what they see as a monolithic Western liberal secularism. More urgently, the present crises of rising religio-nationalisms in the postcolonial world ask us to approach postsecularist arguments that cast piety movements, the strengthening of religio-political parties, and the public reclamations of pristine religious pasts as exemplary of social agency in Islamic states, with skepticism and apprehension.

I gesture here toward the work of the late Saba Mahmood, but also toward other postsecularists, including Joan Scott and Humera Iqtedar. Mahmood's contributions with regards to the Muslim world and Western liberalism have been particularly valuable for the Euro-American academy, but also resonate with scholars in the Global South. Mahmood is best known for her multifaceted study, *The Politics of Piety: The Islamic Revival and the Feminist Subject*, which argued that feminine acts of religious submission can and should, in fact, be considered as acts of agency and self-determination. The study, based on extensive fieldwork with the female followers of an Islamic revivalist movement in Egypt, challenged the Western feminist ideal of agency as a possibility that demanded resistance and freedom. Reading the latter condition as an assumption of contemporary scholars, even nonprofit organizations, liberal governments, and rights activists, Mahmood posits that the "natural status accorded to the desire for freedom in analyses of gender runs the risk of Orientalizing Arab and Muslim women all over again."[24] Muslim women who participate and are motivated by these new piety movements, Mahmood argues alternatively, should be treated as agent subjects whose cultivated "forms of desire and capacities of ethical action" stem from "discursive and practical conditions" that may be outside the pale of Western liberal secularism.[25]

As an anthropological study, *Politics of Piety* has critical and continuously relevant ramifications for ethical practices in the field. But if read in conjunction with Mahmood's earlier works, *Politics of Piety* misreads secularity as a principle of a hegemonic and misplaced Western liberalism. Secular culture, as Mahmood sees it, far from liberating often takes on violent means in order to render minor religious subjects "compliant with liberal political rule."[26] Her critique addresses itself both to liberal Muslim citizens in countries such as the United States, but also, ironically, to Sunni majoritarian states such as Egypt, Pakistan, and Afghanistan. While Mahmood's work and her political positions have been celebrated by a number of her intellectual interlocuters, Iqtedar and Scott included, it is a worthwhile exercise to consider the possible implications of her arguments not just for members of the Euro-America academy, but also for scholars and subject citizens in the postcolonial Muslim world.[27] It is worth considering also that resistance against some of her compelling claims has not necessarily come from fellow anthropologists, but from critical humanists as well as scholars of religion and political science.

Mahmood reads the revivalist *Da'wah* movement in Egypt (a lens with which we can examine parallel movements in other Islamic societies that maintain mostly colonial era constitutions) as a means through which Muslim women, through practices such as veiling, segregated gatherings for re-education and proselytization, and deliberate subordination to men on matters such as male polygamy, become agent subjects within what Talal Asad has called the Islamic "discursive tradition."[28] Mahmood, with close reference to Asad, describes the latter not as a fixed idea unable to come to terms with modernity, but as a practice in which the "past is the very ground through which the subjectivity and self-understanding of the tradition's adherents are constituted."[29] In other words, the idea of Islam as a discursive tradition, central to Mahmood's defense of revivalist and associated piety movements, is premised on the assumption of a fixed past, which in this case is defined by the Quran, the Hadith, and the Sunnah, or the known practices of the Prophet Muhammad.

While this past and the significance of its chastity may or may not be open to interpretation, other scholars, including Shahab Ahmed, have argued against its centrality to premodern Muslim societies in particular. My own engagement with Mahmood is urgently informed by how the present moment—one of violent and rising religio-populism in Pakistan and India—is anchored in the longer history of the orientalist *invention* of religious and national pasts in North India. I formulate the concept "religious populism" by drawing on Jan Werner-Muller's recent book *What is Populism?* in which he suggests that the populist wave afflicting liberal democracies of the Euro-American world is marked not just by its anti-elitist turn, but by its *anti-pluralist* inclinations. I show how this moment of religio-populism in Pakistan, narrativized in bestselling Urdu novels, short stories, and television serials (in addition to talk shows and political rhetoric), bases itself firmly within this notion of a sacred foundational moment in Islam. In upholding the idea of a certain past as central to Islamic practice, Mahmood and Asad forego a confrontation with colonial recoding of the originary pasts—religious or other—in essentially *national* terms. The anchor of origin, or the "past" to use Asad's term, allows novelists such as Umera Ahmad and Nimra Ahmad to reject those Muslims they may see as Western or liberal; decry minority sects such as the Ahmadiyya as blasphemers, while extolling women who take up practices such as the veil; and abjure associations with that which may be Western or non-Islamic.

While Mahmood admits that the assumption of a pure religious reclamation is "easy to dismiss," she asks her readers to refrain from casting doubt in a "context where the distinction between the subject's own desires and socially prescribed performances cannot be easily presumed and where submission to certain forms of (external) authority is a condition for achieving the subject's potentiality."[30] Mahmood's defense of piety movements and attendant teachings, thus, is premised on the condition that the observer refrain from questioning the paradigms and social formations within which the subject exercises desire. By sequestering off the terms with which piety movements establish authority, Mahmood absolves herself of the task of both critique and historicization, but also seems to suggest that others also refrain from such intellectual exercises. Mufti has called this tendency *"ethnographic philanthropy,"* or the condition by which the "postcolonial liberal Western subject . . . closes off in advance any possibility of engagement and critical involvement in the postcolonial societies and communities in question."[31] Mahmood's gesture, the closing off of critique, though clearly an example of this kind of philanthropic orientation, eludes the task of delving into the historical processes that have created these socio-ethical conditions.

My use of the term "religio-populist" to describe these evangelical novels, the socio-political influence they exercise, and the associated revivalist ideologies that they prescribe should not be read as a testimony of the secular humanist's "commitment to the poetic resources of the Judeo-Christian tradition," but rather as a means of comprehending the ultimate and most present iteration of the long orientalist literary project in North India.[32] From different vantage points, Mufti and Abbas separately remind us that modern Islam, above all its Sunni rendition, with its legalistic-theological leanings, its totalizing tendencies, its claims of pure origin, and its condemnation of all other claimant forms of practice, Shi'ism included, is symptomatic not of "a return of religion, but of its historical transformations under the conditions of late, postcolonial capitalism."[33]

In this book, I hope to undo Mahmood's gesture through a confrontation with both the present and the narrative pasts that have led to it. Admittedly, the scope of my argument is not limited to piety movements, and this study approaches the specter of religious populism through literary texts. I ask audiences from the Euro-American world and the Global South alike to acknowledge the contemporary state of Islam and Muslim societies as an ongoing condition, the most recent manifestation of the protracted legacies of orientalism in the colony. My project, to borrow Mahmood's own words, is another kind of attempt at "turning the critical gaze" upon oneself.[34]

This critique of a language, culture, and religious practice—all of which remain part of my identity as a Pakistani citizen and a Muslim—is informed by what I see as the deep, colonial roots of piety and revivalist movements, as well as by the broader role they play in the spread of ideologies that distance themselves from terrorism and organizations such as Al-Qaeda or ISIS, but that nevertheless sanction other forms of extra-state violence, including death to apostates and blasphemers, marital rape (by denying women the right to refuse sex to their husbands), and the excommunications of non-Sunni sects from the folds of Islam. These events and ideas do not make for international news, but rather take shape and solidify over some two and half centuries of Urdu prose narratives that are consumed in Pakistan for the purposes of both religious edification and chaste entertainment.

In turning the critical gaze, then, I see myself as the product of various, often conflicting discursive traditions. I am a citizen member of a state where the often-violent expression of religious populism has become a quotidian event. I am, both as a historical subject and as an individual, implicated in the questions that this book raises. To trace the literary past of modern Urdu is a simultaneous exercise in tracing the increasingly rigid ideals of *who* in Pakistan can lay claim to the title of Muslim. In tracing the troubled past and present of a language and literature I am meant to consider as *my* "national" language and literature, I am forced to acknowledge the mechanisms of their creation, but also to confront the *homelessness* that accompanies this acknowledgment. My confrontation with the now indelibly linked *national* language, literature, and religion in Pakistan is an inadvertent confrontation with narratives of identity that I cannot disassociate or tear from my person at will—Pakistan, Islam, Urdu—but that designate those who dissent or doubt as apostates and traitors.

A History of Literary Populisms

The single interrogative thread *"who is a Muslim,"* which runs through the works I examine, originates not in the Indo-Persian cultural complex where much of this work is inevitably located but in late Enlightenment Europe, specifically, eighteenth-century England. Whether we turn to the proliferation of the literary genre known as the oriental tale in the early decades of the eighteenth century or the scholarly orientalist tracts on "Asia" in the latter half, the attempt to codify "Muslim" in or against the idea of a nation is endemic. While Urdu poetry, an older and more complex formation, also takes up the question of Muslim selfhood through stalwarts such as Hali and Allama Iqbal, the particular trajectory of prose fiction following the English oriental tale as well as the *scale* of its reach in the twentieth and twenty-first centuries demand a close and careful study. On a formal level, I chart the English oriental tale's transformation over the course of almost three centuries as it journeys from the European Republic of Letters to the Indian colony. In doing so, I also trace the transformation of Urdu, a once elite aesthetic register of the Indo-Persian world to a modern vernacular for the Muslims of the Indian subcontinent. Cementing the conjoined histories of an English literary form and an Indo-Persian linguistic register is the chrono-spatially fluid figure of the Muslim, or as his orientalist title goes, the Mahometan.

In the first chapter, "Mahometan/Muslim: The Chronotope of the Oriental Tale," I argue that we read the vogue that surrounded the English oriental tale in the early part of the eighteenth century as one whose effects extended beyond the metropolis. An essential element of the oriental tale, whether we consider Antoine Galland and Grub Street's *Arabian Nights' Entertainments* or Francois de la Croix's *Turkish Tales* (1707) and *Persian Tales* (1710), is the chronotope of the Mahometan. The imagined counterpart of the Ottoman or Mughal Muslim kings, the Mahometan is a figure that defies Enlightenment modalities of ancient time and geographic origin. In these works and others, including Frances Sheridan's *History of Nourjahad* (1767), the chronotope, the "organizing center" of a literary genre, is defined by the absence of an originary space and time for the Mahometan.[35] A ubiquitous figure in the English oriental tale, the Mahometan is constructed as a homeless potentate, a traveling merchant, an itinerant dervish, a wanderer. Validated and expanded in the orientalist scholarship that flourished in the early days of the Indian colonial project, the Mahometan/Muslim functions in opposition to the "chronotope of the indigenous," a term premised on the orientalist "notion of indigeneity as the condition of culture."[36] These competing *literary* chronotopes complicate what Mikhail Bakhtin envisions as the "assimilating of an actual historical chronotope" into literary narrative.[37] The chronotope of the Mahometan/Muslim unfurls from within various English orientalist fictions and poems, traveling to scholarly documents, informing colonial laws and institutions.

The second chapter, "Hindustani/Urdu: The Oriental Tale in the Colony," traces the oriental tale's early nineteenth-century travels from the metropolis to the North Indian colony and the subsequent transformation it effects on premodern Urdu. I examine the scholarly writings of the celebrated philologist, William Jones, best-known for his 1784 so-called discovery of Sanskrit as the foundational language of an ancient Indic civilization. Less known is Jones's elaboration of the chronotope of the Mahometan in which he designates Islam as a non-national movement, a false sign blotting a landscape of an otherwise ancient nation. Jones's successor, John Gilchrist, however, changes the direction of the orientalist philological project, investing English resources to develop Indian vernaculars, the most visible of which is Hindustani. Claiming Hindustani to be one and the same with Urdu, Gilchrist patronized the production of a new vernacular literature in Hindustani whose foundational texts mirrored the English oriental tale and sought to inculcate an acquiescent morality within young officers and native subjects alike. Authored by natives working in the colonial institution of Fort William College (established 1800), these works collapse the Mahometan of the oriental tale with the North Indian Muslim, rewriting the historical presence of the latter in India as symptomatic of an itinerant, dislocated potentate. The articulation of the chronotope, therefore, becomes a moral articulation of the colonized self by the native subject. At a distance from the colonial ambit, however, examples of a courtly Urdu *adab* persist, exposing the contrived nature of Fort William narratives. Unattached to religious morality, existing in alternative geographies, stylized for effect and recitation, these narratives are slowly excised from the native imagination by the systematic promotion of the new prose literature.

"Nation/*Qaum*: The 'Musalmans' of India," the following chapter, argues that in the decades following the Mutiny of 1857, the marauding potentate of the oriental tale has to be reformed in order to occupy the molds of bourgeois subjectivity in the high colony. The oriental tale is rewritten as a set of didactic and realist fictions within which the once unstable protagonist, the Mahometan, now takes the form of the bourgeois Muslim. This second stage of literary invention in the colony—patronized by the Government of India but realized by native subjects—recasts a once-aristocratic, culturally cosmopolitan individual as a compliant cog in the colonial machinery. Reinventing Muslim women as socio-religious reformers, writers such as Deputy Nazir Ahmad, Altaf Hussain Hali, and Abdul Halim Sharar offer a believing, yet rational Muslim subject, whose earlier flaws are attributed to his assimilation in India and his relations with peoples outside the fold of Islam. The reformist moment, for the most part, is lauded as having inaugurated realist and historic fiction-writing in Urdu, with Nazir Ahmad's domestic stories frequently being cited as early prototypes of the "novel," while Hali's disavowal of the ghazal in favor of the single-theme, natural *nazm* form is also counted as literary development. Yet what often goes unquestioned in this celebration of

Urdu's attainment of the novel is its transformation of the Indian-Muslimness, a cosmopolitan condition, into a *qaum* or a nation whose origins lie outside of India.

In Chapter 4, "Martyr/*Mujāhid*: Muslim Origins and the Modern Urdu Novel," I examine how the chronotope of the now-Muslim travels into the twentieth century through what is now a large network of Urdu literary journals and print novels. While this period is best-known for the subversive works of All-India Progressive Writer's Movement, a Bloomsbury-inspired collective in India, the powerful, looming influence of a parallel set of Muslim *nationalist* writers—Rashid ul-Khairi, Nasim Hijazi, and Razia Butt—has gone unnoticed in literary histories both in the Euro-American academy and in Urdu. Written and published from around the 1920s to the 1970s, the novels of these nationalist writers resituate the once-itinerant, despotic Mahometan in terms offered by colonial modernity: nation, state, language. Within these mainstream works, which include Hijazi's wildly successful *Muhammad bin Qāsim* (1945) and Butt's enduring *Bānō* (1971), the Muslim *qaum*, or nation, is envisioned in terms of a single origin and its onward history: the caliphate, or Mecca, and the revived relevance of *mujāhids*, or warriors who fight in the name of Islam for the purpose of creating a separate Muslim state called Pakistan. A far cry from contemporaries such as Manto or the mutinous *Angārē* group, these nationalist writers cultivate the nascent ideas of nationhood propagated by earlier reformists into a powerful narrative of Muslim selfhood in the young Pakistan.

The inherent instability of the Mahometan/Muslim chronotope, however, does not permit an extended commitment to national territories. By the twenty-first century, seventy odd years into Pakistan's existence, the cobbled ideals of nationhood and state implode into a radically reimagined Muslimness that I elaborate upon in Chapter 5, "Modern/Mecca: Populist Piety in the Contemporary Urdu Novel." Enabled and legitimized within a number of popular novels and television serials authored by bestselling writers such as Umera Ahmad, Nimra Ahmad, and Farhat Ishtiaq, the "new" Muslim, predominantly signified by young women, is the contemporary reincarnation of a *salafī*, an early convert and companion of the Prophet Muhammad. In these religio-populist novels, the true Muslim protagonist actively rejects those outside the fold of Islam, including religious minorities, and renounces all that is Western, such as clothing and occupations, all the while reinventing the self in the image of the early Meccan community of converts to Islam. This exclusionary, often violent discursive formation marks the coming-of-age of a widespread religious populism in the domain of vernacular literature.

1 / Mahometan/Muslim: The Chronotope of the Oriental Tale

More than a century ago now, Martha Pike Conant, a doctoral student at Columbia University, undertook a study of the oriental tale in which she demarcated the literary form as constituted by "all the oriental and pseudo-oriental fiction—chiefly prose that appeared in English, whether written originally in English or translated from the French."[1] Oriental, the framing adjective, Conant elaborated, pertained to "those countries, collectively, that begin with Islam on the eastern Mediterranean and stretch through Asia."[2] Borrowing verbatim from Antoine Galland, the self-professed discoverer and translator of the *Arabian Nights* into French, Conant further suggests that "'Oriental,' then, includes here what it included according to Galland [. . .]: 'Sous le nom d'Orientaux, je ne comprends pas seulement les Arabes et les Persans, mais encore les Turcs et les Tartares et presque tous les peoples de l'Asie jusqu'à la Chine, mahometans ou païens et idolâtres.'"[3] We can ask what it means to "begin with Islam," but for now it should suffice to say that Galland and Conant delineated the orient as a set of Muslim territories that extend east from the Mediterranean, and home to, as Antoine Galland writes, Arabs, Persians, Turks, Tartars, and all the people of Asia until China, "Mohammadans," pagans, and idolaters included.[4]

What is the oriental tale, then, if the orient is constituted in these apparently ethno-religious and geographic terms? By logical derivation, the oriental tale is the name for fictions *in English* that claim origin in— or by way of their plot, characters, or location are somehow *of* the orient—a non-Christian, in fact, Muslim geography that lies to the east of Europe. Conant's generous definition serves the purpose, in fact, gathers for contemporary readers a large part of the structures that have informed that eighteenth-century literary phenomenon we now know as the oriental tale. Taking on a range of fictions that include the Grub Street translation of Galland's *Mille et Une Nuits* (~1707), the instructive stories that appeared in weekly journals such as *The Spectator* and *Rambler* for much of the 1710s, as well as later, more complex, Gothic renditions such as William Beckford's *Vathek* (1787), Conant describes a multifarious narrative that seemed to defy conventional notions of genre and origin. The critical attribute of the oriental tale, then, is its deliberate affiliation with spaces or people designated as the same. Assuming the orient to be an established space from the very outset, Conant directs her readers away from an interrogation of its members and territories, pointing instead toward the European Republic of Letters, the true home of the form in question.

In recent years, Conant's small, but comprehensive book on the oriental tale appears as a frequent citation in contemporary works on eighteenth-century fiction forms. While the unrelenting efforts of postcolonial intellectuals have forced us to rethink grouping large swathes of people and traditions under the term "oriental," what remains unchanged from Conant's conception of the oriental tale are the limits of its influence. Contemporary scholarship *still* sees the oriental tale functioning largely within a world defined by its Englishness. It is translated into, or originally composed in English; its inspirations are other English or European narratives about the East; and its circles of influence are largely constrained to further literary developments within England.

Alternatively described by James Beattie, the eighteenth-century Scottish poet and moralist, as the "Oriental fable," the oriental tale also became affiliated—albeit as a lesser form—with the Aesopian tradition that itself commanded significant influence in Restoration England.[5] Like the English fable, "an amazingly diverse assortment of literary exercises undertaken in Aesop's name," the oriental tale also served a variety of purposes—cultural, domestic, political—mostly through the evocation of an Arab or Persian writer named briefly in the English or French translator's introduction.[6] Arriving in a reading metropolis where fairytales, or oral lore such as the stories of Tom Thumb and Robin Hood, had been pushed to the social peripheries, while more informative, moral, or knowledge-oriented genres had gained ascendancy, the oriental tale achieved the vogue that it did, in part at least, because it stood as a bridge between these two otherwise removed categories. That is to say, its English authors and translators believed it to be "less insipid" than animal fables, while containing all the "Beauties without the extravagance of our own tales of the Fairies."[7] Despite the fact that some of the most heavily circulated oriental tales in eighteenth-century England were translated from French originals, their popularity and their afterlives attest to their significance in the formation of an English nationhood. If the novel achieved this through dedicated realism, the oriental tale took on this task by proclaiming itself as moral and informative, an allegory for the domestic performed by the exotic and the fantastic.

Much like its nineteenth-century scion, the novel, the oriental tale fast became a frequent member of popular magazines and weekly periodicals and papers such as the *Flying Post, The Spectator,* and *The Gentlemen's Magazine,* a staple script for cheap, nightly theatrical performances in London, and eventually a recurrent event in women's magazines. This last aspect of the oriental tale, mostly a footnote or passing mention in studies of the form, is a significant one. A work such as *Arabian Nights Entertainments,* for example, made for convenient fodder for eighteenth-century chapbooks, thus achieving a much wider circulation in English society than either the oral folklore that was commonly associated with a newly literate working class or the higher literary forms—essays, poems—that were preferred by a more aristocratic or socially aspiring order. Early reprints of the *Arabian Nights,* Paolo Lemos Horta tells us, most often appeared as "cheap bootleg editions, some just one story long, produced with a popular audience in mind and with little concern about the accuracy of the translation."[8] In other words, various versions of the same volume could be read across social class and gender in edited, pirated, or abridged forms, unlike many texts from elite or high culture, which normally appeared as "poetry and drama, moral essays and prose satire."[9]

Recent studies of the oriental tale, including the nuanced and comprehensive projects of eighteenth-century scholars, the late Srinivas Aravamudan and Ros Ballaster, revisit this literary form with the intent of explicating the at times renegade, dissident role it played with relation to mainstream narratives of its time. Aravamudan, in a number of articles and two fine books, illustrates the contradictory posture that the eighteenth-century oriental tale took with respect to the emergent novel.[10] Ballaster's position, articulated through a full-length study of the oriental tale, asks us to consider this form in terms of the political and social complexities that marked the long eighteenth century. Fiction, for much of this period, is the dominant means for France and England to understand and negotiate national politics and social morality as well as the vast swathes—trading and political allies or rivals—that were collectively referred to as the Orient.[11] At the heart of these diverse critical arguments by Conant, Ballaster, and Aravamudan, however, is a single concern: what role did the eighteenth-century oriental tale play in the longer history of an emerging *English* literariness? That is to say, if Conant's reading of the oriental tale marks its instrumental role in the rise of English Romanticism, then Aravamudan and Ballaster read this form as carving an uneasy, but ultimately complicit, relationship with the idea of nationhood as well as with England's imperial aspirations.

Aravamudan's contributions on the import of the oriental tale in England are an invaluable point of departure for this study. In a redemptive reading of the oriental tale, Aravamudan asks us to consider the oriental tale as a form that, like the novel, also "constitutes nationalism, but differently."[12] Unlike the novel, it "generate[s] a two-way cultural process of dissemination as well as the consolidation of aesthetic values."[13] Aravamudan's celebration of the oriental tale as a form that brings forward a "different set of questions concerning nationalism, cosmopolitanism, and transculturation," however, rests on a problematic position that postcolonialists have adopted with respect to Edward Said's eviscerating critique of the totalizing discipline we know as "Orientalism."[14] Oriental fictions and tracts from the eighteenth century, Aravamudan argues, instigated a critique of the self, as well as of the hegemonies of nation and state that more insular genres such as the novel, in fact, bolstered. Aravamudan's project—one in which he certainly was not alone—was based on the premise that Enlightenment Europe's interest in the orient had utopian aspirations, motivated by self-reflection, thus prompting a "fluid circulation of endocultural and exocultural processes."[15] To put it simply, texts, fictions, and travel narratives that took the orient as their center but demonstrated a committed critique of the self, or took a stand against slavery, constituted a positive orientalism as well as a positive nationalism.

Aravamudan's persuasive stance on the oriental tale stands as long as the literary history of English is considered a cocooned event with a singular trajectory. If we consider English "not merely as a language of literary expression, but as a cultural system with global reach," then the pivot of the oriental tale also shifts.[16] Once decentered from the orbit of a single literature or language, the oriental tale is forced to confront the English version of its origins as well as the journeys it takes from the European Republic of Letters toward colonized "orients." Thus, Aravamudan's claim, that "oriental tales, pseudoethnographies, sexual fantasies, and political utopias" that "speculated about a largely imaginary East" were "experimental, prospective, and anti-foundationalist," also asks us to recall that these productive attributes were available only through exercises in allegorical reading.[17] More important, the political and social concerns addressed in these progressive forms are proper to French and English audiences. For most readers, these stories were literally just tales about a distant orient. The oriental tale is thus a literary form whose cosmopolitanism—to use Aravamudan's word—masks a nation-centeredness that is usually contained in the allegories and moral precepts of the form. Consumed across literate social classes and integrated with the rise of journalistic impulses that had become an indispensable part of public life, the oriental tale was distinct precisely because, for its metropolitan audiences, it was as fantastic as it was authentic, truthful, and moral. The story that this chapter tells continues not in England, where the oriental tale is slowly superseded by the novel, but in colonial North India (and eventually contemporary Pakistan), where this literary form is introduced and systemically canonized over the course of the nineteenth century.

Our present moment—coincidentally defined by the rise of populist movements across Euro-America and postcolonial states in South Asia—demands a more nuanced and critical reading of the oriental tale as a popular national genre distinguished by its worldly aspirations. To go back to Conant, what does it mean to say the "Orient begins with Islam?" Was the *vogue for the oriental tale*, a much-used phrase, merely a vogue? Is it enough to try and rehabilitate eighteenth-century English attitudes toward the Muslim East by attempting to cast one literary genre as liberal, even dissident? Is this ostensibly worldly, progressive moment ultimately insular or nation-centric? In the case of the affirmative, we must also interrogate the relationship the oriental tale in English forges with the so-called oriental spaces it claims as its origin. And finally, if the oriental tale exceeds the bounds of the metropolis, what are the terms of this excess? That is to say, is the circulation of the oriental tale an unregulated accident, or does it take place within the systems and institutions of a once-colonized world? To read the oriental tale as a sign of *translatio*, or intercultural exchange, as Aravamudan does, is to elide its historical presence and enduring influence in both the metropolis and the colony. It is a form that inevitably contributes to the twin projects of British national reification and imperial expansion, which are mediated largely through the performative specter of the then-Islamic East. Despite its worldly, but other times naïve, demeanor, the moment of the oriental tale is a decisive event in the intertwined histories of orientalism and its constitutive literary and cultural forms.

When I say the moment of the oriental tale, I am referring to roughly the first half of the eighteenth century in England, when volumes such as Francois Petis La Croix's *Persian Tales* and *Turkish Tales* (1710), Thomas Guellette's *Mogul Tales* (1736), and Frances Sheridan's *History of Nourjahad*, all inspired by the raging success of the *Arabian Nights Entertainments*, flooded the English literary market, the scope of their readership ranging from the working to the aristocratic classes. Though not normally considered significant in studies of orientalism—the discipline or the discourse—the oriental tale is instrumental in the imaginative invention of a particular kind of orient. The critical impulses of the oriental tale are not restricted to England, and therefore, I read the oriental tale *against* the idea that it is archive only to English and Anglophone literatures. I read it as a moment that must be read *into* the mainstream archives of modern vernaculars such as Arabic or Urdu, both wrought by colonial pasts.

The oriental tale invents and is organized around what I call the *chronotope of the Mahometan/Muslim*, the relational unit of time and space that is essential to the form and meaning of this literary genre. The oriental tale is inevitably located in the imaginary space I call the *Mahometan* Orient and its protagonist is a Mahometan, who in later forms gives way to the category of Muslim. The Mahometan and, by extension, the Muslim are constituted as itinerants, devoid of civilizational, racial, or even linguistic origins, a figure who is unlike other "Orientals," Hindus, for example, and above all, in contradiction to Enlightenment ideals of nationhood. It is this set of time-space relations that replicates in vernacular oriental tales and the later fiction forms that arise from the dominance of this form in the Indian colony. Though the chronotope of the Mahometan/Muslim does not necessarily dictate the plot or the allegorical lesson that oriental tales often have for English audiences, it informs the arrangement of the oriental tale, the orientation of its characters, and the possibilities of representation in the narrative. It is the particular configuration of this chronotope that distinguishes the oriental tale from earlier English and continental representations of the Muslim East.[18]

I use the term "Mahometan," and not Muslim, Islamic, or Arab, to emphasize the *imaginative* construction of a historic, lived geography and peoples by the greater orientalist project.[19] As a concept, Mahometanism is a European invention, a title that Said explicates in *Orientalism* as a crude conflation of Islam as an imitation of Christianity. In the oriental tale, the Mahometan Orient is constituted by the vast territories that ranged from Egypt to China and whose historic associations with Islam allowed for them to be represented through a limited set of conflated signifiers: sultan, caliph, wives and harems, viziers, merchants, belief in

Mahomet, empire. Places and cities such as "Baghdad," "Persia," "Damascus," "Cashmire," and "Egypt" are all part of the homogenous geography of the Mahometan Orient, merchants and sultans constantly moving from one part to another. Particularized for Western consumption, the Mahometan Orient of the oriental tale exists as an extended empire that houses the caliph/sultan figure and serves as a playground for his barbarisms and sexual fantasies, as well as his eventual reformation. At odds with the rational Enlightenment ideals of origin, nation, and modern state, the histories and uncontained geographies of *this* orient—as compared to other, later orients, the Indic or even Semitic, for example—are fantastical and unreal. The Mahometan Orient, then, was the imaginary spatial formation that lent itself to popular consumption through its seeming disconnect with English society.

Within the vast imagined territories of the Mahometan Orient, the Mahometan appears in the various identities of caliph and sultan, and, at times, merchant and dervish. In many of his guises, including that of caliph, he indulges in the multiple identities made possible by masquerade. Whether despot or dervish, the Mahometan is inevitably an itinerant, a nomad, who imposes himself upon foreign lands through the force of conquest or through the exploitation and wiles of mercantilism and disguise. As a "Mahometan," he follows Mahomet, a prophet who is cast as a posturing despot in various orientalist works, the most prominent among them Voltaire's *Le fanatisme ou Mahomet, le prophete* (1736). The territories within which this figure moves are always empire formations: Ottoman, Safavid, or Persian. That is to say, the Muslim is not native to the lands or territories that he inhabits. He is *non-national*, unable to lay claim to a single civilization, a native language, or an aboriginal people (this particular contradiction is fleshed out more scientifically in the second half of the eighteenth century). Conspicuously unattached and undomesticated, the Mahometan, even if married, is sexually deviant by English standards, indulging in multiple wives and concubines, marrying at will in different locations, other times deceived and tricked by oriental women in the style of Schahriar's first unfaithful queen.

Sometimes of humble origins, other times as princesses and queens, female characters in the oriental tale are either wise and virtuous, *or* sexually deviant and adulterous, their deception often causing a sultan to unleash his brutality upon innocent citizens. While women such as Scheherazade and Nurse Sutlememe from the *Persian Tales* are speaking figures, their virtue is made apparent only by their story-telling abilities and their success in reforming a barbarous sultan or recalcitrant princess. More common are women such as Schahriar's first queen, whose infidelity unleashes the anger of the sultan upon all the virgins of the empire; Canzada, the sexual predator in the frame tale of the *Turkish Tales*; and the multiple enslaved women whose work seems to be to seduce wandering Mahometan men. The female characters of the oriental tale are never outwardly identified as Mahometan, nor do they seem to indulge in religious rituals such as prayer and ablution, as their male counterparts often do. In other words, the female subject of the oriental tale replicates masculine itinerancy through the sexual license of her body by offering herself to black slaves and her stepsons, and through polygamy, which is often inadvertent.

The Mahometan Orient, as it unfolds in the oriental tale, is a space of constant transgression. These various transgressions are incurred through empires that forcibly rule over various peoples, men who are in a constant state of movement, which is largely physical but often supplemented by assumed identities and changed bodies, or women who cross the bounds of home and marriage through adultery and infidelity. The oriental tale, defined by the chronotope of the Mahometan/Muslim, becomes the stage for a variety of metropolitan concerns by way of a foreignness that is constructed as both intimate and exotic, a marked departure from Tudor and Jacobean plays and poems about Islam. The overt heterogeneity of the oriental tale as well as the duality of its protagonists allowed it to exist as a popular genre, entertaining, at times moral, and simultaneously to represent higher aesthetic or philosophical concerns. Despite the absence of domestic attachments or national origin for the protagonists of the oriental tale, the genre becomes significant in the negotiation of English domesticity as evidenced not just in works such as the *Persian Tales*, but most noticeably by the frequent appearance of oriental tales and anecdotes in women's magazines. If the romance and "pleasant histories . . . were singled out as fit for only lower-status readers, including women, servants, and eventually children," then the oriental tale for much of the eighteenth century achieved an unprecedented status as a "popular" form, permitting readers from across intellectual and social classes to partake in the variety of narrative possibilities it offered.[20]

Given the literary-historical ambitions of this book, I turn to the work of Edward Said in *Orientalism*, despite the recent multitude of scholarly critiques decrying Said's arguments. I do not need to rehearse Aravamudan's, Ballaster's, or even Felicity Nussbaum's arguments, which suggest that *Orientalism*, possibly inadvertently, led scholars to denounce the oriental tale as a genre, and thus permitted only limited views of the long eighteenth century. Said does not identify the oriental tale as a specific genre; much of the early discussion in *Orientalism* remains focused on European attitudes toward Islam from as far back as the medieval period. In part, I premise my argument in this chapter and others, in a perhaps elementary manner, on Said's own admission that *Orientalism* is "far from a complete history or general account of Orientalism." "All I have done," Said clarifies in his introduction, is "merely to suggest the existence of a larger whole, detailed, interesting, dotted with fascinating figures, texts, and events."[21] Critics of Said's formidable volume have pounced on this supposed deficiency but to little effect. The oriental tale and the Mahometan Orient are both categories that emerge as precursors to the period of high imperialism, which is, of course, Said's main concern. Here, I offer a close account of the early decades of the eighteenth century during which English identity at various levels is negotiated through the oriental tale and the ubiquitous chronotope of the Mahometan/Muslim.

The second premise that informs this chapter pertains to the fact that Said's *Orientalism* mostly takes stock of the "Islamic Orient." Using self-experience as a reason to limit, Said mostly stays close to the territories he deems part of this particular orient—Egypt, Palestine, modern-day Syria, Iraq, the Maghreb. But representation is not the end of orientalism, and neither is the Islamic Orient a stable category. The Mahometan Orient (to use my amended term), as it is constructed in the oriental tale, is a moving empire, extending from Persia to China, or from Cairo to Damascus in any given story. Unfixed, the Mahometan Orient shifts variously in the several hundred tales that were published during the eighteenth century, taking with it its constitutive structures of despotism. It is premised on Mahomet as a figure in the European imagination. Described even in early Christian scholarly exercises such as Humphrey Prideaux's *Life of Mahomet* (1697), Mahomet is a wily trader and imposter who is able to invent a new religion almost entirely through pretense and performance.[22] It is this imagined Mahometan Orient, and not historic, lived Islamic societies, that can smoothly imitate English society while remaining at a distance from its actual geography and interests.

On its own, perhaps, a Mahometan Orient would have been deemed harmless, but the rise of a competing oriental ideal, that is, the Indic, is a turning point within the longer history of British orientalism and its imperializing bent. For the most part, the Indic Orient gains consequence in the late eighteenth century through the scholarly work of orientalists such as Nathaniel Halhed and William Jones, and through its linguistic revitalization of the Aryan hypothesis. In the seventeenth and early eighteenth centuries, Ballaster argues, India was described by early travelers as a "kind of physical fairyland, rich in minerals and precious stones," and in other narratives as "a space of the marvelous, a dreamscape for the Christian pilgrim."[23] While the Indic Orient indeed entered the English cultural imagination in a decisive fashion only after the success of Jones's translation of the Sanskrit play, *Sakuntala* in 1789, its initial interactions with the Mahometan Orient are hardly inert. In the high moment of the oriental tale, the Indic Orient travels to the Mahometan Orient in the form of santons, or mystic devotees; giaours, or monsters; and through knowledge of the dark arts, all of which seem to bring the Mahometan protagonists to grief in some fashion or the other.[24] While the oriental tale lacks the scholarly sophistication that later orientalists would bring to the question of India, it offers the Indic Orient as a space that is inhospitable, even destructive to the Mahometan who ventures toward it, codifying Anglo-French perceptions of the Mughal presence in India into its stories. India is referred to variously in the oriental tale, sometimes as "the Indies" or India. In some cases, the "Indies" can also refer to a vague space extending forth from the Ottoman East.

Toward the close of the eighteenth century, as the next chapter shows, the Indic Orient is seen as having "poured forth," recast as a long-lost civilization, the cradle of ancient cultures that British orientalism had discovered and that could only be revived for modernity through the efforts of a British Empire in India.[25] To borrow from Aamir Mufti, the Indic Orient was subsequently generated through the "chronotope of the indigenousness, a temporal structure of deep habitation in ancient time," by way of which the Hindus, deemed the descendants of an ancient Sanskritic civilization, were crowned as the natives of the territory the English called India.[26] It offered a new source to replace biblical lands and languages whose Judaic claims interrupted the emergent ideals of a European Aryan identity. The Mahometan Orient, on the other hand, evolves in the space of the oriental tale as the contradictory medium through which late eighteenth-century England defines certain ideals of nationhood against the face of an empire that shuttles between despotism and barbarism. It is worth noting as well that while the Indic Orient featured in several late eighteenth-century novels, including Phebe Gibbes's *Hartly House, Calcutta* (1789), the Mahometan Orient remains proper to the oriental tale.

Given that the oriental tale or fable, to use Beattie's term, for at least the first half of the eighteenth century, orbits largely within France and England, we may correctly assume that the form was *intended* for Western consumption. Like the early novels of the eighteenth century—*Robinson Crusoe* (1719), *Moll Flanders* (1722), or Samuel Richardson's *Pamela* (1740)—oriental tales such as the *Persian Tales* and *Turkish Tales* were also accompanied by moral lessons that were either announced in the prefatory remarks made by the author masquerading as translator or were part of the fabular narrative that followed. Whether English reading audiences stood to benefit from the "examples of vertue and vice" in the *Arabian Nights*,[27] or the "most exalted notions of virtue" in the *Persian Tales*, the oriental tale, true to the demands of English society and literary markets was hardly pure entertainment.[28] Unlike the novelistic hero, the Mahometan protagonist of the oriental tale was usually a sultan or caliph, or occasionally a queen or princess in the harem. Reformation or domestication, both of which were stated functions of the novel as well, thus functioned with a dual purpose in these works. On the literal level, the frame tales of the *Arabian Nights*, *Persian Tales*, and *Nourjahad* were the stories of despotic or royal figures in need of domestication and moral edification. Allegories that highlighted *English* fears around despotism, wasteful and bad women, or trade concerns, or alternatively exemplified social virtues, frame tales as well as the sequences within, came together as reformative or cautionary works for an English reading public.

In the sections that follow, I suggest that the chronotope of the Mahometan/Muslim is codified in the frame tales of works such as the *Arabian Nights Entertainments*, *Turkish Tales*, and *Persian Tales*, volumes that were published within a few years of each other and whose widespread popularity gave rise to more sophisticated, complex stories and plays, including Voltaire's *Mahomet* and Delariveire Manley's *Almyna* (1707). I read major characters such as Sindbad and Haroun al-Raschid, merchant and caliph, as prototypes for the itinerancy and masquerade that become integral parts of the Mahometan protagonist. Sindbad, I argue, performs and justifies early colonial forays to India and East Asia for England. Other Mahometans based on Sindbad, most visibly, Aboulfouaris of the *Persian Tales*, however, exemplify how the prototype of the merchant evolves into a figure forever unmoored. The chronotope of the Mahometan takes on further complexity in popular stories such as that of Fadlallah and Zemroude, where its geographical limits are defined against a slowly unfolding Indic Orient. Finally, the emergence of the English novel, with its proclivity for the domestic, signals the maturation of the chronotope. A sign, a synecdoche, a meaning-laden reference for the Mahometan Orient, the chronotope of the oriental tale, as it appears in the English novel, is definitive of all that an emergent national consciousness in England seeks to define itself against.

Reframing the Mahometan: The Politics of the Oriental Tale

The publication and wild success of Antoine Galland's *Mille et Une Nuits* in France and, soon after, the anonymously translated *Arabian*

Nights' Entertainments in England have long been lauded as a singular moment, described by Sari Makdisi and Nussbaum as inaugurating "a genuinely open-minded obsession with the East."[29] Arguing that "European writers embraced the new world opened up to them by the *Nights* with unreserved enthusiasm," Makdisi and Nussbaum draw up a hopeful picture of East-West exchange, and of an English canon forever altered for the influence of the *Nights*.[30] Makdisi, Nussbaum, and other major scholars of the eighteenth century, including Aravamudan, and Ballaster, have repeatedly argued for seeing the moment of the oriental tale as a uniquely positive event in the longer history of Europe's relations and perceptions of the Muslim East.

The optimistic rhetoric of newness that accompanies laudatory studies of the oriental tale suggests that works such as the *Arabian Nights* or *Persian Tales* somehow opened up alternate ways of imagining the Muslim East, giving English and French readers different perspectives, and indeed, *knowledge*, of the various peoples and practices from Islamic societies in the East and North Africa. Yet, if we examine works such as the *Nights* and the many fictions it spawned within a mere decade or so of its publication, what we find is not newness or a refreshing orientation of its Muslim subjects but rather a *rearrangement* of the popular and literary perceptions around Islam that were endemic to the Renaissance and that continued to gain impetus in Tudor and Jacobean England.[31] What the oriental tale actually marked, we can say, was the *domestication of the Mahometan* from a barbarous, genuinely feared antagonist of Europe and Christianity to an exotic other, reduced in military might and at a safe physical distance from England's and France's borders. The formation of the chronotope of the Mahometan is a function of this domestication: The rapacious, intractable Tamerlaine of Christopher Marlowe's *Tamburlaine the Great* (1587) progresses into Schahriar, or Hasikin of the *Turkish Tales*, monarchs who can be tamed by fictions and tutored in governance by their subjects. Likewise, characters within the unfolding stories of these collections play out both their own foreignness as well as English concerns.

Muslims had long occupied a place in the popular English imagination, as Samuel C. Chew's excellent study *The Crescent and the Rose* (1937) tells us. By the height of the Tudor period, an Englishman

> of average education and intelligence had in mind the conquests of Tamburlaine and his humiliation of Sultan Bajazet; the heroic resistance of Scanderbeg; the fall of Constantinople and the ruthless cruelty of Mahometan the Conqueror; the alternatively advancing

and retreating tides of Turkish forces in the Balkans and Danube country (these aggressions and recessions confusedly remembered); the overrunning of Greece and the islands of the Aegan . . . [32]

The list continues, concluding with the fact that "history merged into legend and romance," the roving Turks somehow representing all Muslim pasts and people.[33] If by the beginning of the seventeenth century, Shakespeare popularized the Turk as a traitor and liar, mainstreaming idioms such as "turning Turk" and "or else, I am a Turk," then by the end, John Dryden had rewritten Muslim rulers across history as drowned in lust, unable to rule over their own kingdoms. Dryden's plays, particularly *Aureng-zebe: A Tragedy* (1676) and *The Conquest of Granada* (1672) reflect also the receding threat of the Ottomans to Europeans that finally came to a head in 1683 at the Battle of Vienna, a victory for the Hapsburgs.[34]

Thus, when Antoine Galland claimed that he had translated the *Mille et Une Nuits* from an original Syrian manuscript, he was no longer presenting his audiences with stories of their dark conquests or the specter of Europe's own vulnerability to Ottoman armies. In telling the story of Schahriar and the thousand stories that conquered his barbarism, he was giving his readers a Mahometan, who though inherently foreign and still master of his properties, was no longer a threat. The sources and *ur*-texts of the *Nights* have been debated for some time now, but Muhsin Mahdi, a leading historian of the text, has rejected the idea that Galland's French text was a translation in any sense of the word.[35] Madeleine Dobie, Marina Warner, and Aravamudan, on the other hand, approach Galland's work as a "familiarizing translation," asking contemporary audiences to read the French translation as a moment of intercultural contact and exchange that flowed from East to West.[36] Horta's recent intervention in this debate recasts the *Nights* as a collaboration between Galland and a young Syrian man, Hanna Diyab, who had traveled to Paris from Syria, suggesting that the *Nights* had emerged from "networks of transcultural creativity."[37]

The scope and detail of these debates are commendable but obscure the *moment* that the *Nights* and its spawn inaugurate in England. The moment of the oriental tale is distinguished by its orientation toward the Muslim East or the Mahometan Orient as the site of "pleasant and diverting stories," a seemingly far cry from the violence and darkness that marked earlier fictions.[38] This moment is marked by a new trend in French and British orientalisms, where narratives and stories from the "Orient" or the "East" are "discovered" or unearthed from their original locations, translated by a single orientalist, and brought to Europe. In the case of English readers and writers, Galland's introduction to the *Nights* emphasized its moral utility, making it consistent with other contemporary works. It is ironic, at the very least, that contemporary editions—most noticeably Robert L. Mack's 1995 edition that apparently offers the entire "original version of the *Nights*"—leave out the preface contained in the early French and subsequent Grub Street editions. I suggest, then, that we turn to the prefaces and frame tales of the *Nights* and other volumes in order to understand the terms under which this genre comprehended the Mahometan, terms that rearrange a longstanding antagonism into oppositional parts: nation and empire, domesticity and itinerance, truth and deception, reason and superstition, excess and moderation.[39] The chronotope of the Mahometan is constituted by the latter category of each set.

Galland's "Translator's Preface" sets up the oriental tale as both fact and fiction. In introducing his audiences to a "prodigious quantity" of stories "whose variety is surprizing" and "whose connection is so wonderful," he offers a Muslim East made up of "Persians, Tartars, and Indians," authored by the Arabs, and whose "customs and manners" included "as well Pagans as Mohametans."[40] Stripped of the Ottomans, or Turks (even the *Turkish Tales* are not about an Ottoman sultan), the Mahometan Orient, "from the sovereign to the meanest subject," can now "speak" and "act" for English and French readers in a fashion that is "pleasing."[41] Though the Turk himself almost rarely enters the oriental tale, cities from the Ottoman empire—Damascus, Baghdad, and Basra—are an integral part of the Mahometan Orient's geography. The author of the *Nights*, "an anonymous Arab" whose very existence Galland throws into doubt, is blurred between fact and fiction in a manner synonymous to the stories that are to follow.[42] As the new master of the text, having rendered it from "Arabick" into the "niceness of the French tongue," Galland is no longer imagining the Mahometan Orient in the manner of his predecessors; rather, we can say he is converting it from its previous antagonism into a compliant otherness, open to new meanings in the wake of altered relations.[43]

The territories of Schahriar, the infamous sultan of the frame tale, extend from Persia as far as China. Though generally a well-loved and fair ruler, the infidelities of his sister-in-law and his wife "persuaded" him "that no woman was chaste," and in the wake of his betrayal, he decides nightly to take a wife and daily to kill her.[44] In his "unparalleled barbarity," Schahriar is one of many Mahometan sultans, caliphs, and rulers of the Mahometan Orient whose laws have to be met with "blind obedience" from his subjects.[45] The frame tale of the *Nights* is the story of this sultan's conversion from the classic Mahometan traits of barbarism and savagery to a docility induced by the brave Scheherazade, the daughter of Schahriar's grand vizier.

A close look at Scheherazade, as she appears in both the English and French texts, reveals a character constructed in accordance with Enlightenment mores, rather than those fitting an oriental queen. Not only is she beautiful, but she is described by the narrator as possessing "courage, wit and penetration, infinitely above her sex."[46] Her education, however, sets her apart from oriental women and their European counterparts, for she is well-versed in "philosophy, physic, history, and liberal arts," in addition to being a poet par excellence.[47] When she announces to her father her plan to marry the sultan, she does so with the knowledge that, should she die, "my death will be glorious," and in the case of success, "I will do my country an important piece of service."[48] Over the course of the thousand or so nights that Scheherazade passes with Schahriar, the Oriental despot will be tamed by the strategic fictions of a character trained in a distinctly European curriculum of liberal arts and sciences. Unlike a typical Oriental subject who at this time was believed to have lyric skill but little other learning, Scheherazade has a European intellect as well as a poetic talent.[49]

More enduring is the other oppositional quality Scheherazade possesses. Unlike Schahriar, the sultan, she is *of* a place and people. She sees herself as part of a *country*, the word Galland uses is *patrie*, fatherland, a place to which one filiatively belongs.[50] She exists under the sign of the indigenous, while Schahriar remains foreign, a Mahometan sultan.[51] Schahriar, the master of many domains, belongs to no place in particular, and though he possesses many countries or cities, none possess him. His adulterous queen, likewise, defies any domestic ties by participating in orgies with black slaves, though her particular lover, Masoud, enters and exits the palace by climbing through the trees that surround it. Schahriar and his household, in their distinctly *non-national* orientation, thus, establish the chronotope of the Mahometan that I have suggested is critical to the formation of the oriental tale.

The frame tale of the *Nights*, though literally the story of a heroic young woman, is also the story of how Enlightenment ideals can overcome the savageries and barbarities that lie outside of it. A simpler example of this occurs in La Croix's *Persian Tales*, translated into English by Ambrose Philips, the poet and politician, who dedicates the volume to the Duchess of Gondolphin, a lady "allied with two glorious patriots," the one who brought England glory against the French, while the other led it to economic prosperity.[52] Describing the tales that lie within as "designed" to "reduce a young princess to reason," Philips simultaneously also likens them to "little epic poems," in which the "characters and the passions ... are taken from nature."[53] Though many eighteenth-century poets and novelists were obsessed with the idea of epics, Philips himself preferred the pastoral form, arguing that forms such as the epic "by the vehemency of their emotions, raise the spirits into a ferment."[54] Formally, too, Philips hints, the oriental tale was a reflection of its Mahometan subjects who, over the course of the narrative, are to be contained by the superior ideals of reason and rationality.

Considerably simpler than the frame of the *Nights*, the *Persian Tales* begins with the story of the Princess Farrukhnaz, the daughter of the king of "Cashmire," whose famed beauty has attracted the princes of all the neighboring domains. Just before the princes arrive to compete for her hand, Farrukhnaz dreams of herself as a doe being abandoned by a stag she has just saved from death. Interpreting this dream as being sent by "Kefaya," who we are told in a footnote was "an idol formerly worshipped in Cashmire," she refuses to marry any of her suitors. The task of converting her from her irrational state falls upon her nurse, Sutlememe, who "weans" her young charge from her dreams through the "Reason" of entertaining stories.[55] Though the people of Cashmire are described as idol worshippers, Farrukhnaz eventually settles on marrying the Persian prince, Farrukhschad, aided and abetted by a number of rather rational dervishes, religious figures generally associated with Islam in the oriental tale. The conversion of the oriental through "reason" or science finds even fuller elaboration in Sheridan's *History of Nourjahad*, in which the Sultan Schemzeddin humbles his successor, the arrogant Nourjahad, through an elaborate, scientifically organized set of illusions intended to reform a subject drowned in his desire for wealth and immortality.

It is in the *Turkish Tales* that the subject of the Turk enters the oriental tale, though only briefly for the frame tale and the stories that follow are located as part of Persian chronicles. The anonymous translator's introduction to the stories alludes constantly to the degraded "character" of the Turks. The point of the stories is to cure a prince "too much addicted to women."[56] Turkish women, the supposed undoing of Turkish men, have no care for "Menaces of Mahomet, and his Alcoran," a breed not unlike Schahriar's unnamed adulterous queen.[57] The Turk is no longer a violent, deceitful conqueror but is recast in terms of his blind attachment to women, while the women themselves are a faithless, unrooted breed. Thus, the frame tale of the *Turkish Tales* is the story of the Persian queen, Canzada, who begins to lust after her stepson, the Prince Nourgehan. The Prince, like Scheherazade, is distinguished by his learning in both letters and athletics, as well as his spirituality. One day, just as he has begun a forty-day pledge of silence, Canzada throws herself at him, promising that once his father is dead, she will marry the young prince. Angered by his refusal, Canzada goes to the sultan, accusing his beloved son and successor of trying to ravage her. Believing the queen against his son, whose vow of silence is a secret, the Sultan Hasikin decides to kill his son. His viziers, suspicious of the queen, begin to delay Nourgehan's execution through a series of stories about the infidelity of women. Canzada, however, often interrupts with stories that belie the lessons of the vizier's tales and instead tell of violent sons.

As in the case of earlier works, the preface and frame tale of the *Turkish Tales* emerge out of and further make the chronotope of the Mahometan Orient. Titled and supposedly told by the Turks, the stories unfold from the events taking place at Hasikin, the Persian sultan's palace, while his son's spiritual teacher, Aboumaschar, an astrologer, retreats to a subterranean cave. The makeup of the frame tale betrays an unreal geography that extends outward in terms of empire, for Hasikin rules "all Asia," but also upward to the sky and downward into the earth, as symbolized by the astrologer.[58] While we can read this, on the one hand, as symbolizing the seemingly endless territories within the Mahometan Orient, it also gestures to the instability of the characters who populate these territories. Though a later tale, William Beckford's *Vathek* (1786) likens astrology to the desire of conquering even the heavens, an interest that eventually leads to the undoing of the Caliph Vathek. But the narrative structure itself, a tussle between the viziers, who stand for the Prince Nourgehan's innocence, and Canzada, whose duplicity may be revealed should the prince live, exemplifies the tussle between falsehood and truth that plays out in the oriental tale. Truth, here, is contained in the worldly figure of Prince Nourgehan, who, like Scheherazade, is "skilled in the Characters of several languages," "excelled in drawing the Bow," and was the "Master" of almost all known "Sciences," while Canzada, with her uncontrollable passions, and the naive Hasikin embody the power of falsehood.[59]

Collectively, these volumes, among others, became critical in establishing the Mahometan Orient as a spatial imaginary, an amalgamation of various Islamic empires, Persian, Ottoman, and Mughal, but also one that appears to exist in *false time*. The Mahometan is thus conceptualized by James Beattie as an "Eastern Prince [who] happens to be idle... and at a loss for expedients to kill the time, he commands his Grand Visier or his favorite to tell him stories."[60] Imagined as existing against ancient or civilizational time, and subsequently excluded from trajectories of progress that defined Enlightenment thought, the non-national

Mahometan's time itself is a fiction, the last an obvious condition of the oriental tale.

The Mahometan on the Move: Trade and Masquerade in the Oriental Tale

The chronotope of the Mahometan develops further in the stories of Sindbad, the famous traveler, and Haroun al-Raschid, the wise caliph, both of whom feature prominently in the *Arabian Nights*. Like Schahriar and Scheherazade, Sindbad and Haroun give rise to a series of other characters, whose adventures are based on the conditions of itinerancy and masquerade. That is to say, characters such as Aboulfouaris, Sultan Schemzeddin from *Nourjahad*, and later, Vathek are all constructed around the instability of the Mahometan in both place and person. Itinerancy and masquerade often find themselves hand-in-hand, deception and false identity, as exemplified by Haroun, coming in handy to restless travelers such as Sindbad. Beginning from the *Nights*, and onward, any number of Mahometan protagonists roam a vast geography armed with a fluid identity that shifts from king to mendicant, merchant to slave, depending on the circumstances. A far cry from the rapacious hordes that stood in for Muslims just a century or so back, the travelers of the oriental tale offered a number of lessons to English readers, including the benefits of virtue, moderation, and a cultivated wit. Sharing some qualities with heroes of chapbooks and local lore, the Mahometan traveler at times demonstrates that "the disadvantage of birth can be overcome by merit."[61] Successful travelers such as Sindbad and Aboulfouaris "triumph over the chicanery of foreigners" by remaining faithful to English virtues.[62] Despite this domestication, however, the Mahometan's inability to claim belonging to a single place, people, or person remains the premise upon which allegory becomes possible.

Versions of the Sindbad story are present in the Bulaq and Calcutta manuscripts of the *Alf Layla*, their theme consistent as one of hardship during travel followed by comfort and conclusion. Within Galland's telling, though, the story of Sindbad reads as that of a Mahometan protagonist imagined within European bounds. In the Galland and Grub Street volumes, Sindbad is cast as a shape-shifting adventurer enabled by his association with Islam, but also as a curiously European figure, who has both the spirit (and stories) of Odysseus as well as the commercial instincts of a modern traveler going from West to East. The son of a wealthy merchant, Sindbad is introduced to us as "that famous traveler who has sailed around the world."⁶³ In an attempt to remake his fortunes after squandering what was left to him when his father dies, the young Sindbad takes up the only profession that male protagonists in the Oriental tale seem to have, and thus joins a group of merchants headed to the East Indies from Persia.

Sindbad's geographical descriptions of the many strange islands he visits are vague and, on occasion, approximately situated, not surprisingly given that his interests are distinctly European. Over the course of his seven voyages, we come to know that he trades in spices such as "the wood of aloe," "pepper," "nutmegs," "cloves," "ginger," "pearls," and "diamonds."⁶⁴ His encounter with the one-eyed savage during his third voyage gains much from Odysseus's encounter with the Cyclops. Presaging the onset of high colonialism, Sindbad too masters the various places he visits, conquering the land and natural geography (as in the case of the rocs and elephants) and overcoming local resistance—the Old Man of the Sea and the apes on the coconut trees from his fifth voyage. He brings technological advancements to the far-away island of his fourth voyage where he teaches the people to ride with stirrups and bridles. By the time of his seventh and final voyage, he is an ambassador, helping forge alliances between the Caliph Haroun Alrashid and the unnamed King of Serendib.

Though Sindbad is in part a fictional archive of French and English trade practices in what is now South India and East Asia, his "Mahometanism" is an essential part of his story. There is no romantic narrative of discovery attached to his travels. Rather, he is a merchant, a profession that as mentioned earlier, recurs in the *Nights* and the oriental tales that follow. Perhaps the only other—comparatively occasional—vocation available to the Mahometan in the European imagination is that of a tailor, normally one that represents poverty and social marginality. The question of the traveling trader, on the other hand, is an important one that, though explicated in detail in the works of historians such as Sanjay Subrahmaniyam among others, demands some context here as well. During the seventeenth and early eighteenth centuries, European—particularly English, French, and Dutch—trade with Muslim traders flourished. To quote Gerald MacLean, "trade and travel took Muslims into the Eastern Mediterranean, the Indian Ocean, all the way to the China sea."⁶⁵ Yet Muslim travelers, diplomatic and merchant, were never allowed to establish anything close to the "settlements of Britons in Algiers, Istanbul, Hormuz, and Surat."⁶⁶ Neither did the English allow or encourage complementary settlements in England itself, choosing to keep Muslim merchants from traveling to Europe. When we read Sindbad in the light of a seemingly secular Europe's trade history with the Ottoman,

Mughal, or Safavid empires, his figure reflects both a European anxiety around Muslim trading communities and Europe's imperializing attitudes toward foreign territories.

As a "Mahometan," Sindbad is marked by his nomadism: "think no more of thy own country," one king tells him, and simultaneously commands him to marry a woman of the island.[67] The relevant footnote informs readers that Sindbad "was a Mahometan, and they allow polygamy," thus explaining his changeable identity by way of Mahometanism, or European perceptions of Islam.[68] At other times, Sindbad maneuvers and manipulates island natives through his knowledge of Arabic, attracting help from the black inhabitants through his prayer to the Almighty. Though Sindbad himself eventually returns to Baghdad, most of the other nomadic Muslim protagonists from tales that follow never return home. The original traveling Muslim, Sindbad, pioneers an entire plotline for the oriental tales—as well as the orientalist scholarship—that were to follow: the inability of the Muslim to claim a single space as his home.

Though Sindbad's travels inspire a number of other characters, Aboulfouaris, the "Great Traveler" of the *Persian Tales*, comes to embody the particular problem of Mahometan itinerancy in the oriental tale.[69] Given that Aboulfouaris's adventures are centered on the theme of a husband's fidelity—as the frame tale of the *Persian Tales* dictates—many of his travels are directed around the quest to earn or return to his wife, Canzada. Like other fictional Mohametans, Aboulfouaris is a merchant from Basra, whose adventures begin when he sets out on a journey to Serendib and Surat. Upon landing in Serendib (modern-day Sri Lanka) and successfully concluding his business, he chances upon a beautiful lady, Canzada. The latter, a "Guebre" or Zoroastrian, though suitable as a mistress cannot be taken as a wife by the Mahometan Aboulfouaris.[70] Angered by his rejection of her proposal, Canzada decides to punish Aboulfouaris by selling him as a slave to some nobles of Golconda. The ship carrying Aboulfouaris and his new masters to Golconda veers off course, taking its travelers to an unmapped sea, further even from the Philippines and Java, where they are deceived into taking on board a "monstrous" man, who in his appearance, appetites, evil propensities, and physical capabilities presages the Indian Giaour in Beckford's Gothic tale, *Vathek*.[71]

The cursed crew gets reprieve from this terrible alien when a roc picks up the invader and throws him to his death. Upon their arrival in Golconda, Aboulfouraris's new master, impressed by his charge, decides to convert to "Mahometanism" and offers his daughter to Aboulfouaris.

THE CHRONOTOPE OF THE ORIENTAL TALE / 41

He soon discovers that the girl is unwilling to marry him, and after rearranging both his and her affairs in Golconda, Aboulfouaris sets off toward Surat with the intent of returning home to Basra. In Surat, he is befriended by a deceitful man who adopts Aboulfouaris, declaring him his heir, much in the style of the sorcerer turned uncle from the story of Aladdin. Keeping with that pattern of mentor, he abandons Aboulfouaris in the pit from which he directed him to draw treasures, announcing that every year a new "Mussulman like thee" comes to die in the pit. Aboulfouaris prays for salvation, and eventually finds his way to a shore where a ship rescues him. Once he escapes from the particular snares of the following island, Aboulfouaris finds himself in Serendib again, only to discover that Canzada had married another man, and upon his sudden death was about to become a *sati*. Canzada, however, manages to evade her fate as dictated by this "terrible custom,"[72] and she and Aboulfouaris reunite, escape from Serendib, find their way to Basra, where she converts to the "Doctrine of our Great Prophet," and marries her faithful lover.[73]

The second phase of Aboulfouaris's travels begins after some years of domestic bliss when the need arises, in the wake of his father's death, to remake the family fortunes. His journey to Golconda is fruitful, but on the return the ship is washed against an unknown island, and this time around, the traveler is taken captive by a group of cursed genies who are marked by their "contempt" of "the Alcoran and Mahomet."[74] Later, rescued by a group of good genies amongst whom he is allowed to practice and preach Islam, Aboulfouaris continues his journey homeward on the back of an afrite, a devil-like monster. Diverted on the way to a strange island where he is roped into helping the afrite achieve his dark purposes, Aboulfouaris is trapped in a series of gloomy courts within which lie the corpse of the prophet Solomon; the Dedgeal (or Dajal); a passage of murals recounting all the victories of Islam gained by the prophet Muhammad; a garden with the *houris* and companions of the prophet, as well as several other prophets, including Elias. Eventually, with the help of the prophet, Kheder, Aboulfouaris returns to Basra only to find his wife, Canzada, married to another man, and himself unrecognizable to all who knew him. After a protracted effort, he is finally identified and Canzada is restored to him. But his end is not a happy one for Canzada remains in love with the man she temporarily married. We find Aboulfouaris telling his story to the king of Damascus while ensconced in his tent during yet another journey.[75]

Sindbad's journeys in the *Nights*, in comparison, appear to conclude after his seventh voyage, though his adventures had been recorded in gold letters by the Caliph Haroun al-Rashid as an example for all to behold.

Ballaster reads Aboulfouaris's story as a narrative on India, where Canzada, a "chimerical, protean creature," is synecdochal of "India for the seventeenth and eighteenth-century European imagination."[76] Centered by the performance of *sati* that occurs in the first half of the tale, Ballaster argues, "Canzada/India is a shape that shifts elusively from the desiring subject . . . the 'dream of men awake' to the immense riches and power offered by the territory of India, but also to a risky alterity that may finally evade the covetous grasp."[77] There is no denying the fact that in these early oriental tales, India and associated territories are evoked as dark yet desirable. For the Mahometan protagonists of these tales, however, India becomes an antagonist, often invading the Mahometan Orient through covert practices such as the dark arts, warning the Mahometan against entering its alterity. Aboulfouaris's story precedes the powerful orientalist reconceptualizations of India by scholars such as William Jones. What this and a set of stories with similar lessons that I discuss directly offer is an early version of the English narrative that India was somehow a geographically distinct orient from that which was imagined as Mahometan. That is to say, despite the fact that much of the Company's negotiations and battles during the seventeenth and eighteenth centuries were with Mughal rulers, Company officials continued to refer to them as "Moors," designating them as foreign and temporary invaders of India.

In Ballaster's reading, Aboulfouaris's patience is an allegory for Christian virtue in the face of danger and temptation, a possible example also for Englishmen traveling to India. But the fact that this allegory plays out through a Mahometan figure prompts a reconsideration of the text's literal meaning. On this most obvious level, Aboulfouaris, the Mahometan protagonist, is born into the profession of a merchant, which, of course, takes him on journeys across the Mahometan orient, as well as into part of India. After overcoming numerous obstacles, physical and spiritual, he returns to the place he believes to be his home. While some Mahometan merchants never return to the place they originally departed from, Aboulfouaris is among those whose return is marked by an uneasy domestic arrangement that augurs no happiness for the weary traveler. While Aboulfouaris's virtues represent Christianity, his actions and the world around him, particularly its darker elements, are all imagined and appropriated under the label of Mahometanism. More significant, however, is that despite recovering Canzada, not once but twice, Aboulfouaris remains unmoored. Knowing Canzada to be in love with her other husband, Aboulfouaris continues to travel, as is his destiny.

Part of Sindbad's and Aboulfouaris's success in their travels depends on their ability to disguise themselves, a Mahometan trait that is embodied by Haroun-al-Rashid, the caliph of Baghdad. Also present in d'Herbelot's *Bibliotheque*, where he is recounted as having made the pilgrimage to Mecca on foot, Haroun's role in the *Nights* almost always begins with his attempts to traverse his city by night in the disguise of a merchant or beggar. We encounter Haroun early on in the stories of the sisters Zobeide and Amine, and the three calendars, who have traveled from various kingdoms to meet Haroun and avail of his generosity. What is remarkable about this set of stories is that almost every character indulges in disguise, altering their actual identity for various reasons. Beginning with Haroun, who, we are told, was "accustomed to walk in disguise very often by night that he might see with his own eyes if everything was quiet in the city," to the "calendars," or wandering mendicants, who used to be princes, to the two bitches that Zobeide whips each night, once her sisters, the entire sequence hints at the Mahometan Orient as a place of unfixed and volatile identities.[78] The calendars, once princes and heirs to various kingdoms, are distinguished on account of their devotion to Mahometanism—one a famed scholar of the Quran, the other a secret convert in his father's idol-worshipping kingdom. The very state of being a Mahometan "calendar," the English appropriation of the Arabic *qalandar*, whose basic meaning implies one who has abandoned worldly pursuits, becomes implicated with the act of endless travel in the oriental tale.

While the sequence of Zobeide and the calendars attests to Haroun's generosity, another set of stories in the *Nights*, those of Ganem and Fetnah, show Haroun as a caliph whose jealousy often misleads him into cruelty. Ganem is the son of a Damascus merchant, whose sudden death leaves the family with a number of brocades destined for Baghdad. Though Ganem's mother tries to dissuade him from traveling, "an inclination to travel . . . edged him to set out" toward Baghdad.[79] Upon reaching Baghdad, Ganem mistakenly finds Fetnah, a slave-girl belonging to Haroun who has been buried alive by Zobeide, his wife, out of jealousy. Ganem saves Fetnah, nurses her back to health, and eventually brings her to his mother's house, from where she is able to tell Haroun, who believed her to be dead, that she is alive. But Haroun, convinced that Fetnah had been unfaithful to him, has her sentenced to imprisonment in a tower, while Ganem's house is burnt down and his mother and sister shamed on the streets, taken prisoner, and then finally set free to wander impoverished. Ganem is saved by Fetnah's warning. Upon realizing Haroun's intent, she told him to "put on the habit of a slave and daubed him with soot," thus allowing Ganem to walk away from the house unnoticed when Haroun's army comes to arrest Fetnah.[80]

It is only when Haroun hears Fetnah reminiscing one evening about Ganem's honorable treatment of her that he decides to forgive all. Fetnah is freed, Ganem's mother and sister are recovered, but Ganem's whereabouts remain unknown. Eventually, Fetnah receives news of a sick man taken in by a jeweler's syndic who was unable to identify himself to his caretaker. The man is Ganem, who is almost unrecognizable due to his illness, but under the care of Fetnah and his host, he finally comes to himself and is able to relate how, while hiding in small village, he fell ill and finally had to be tied on a camel's back and brought to Baghdad for treatment. The story resolves by Haroun gifting Fetnah to Ganem, himself marrying Ganem's sister to punish the jealous Zobeide, while also arranging for his widowed mother to be married to one of his viziers.

Haroun's other appearances include his encounter with Aboul Cassem, a man known for his generosity and largesse, incidentally a merchant forever displaced from Cairo, the city of his birth. Disguised as a traveler, Haroun avails Cassem's legendary hospitality, but also helps him in reuniting with Dardane, a well-to-do woman from Damas who had been sold into slavery by her mother. An unstable caliph, sometimes the subject of reform himself, other times helping reform others, Haroun is the ruler who sends Sindbad on his missions, forging diplomatic relations with other kings through this single ambassador. Haroun's frequent appearances in early and late oriental tales, as well as his well-known historical relations with Charlemagne, make him a stock character of eighteenth-century English fictions and essays. For the most part, Haroun doubles as Mahometan, who also performs the role of an ideal ruler. On the one hand, he stands for the inconstancy, the disguise, and the deception that Mahometan protagonists of the oriental tale invariably practiced, but for English readers, he offers the model of an ideal ruler, an inadvertent instrument of critique of the late Restoration king, James II.

One of Haroun's enduring reincarnations is the Sultan Schemzeddin of Sheridan's *History of Nourjahad*, who sets up an elaborate stage designed to bring his arrogant successor, Nourjahad, to task. When Nourjahad declares to Schemzeddin that he desires worldly pleasures above those of heaven, Schemzeddin decides to test him by offering him riches as well as immortality. Disguised as a heavenly angel, Schemzeddin appears in Nourjahad's bedroom while Nourjahad sleeps and upon waking him offers him a vial that will grant him his earthly desires. The single condition that the angel imposes on Nourjahad's immorality is that on occasion he will experience extended episodes of deep slumber. From then on, an elaborate drama plays out in which Nourjahad, believing himself to be the master of limitless wealth, begins to give in to his appetites for wine and women. Knowing Schemzeddin's displeasure, he is restricted to his estate where he is entertained by a number of servants and slave-girls. At the height of his arrogance and boredom, Nourjahad embarks on "one of the most extravagant projects . . . that ever entered the imagination of man."[81]

Setting up a masquerade within Schemzeddin's masquerade, Nourjahad decides to stage an Islamic paradise in his own gardens. His concubines would play the "beautiful virgins that are given to all true believers," his most beautiful mistress would be Cadiga, the favorite wife of the prophet, and he himself would fulfill the part of "Mohamet."[82] But even as the fountains in his garden begin spouting milk in place of water, Nourjahad falls into one of his slumbers and awakens to find his slave-girls aged into old women, his trusted servant, Hasem, dead, and the son borne by his favorite slave, Mandana, disappeared after robbing him of his wealth. Undeterred by these events and failure of his masquerade, Nourjahad becomes "peevish, morose, tyrannical; cruelty took possession of his breast."[83] Finally, after a drunken fit of temper in which he kills his last faithful servant, Cadiga, Nourjahad falls into yet another deep sleep.

Upon waking, he finds a man by his side, who identifies himself as Cozro, the brother of the dead Cadiga, who had made her brother promise to care for her depraved master instead of punishing him. Subsequently, it was Cozro who had begged Schemzeddin for clemency, and now that Nourjahad had awakened, he was ready to depart, leaving Nourjahad "condemned to wander in an unknown land."[84] It is at that moment that Nourjahad finally repents. In order to show that he is a changed man, he begins, with Cozro's help, a widescale effort to distribute alms across the city. His good deeds and changed persona finally lead him to Schemzeddin, who upon forgiving him, reveals that "thy guardian genius was all a deception and a piece of machinery by my contrivance."[85] What Nourjahad believed to be a lifetime was, in fact, only the matter of some fourteen months, a masquerade carefully surveilled, directed, and at times, even performed by the Sultan Schemzeddin. Believing Nourjahad's repentance to be sincere, Schemzeddin makes him the heir to his throne and so the tale ends.

As in the case of many such oriental tales, *Nourjahad*, too, has been read as a progressive text, Nussbaum suggesting that the tale illustrates the ills of domestic confinement, whereas Aravamudan and Mita Choudhry have read the work as posing a challenge to genre boundaries. My point is quite simple: *Nourjahad*, a text that is considered literary, even critical of national practices, is constructed around the spatial and temporal conditions of the Mahometan Orient: empire and false time. Though Schemzeddin's elaborate stage exhibits a scientific sophistry that Haroun's masquerades do not, the basic premise of the caliph or sultan governing, surveilling, and reforming through disguise remains in place. Other standard elements that I have not chosen to privilege include opulence, lustfulness, and hedonism, though these do not constitute the chronotopic makeup of the oriental tale. Within these varied stories, the evolving chronotope of the Mahometan acquires flesh: the empire-nation tension from the *Nights* is expanded in the forms of Sindbad and Haroun. The stories of Aboulfouaris and Nourjahad, despite relaying specific English concerns, rest upon the basic elements of earlier oriental tales: masquerade, despotism, and itinerance.

Dark Magic and Transmigration: The Indic Undoing of the Mahometan

For the most part, the Mahometan of the oriental tale is confined to the Mahometan Orient, the vast space that seems to extend continuously from Cairo to Cashmire. Despite his extensive, often endless travels eastward, however, the Mahometan protagonist is barred from one space: the Indic Orient. By the early eighteenth century, long-circulating, conflicting arguments in Europe regarding India as either the site of ancient knowledge on Abrahamic religions and other historical mysteries or, alternatively, as the home to idolatrous sects whose philosophies were premised on transmigration had found their way into oriental tales as well.[86] Travel accounts offering details of the Mughal courts, penned by explorers such as Francois Bernier and Jean-Baptiste Tavernier were available in English by the end of the seventeenth century. India, though still not fully colonized, nevertheless had begun to take definite shape in the English imagination.

While travelers such as Sindbad and Aboulfouaris traveled to ports such as Golconda and Serendib, their journeys to these outlying parts of the Indic Orient were fraught, and the conditions they faced necessitated return to the Mahometan Orient. In the heyday of the orient tale, the Indic Orient is a lurking presence, described by Ballaster as a "duplicitous fiction," the site of "master tricksters."[87] For the Mahometan protagonist, however, the Indic Orient is a warning, a dark but sacred territory that threatens to destroy the masquerading despot should he attempt to traverse its bounds. For a good part of the eighteenth century, India was popularly seen in England as the reason for the rise of newly rich nabobs who threatened the domestic and political order of the metropolis upon their return from the colony. This well-known perception may well be one explanation for the early fictional construction of the Indic Orient—one that persisted in many stories and even some novels—but its animus toward the Mahometan in the oriental tale has more complex bearings.

While England's dealings, from as far back as Thomas Roe's embassy to the emperor Jehangir to the Company's interactions with Aurangzeb, had been with Mughal rulers, a single narrative around this dynasty persisted in England and France within which we can see much of what I have attempted to describe take on material significance. To borrow from Francois Bernier's travelogue from his days in the Mughal territories:

> The Great Mogul is a foreigner in Hindoustan, a descendent of Tamerlane, chief of the Moguls from Tartary, who, about the year 1401, overran and conquered the Indies. Consequently, he finds himself in a hostile country, or nearly so, a country containing hundreds of Gentiles to one Mogul, or even to one Mohametan.[88]

Bernier's account was a popular one, translated into English around 1671, believed also to be a source for Dryden's own *Aureng-zebe*. The Mughal ruler of India, by this account, follows the general prototype of the Mahometan despot: foreign and itinerant. But unlike fictional rulers such as Schahriar, Haroun, or Hasikin, who remained within the Mahometan Orient—incidentally no longer a threat to European interests—the "Mogul" rules in a "hostile" geography. Appropriating this general and oft-repeated conception of India, the oriental tale imaginatively codifies the perceived condition of the Mughal emperor in cautionary terms of ruined Mahometan empires.

The final element of the chronotope, then, posits that the Mahometan, in all his various forms—posturer, nomad, despot—cannot inhabit the Indic Orient. To put it another way, the Indic Orient of the oriental tale is starkly separated from the Mahometan Orient through the constitutions of its characters and its people. How can we read this destructive antagonism between orients: the one, signified by its empire-like formation and its itinerant, masquerading subjects, and the other, a place of possibility that, though mysterious, is home to vast stores of wealth and knowledge? As a construct, the Mahometan Orient, marked by its false time and space, simply could not cohere with the Indic. The latter, in contrast, was a territory whose "Gentiles" were rumored to be the "direct descendants of Abraham," and that housed "ancient scriptures," believed to be the key to the Mosaic narrative.[89] Captured by Raymond Schwab, the French letterist, the Mahometan Orient, "much of a piece with the empire of the caliphs" in the *Arabian Nights*, lacked exactly what India offered to Europe: "remoteness, nobility and a sense of the archaic."[90] The vague incompatibility of two invented orients is formally theorized by later orientalists in India, ironically, using some of the terms that the oriental tale provides. In the stories of Fadlallah and Zemroude, and Beckford's *Vathek*, the Indic Orient—personified as santons, or Hindu devotees—ventures to Mahometan territories, tempting sultans and caliphs with promises of immortality and wealth, but inevitably destroys them when they fail to resist their seductive guests.

The story of Fadlallah and Zemroude first appeared in the *Persian Tales* as a story about a man's fidelity to his wife, while an excerpt from the story was reprinted in the *Spectator* with the lesson that "Consciousness alone and not Identity of Substance" makes a person. Indeed, a pliable plot with many lessons to offer, the story is also a warning to the Mahometan prince against giving in to his curiosity for India. Fadlallah, the prince of Moussel, asks his father to allow him to travel before he has to settle down and marry. En route to Baghdad, his retinue is attacked by Bedouins who, upon discovering his identity, decide to exact a special revenge on him. One of the Bedouin wives, taking pity on Fadlallah releases him from captivity a night before the desert pirates have to move camp. He continues his journey to Baghdad, but upon reaching it, he catches sight of Zemroude, the daughter of the aristocratic Mouaffac, engaged to marry the prince of Basra. Disguised in a "costly robe" and a "turban of Indian muslin," Fadlallah impersonates the prince and ends up marrying Zemroude himself.[91] Not at all unhappy when Fadlallah's deception is discovered, Zemroude helps perpetuate the disguise, even indulging in some masquerade herself.

After living in Baghdad for some years, Fadlallah hears of his father's death and decides to travel back to Mousel to take his rightful place on the throne, which was in the meanwhile occupied by his German cousin, Amadeddin Zengui. But Fadlallah's reign is brief, for soon after returning to Mousel, he befriends a mysterious "dervis," the Indic undoing of the happy couple.[92] The young man, who fast becomes the "principal favorite" of Fadlallah, tells him of his travels to the Indies where he had seen a "great many curiosities and wonderful things" and during which had become close to an "aged Brachman," a man acquainted with the "most hidden powers of nature."[93] One of the many "secrets," the devious dervish learns from the Brahmin is the power of transmigration, or transporting the soul from one body to another.[94] Overcome by curiosity, Fadlallah insists that the dervish also teach him the secret of transmigration, and after several refusals, the dervish gives in. By leaving out the words for returning to one's own body, the dervish ends up occupying Fadlallah's body, while the prince himself is in that of a wounded doe. Disguised as Fadlallah, the dervish returns to the palace and to Zemroude who knows nothing of what has transpired. After a series of bodily migrations, Fadlallah finally manages to return to his body and kill his false friend, but when Zemroude discovers the deception she has suffered, and the adultery she has inadvertently committed, she dies, leaving Fadlallah alone. Fadlallah abdicates from the throne and spends the rest of his life as a wandering mendicant.

Allegorically, Fadlallah's story "suggests parallels between the Persian seraglio and the court of Louis XIV in France, both spaces of intrigue, duplicity, sexual and political plotting."[95] In the case of its abridged reprint in the *Spectator*, the story served as a philosophical and political reflection for the bourgeois Englishman. Derivative in form, the chronicle of Fadlallah and Zemroude has, at its center, a male protagonist who, like Sindbad, travels at will, and like Haroun, facilitates his physical and social mobility through disguise. In a sharp contrast to other characters in the oriental tale, however, Fadlallah, a Mahometan prince, pursues India, here signified by certain forms of knowledge with which the dervish tempts him. The pursuit of this mysterious entity costs Fadlallah both his person and his kingdom, leaving him forever a mendicant. Fadlallah and other Mahometans, including Aboulfouaris, seek proximity to India, a harsh end that stands in stark comparison to the happier situations that territorially compliant characters such as Schahriar and Sindbad find themselves in.

Though India and the dark arts also make an appearance in the story of Chec Chahubuddin from the *Turkish Tales*, a more precise example of the maturation of this contradiction between Mahometan and Indic appears in *Vathek*. The story of the Caliph Vathek details the events in the life of the protagonist and his final fall into the caverns of hell. Vathek is the ninth caliph of the Abassid caliphs, the ruling dynasty that claimed to be the direct descendants of "Mohamet" (as narrated in the *Bibliothèque*), taking control from the "Ommiades" by accusing them of "usurping" what was "heritage" to the former group.[96] The name Vathek is a corruption of al-Vasiq, the ruling Abassid caliph from 842 to 847 A.D.

The chronotope of the Mahometan culminates in the figure of Vathek, a caliph whose role the footnotes of the story tell us "implies the three characters of Prophet, Priest, and King," and who, instead of living in a single palace, moves around within five different palaces, each dedicated to the pleasures of a different sense.[97] A man of excesses, Vathek "wished to know everything; even sciences that did not exist," an end for which he decides to build a tower that literally seems to carry him beyond the earth and into the "mysteries of astrology."[98] His desire to outdo his humanly limits and his "irreligious conduct" are "beheld with indignation" by the "great prophet Mahomet," who decides that Vathek's excess must become his undoing, going so far as to send his Genii to expedite the construction of the tower. When Vathek finally climbs atop the completed tower, he beholds "men not larger than pismires; mountains, than shells; and cities, than beehives." In his own estimation, "he was almost ready to behold himself," interrupted only by the presence of the stars that shone above him.[99] While Vathek is *exterior* to all that he beholds—pismires, shells, beehives, all suggestive of defined, bounded communities that *exclude* the caliph—Mahomet is an imposter of a prophet, who misleads his subject instead of counseling him.

Vathek's forays into astrology lead him to believe that the "most marvelous adventures, which were to be accomplished by an extraordinary personage from a country all together unknown," awaited him.[100] To that end, when a stranger arrives in Samarrah, "a man so abominably hideous" and of "so horrible a visage" that all who see him recoil, Vathek, despite his own disgust, decides to welcome him to the palace.[101] The man identifies himself as a Giaour, "an Indian; but from a region of India, which is wholly unknown."[102] He shows Vathek "sabres ... enriched with gems that were hitherto unknown" that "emitted a dazzling radiance," covered with "uncouth characters engraven on their sides," a script that arrests the caliph's attention immediately.[103] Vathek's obsession with the Giaour and the mysterious letters makes him ill to a point that he abandons all his pleasures, poring over the sabres daily until one day the Giaour finds him alone. He commands Vathek to "devote thyself to me ... abjure Mahomet," in return for which he would show Vathek "in immense depositories, the treasures which the stars have promised."[104] Vathek agrees, and a series of events follow that signal the unraveling of his empire.

Vathek's obsession with the Giaour leads him to abandon his own kingdom and travel across the Mahometan Orient, but the journey does not end with the treasures of India. Instead, the Giaour reveals himself to be "Eblis," a satanic spirit, and Vathek meets his end in a monstrous cavern that seems to stand for hell itself. A number of other characters, including a benign Emir, his beautiful daughter and Vathek's own sorceress mother, play a role in the story, but none as compelling as that of the Giaour from India. While the version of events presented in this discussion is an abridged one, my interest remains in the overwhelming role that the Indic Orient plays in the annihilation of the Mahometan protagonist and his territories. As a character, Vathek is certainly not likeable, but unlike other barbaric sultans, an enlightened domestication becomes closed to him when he pursues knowledge and territories that extend beyond the Mahometan Orient. Neither can Vathek be reformed or dissuaded by way of stories from his curiosity for the treasures and secrets of India, for the latter differently from the territories of the Mahometan Orient, resists any attempts on the part of the Mahometan to colonize it.

A somewhat later tale than others discussed here, *Vathek* deploys every aspect of the Mahometan chronotope to produce a narrative whose allegorical possibilities range from bad governance to sexual deviance, the performance of which is undertaken by the Mahometan protagonist. Taken as part of a progression of stories and characters that include Fadlallah, Aboulfouaris, Chech Chahabudin, *Vathek* ultimately points us to the impossibility of the posturing, itinerant, and despotic Mahometan—Ottoman or Mughal—to lay claim to the Indic Orient as the English imagination constructs it: the seat of ancient knowledge, perhaps even Abrahamic truths, populated by a Gentile people destined for Christianity. It seems redundant to recall that by this point, India was a flourishing site of lived Islam, the so-called "Gentiles" of Bernier's narrative part of a fluid Indo-Persian religio-cultural complex. Scattered, even inconsistent, the interactions between the Mahometan and Indic Orients that take place in the oriental tale are gathered into a cohesive, scholarly narrative by William Jones within a year or so of *Vathek*'s publication.

By the latter decades of the eighteenth century, both the oriental tale and the chronotope of the Mahometan had become ubiquitous symbols in English culture. Independently composed volumes of oriental tales or single stories such as Thomas Moore's political allegory *Lalla-Rookh* (1817) and Lord Byron's romance *The Giaour* (1813) persisted, but to a large extent, the domestic novel had assumed the reigns of national narrative. Within the novel, what was once a definitive chronotope became a synecdoche for all that is oppositional to English virtue. In Samuel Richardson's *Pamela* (1740), Pamela declares herself to be above those who may trade their honesty for "all the riches of the Indies," while in *Clarissa* (1748), the evil Lovelace compares himself to a slave and his captive, Clarissa Harlow, to an "eastern monarch." In Henry Fielding's *History of Tom Jones* (1749), Tom Jones fantasizes about turning down "Circassian beauties" for the village squire's daughter, Sophia. By the end of the eighteenth century, novels about Warren Hastings's India, including

Gibbes's *Hartly House, Calcutta* and Elizabeth Hamilton's *Letters of a Hindoo Rajah* (1796), rewrite the chronotope as historical fact for the English reading public. Relegated to minor, low-brow popular forms such as the chapbook, the fantastic Mahometan endured as an image: Bluebeard, the infamous wife-killer, began to be dressed in Ottoman robes; brightly illustrated copies of Sindbad's and Aladdin's adventures circulated as penny fiction.

This is not to say that chronotope of the Mahometan, as it emerged in the once-dominant form of the eighteenth-century oriental tale, vanished entirely. Much of the point of this chapter, at the risk of seeming descriptive, has been to explicate the construction of the Mahometan as a figure in a space and time delineated by Enlightenment ideals. Similarly, for those weary of critics and scholars who continue to engage with the discipline and legacies of orientalism, this chapter may read as a simplistic rehearsal or elaboration of arguments contained in Said's *Orientalism*. My extended argument, however, should not be misread as a recounting of various oriental tales and their biases against Muslims. What I hope to have done is to have elaborated the underlying narrative structure of the oriental tale as uniquely constituted by the elements of a time and space that are in contradiction with the moment in which they are invented. The Mahometan chronotope, as I call it, materializes in the English oriental tale as a non-national, shifting space whose inhabitants themselves are fluid, unattached beings. Over the course of the late eighteenth and nineteenth centuries, this chronotope travels past the limits of domestic fiction to other orientalist forms, including scholarly tracts and vernacular oriental tales.

2 / Hindustani/Urdu: The Oriental Tale in the Colony

By the second half of the eighteenth century, the flourishing vogue for the oriental tale in the metropolis was superseded and eventually supplanted by the domestic novel. This is not to say that the Mahometan Orient was no longer a concern in the English popular imagination. The Mahometan remained a reference in the domestic novel as well, but English knowledge-production and imaginative forays with regards to the orient had largely shifted elsewhere. Not entirely a new sphere in the history of European knowledge-practices, orientalism as a serious academic discipline in England took hold in the mid-eighteenth century, with universities such as Cambridge and Oxford expanding their programs in Hebrew and Arabic to bring in Persian as well. But what we call British orientalism—the comprehensive eighteenth- and nineteenth-century scholarly effort to know territories ranging from Egypt to India in their totality—did not unfold in isolation from the oriental vogue that had taken over metropolitan popular culture in the previous decades. That is to say, academic and scholarly knowledge practices spearheaded by individuals and imperial institutions in colonial territories were not disconnected from the domains of popular and high literary culture in England. We can say, in fact, that the oriental tale gained renewed prominence within the scholarly endeavors that accompanied the expansion of the East India Company interests in the Indian subcontinent following the English victory in the Battle of Plassey in 1757. British orientalism, with its deliberate interests in language, law, religion, and literature in India, appropriated and repurposed the Mahometan chronotope for the philological project that was so essential to colonial expansion.

Spearheaded by Warren Hastings, the first English governor-general of the Company's holdings in India, the orientalist effort in India saw itself as essential to the Company's new role as the rulers of Bengal, as well as the subsequent territories it added to its holdings. Extended as it may have been, the project of the Calcutta orientalists—as the group working under Hastings's patronage has been called—indelibly transformed the realm of language and textual practice in India from a fluid, regional complex evolved from Indo-Persian-Arabo-Turkic exchanges to an insular set of languages divided across religio-national lines. This was not achieved solely within the two decades that orientalists such as Nathaniel Halhed, William Jones, and Charles Wilkins attempted to revive what they believed was India's classical past, but over the course of half a century or so of expansive efforts on the part of a number of Company officers. The efforts of some two generations of British orientalists in Calcutta culminated in the colonial education system for natives, a nexus through which the so-called knowledge of the Calcutta orientalists was employed in the creation of a new subject whose identity—linguistic, aesthetic, even legal—was reconstituted entirely on religious lines. Visible today in the divided registers of the modern vernaculars, Urdu and Hindi, but also in the antagonistic South-Asian identities of Muslim and Hindu, the "tectonic shifts in language, literature, and culture," caused by the orientalist project in India, to quote Aamir Mufti, had at their core two oppositional chronotopes: the Mahometan, as I have described it in the previous chapter, and the "chronotope of the indigenous," as Mufti has termed it.[1]

I argue in this chapter that the Mahometan chronotope travels to India through the efforts of orientalist scholars and institutions, preeminent of which are the Royal Asiatick Society of Bengal, established by William Jones during the Hastings era, and Fort William College, a language school for English officers, set up at the bequest of John Gilchrist, an entrepreneurial polyglot. It is reaffirmed through the discipline of "literature," a vital part of the education curricula in the network of colonial schools and colleges intended for the preparation of natives for service under Company, and subsequently the British Government of India. Visible in the oriental tale, the idea of the Mahometan is further given flesh by the Calcutta Orientalists in scholarly tracts, as well as in "vernacular" oriental tales, the particular project of Gilchrist and his Fort William colleagues. Overwriting what can only be described as a historical, lived reality of Muslims in India for many centuries, the extended orientalist project ruptures extant aesthetic and linguistic practices by attempting to classify them according to religion, itself a fluid category prior to the colonial moment. To see it another way, the concept of what it meant to be a Muslim or Hindu in India was formally defined for the first time by the colonial state through the categories of language and literature.

My interest, in particular, remains with the chronotope of the Mahometan, its entry into the North Indian literary sphere by way of what I argue is a vernacular oriental tale, and its transformation of Urdu, once an elite linguistic register, into a religiously aligned formation. To be very clear, the oriental tale was never *returned* or *revived* in the orient or colonized spaces by the wave of British orientalists in Calcutta during the late eighteenth and early nineteenth centuries. Rather, a new category—literature—invented and cultivated by British orientalists in India, overwrote existing aesthetic and textual traditions through its promulgation of morally inclined fictions, simplistic versions at best of the English oriental tale.[2] In this chapter, I trace what appear to be three phases through which the chronotope of the Mahometan moves from the English imagination into the colony, reorganizing what we can approximately call socio-aesthetic affiliations into rigid religious identities.

The initial phase is marked by the absorption or the appropriation of the Mahometan chronotope into the authoritative orientalist scholarship that was produced in India during the governor-generalship of Warren Hastings. Authorized and published by the Asiatic Society and its annual publication, the *Asiatic Researches*, the ambitious projects of Jones and fellow orientalists were deemed essential to the Company's mission in India and celebrated for the insight they provided the English into native laws and culture. Jones was also a well-known poet and literary theorist of sorts (if that term may be backdated) before he left England. His volume *Poems, Consisting Mainly of Translations from Asiatick Languages* (1772), exemplifying the oriental vogue that had taken over England, is also one of the first exercises that attempts to link the poetics of a language with the character of its people. Upon arriving in India, Jones's philological efforts, though focused on the question of the Indic, situate the Mahometan in terms of its relation to the former. Best-remembered for his translation of the ancient Sanskrit play *Sakuntala* (1787), Jones's famed "Discourses," presented to the Asiatic Society members between 1784 and 1790, attest to the fashion in which what seemed to be harmless tropes of a popular fiction and travel accounts are formally codified in theoretical and scholarly documents.

The second, more transparent phase of this movement is steered by John Gilchrist and takes place at Fort William College during the years 1800 and 1810. The self-proclaimed discoverer of the "grand popular language" of India, Gilchrist spent several years of his eclectic career in India at Fort William College where he worked tirelessly on the invention of a literature in "Hindustani," the crude spoken register he believed could serve as a universal vernacular in colonial India.³ Deriving this title from the Persian word for India, Hindustan, Gilchrist defines Hindustani as the language that has resulted from "the repeated, successful invasions by the Moosulmans."⁴ In Gilchrist's words, it is the adulteration of Hindwee, the "once pure speech," "the language of the Indian Arcadia," with the Arabic and Persian of the invading Mahometans.⁵ Unlike Jones, whose efforts were focused on the discovery and revival of this pure Arcadia, Gilchrist's entrepreneurial drive led him to focus, quite literally, on inventing Hindustani as a universal vernacular in India. Not only did the propagation of Hindustani meet with resistance from natives outside the colonial ambit, even within the College it was confronted with the parallel invention of Hindi, a Sanskrit-leaning version of the vernacular favored by Gilchrist's colleague, Henry Colebrooke, a mentee of Jones and an ardent Sanskritist.

Replete with printing presses, Orientalist scholars/professors, and *munshīs* (native scribes) the College, under Gilchrist's leadership, patronized the composition and publication of a large number of so-called "literary" works in local languages such as Bangla, Persian, Tamil, and most important, Hindustani.⁶ Gilchrist's invention and patronage of Hindustani as a vernacular, complete with a literature, mark a new phase in the complex history of the oriental tale during the long eighteenth century—now in the heart of the colony. I focus specifically on the composition and promotion of a single and deeply influential text, *Bāġh-o Bahār*, or the Garden and the spring (1804), a vernacular oriental tale in which the orientalist term "Hindustani" becomes irreversibly conflated with Urdu, at that moment a name for the elite literary register preferred in Delhi and Lucknow that the orientalists, on account of its Persio-Arabic borrowings, associated with Islam. This event, often clumsily ascribed to Gilchrist, is perhaps better understood in terms of the broader politics of Fort William, though Gilchrist's role does remain central to the emergence of the vernacular we now know as Urdu.

The third phase of this movement from metropolis to colony occurs when the Fort William College curricula are transplanted upon a colonial education system for native subjects. The culmination of Jones's and Gilchrist's efforts, this nexus of schools and colleges is directly evolved from the "research" produced by institutions such as the Asiatic Society, Fort William College, and English missionary activity in India. Intended for the reeducation of the natives, or in some versions, the revival of an Indian civilization, the Eurocentric category of "literature" is introduced to Indian natives within the Government of India's new education system. Reflected in the various debates between the orientalists and their naysayers, the Anglicists, literature is that body of texts in a language that reflects the national character and ethos of a people, but in the case of Indian languages—as both groups see them—non-existent or deplorably lacking in body and character. The vernacular oriental tale, manufactured at Fort William, then, is classified as a *literary* object in Hindustani, erroneously considered the same as Urdu, and designated as embodying the collective nature of India's "Mohametans," or Muslims. Likewise, the Sanskrit-leaning register of the vernacular, Hindi, is cultivated as a vehicle for the revival of ancient Sanskrit literature, the sacred inheritance of Indic Orient. An alien category for native elites for whom the concept of aesthetic expression held profoundly different meanings, the Enlightenment ideal of "literature" and its derivative concepts became central to the twin colonial projects of vernacularization and moral disciplining.

These successive "movements" of the oriental tale from the European Republic of Letters into the colony ostensibly appear, and have recently been read, as examples of "*translatio* or transmission" whereby "texts moved across languages with relative ease and without much explanation."[7] They are, in fact, seminal to the rise of a national consciousness within Urdu and Hindi prose writing in the nineteenth and twentieth centuries. In short, the oriental tale is not, in fact, an "oriental," "Eastern," or "Indian" literary form. For those there are other names with other implications, including the different varieties of Persian and Urdu fantasy known as *dāstān* and *qiṣṣā*. But it is the metropolitan oriental tale dressed in the vernacular, not these local forms, that has commanded a significant impact on North Indian prose fiction over the past two centuries or so. In particular, the oriental tale was a foundational genre in the imperially mediated, identitarian emergence of the divided North Indian vernaculars, Urdu and Hindi. Though this book remains focused on the transformation of the Mahometan chronotope in modern Urdu, its counterpart, Hindi, historically fashions itself *against* the myth of the Muslim invader. In the colony, the oriental tale was more than a renegade or popular literary form. Patronized by imperial institutions, it enjoyed a renewed license and cultural purpose in nineteenth-century North India.

William Jones and the Mahometan Chronotope: India Against Islam

Jones, a prolific and influential orientalist of the modern period, for much of the nineteenth and twentieth centuries has been described as the savior of Indian culture and the "father of modern linguistics," his best-known achievements being the mastery of Sanskrit and the subsequent theorization of the "Indo-European" linguistic family.[8] Much energy has been expended applauding, and recently interrogating, Jones's philological achievements in India, but there is little engagement with his literary essays, poems, and scholarly discourses—almost all of which are concerned with the Mahometan or Indic Orients. Though my concern is largely with Gilchrist and Fort William College, Jones and his views on Muslims and Islam as a vital part of what he referred to as the "vast regions of Asia" must preface any further engagement.[9] Hardly a lone figure in terms of his intellectual leanings, Jones is a classic product of the Enlightenment, his understanding of language and its supposed ties to nation and origin inspired by the German Romantic Johann Gottfried Herder as well as by Voltaire, an early Indophile. Likewise, his work formed the basis for the intensely language-focused work of later German orientalists such as Max Muller, not to mention the linguistic-racial developments conceived by Ernst Renan with regards to the Hebrew and its links to the Jewish race.[10]

Prior to his arrival in India, Jones studied the classics at Oxford, dabbling in poetic translations, even composing verses of his own that his ardent biographer, Garland Canon, claims were "on a par with Dryden and Pope."[11] Though skilled in Latin and Greek, Jones eventually turned toward Hebrew, then Arabic, and finally to Persian, each of these "Eastern" languages ostensibly offering a poetic wealth that he found lacking in their European counterparts. Nevertheless, Persian and Arabic, given the Company's growing investments in India also made for a lucrative career in translation and instruction. Jones cultivated both, especially the former, even producing a Persian grammatical guide in 1771. In little over a decade, he arrived in Warren Hastings's Calcutta to serve as a junior judge. In Calcutta, Jones underwent a rebirth of sorts, his previous interests utterly overwhelmed by the challenges of establishing a standardized English legal system that would be based on the religious laws of Hindus and Muslims.[12] On encountering the vast linguistic and expressive diversity of India, Jones, as Mufti puts it, experienced a "philological sublime," brought on by the cultural landscape of "infinitesimal and dynamic differentiations and of seemingly infinite proportions."[13] This encounter is historically commemorated by ascribing to Jones the honor of having "discovered" Sanskrit, the foundational unit of the chronotope of indigeneity. Jawaharlal Nehru, for example, thanks Jones for his "gift" in his autobiography, *The Discovery of India*. But Jones's Indological research central to the emergence of modern nationalist and origin-thinking in the Indian subcontinent, cannot be parsed as unrelated from his and other contemporary conceptions of Muslims and Islam at the time. The Mahometan chronotope, the structural core of the oriental tale, reappears in a variety of well-circulating, scholarly works on the subject of India, both bodies of representation in conversation and confluence with one another. We can say that the Mahometan chronotope, once materialized in the oriental tale, is subsequently confirmed in orientalist attempts to conceptualize the Indic Orient. The Indic Orient, as it unfolds in Jones's writings, is imagined *against* the existing chronotope of the Mahometan.

A product of his times, Jones, in his scholarly works, reiterated much of that which abounded regarding the Mahometan orient in popular fictions and even more highly regarded works such as Voltaire's essays and plays. By the second part of the eighteenth century, the intersection of the scholarly with a large reading public was enabled by the various journals and newspapers that abounded in London and other metropolitan centers. A newspaper such as the *Whitehall Evening Post*, a tri-weekly founded by Daniel Defoe, along with publishing obituaries, moral-bearing oriental tales, news, and public announcements would also publish scholarly lectures or longer essays as part of its section "Sunday Amusements." In a February 1785 issue, the *Post* published parts of the orientalist and theologian Joseph White's Bampton Lectures at Oxford, attractively titled "Comparison between Christianity and Mahometanism." In White's essay, Mahomet is a merchant who countered his early troubles by taking "flight," as opposed to the "domestic privacy" and "public miracles" that distinguished the young Christ.[14] As the many sultans of the oriental tale do, Mahomet "allured his followers with the glories of a visible monarchy and the splendor of temporal dominion."[15] Volumes bearing titles like *The History of Mahomet, That Grand Imposter* took up the task of serving as scholarly biographies of the Prophet Mohammed. Bearing a loose resemblance to the various Mahometans that populated the oriental tale, Mohammed, the prophet, is Mahomet, the imposter and itinerant in scholarly endeavors as well.

In his comparatively early but deeply influential volume *Poems, consisting chiefly of translations from Asiatick Languages* (1772), Jones composed and loosely adapted a number of moral poems clearly inspired by the English vogue for the Mahometan Orient. With names such as "Solima: An Arabian Eclogue" and "The Palace of Fortune," in which "camels bounded," alongside "swift ostrich," and "soft tents," in and out of an English bucolic made up of "life-breathing glades," "meadows ever green," and "lily, pink, and rose," Jones's oriental poems well-suited a reading audience still desirous of experiencing the "Asiatick luxury" they represent.[16] Attached to this longish collection of "imitations," or translations, are two critical essays on the nature of poetry, deemed by M. H. Abrams as the earliest rendition of the "expressive theory of poetry."[17] Though largely written about with respect to their significance for poetics, Jones's essays also reveal an intellectual continuity with existing theories of Muslim origin.

"On the Poetry of Eastern Nations," Jones's first essay, argues that the Quran is a poetic movement, an argument that Jones would later, under the influence of Voltaire, develop with a greater political bent. "It is not sufficient that a nation have a genius for poetry, unless they have the advantage of a rich and beautiful language, that their expressions be worthy of their sentiments," Jones argues.[18] The "Arabians," possessing both, are thus the exemplar, and Arabic poetry, as evidenced by "Solimah," a distinct reflection of their nature. In particular, the Arabs having to suffer the heat of the desert, value, above all, in their poetry, "freshness" and "verdure," often appearing in the form of "a green meadow" or "a beautiful woman."[19]

Before becoming Mahometans, the Arabs had a "national" character, one manifestation of which is "the fondness of the Arabs for poetry and the respect which they show to the poets."[20] "Mahomed, who was himself a poet," Jones suggests, composes chapters of the "Alcoran" to win converts among this lyrical nation.[21] Knowing full well the character of his people, Mahomet "described the pleasures of heaven to them, under the allegory of cool fountains, green bowers, and black-eyed girls, as the term 'Houri' literally signifies in Arabick."[22] He continues the story of Islam's rise in Arabia by suggesting that Muhammad was an accomplished poet whose compositions—that is, chapters of the Quran—won him converts when rival Arab poets declared his verses to be "divine."[23]

What Jones does with the category of "Arab," as approximately national, and Mahometan, as falsely religious, requires careful parsing. Islam, upon its founding, exists as a spurious superstructure *above* the original, organic Arab national identity, one whose "genius" is the result of its geography and climate.[24] Early Arab converts to Islam surrender to the power of Mahomed's poetry, relinquishing enmity under the influence of the poet's verses, much in the fashion that barbaric sultans such as Schahriar relented under Scheherazade's masterfully told stories. Across the Arab Peninsula, and into Persia and Tartary, as Jones calls these regions, "the religion and language of Mahomed" spread, transforming, above all, the poetic traditions of these otherwise different peoples.[25] Though generous, when compared to the crude comparison offered by White and any number of like-minded orientalists, Jones's conceptualization of Islam as a structure that overwrote national languages and traditions expands the prescriptive possibilities of the oriental tale. Islam and its attendant threats to Europe are contained within the realm of a poetics that replicates the formative core of the Mahometan chronotope.

The second instance where Jones reaffirms this conceptualization of Islam occurs a decade and a half later. By now in Calcutta, crowned the discoverer of the ancient language Sanskrit, Jones embarks on his famous "Discourses," annual speeches delivered to members of the Asiatick Society in Bengal on the linguistic and ethno-racial affinities between what he called the "five principal nations" of Asia.[26] In some eleven or so discourses on the various Asiatic "nations," Jones is largely dedicated to the Hindus and to what he believed to be the Indo-European language complex. Though the Asiatick Society aimed to command sweeping and comprehensive knowledge of India, ranging from its languages and peoples to its flora and fauna, Jones remained largely concerned with the "Histories of India ... confined downwards to the Mohammedan conquests at the beginning of the eleventh century, but extend[ed] upwards, as high as possible, to the earliest authentic records of the human species."[27] India and the Hindus, Jones believes, "in some early age, were splendid in arts and arms, happy in government, wise in legislation, and eminent in various knowledge."[28] The "Mahommedan conquests" of India are discarded as a false period in the history of this place and its people. In imagining India as distinct and its people, the Hindus, as the scions of an ancient civilization, Jones becomes the first European scholar to "conceive" of the subcontinent "as a single cultural entity, a unique civilization with its roots in the Sanskritic and more particularly Vedic texts of the Aryans."[29] The importance of this theoretical reiteration of the Indian subcontinent into the originary cradle of a people Jones calls the Hindus begins the systematic invention of the imagined entity I have referred to as the Indic Orient, a site that has earlier appeared in the oriental tale as secretive and antagonistic to Mahometans. Distinct from the Mahometan Orient, the Indic Orient is ancient and its people, the Hindus, indigenous.

"On the Arabs," the fourth discourse, marks the coming of Islam as the "Mahomedan Revolution," a movement that ended the "stupid idolatory" that was prevalent amongst the "lower orders."[30] Arabic, the ancient languages of the indigenous peoples of the Arab peninsula, we know from the earlier essays, is usurped by Muhammad through his skill in poetry. In this later "Discourse," Islam, characterized as a political moment, is utterly devoid of ancient origins, at odds with Jones's Herderian ideals of *volk* and nation. Islam is a not a people or a civilization in the manner of Hinduism, or even Judaism, for that matter. Jones claims that when told by an Arab that the Ka'abah in Mecca was built by the Prophet Abraham (from whom Muslims believe their religion to be descended), he corrected the Arab by informing him that Abraham "was never there [Mecca]."[31] Geographically false, a lyric movement, Islam is at best a revolution, ongoing until the arrival of the next great poet. Much more could be explored from Jones's grand corpus of letters, poems, essays, and translations, but these brief selections from both his early works and his revered Indological research testify to the precise categorization of orients, Indic and Mahometan, which would, within less than a century, bloom into the irrevocable religio-linguistic divisions of Urdu and Hindi in India.

Across Europe, the recovery of India's ancient civilization and language was celebrated for its potential to revive Western culture. Jones's much acclaimed translation of the ancient Sanskrit *natak*, *Sakuntala* in 1789 firmly established him as the savior of Europe's arts and sciences: Herder believed he had found the "mistress of my heart," while Goethe, equally rapturous, modeled his opening of *Faust* on Kalidasa's play.[32] India, Jones offering to Europe, was a seductive, alluring mistress whose attainment would reinvigorate spirits sobered by the rationalism of the Enlightenment. While Mahometan Orient was "a companion, ancient and familiar," as Raymond Schwab put it, the Indic Orient spun by the Calcutta orientalists brought to Europe a second renaissance, a rebirth of its own arts and culture, but also a relocation of the Mahometan Orient as an invader of the Indic.[33] Jones died in 1794, living through the governorships of both the deposed Hastings and his successor Charles Cornwallis. During his time in India, Jones undertook the production of the massive *Laws of Manu* as well as a law book for Muslims, efforts that have been lauded by biographers such as Michael J. Franklin, who describe this knowledge as a "cooperative process" between Jones, Brahmin pundits, and maulvis.[34] But these works and their subsequent imposition in the colonial state only served to further delineate an emerging set of national identities.[35]

John Gilchrist and the New Vernaculars of India

As the Jones-inspired "oriental renaissance" spread across Europe, Paris, Frankfurt, and Berlin, becoming as involved as London, Jones's most important successor, John Gilchrist, focused his efforts on the Indic Orient as the actual site of the Oriental renaissance. Until well into the 1790s, the official languages of communication between the Company and the native population in India remained Persian and Bangla. Gilchrist, initially a doctor in the Royal Navy, soon shifted careers, first becoming an indigo farmer, and subsequently, a textbook writer, publishing book after book on a language he called "Hindostanee," which he believed was the common vernacular of India. By the close of the eighteenth century, he had authored several poems, *A Grammar of the Hindostanee Language* (1796), *The Oriental Linguist* (1798), and several shorter tracts on the importance of his discovery. Aggressively marketing his books to Company officials, Gilchrist eventually managed to convince Lord Wellesley, the third governor-general of India, to establish Fort William College in Calcutta in 1800 for the purposes of training English officers in the native languages, "Hindustani," Persian, Braj, and Bengali among others.

Wellesley and Gilchrist expanded the official focus of the greater Indological project established by Jones from the discovery and learning of classical languages (as was the ambition of Warren Hastings) to the standardization of modern vernaculars more fitted for governance. Consolidating several decades of orientalist research in India, Fort William was created to train Company officers to act as "statesmen ... Magistrates, Judges, Ambassadors, and Governors of Provinces" in Company territories.[36] While it also provided instruction in the sciences and European classics, its chief function was to familiarize young Englishmen arriving in India with the diversity of native languages. With self-taught scholars such as Gilchrist and Henry Colebrooke steering the nascent language departments at the College, the ideologies underpinning the language curricula could often be ascribed to the powerful opinions of a single orientalist. Under the influence of the self-styled linguist, Gilchrist, the College also manufactured a series of short, instructive tales in these vernaculars as textbooks for the education of English officers on the language and nature of the Indians. Twentieth-century scholarship on Fort William College has naively tended to laud the institution for its role as "chief patron for an indigenous literary and cultural revival" and to credit its particular influence in the theoretical founding of the modern languages of Hindi and Urdu.[37] This last issue, the founding, or invention, of Hindi and Urdu as distinctly modern, religio-national languages is an important one and is directly linked to Gilchrist's perceptions of the vernacular he called Hindoostanee.[38]

Building upon the arguments of his predecessor orientalists, Gilchrist embarked on his classification and definition of Indian languages with the premise that "Sanskrit" was the "grand source" of all language and literature that were indigenous to India.[39] Languages or registers that utilized Persian, Turkish, or Arabic sources, "Hindustani" the most prominent among them, were considered adulterations of Indic purity by the Mahometan invaders.⁴⁰ Gilchrist elected to reserve Hindi and Hindavi, variable terms for the broad vernacular, for "the old language of India which prevailed before the Moosulman invasion," the "exclusive property of the Hindus alone."⁴¹ Presuming that the "Moosulmans will be more partial to Arabic and Persian," while the "Hindoos will naturally lean most to the Hinduwee," Gilchrist envisioned Hindustani as the "middle or familiar current style between them."⁴² His simplistic understanding of this vernacular derives from a standard history of English at the time, the latter believed to have formed after the original Saxon had been mixed with French and Latin of the invading Normans. In choosing to develop Hindustani, the purported future English of colonial India, Gilchrist substitutes national identity, as it had emerged in Enlightenment Europe, this time with *religious* identity as the marker of linguistic difference.

Given that Hindustani bore no real merit for the natives, Gilchrist naturally found that "there is not a prose work now in existence of sufficient worth or accuracy" with which to teach the students at Fort William.⁴³ This, combined with his intention to "form such a body of useful and entertaining literature in that language" as to raise Hindustani to a platform reserved only for the classical in Europe, though transformative events, as I explain directly, betray the stark conceptual distance from which an administrator such a Gilchrist beheld language in India. For one, the vernacular that Gilchrist hoped to develop has best been described by Alok Rai as an "infinitely varied common tongue" that altered register, meter, and syntax according to class, region, even age and gender, leading to countless permutations.⁴⁴ Likewise, if we are to locate what Gilchrist called "literature," we find a wealth of texts whose merits lie in their aesthetic finesse and their style, but not necessarily their morality or didacticism. One of the major aesthetic registers of the moment, Urdu, an elite, rule-governed style of speaking and writing, heavily inflected with Persio-Arabic borrowings, offers many examples of both lyric and prose, but most of the extant texts went unnoticed by Gilchrist.⁴⁵ To be clear, despite its borrowings, Urdu, as it emerges, like other elite variants of the vernacular, did not identify strongly with Islam or signify the religious attachments of the speaker or writer. Similarly, the term "Hindi" was often used interchangeably with Urdu and did not originally imply an attachment to Sanskrit or to Hinduism.⁴⁶

What Gilchrist sought to invent, then, was a "literature" utterly removed from that which constituted *adab*, or *sahitya*, both words, the former Persianate, the latter Sanskritic, signaling in different ways the elaborate sets of practices, ideas, and etiquettes that went into the poetics of art-making in pre-colonial India.[47] His particular project, as he saw it, was to "promote Oriental literature" by "bestowing ... useful" works upon "Hindoostanee."[48] The bland nature of this project is made apparent in two works, *The Oriental Fabulist* (1803), a translation of Aesop's fables into Hindustani, Bangla, the variant register, Braj, and Sanskrit, and *Bāġh-o Bahār*, a purported translation of a set of Persian stories into Hindustani by the College *munshī*, Mir Amman. Simple, didactic texts such as these replicated the oriental tale, conformed with Gilchrist's vision of an ideal Hindustani literature, circulating at odds with those works that did, in fact, command aesthetic reverence in North India, a process that I trace over the next few pages.

The Oriental Fabulist adapts Robert Dodsley's 1781 translation of Aesop's fables into a textbook form, where the English version of each fable is followed by Romanized translations in the aforementioned vernacular registers. Though Aravamudan reads earlier fables in English, including *The Fables of Bidpai* (1688), as productive by virtue of the wealth of meanings offered by their "openly indirect" narrative "readerly hermeneutics," he is wary of the potential for moralizing that Dodsley brought to the fable in the eighteenth century.[49] Rendered in a simple style and with a moral attached, Dodsley's fables found special favor with Gilchrist who saw their didactic potential indispensable to the literary project of Fort William.

From his introduction to the *Oriental Fabulist*, it is apparent that Gilchrist's interest extended beyond his target audience at Fort William College. His hope is that "the translation of these Fables has now diffused a taste among the Hindoostanees for such exercises, which may yet be attended with the most beneficial consequences, on the literature of India."[50] Not only for the English officer students at the College, Gilchrist's translation of Aesop's fables was intended also as a model for the natives to emulate in their future "literary" compositions. At other points, he recognizes the utility of "short, amusing lessons or stories" for the purposes of language instruction, but his broader vision is fixed on the prospect of "the Orient gleam of learning in the days of Hastings and Jones [being] totally eclipsed by that precocious dawn in Eastern lore apparent now."[51] Gilchrist's "Hindoostanee" and the works that subsequently populated it were intended to transform the literary landscapes of both the Indic Orient and Europe. Though at odds with the revivalist practices of the Hastings generation of orientalists Gilchrist's ambition to develop "Hindoostanee" as a universal vernacular reiterated his predecessors' core edicts regarding the origins of language in India.

Gilchrist's "polyglot" translation, as he referred to it, affixes a lesson to each fable, imbuing what he sees as a suitable type for an oriental literature with renewed purpose. In the second fable, the Republic of Frogs repeatedly asks for a new king until Jupiter finally grants it a crane that eats all its inhabitants. The lesson: "Tis better to bear with some defects in a mild and gentle government than to risque the greater evils of tyranny and persecution."[52] This edict echoes the countless refrains on the part of Jones and his predecessor Halhed regarding the bane of Muslim rule in India, a period that was largely written off by English orientalists as the dark ages of the Indic civilization. The seventeenth fable teaches that "the utmost extent of some men's gratitude [is] barely to refrain from oppressing and injuring their benefactors."[53] The thirteenth, in which a stag's vanity leads him to his own death, instructs, "We often make a false estimate in preferring our ornamental talents to our useful ones."[54] The lessons, as is obvious from this representative selection, seem to reflect an early orientalist and imperial anxiety to justify colonial rule (visible also in Gilchrist's other writings).

The final lesson is an important one in terms of its bearing upon the nascent literary tradition that Gilchrist hoped to cultivate: prose fiction in "Hindoostanee." For this purpose, Gilchrist makes the vernacular oriental tale instructive in both style and content, a stark departure from the elaborate style that signified aesthetic expression higher registers such as Urdu or Braj-bakha. Over the course of the nineteenth century, this desire for an "unaffected," or unornamented, language marked battle lines between the imperial invention of literature in North India and the extant traditions of textual aesthetics. Well-known, of course, is the shifting literary preference in England for a "language, unaffected and simple."[55] Visible in the Grub Street translation of the *Nights* and in popular oriental tales, this stylistic mode was a particularly pervasive feature of the Scottish Enlightenment. It found almost immediate currency in England, and its broad appeal suited it for linguistic education in the colony. For North Indian aesthetes away from the colonial ambit, this new style was inadmissible, later leading to a series of ruptures around the meaning of the term, "Urdu."

The Oriental Tale in Hindustani/Urdu: The Case of Mir Amman's *Bāġh-o Bahār*

In 1803, Gilchrist commissioned Mir Amman, a senior *munshī* at the College, to compose a work in Hindustani such that it would be suitable for English officers learning the language. We can presume from our reading of the *Oriental Fabulist* that the commissioned text was to be simple, entertaining, morally inclined, but, above all, representative of Hindustani, the spoken language supposedly born of Mahometan invasions of India. In other words, what Gilchrist commissioned was an oriental tale in vernacular. Indeed, the story of four dervishes, incidentally all princes from various parts of the Mahometan Orient, with a series of morals clumsily tacked together at the end, *Bāġh-o Bahār* (also known by its alternative title, *Qiṣṣā-e Čār Darvēsh*) is like any volume of oriental tales to be found in eighteenth-century England. In the Indic Orient, however, it is the first imprint of the Mahometan chronotope in a language Gilchrist had ironically intended as the *universal* vernacular of India, but that by his own definition contradicted the condition of indigeneity upon which the Indic chronotope had been designated. In other words, the very basis of the new Hindustani literature, as Gilchrist envisioned it, existed at odds with the orientalist conception of India as the birthplace of an ancient, Sanskritic civilization. Ostensibly a modest errand, *Bāġh-o Bahār* became (or was promoted to be) one of the most influential texts to be produced at Fort William College, irreversibly altering the history of Urdu prose, a register it had little to do with at the moment of its publication.

Lauded by Gilchrist as exemplifying the "plain and perspicuous style" that he sought to inculcate in Hindustani literature, Mir Amman's Fort William debut, in the manner of the English oriental tale, also "contain[ed] a pleasing description of the manners and customs of Asia."[56] But what Gilchrist saw as a successful exercise in literary innovation, native aesthetes and readers of *Bāġh-o Bahār* would see as a degradation of the elite style. In his introduction to the "Story of the Four Dervishes," as the volume's alternative title translates, Mir Amman made two definitive claims, the consequences of which reverberate in vernacular literature even today. He had written the *qiṣṣā* of *Bāġh-o Bahār*, Mir Amman claimed, "in pure Hindustani speech, which was spoken by the people of Urdu: Hindu, Muslim, men, women, children and elders."[57] His second claim, penned at the request of Gilchrist, presents Urdu as the legacy of longstanding Muslim conquests in India, rather than the result of several centuries of fluid Persian and Ottoman exchanges in the region. The latter, despite having been proven as erroneous by scholars of the history of Urdu, including Shamsur Rahman Faruqi and Frances Pritchett, remains an excellent example of how Urdu—an elite, not religious register— became a casualty of the Mahometan chronotope. Lest my usage of this literary term be misread, I do, in fact, mean that the place of Urdu in Indian aestheticism was subsumed by the narrative that it was a language that owed it existence to foreign invaders—Tamerlane, Mahmud Ghaznavi, Mughal rulers—and had no claims to indigeneity in the way that Sanskrit, or the emergent, Hindi/Hindawi did.

Mir Amman's initial claim also carried little merit. His conflation of Hindustani—really, an orientalist term for the spoken register—with the language "spoken by the people of Urdu" is a contradiction, for the latter phrase refers to Delhi, the cultural center that Mir Amman himself was from. The term "Urdu" for much of the eighteenth century was relevant mostly to the rival court cultures of Delhi and Lucknow. The term itself did not imply a language or even a broadly used linguistic register until late in the eighteenth century. Its usage in what we can roughly term pre-colonial texts, or texts at a distance from the colonial ambit to be more accurate, most often referred either to the royal corridors of the city of Delhi, or to the dialect of a select population of Delhi, or Shahjanabad, as it was then known.[58] While the Persian (*nastaliq*) script was preferred, it was not unknown to find Urdu written in the Indic *devanagari* as well. A more direct contextualization of the term Urdu appears in Inshallah Khan Insha's *Daryā-e Laṭāfat*, or the Ocean of refinement (1803), a slim, somewhat satirical, but veritable guide to the language of the "great men and the pure of speech."[59] Covering variances in grammar, sources, and commonalities with Turkish, Persian, Punjabi, and Braj, among others, and even the letters of the script, Insha, a Lucknow poet, nevertheless maintains a focus on what to him is the defining feature of an Urdu speaker: *faṣāhat*, or a pure, elevated, and eloquent style of speech and composition.

Despite Mir Amman's claim that the language of *Bāġh-o Bahār* was *ṭhēṭh* or chaste, its colloquial, one-register-for-all defied the particularized rules of Urdu usage, a matter I explore in detail in the next section. His classification of the work as a *qiṣṣā*, an intricately narrated, often oral rendition of a story, is a wide approximation for this Indo-Persian fiction form was distinguished, among other features, by its alternative teleology and "amoral" worldview.[60] Though Mir Amman traced his knowledge of the tale directly to the medieval saint Amir Khusrau, it is safe to say the actual text is a loose adaptation of a highly stylized rendition of the circulating *qiṣṣā* of four dervishes composed for the Oudh nawabs, Siraj ud-Dawla and Asif ud-Dawla by Mir Muhammad Hussain Ata Khan Tahsin around 1795 (possibly earlier), titled *Nau tarz-e murassā*, or the New gold-embroidered fashion. Mir Amman neither acknowledges his debt to Tahsin, nor attempts to obey any of the etiquettes of the *qiṣṣā* tradition.

The narrative structure of *Bāġh-o Bahār* resembles the English *Arabian Nights' Entertainments*, its moralizing bent clearly modeled on the English oriental tale. The interconnected tales of *Bāġh-o Bahār* are roughly set in the Persian and Ottoman empires. Four princes turned dervishes travel from Yemen, Persia, and China, crossing paths with one another and with King Azad Bakht in the city of Constantinople. The theme of four travelers conveniently conforms with the inevitable itinerancy that marked English oriental tales set in the Mahometan Orient. As in the case of the *Arabian Nights* and *Persian Tales*, the travelers are either sultans or princes, or wealthy merchants remaking lost fortunes by traveling the vast expanses that lie between cities such as Baghdad, Isfahan, and Damascus. Their adventures and mishaps are mutually resolved at the end of the narrative through the intervention of the King of the Fairies, a powerful but just monarch. While there is nothing particularly distinctive about the stories that are borrowed from a number of circulating Persian, Arabic, and Urdu fictions, it is the appropriation of these stories into an English literary modality that distinguishes *Bāġh-o Bahār* from other contemporary vernacular or Urdu texts that were written at a distance from the colonial center.

Tacked on to the individual stories of each of the dervishes is a lesson that addresses their various states of desperation. Delivered by a mysterious horseman bearing the Caliph Ali's sword, these platitudes exemplify the stirrings of a marked literary morality that until this moment had hardly been a defining feature of Urdu prose fiction. At the darkest moment in the story of the first princely mendicant, the mysterious savior appears to say: "to be hopeless is to be a nonbeliever.[61] Another is told, "while there is breath [in one's body], there is hope." Similarly, as the fourth is about to throw himself from a mountain, the horseman tells him "not to despair of the way to God."[62] Each time the horseman appears in front of a dervish, the essence of the instruction remains the same: The good will be rewarded upon reaching the destination their caliph-like savior directs them toward. The story of the four dervishes closes with a little prayer by the author-narrator figure, asking that all wanderers find their rightful destination, a barely veiled reference perhaps, to Mir Amman's gratitude to the Company for employment and a salary.

This is not to say that prior to *Bāġh-o Bahār* Indo-Persian narratives, fictions and other were bereft of moral or spiritual contemplation. The thirteenth-century *Gulistan* by the Persian poet Sa'adi, for example, was styled as an exercise in which stories, poems, and anecdotes were a means to arrive at deeper understandings of the human condition. In *Bāġh-o Bahār*, however, there is a broad resemblance to Gilchrist's fables, the turn to purposeful moral edicts delivered under the slowly formalizing sign of Islam, or "Mohametanism," signifying an artificial distance from fictions written outside of the colonial ambit. There are several eighteenth- and early nineteenth-century "Urdu" prose texts, including several aforementioned, composed outside of Fort William College, that illustrate the extent to which colonially sponsored texts were removed from existing literary contexts. Such contemporary works, which also include Inshallah Khan Insha's *Rānī Kētakī kī Kahānī*, or the Story of Queen Ketaki, and Isvi Khan Bahadur's *Qiṣṣā-e Meher Āfrōz-o Dilbar* (c. 1731–55), did not take morality or literary reform as direct parts of their aesthetic exercise. The former, Mufti reminds us, undertakes the challenge of writing in a register purged of high Persianate vocabulary without falling to the level of the "rustic," or "*bākḥā*," an exercise in stylistic possibility rather than religious excommunication.[63] The latter, Bahadur's *qiṣṣā*, the love story of a prince and fairy, combines Braj with the higher Persian style. The second part of this text has been described as "a hotch-potch of advices on all kinds of matters given in a most unsystematic manner."[64] The other venerable example, which I discuss at length further on, is that of the *Dāstān-e Amīr Ḥamzā*, until this point largely an oral text recited in a variant register by the *dāstān-gōh*, or storyteller. Similarly, the grand dame of Urdu, the ghazal, though variously printed by the Hindostanee Press, did not succumb or reorganize itself to suit any pedagogical aspirations the publisher may have had.

The systematic lesson of goodness and obedience necessarily meriting salvation or happiness presented by way of fiction in a colloquial or universalizing register, then, enters the Urdu tradition through the literary standards introduced by the orientalist scholars of Fort William. *Bāġh-o Bahār* thus is the consequence of the grafting of the English oriental tale's chronotope upon extant modes of storytelling and vernacular practices. Contemporary scholars of South Asia, most notably Pritchett, have leaned toward reading this text in a structuralist fashion, ignoring to a large extent the historical intricacies of its production. In her pioneering monograph, *Marvelous Encounters: Folk Romance in Urdu and Hindi*, Pritchett categorizes the Fort William texts as "the first written North Indian *qiṣṣās*," indirectly acknowledging their departure from the orality that was definitive of the *qiṣṣā* and *dāstān* tradition.[65] In other words, her reading of *Bāġh-o Bahār* assumes a Eurocentric literary evolution at odds with the contexts from which the text emerges. The tight morality and designated ending of the dervishes' stories seem incongruous when compared with the often purely entertaining twists of the *qiṣṣā* tradition, one that flouted consistency thanks to its mainly oral recitations. An excellent parallel, instead, is the set of "Hindi" fiction texts sanctioned and printed at Fort William that Rashmi Bhatnagar has argued "were part of a larger project to protect English boys from the plebeian life in the Calcutta bazaars ... and to insulate them from pernicious ideas associated with the French Revolution."[66] *Bāġh-o Bahār* barely accords with the aesthetic sensibilities and fiction forms that flourished in eighteenth- and early nineteenth-century Urdu. The Mahometan chronotope, a transplanted pedagogical instrument, now protrudes into an unaccustomed aesthetic and linguistic milieu. Oriental tales were popular and exotic, implicitly renegade fictions in English, but when cast into the varied, yet exacting North Indian language complex, they ruptured the nuances of local registers and irrevocably altered narrative forms and content.

Against Hindustani:
The *Dāstān*, the *Qiṣṣā*, and Fort William College

At first, works such as *Bāġh-o Bahār* circulated within Company circles only. By the second and third decades of the nineteenth century, however, many of these works had traveled across to North Indian princely states and Company protectorates. The obvious route for this widespread circulation was the growing nexus of schools and colleges run under the Company that used the Fort William curricula to re-educate native subjects.[67] In its initial days, however, this still nascent colonial literature met with serious opposition both from texts composed *at* Fort William College, and more vociferously, from those composed at a distance from colonial circles of influence. Two texts, in particular, stand out for their commitment to the elite register of Urdu, but also to traditional forms of storytelling, the *qiṣṣā* and *dāstān*, neither of which can be approximated to the oriental tale, or as I have argued earlier, to a work such as *Bāġh-o Bahār*. In the first case, Rajab Ali Beg Surur, a Lucknow courtier, attacks Mir Amman for presuming to conflate Hindustani with Urdu, a move that inadvertently allows for *Bāġh-o Bahār* to be misread as representative of a new style in Urdu. The second work, an Urdu rendition of the famed Indo-Persian *Dāstān-e Amīr Ḥamzā*, penned at Fort William College by the *dāstān-gōh* or *dāstān* teller, Khalil Khan Ashk, defies the colloquial standards of Hindustani, respecting the stylistic demands of the narrative form. But the opposition that these texts posed to the growth of Hindustani is soon quashed by the colonial state.

Around 1830 or so, Surur, a poet and aesthete in the court of Nawab Naseeruddin Haider, taking offense at the language in *Bāġh-o Bahār*, penned *Fasānā-e 'Ajā'ib*, literally, the story of wonders, in a classical, highly stylized diction. At liberty from colonial edicts on morality or narrative simplicity, Surur's *qiṣṣā*-like narrative is both a celebration of Lucknow's court and courtly aesthetics and an elaborate fantasy properly modeled on the Persian *qiṣṣās* that were popular in the courts of North Indian *nawabs* and princes. Prince Jan-e Alam's quest to find a woman of incomparable beauty in a world of enchantments, talking parrots, and fairies, self-identifies, we can say, with extant modes of storytelling rather than leaning toward the moral righteousness that Mir Amman had deliberately inserted in *Bāġh-o Bahār*. To be more explicit, Surur's concern is not with Islam or Muslims, but with a particular style of storytelling in an Urdu tradition that predated the Fort William College innovations.

A key text in the creative historiography of the term "Urdu" is Surur's introduction to *Fasānā-e 'Ajā'ib*, often read as an offering to the nawab of Lucknow, as a plea to end the author's exile from his beloved city. Describing the fantasy, Surur calls it "a *qiṣṣā*, a story [. . .], a book of fancy. Each enviable page is a garden unto itself, the zenith of springtime . . . The perceptive, the exacting [. . .] should see this manuscript and what is written in it for themselves. I have let flow a river of *faṣāhat*."[68] Surur's focus, it would appear, is on the finesse of the narrative style, rather than on the plot or characters. But this is not just any exercise in style. It is premised almost entirely on *faṣāhat*, or the eloquence and chastity of its language, and he asks readers to "nourish and correct" his story where they "encounter an error or mistake."[69] Surur concludes with an attack on Mir Amman: "He [Mir Amman] writes that he is a crumbled brick from Delhi, but he has broken the hands and feet of idiom."[70] The ambitiously titled *Bāġh-o Bahār*—and here Surur puns on Mir Amman's metaphoric use of a garden and spring in his title—is a "thorn in the flesh," a "mangled" version of the language of Shahjahanabad.[71] Mufti has called his wittily worded, clever repartee a stinging "repudiation" of Fort William's conversational style.[72] But Surur's derision of Mir Amman's style inadvertently becomes a recognition of the latter's claim to having written *Bāġh-o Bahār* in Urdu.

Instead of remaining a simple story for the edification of students at Fort William, *Bāġh-o Bahār* now entered and forged an uncomfortable place in the Urdu aestheticism proper to the Delhi and Lucknow rivalry. Surur's misreading, then, must be taken to be the first act of resistance against the colonial recodification of the term "Urdu" from its initial implications of an elite, aesthetically defined style to one that was common and colloquial. For want of a better word, "misreading" here signifies the possibly misplaced context or intention upon which Surur bases his criticism of *Bāġh-o Bahār*. The Lucknow aesthete interprets Mir Amman against or with apparent disregard to the colonial patronage that is directing the tone and plot of the work. Yet the acts of reading and response enable the admission of Mir Amman's artificially constructed work as an innovative exercise in Urdu as it was understood outside of colonial precincts. *Fasānā-e 'Ajā'ib* gained fame somewhat belatedly, benefiting greatly once Sharaf-ud Daula became the ruler of Lucknow, following Naseeruddin Haider's death and the temporary chaos that ensued. By the 1850s, Surur's book had become an "example" for *qiṣṣā* writers still composing in the high register.[73]

As Naiyer Masud, one of Urdu's great modern fiction writers, argues, Surur, according to the "popular tastes of his time," had celebrated elements of the *qiṣṣā* tradition, including "love and passion, battles and wars, magic and secrets" (*'ishq-o muhabbat, jang-o jadal, tilism-o asrār*), without any of the didacticism of Mir Amman's work.[74] Subsequently, *Fasānā-e 'Ajā'ib* was mainly read and applauded by the courtly and elite speakers of Urdu. In 1854, it also seems to have found its way to the native education system set up by colonial administrators, but remained largely unappreciated, one inspector deeming it "not the best of textbooks" and "too difficult for the boys generally" (but easily read by those adept in Persian).[75] In an 1863 report, one inspector "take[s] exception" to *Fasānā-e 'Ajā'ib* reaffirming its place on a list of "not desirable books to place in the hands of students."[76] Within a few years, however, Surur, in what was probably a time of financial stress for him, sold his book and its rights to the local Naval Kishore Press, benefiting from the still unaltered popular tastes.

Carefully written out of the Fort William archives is its patronage of one of the earliest print versions of the *Dāstān-e Amīr Ḥamzā*, a gargantuan project undertaken by Ashk, another *munshī* at the College, in 1803. While Mir Amman's work occupied a prominent place both at the College and the later language curricula of Company-owned schools, Ashk's telling of the *dāstān* is scarcely mentioned in Gilchrist's chronicles of the College and subsequently missing from school syllabi as well. Partially on account of form—the *dāstān* is a tortuously long, geographically otherworldly, and utterly unconcerned with morality—and partially on account of register—it could not really be told in a leveled language—Ashk's tome was soon discarded by Gilchrist from the literary canon of the new Hindustani. In other words, the *dāstān*, a flourishing Indo-Persian narrative form, could not conform with the domesticated, generic bounds of the oriental tale.[77]

Ashk's preface to his work stands in direct contrast to Mir Amman's: "At the request of Mister Gilchrist . . . for the benefit of beginners, I wrote this *qiṣṣā* of the Hindi language in the language of *Urdu-e Mu'allā* so that it is easy for the honorable young scholars to read."[78] Ashk refers to the language he is writing in as Hindi, the title Gilchrist had already designated as the name for a "Hindu" register, devoid of Arab and Persian borrowings. Though the systematic Orientalist reclassification of Hindi as the Sanskrit-heavy version of the language had already begun at the College, Ashk does not distinguish between Hindi and Urdu. Here, he uses the term *qiṣṣā* loosely, merely to indicate that the ensuing narrative is part of a longer story. Yet his language once narrating the *dāstān* is far from leveled or colloquial. Its shifts in tone and diction are prompted by events in the story rather than the requirements of a non-native, pupil audience. The birth of the new king is one example:

> When nine months had passed, and the day had risen on the clock, a eunuch came from inside the palace, softly whispered something in the king's ear and left. The king ended the court that very moment and retired. He sent for the venerable and noble Hamza, and informed him that the birth he had expected for some time had happened; a boy has been born in our house... The fountain of drink that for some years now had dried out, today, on its own, flowed with water, and on account of this happy event, the venerable and noble Hamza named the boy Naushervan, and some narrators say that at the moment of birth, the king held a goblet of wine, and Hamza said to the king in the Persian language, "O Majesty, let the wine flow."

> *jabkē nau mahīnē guzar ga'ye ēk rōz g͟harī par din čaṛhā kē mahal kē andar sē ēk k͟vājā sirā āyā aur kuč̣h āhistā sē bādshāh kē kān meiñ keh kar čalā gayā bādshāh nē usīvaqt dīvān bark͟vāst kar kē k̤alvat kīyā aur k͟vājā bazar hamzā kō bulvā bhējā aur farmāyā tum sā'at kō tavalud kē sādhō hamārē g͟har meiñ bēṭā huā čāhtā hai... jō čashmāh k̤āẓ jō kō'ī bars sē sūkh gyā thā, āj k̤ud bak̤ud pānī ā gayā aur ravān huā bazar hamzāh nē bamujab isī k̤ushī naushērvān nām rakhā aur b'aźē rāvī kehtē haiñ keh tavalud kē vaqt bādshāh kē hāth meiñ jām-e-sharāb kā thā bazar hamzāh nē zubān-e fārsī meiñ bādshāh sē kahā ī qiblāh-e 'ālam nōsh ravān kun...*[79]

Shifting into Persian to narrate Amir Hamza's quip, and preferring a more refined Persian vocabulary to describe Naushervan's birth, Ashk does not simplify his style for the benefit of an elementary reader. Far from communicating a precise grammar or set of rules for language, Ashk favors a tone that maintains the orality so vital to the *dāstān* form. Rich with the multiplicity that populates the *dāstān*, this moment in the longer narrative where the prophetic birth of the long-awaited prince finally takes place is unconcerned with the religious law or moral pedagogy. Naushervan's birth is relevant only to the narrative of the events of his life within the longer cycle of *Amīr Ḥamzā*. Simultaneously joyous, unifying, sad, crude, and even fantastic, the birth signals a new era for the Persian Empire as the lives of Naushervan and his savior Hamza finally coincide. The awareness of the *dāstān* is restricted to the world of Amir Hamza and his adventures, and its style is compelled absolutely by a dramatic and gripping recitation of these events.

In purely formal terms, a work such as *Amīr Ḥamzā* could not reconcile with the rather pedestrian generic demands made by Gilchrist and the College administration. As Shamsur Rahman Faruqi argues in his powerful study of the *Amīr Ḥamzā* cycle, the elusive and arcane demands of a narrative form such as the *dāstān* prevented easy replication. Though *Bāġh-o Bahār* could boast the "magic, charms, demons, [and] fairies," it did not replicate the spiraling world of battlefields (*razm*), realms of enchantment (*tilism*), loyal tricksters ('*ayārs*), rules and performances of love (*bazm*), and destiny essential to the *dāstān*. It lacked the almost "interminable length"; the "highly artificial, dense, and often (in order to stir the audience), tortuous language"; the frequent reiteration of the same event; and the mercurial nature of the extended narrative.[80] The Fort William moment reconfigures literary hierarchies in North India such that the pre-existing tradition of *dāstān-gō'i*, which included both the recitation of the *dāstān* in court and the writing down of the *dāstān* for that purpose, yields to fable-like compositions whose style and themes were officially sanctioned by the College.

As a prose form "intended for oral narration," the *dāstān* contains "examples of all kinds of prose" and is "a treasure of words, terms, and idioms."[81] Ashk was not the first to render the *Dāstān-e Amīr Ḥamzā* in writing, but his version was certainly the first to go to print at the Hindoostanee Press set up by Gilchrist.[82] Despite the popularity of the *dāstān* in the higher echelons of North Indian society at the time and its well-documented mass appeal in urban centers such as Delhi, Gilchrist displayed mixed feelings toward Ashk, "who now considers himself the Hereditary Story Teller of the Emperor, Princes, and Nobles of India."[83] For Gilchrist, the *dāstān* was an "inexhaustible fund of legendary narrative and diversion" appreciated by "the patrons and admirers of the Hindoostanee"; nevertheless, "Oriental knight errantry and Harlequinism can hardly possess many charms for the present age."[84]

Entertaining, but stylistically too rich and morally disinclined, the *Dāstān-e Amīr Ḥamzā* defied the ideals of the English oriental tale. Neither could this form be contained by the time-space relations of the

Mahometan chronotope. In spite of its dynastic heroes, the *dāstān* is deeply secular; its narrative boundaries porous, welcoming a multitude of characters; and its traditions, far from being governed by a perceived Islam, spontaneous and riotous. Yet *Dāstān-e Amīr Ḥamzā* failed to find favor with the nineteenth-century metropolitan and colonial patrons of "oriental" fictions. The written rendition of the *dāstān* remained outside the literary canon assembled at the College and was brushed aside by subsequent administrators of the native school language syllabi.[85] With a hero as volatile and unpredictable as the tricksters, or *'ayārs*, that accompany him in his quest, the *dāstān* did not provide students with the placid moral frame that the vernacular oriental tales were intended to impart. Toward the close of the century, the *dāstān* and the practice of *dāstān-gō'i* had all but disappeared from North Indian culture, despite valiant efforts on the part of the local publishing giant, Naval Kishore, to preserve the form by issuing a massive forty-six volume edition of *Amir Ḥamzā* in 1893. Though Naval Kishore made money from this venture, more profitable were the reprints of various Fort William College works because of the canonical status they had acquired as staple textbooks in the higher education system.[86] *Bāġh-o Bahār*'s mistaken entry into the Urdu prose tradition was not forgotten; however, even nineteenth-century writers, most noticeably Abdul Halim Sharar, remained critical of its claims, citing its readership as influenced entirely by imperial education.[87]

In place of the *dāstān*, compliant, Fort William–approved volumes such as *Bāġh-o Bahār*; Haider Buksh Haideri's *Ārā'ish-e Mehfil*, or the Ornament of the assembly (1803); Mir Amman's other translated work, *Ganj-e Ḵūbī*, or A treasure of virtue (1811), a loose adaptation of a medieval Persian treatise on princely ethics were prescribed and taught as the literature of Hindustani in the Company-run networks of schools and colleges. *Ārā'ish-e Mehfil* is a Persian translation of the stories of Hatim Tai, the Arabian prince unparalleled for his generosity and kindness to strangers, keeping well with the gentle morality and basic narrative style that Fort William curriculum preferred. Other works of note include the *munshi*, Maulvi Ikram Ali's translation of the Arabic text *Ikvān-us Safā*, or Brothers in purity, into Hindustani in 1811. By this time, Gilchrist had returned to England, never to see India again, and his successor, Captain John William Taylor, as identified by Ikram Ali, asked the latter to translate *Ikvān-us Safā* "into Urdu," describing it as a "very simple language, free of any abstract words," keeping with Gilchrist's concept of a vernacular.[88] In this work, men and animals debate with the king of the genii as a mediator as to who is the most enlightened species to walk the earth. Like other important Fort William texts, the *Ikvān-us Safā* also follows a simple, fabular format, and though Ikram Ali's translation was deemed erroneous by Duncan Forbes, one of Gilchrist's influential and prolific successors, it remained a constant in the Urdu curricula for much of the nineteenth century. Remarkable, if we peruse these works, is the fact that not a single one allows for a Muslim tradition to be located within the broader Indo-Persian complex. Stories about and for Mahometans, this rather homogenous set of works suggests, come from outside of India, and are, in fact, *translated* into Urdu, the branch of the vernacular associated with India's Muslims.

Hindi, reinvented by Colebrooke as the Sanskrit-leaning version of the vernacular, now claimed works such as Lalluji Lal's *Prēmsāgar*, or the Ocean of love (1803), and *Baitāl Paĉīsī*, or the Fifty demons (1805), as exemplary of its own modern literary texts. The former, like *Bāgh-o Bahār*, in addition to its moralizing fiction, made literary-historical claims, the foremost among them being what Bhatnagar describes as "consigning to prehistory the philological revolutions of the Indo-Islamic millennium."[89] In other words, while Mir Amman wrote the history of Urdu in the Indian subcontinent as dictated by the Mahometan chronotope, an orientalist construct, another *munshī*, Lalluji Lal, in the same vein, invented a register that he claimed was "purged" of the language of the "*yavanās*," or foreigners, writing the Hindi register in terms of the chronotope of indigeneity.[90] It is at Fort William, Bhatnagar has so meticulously shown, that the process of reading Sanskrit texts such as the *Bhagvad-Gita* and the *Puranas* as the "Bible of the Hindus" is instituted, leading, as we well know, to the production of Hindi as a modern vernacular on religio-national lines.[91]

Literature in Colony: Creating a Canon for Hindustani

The deliberate codification of the Fort William oriental tales as constitutive of a "literature" in the newly standardized vernacular, "Urdu," could never have been achieved without the ambitious and extensive network of Company and later Government of India schools for Indians set up in the various presidencies administered by the English. It is within the grand institution of colonial education that the term "literature," as it was understood in England, took form in North India. In other words, literature, as we know it today in postcolonial states such as India and Pakistan, is a *modern* category, starkly different from premodern aesthetic traditions of the Indo-Persian world. To qualify the matter further, literature as it was envisioned in the colony was derived from the idea of an English literature as it had recently emerged in England, a carefully curated body of works "from Chaucer to Milton" that reflected a national identity distinct from the Continent.[92] Gauri Viswanathan's classic work *Masks of Conquest* argued that the idea of English literature was inseparable from the colonial endeavor, its canon determined by the civilizing mission above all. Viswanathan's history of the rise of English literature focuses on the careful curation of English texts in Indian school and college syllabi (much like what Bhatnagar argues ensued at Fort William) as a "defensive mechanism" against native rebellion and English anxieties regarding their own vulnerabilities in India.[93] But even as an English literature was being established alongside the growing colony, two bodies of vernacular literature—Hindi and Urdu—had already taken shape at Fort William. The shape of these literatures, over the course of the nineteenth century, is determined against and in conversation with the English ideal of literariness.

The first landmark in the colonial education program is generally considered to be the Charter Act of 1813, which promised "a sum of not less than one lakh rupees in year . . . applied to the *revival and improvement of literature*, and the encouragement of the learned natives of India, and for the introduction and promotion of a knowledge of the sciences among the inhabitants of the British territories in India . . ."[94] I repeat here a question that Viswanathan has already asked and answered: Why literature? Why was a body of written works, consisting largely of moralizing stories, considered central to Company's, and later, the Government of India's presence in the subcontinent? Viswanathan argues that English literature came to "perform the same functions of those social institutions (such as the church) that, in England, served as the chief disseminators of value, tradition, and authority."[95] In the case of the newly formed vernaculars, Urdu and Hindi, the act of inventing literary canons follows a different pattern. At Fort William, as Bhatnagar has argued, the chosen works are an attempt at "linguistic discipling" of first, young English officers, and subsequently of natives. But vernacular "literatures"—if we may call them that—are deliberately curated, particularly in the case of Hindustani/Urdu, against what is perceived as an "oriental," or specifically, Mahometan identity. That is to say, the literatures and literary texts patronized by the colonial government became the means through which North India's cosmopolitan Muslims were made to understand themselves as *Mahometans*, and subsequently to grapple with their presence in India through a sense of their foreignness, their opulent despotism, and their itinerance. The new vernacular literatures, then, permitted the exercise of colonial authority by way of their supposed inadequacy and moral paucity.

This crisis reaches a head in the decades following the Mutiny of 1857 (a moment I discuss in intricate detail in the following chapter), the groundwork for which, I argue here, is laid in the first half of the nineteenth century. The history of literature as a discipline in North India is usually overshadowed by discussions on the disagreements between Anglicists and Orientalists; the former wanted English to be the sole mode of instruction, while the latter invested in developing the vernaculars into modern, scientific languages. What goes unnoticed is the agreement of both on one thing: that *native* literatures were lacking in moral and aesthetic fiber. Thus, the grounds of contention between the two schools were premised on the option to "cultivate, liberally and judiciously" a native literature, or to succumb entirely, as the Anglicists wanted, to English as a medium of instruction and exchange.[96] What persisted, in spite of these disagreements, was a native education in two literatures: English, and for Muslims, the Gilchrist version of Urdu or Hindustani, while Hindus were largely directed toward Hindi.

The colonial reinvention of literature as complicit with the missionary zeal for religious conversion and reformation is no secret. Viswanathan's work has shown the powerful affiliation of early versions of the English literature curriculum with Christianity, and Parna Sengupta's *Pedagogy for Religion*, a study of late nineteenth-century Bengal, suggests that colonial pedagogy in the vernaculars had a powerful effect on the enunciation of religious reform for both Hindus and Muslims. But in the early decades of the nineteenth century, the Orientalists remained focused on two strains of literary reinvention: revival, in the case of a Hindi literature, and improvement, in the case of the nascent Hindustani/Urdu literature. The hope, as H. H. Wilson, an orientalist and administrator of the public instruction system, put it was for the natives to have "a literature of their own ... the legitimate progeny of that of England, the living resemblance, though not the servile copy, of its parent."[97] In other words, whether improved or revived, the vernacular literature in question, as evident from the earlier half of this chapter, had to be modeled on its counterpart ideologies in English.

In the decades following the decline of Fort William, it was indeed English literature that Orientalists and Anglicists alike turned to. For the former, English was one way to inspire works in the vernacular, whereas for the latter, English was the means through which a "a class of persons qualified by their intelligence and morality for high employments in the civil administration of India."[98] Though Thomas Babington Macaulay's infamous "Minute on Indian Education" (1835) remains by far the most-quoted document in scholarly studies on colonial education, a more specific view emerges in a letter written in the same year from J. C. Sutherland, the Secretary-General for public education, to James Prinsep, secretary to the Asiatic Society. Amenable to the idea that "the great body of the people must be enlightened through the medium of their own language, and that to enrich and improve these, so as to render them the efficient depositories of all thoughts and knowledge, is an object of the first importance to be kept prominently in view," education directly in the vernacular or the "learned languages," would not achieve the desired ends. Instead, Sutherland suggests that,

> The Foreign literature must be studied in itself, and if it be stored with superior Knowledge and capable of imparting a new vigour and capacity of thought, an indigenous and independent Literature will arise from it, and become the medium for diffusing knowledge through the body of the people, in the forms most suitable to their National circumstances, Character and wants. It is by rousing and strengthening the mind of the Educated classes for original efforts, that the general extension of national Education can alone be accomplished.[99]

What the letter suggests, then, is the re-education of a pliable bourgeoisie that would then take it upon itself to redirect the "career of National Civilization" in India.[100] Echoing Gilchrist's core argument from three decades earlier, it concludes with the assumption that "when the power of forming enlightened and enlarged ideas, and the desire to give expression to them shall first have been secured, a language fit for their expression will soon be framed . . ."[101] In the case of Hindustani, now akin with Urdu, the effect of the so-called "foreign literature," English, really, was the creation of a specific—and at this point contradictory—set of attitudes toward the still-minor Fort William canon, as well as the significantly larger body of works that lay outside of the colonial formation.

To populate and develop Urdu as a vernacular, public administrators had initially turned to the Fort William curriculum, grafting texts such as *Bāġh-o Bahār*, *Ikvān-us Safā*, *Ārā'ish-e Mehfil*, and even Gilchrist's late *Rissalah* or Rules of Hindustani grammar (1820) onto syllabi for the natives. The core of the Hindustani or Urdu curriculum at an institution such as the Benares College in 1851 consisted of *Bāġh-o Bahār*, Surur's *Fasānā-e 'Ajā'ib* (soon removed), whereas at the Agra College, *Bāġh-o Bahār* was paired with Gilchrist's *Rissalah* from at least 1845 to 1851.[102] Native students, we can surmise from these pairings, were learning grammar anew in the colonial system. In 1857, the Urdu texts for the entrance examination to Calcutta University were *Bāġh-o Bahār* and *Gul*

Bakaulī, another *qissā* printed at Fort William, while the Arabic texts were *Alf Leila* and *Nafhat al-Yaman*, the latter an eclectic set of stories, several of which overlapped with those of the former. It is only in the last decade or so of the nineteenth century that *Bāġh-o Bahār*, long a staple text on school and college syllabi, is relegated to younger students. The early efforts on the part of the administration to advance Urdu as a vernacular medium for broader instruction in the natural and social sciences, however, were not restricted to just placing particular texts on the curriculum.

At the Delhi College, an institution intended for an elite class of natives, one examination question asks the student to elucidate how "literary compositions" in English and Urdu differed from each other. In response to this question, a student by the name of Surroop Narrain answers, his reference clearly to ghazal poetry: "The subject of which the Urdu writers treat frequently is love, their compositions always filled with exaggerations, and their attention is seldom directed towards any scientific or historical objects."[103] In comparison to English, the student continues, the Urdu style is "florid," and the language can often be "so abstruse and difficult as to puzzle the best scholar."[104] Examination questions at Agra College testing the proficiency of students in "Oordoo" during the 1840s often asked for translations of *Bāġh-o Bahār* into Persian.[105] In the examination report for Agra College from the same decade, C. C. Jackson and William Muir jointly advise that to "remedy" Urdu's immaturity:

> the students in the two Senior Classes be employed . . . in translation into Oordoo from the best models of English composition, for instance the Spectator, Speeches of English Orators, or from Indian or English History and that their translations be subjected to correction in their presence by the best Oordoo Moonshee, and, after lapse of a fortnight, be again turned into English without aid from the original.[106]

Only through perpetual acts of translation and retranslation, these pedagogues seem to believe, could Urdu be "remodeled" for the "purposes of Narrative and Science."[107] James Ballantyne's remarks from the 1848 examinations at Benares College betray, quite explicitly, the fabricated, synthetic nature of the imperially patronized register: "The best way to teach Oordoo in the College would be to make the Moulvee give his instruction chiefly under the form of lessons in Persian," the report advises. "The boys grudge the time spent in learning Oordoo, because when they go home they may expect praise and admiration for having read Sanscrit or Arabic, or English, or Persian, but not for Oordoo."[108]

Persian, the language of the courts until replaced by Urdu in 1837, and of instruction in native schools prior to their incorporation into the colonial system, remained a constant obstacle to the growth and realization of the latter until as late as the 1870s. In the education report for the 1864–65 year, Matthew Kempson blames the native "moonshee" for "forgetting" his "duty" to "favor" the "grammatical study of the Vernacular." The *munshī's* "repute, considered from a Native point of view, depends on Farsiyat and Arabiyat."[109] As a result of this dismissal of Hindustani/Urdu, the Indian student "acquires a habit of regarding his ordinary speech as incapable of conveying in an elegant form, the ideas of the author he is engaged in studying."[110] Clear from these reports is the utter disjoint at which the colonial education system functioned from native, here, clearly elite, linguistic practices. Even as colonial administrators expressed concern about the literary development and adoption of Urdu as an all-purpose vernacular, native elites continued to attach prestige to other registers and languages. But the eventual success of the colonial vernacular project is foretold in attitudes of native students, such as Narrain, whose examination essay betrays the demands of his studies. That is to say, even as the Fort William texts are promoted in the colonial curriculum, their thematic and stylistic inadequacies are made part of the same. "Oordoo," the erroneous name for Hindustani, the colonially manufactured vernacular, is at once the object of colonial patronage as well as the object of its critique. The onus, as these examination reports betray, is on the native subject to reinvent this vernacular in the image of English.

In this third phase of the movement of the Mahometan chronotope into the orient, the oriental tale though transplanted onto colonial curricula in language and literature is cast as the intimate representative of North-Muslim culture. The Mahometan of the oriental tale, both English and vernacular, is presented to native subjects as the mirror-image of the North Indian Muslim by way of a carefully curated school syllabus that becomes the canon-making instrument of modern Urdu. By the late 1830s, in an institution such as Agra College, "Hindu departments" were for students who associated themselves with that religion, whereas "Muslim departments" were made to teach in Persian and Urdu.[111] The former, taking Hindi as the pedagogical register, used Fort William editions of the *Mahabharat* (1802?) and the *Ramayan* (1811), while the latter, of course, depended on *Bāġh-o Bahār* and *Ārā'ish-e Mehfil* for instruction. We can see, quite literally, the institutionalized system by which language, literature, and religion become inseparable categories in colonial North India. In particular, what unfolds through the construction of literature as an essential part of the civilizing mission is an altered meaning of what it meant to be a Muslim in the Indian subcontinent.

"The Best and Cheapest Book in the Hindustani Language": *Bāġh-o Bahār*, Textbook and Translation

As a staple textbook in this slowly expanding network of colonial schools, *Bāġh-o Bahār* underwent at least three major translations into English, as well as several Urdu editions for pedagogical purposes.[112] By 1860, it had become a mandatory text in "all Government Colleges and Schools in which Oordoo is read."[113] Its prominence in the curriculum and the pioneering place it had been given in modern Urdu literature did not prevent its orientalist translators and editors from locating its worth with respect to English literariness. Rejected by native aesthetes, this vernacular oriental tale, though celebrated in the colony *and* the metropolis, is canonized as the perfect example of a *Mahometan literature*. While Mahometan literature, or oriental tales about the Mahometan Orient, were entertaining both in English and in the vernacular, the apparent absence of a rational, English morality in the latter became the root cause of its inadequacy in a colony that demanded increasing subordination from its native subjects.

In 1813, Lewis Ferdinand Smith, an orientalist and Company officer, undertook the first translation of Mir Amman's book into English in an attempt to aid English students of Hindustani with their efforts. Lauding the work as "the best and the most correct that has been composed in the Urdu language," Smith tells his readers that the work contains "various modes of expression in correct language" and "displays a great variety of Eastern manners and modes of thinking."[114] Lest readers mistake *Bāġh-o Bahār* as a mere language textbook, Smith reminds them that it is a "'Tale,'" an "Asiatic Romance," that like other oriental tales, cannot be "consistent, or free from fabulous credulity," for "the cautious march of undeviating truth, and a careful regard to *vraisemblance* never enters into their [native authors] plan," and as expected, the "wildness of imagination, fabulous machinery and unnatural scenes ever pervade through the compositions of every Oriental Author."[115] Nevertheless, he goes on to assure readers, much like "the *Arabian Nights Tales* the grand prototype of all Asiatic Romances," *Bāġh-o Bahār*, too, can be "read with undiminished pleasure" by the European reader if these various "imperfections" are ignored.[116]

In this introduction, *Bāġh-o Bahār* is classified as a vernacular version of the English oriental tale. Smith's classification and praise for the volume are hardly original; his remarks echo much of what Gilchrist had already said about the work. It is in Smith's footnotes, a scholarly commentary on his part, however, that the "Mahometan" stamp is directly placed on this work. In reference to Mir Amman's traditional obeisance for the Mughal ruler Humayun, Smith comments, "How proud the slave seems of his chains!—but such is the nature of Asiatic minds, under the baleful influence of Asian despotism."[117] Likewise, the presence of fairies, genies, and demons in the stories prompts Smith to tell readers that these otherwise fantastic figures were part of Mir Amman's his "religious creed," evidence that "Mohammedan" readers of the text remained "superstitiously attached to their Religion."[118] While telling the story of the man with the two dogs (one that recurs from the *Arabian Nights*), Smith's footnote reads: "Here I have changed the original a good deal, to render it less absurd and less incredible." Where Mir Amman speaks of the dog as actively "contemplating" (*fikar doṛā'ī*), Smith, in his version, allows "divine instinct" to inspire the dog into saving his master.[119]

Though he remains committed to a literal translation of the work, Smith's commentary is no longer just an echo or repetition of commentaries attached to English oriental tales. It serves as early evidence of the deliberate precarity with which the category of Hindustani or Urdu literature is established in North India. Pitted against the maturing realism of the English domestic novel, the vernacular oriental tale is dated like the English romance tradition, irrational on account of its authors' religion, and deceitful because it lacks a Christian morality. The greater whole *Bāġh-o Bahār* represents in Smith's mind is not merely Urdu, but, in fact, Mohametans or Muslims, their persons, their child-like beliefs, and their affinity for despotic structures of governance. Whereas Lalluji Lal's *Prēmsāgar*, believed to be a translation from an ancient Sanskrit text, is lauded as a display of "the religion of that great nation" from which the Hindus are descended, a religion the translator believes derives from "Gospel History," Islam, or Mohammedanism as Smith would have it, is as fantastic a construction as any other oriental tale may be.[120]

In 1846, Duncan Forbes, a professor at the Calcutta Academy, another language school of Company officers, undertook the task of editing *Bāġh-o Bahār*, which at the time was an essential text for entry into the Company army. Forbes added English-style punctuation as well as a glossary for English students. The project was heavily subsidized by the Company as a result of which Mir Amman's book was no longer just the "best" book to be found in Hindustani but also the cheapest. The Forbes edition went into its fourth reprint in 1860, when *Bāġh-o Bahār* was declared mandatory in all schools and colleges teaching Urdu, but with a caveat. The volume, upon the instruction of William Nassau Lees, the director of the department of public instruction, was to be made "free from objectionable passages," such that would "shock the modesty of an Examiner or injure the morals of the Student."¹²¹ Aware that "a few passages of objectionable nature" are to be found in "all Oriental compositions," Forbes announced that any offending matter had been removed or paraphrased from the latest edition.

One example of Forbes's censorship is visible in the story of the first dervish, who encounters the much-suffering Princess of Damascus during his travels. In love with a young man of easy morals, the Princess tells the dervish of having to observe her paramour's drunkenness with an ugly slave woman. In Maulvi Abdul Haq's definitive Urdu edition of *Bāġh-o Bahār*, the scene reads: "voh pichal pā`ī bhī us hālat mēñ nīčē parī hū`ī nakrē tallē karnē lagī aur dōnōñ mēiñ čūmā čātī honē lagī," translating literally to "the slimy mistress, lying beneath him in the same state [drunkenness], began flirting and coquetting, and the two kissed and licked one another."¹²² In Smith's English translation, the same sentence reads, "the barefaced villain consummated before me his career of infamous indecency with his hideous mistress, who gave herself many airs and appeared very squeamish."¹²³ But Forbes paraphrases the sentence for the revised Urdu edition to read: "vōh pilisht-e bēhayā bhī badmast hō kar us mardūd sē bhī behūdā adā`eiñ karnē lagī."¹²⁴ In his corresponding English translation, we find that "the shameless harlot likewise got beastly drunk and took very unbecoming liberties with that vile youth."¹²⁵

The irony in these prudish translations and alternations is two-fold. The princess's story warns against the evils of imbibing, a tumultuous, celebratory act indispensable to the aesthetics of the Urdu *dāstān* and ghazal. But it is also testimony to the totalizing grip orientalists exercised over modern Urdu from the moment of its inception under Gilchrist to this later point in the canon-making process. Forbes and Smith transform the vernacular oriental tale into something much larger than a set of simple, loosely adapted moral stories.¹²⁶ We must recall that in the initial moment of its manufacture, *Bāġh-o Bahār*, a crudely composed text in a colloquial register, had been deemed a classic of oriental, Asiatic, and Urdu literatures by its imperial patrons. As the anxieties of the colonial encounter with the Muslims of North India gathered, particularly in the years following 1857, the Mahometan oriental is recalibrated as inept and improper, prompting further literary-linguistic disciplining of its communal affiliates.

Bāġh-o Bahār, of course, was just one of the several Fort William texts that became central to the North Indian register we know as modern Urdu. What must be emphasized, however, is the similitude of these imperially sponsored works, and the common source of their compositions. Much of this chapter has focused on the process of how a Mahometan literature is imagined, invented, and subsequently disseminated amongst Muslim native subjects in the colony. On the one hand, there is something of the global or worldly about stories such as *Bāġh-o Bahār* and *Ārā'ish-e Mehfil*, which are authored in a setting like Fort William College, travel all the way to Europe and back, and are celebrated by their various translators and exoticized by their English and French readers. Yet this rather international endeavor is organized by insular principles that privilege the idea of nations and peoples, and in fact, comprehend these categories through the concept of literature. That is to say, the process through which—to put it crudely—the manufacture of a modern prose canon in Urdu takes place is one inherently informed by the Enlightenment ideal of literature as the embodiment of national spirit or *geist*. Masquerading as worldly, cosmopolitan, and traveling, the oriental tale, whether in England or as it is slowly funneled into various overlapping orients, then, seems always to have national or nation-making concerns.

The long arc of the oriental tale from the European Republic of Letters to the Indian colony, then, is far from elemental. While Jones and Gilchrist remain central to the invention of a Muslim identity in India, their legacies gain renewed vigor within the cultural machinery of the native education system. For much of this time, this Muslim identity, where the Muslim is a Mahometan who can be known and recognized from the oriental tale, English or vernacular, does not penetrate cultural spheres that closed themselves to the colonial cultural project. These included the courts of nawabs, the brothels that were the centers of Muslim high culture in North India, as well as *madrassahs*, or indigenous centers of learning. By the second half of the nineteenth century, particularly in the wake of the Mutiny of 1857, much of this changes, and Muslim efforts to resist colonial education give way to an identity that begins to reflect the orientalist imaginary.

3 / Nation/*Qaum:* The "Musalmans" of India

The anxieties around native literature, particularly a Mahometan, or Muslim, one that beleaguered Gilchrist and his successors persisted well into the second half of the nineteenth century, exacerbated by the great uprising of 1857, in the wake of which Muslims—now graduated to the term Musalmans—were deemed the major perpetrators and enemies of the crown in India. As late as 1884, William Muir, an English orientalist and administrator with a special interest in education, wrote of "the vernacular languages of India" as "singularly wanting in sound literature of a useful and amusing sort. Such works as there are, abound, for the most part, in matter of an objectionable tendency."[1] A few years earlier, in an attempt to explain the events of 1857, William W. Hunter, another English civil servant, argued that "the Musalmans of India are, and have been for many years, a source of chronic danger to the British Power in India."[2] Unlike "the more flexible Hindus," the Muslims resisted British education and employment, Hunter believed, the consequences of which bred resentment and enmity for the new rulers of India.[3]

Seen as mired in a religion that took direction from the "Holy City of Arabia," or alternately, in a poetic culture lacking in morally sound "literature," the Muslims became the particular project of the colonial administration in the decades following 1857.[4] In part, this was rather ironic, given that for much of the nineteenth century, the colonial administration had attempted to impress new language curricula and distinct ideals of literature and literariness upon both Hindus and Muslims. Fictions such as *Bāġh-o Bahār* and other Fort William publications remained very much a part of the syllabi in schools and elite colleges, yet the imperial administration was convinced of the increasing dangers of the "unaided prosecution of Oriental learning" that they believed had "produce[d] a people who may talk beautifully, but who think and write most inaccurately."[5] To further that end, a second wave of literary invention, now facilitated and funded by the Government of India, swept over the subcontinent, its specific object: the suddenly disenfranchised and dislocated North Indian Muslim bourgeoisie.

This reversal in the fortunes of the North Indian Muslim elite, who until 1857 had imagined themselves as the rulers of India while Bahadur Shah Zafar II, the last nominal bastion of Mughal rule sat on the throne of Delhi, was nothing short of cataclysmic. An entire society rooted in courtly culture and its attendant practices was now bereft of the institution that had anchored it and that had provided much of its own historical legitimacy in India. As Mufti describes it—quite differently from deadpan nationalist historiographies—this process of "social transformation" was a fitful one, a "reluctant embourgeoisement . . . a dogged and melancholic response to the emergence of a new world."[6] The nature of the crisis and the feelings of impotency and rootlessness that it left in its wake are perhaps best expressed by Mirza Hadi Rusva, the poet and writer:

> We let go of Delhi, now we must leave Lucknow,
> Two cities that were ours, now both lie in ruins
>
> *Dillī čhuṭī thī pehlē, ab lucknow bhī čhoṛeiñ*
> *Dō shehr thē yēh apnē, ab dōnōñ tabāh niklē*[7]

Rusva's verse, one of the many laments of an aesthete immersed in the high culture of Indo-Persian aesthetics, is removed in feeling and impulse from colonial rationalizations of the events, which described a vacuous society obsessed with poetry and sensual pleasures. For poets such as Rusva and Mirza Ghalib, the destruction of Lucknow, the last jewel of Indo-Persian aestheticism in the subcontinent, meant the end of a cultural home and its attendant meanings.

While Rusva and Ghalib mourned the loss of Delhi and Lucknow, a nascent Muslim bourgeoisie, educated in colonial institutions and employed within the colonial economy, undertook the project to socially and politically resituate this bedraggled, embarrassed Muslim elite—the *ashrāf*, as this class had historically been called.[8] The task of men such as Syed Ahmad Khan, perhaps the most influential leader to emerge during this moment of broad religious, political, and cultural reform, was a dual one: to appease the English by assuring them of Muslim loyalty to the crown, and to reconcile an unwilling Muslim elite from shattered illusions of aristocracy to the servitude of a bourgeois existence in the days of high empire. Khan's and other, often oppositional, reformist movements of this period are deeply complex, varying in terms of how they envisioned the future of Muslims in India. While Khan's Aligarh movement positioned itself as a modernizing effort, open to Western ideas, including the rational reform of Muslim practices such that Muslims could become participatory members of the colonial economy, major Islam-centric school such as the Deobandi and Barelvi took antagonistic directions. Of the two latter movements, the Deobandi is the longer standing, tracing its roots to Shah Waliullah, a reformist thinker loosely associated with the Mughal emperor Aurungzeb's court. But in the decades following 1857, the Deobandi reorganized into a mosque movement, its object to reacquaint India's Muslims with their true religious identity, which the founders believed had been corrupted by British and Hindu influences.[9]

Emerging alongside these Muslim movements were Hindu revivalist, or as some call them, "renaissance" movements, including Ram Mohan Roy's Brahmo Samaj, as well as the Arya Samaj, both of which called for a pure society. Given that colonially sponsored reform at this point had become a religion-specific task—Hindu movements reforming Hindus and Muslim groups Muslims—there is no doubt, as Faisal Devji has intimated, that "the idea of modernity had no secular history in India."[10] Despite these differences, however, rising Hindu nationalism, as well as the major branches of Muslim reformist movements, contributed collectively to a single end, a native reiteration of an old English idea: that North India's Muslims were not native to India. This chapter seeks to understand how this idea, referred to in earlier chapters as the Mahometan chronotope—the orientalist chrono-spatial understanding of Muslims as a non-national and itinerant formation—is inscribed within colonially patronized, reformist texts, particularly Urdu fiction during the late nineteenth century.

I focus on the Aligarh movement, named after the city where the first "Anglo-Muslim" university was set up by Khan and his followers. Taking much of its direction from English ideals of progress and social reformation, the Aligarh movement, though controversial at the time, is credited as the major influence behind Muslim nationalist efforts of the twentieth century. As Khan saw it, the solution to the problem of the disgraced and seemingly backward Muslims was in the regeneration of a lost *tehzīb*, a term that roughly translates to civilization.[11] In his writings, the idea of *tehzīb* often seems to imply the modern ideal "culture," which for him encompasses literary works, social practices, historical narratives, and the collective ethic of Indian Muslims. Even more so, Khan is interested in the advancement of what he calls "*qaumī tehzīb*," or the national culture of the Muslim nation, which he argued for much of his later life was a distinct entity in colonial India.[12] Enamored of the British, perhaps also opportunistic, Khan, despite much criticism from the Muslim community, including the Deobandis, took on the role of a native ambassador, propagating ideologies of language and literary reinvention very much in line with Western notions of modernity.

Styling himself as a political leader, Khan was prolific, turning to print to disseminate his ideas to Muslim audiences. Prominent among his many publications were a treatise "The Causes of the Indian Revolt" (1859), *Asar-us Sanadid* (1854), a history of Delhi's Muslim architecture, and from 1870 to 1897, monthly journal he called *Tehzīb-ul Aķlāq*, translated literally as the "civilization of morals," but titled *The Muslim Social Reformer* in English. Deeply influenced by Khan's efforts were a number of other young Muslim men, educated in the English schools, employed by the government, or simply disenchanted with what, when compared to the present, appeared to be a wasted past. Three of these men, convinced by Khan's call for change in varying fashions, became central to the post-1857 reinvention of what colonial administrators called "Urdu literature": Nazir Ahmad, a deputy inspector of education in colonial schools; Altaf Hussain Hali, a poet and scholar; and Abdul Halim Sharar, a journalist and novelist, who rose to some prominence toward the close of the nineteenth century.

Consciously undertaking the task of literary reinvention in Urdu, these writers saw themselves as participants in the larger reform movement, or as it was called by Nazir Ahmad, the *işlāĥ*, or correction of Muslim *tehzīb* or culture in North India. In its original Quranic contexts, *işlāĥ* implied a return or restoration to an earlier moment of moral and religious piety. In the fictions of Ahmad, Hali, and the historical "novel" writer Sharar, the gesture is always toward North Indian Muslims as somehow fallen from an original, right path. The task of these fictions, then, is to enable return to a pristine, unadulterated Islam. Worth stressing at this juncture is the sudden totality and power that the category of *literature*, specifically, a Muslim literature, acquires for social reformers working within colonial structures.[13] Patronized by colonial administrators whose goal was now to rid vernacular literatures of what they deemed fantasy and religious superstition, writers such as Ahmad and Hali offered a rational, colonially compliant Muslim to their readers, whose altered practice was a testament of his *işlāĥ* (correction). Situating themselves as reformers of the Muslim community as well as of the cultural and linguistic aspects of Urdu—that register cleft in two after Fort William College—these writers are historical examples of how the Mahometan chronotope of the English and vernacular oriental tale is internalized and revitalized with new religio-political meaning in the high colony.

In doing so, these writers consciously abandon what we can tentatively think of as premodern, Indo-Persian knowledge systems and aesthetic practices, inseparable in terms of genre or discipline. Until at least the late eighteenth century, terms such as *'ilm* (knowledge) and *adab* (refinement, values, and etiquettes) signified more complex and intertwined functions than their bland translations into English allow. *'Ilm*, in the Islamic world, signaled a knowledge of the hadith, for example, but could also be used to signify the spiritual self-knowledge of an individual. *Adab*, on the other hand, "reflects a high valuation of the employment of the will in proper discrimination of correct order, behavior, and taste."[14] As Barbara Metcalf conceptualizes the term, "It implicitly or explicitly distinguishes cultivated behavior from that deemed vulgar, often defined as pre-Islamic custom."[15] In the heyday of the colony, however, as education and institutions of learning increasingly came under British control, the "dichotomy between literature (now referred to as *adab*) and science or fact (now referred to as *'ilm*)" was taught to Muslims educated in colonial institutions.[16]

The imposition of new knowledge systems begins at Fort William College where, as the previous chapter argues, a category called "literature" was introduced to native subjects. The decades following 1857 mark the inception of a properly domestic Muslim fiction in North India that takes the space of the home as its object, locating it within a larger communal formation that Khan referred to as "*qaum*," or nation.[17] In other words, the North Indian Muslim experience, once exemplary of the subcontinent's religious and cultural cosmopolitanism, is gradually forced to see itself in terms of an alien concept: nationhood. Whereas the structural and narrative concerns of the oriental tales produced at Fort William College may seem far removed from what was now a domestically inclined, religiously reformative set of fictions, these works collectively and continuously come to constitute the literary canon of modern Urdu. The earlier replications of the English oriental tale in the vernacular are thus succeeded by bestselling fictions that engage with the Mahometan chronotope by rewriting its terms to produce a modern, Western-styled literary canon for Muslims. For the second time in one century, then, a new iteration of "Mahometan" literature is produced in the North Indian colony, this time in order to act as an antidote to the poor influences of predecessor works.

Didactic fictions such as Ahmad's *Mirāt al-'Arūs*, or the Bride's mirror (1868), and *Taubat al-Naṣūḥ*, the Repentance of Nasuh (1872), Hali's

Majālis un-Nisā, Gatherings of women (1875), or Abdul Halim Sharar's sensational novel, *Flōrā Flōrinḍā* (1899), attempt to rehabilitate the imagined figure of the Mahometan—opulent, despotic, itinerant, a foreigner in India—into a modern Muslim, a bourgeois subject whose historical origins lie in Islam's glorious past. The narrative reconstruction of this subject organizes within the colonially learned terms of nation and nationalism, ubiquitous in literature and history curricula of native schools. But in place of an ancient civilization, the North Indian *ashrāf* trace their origins to the founding moment of Islam, thus imagining a modern nation in entirely religious terms.[18] Over this period of late nineteenth-century literary and cultural reform, the Mahometan chronotope is reaffirmed in increasingly nationalist terms. The origins of North India's Muslims lie in Islam's various glorious pasts. India is recast from a home to the geographic site where Islam is corrupted, and subsequently, the Muslim home must become the space where a chaste Islam can be cultivated.

The great shift visible in reformist fictions, beginning with Ahmad's conduct book–like works, is that of subject. If the vernacular oriental tale took the male Mahometan as its protagonist, reformist revisions focused on Muslim women. This had much to do with colonial demands, as I will elaborate on later in the chapter, but also with what Partha Chatterjee describes as the "new politics of nationalism."[19] In the case of the Muslim community, particularly as it appeared to the Aligarh group (itself made up of varying opinions), the need for women educated in a more Western style sprang, in part, from colonial demands for transparency regarding the nature of instruction available to Muslim women. Quite plainly, the colonial government believed that "an ignorant Mahomedan mother transmits the fanatical bigotry characteristic of her people," and thus sought to incentivize and encourage a suitable education agenda for Muslim women modeled on equivalent modes in England.[20] But class anxieties amongst this young bourgeois class also had much to do with more traditional images of women associated with the *nawab* and older elite Muslim culture, embodied largely in the figure of the courtesan, or *tavā'if*.

Trained in the poetics of Persian and high Urdu, classical dance, and music, well-read and well-spoken courtesans had long been a part of Muslim life in North India. With the decline of the *nawab* (princely classes) and the subsequent rise of a small but influential Muslim bourgeoisie, the cultural practice of visiting brothels and keeping long-term courtesans as companions was no longer an accepted or necessary social practice. Respectability, as it were, came to belong to the wife, the keeper of the home, rather than women outside of the new family. Finally, as Devji has so succinctly elaborated, the reformed *ashrāf* "created themselves in and through the colonial order as a distinct 'Islamist' or 'revivalist' polity," whether Aligarh, Deoband, or other school of thought.[21] Given their reliance on *shariah* thought, "every one of the reformers viewed the woman, for example, as the agent of a sinister, debilitating corruption that attacked vulnerable Muslim men from the inside, paganizing them and rendering them unable to defend the faith."[22] The solution to this, at least in the case of the Aligarh school, was to "hegemonically incorporate" the Muslim youth and women "into the new *sharīf* polity by education or Islamization."[23] Once incorporated, Devji argues, the woman could become the protector of masculine virtue from the home, rather than herself be a source of disruption.

Given the diversity of reformist movements that had taken root in the nineteenth century, the major fictions of this period were hardly homogenous. Nazir Ahmad's *Mirāt* and *Taubat*, for example, echoed many of Syed Ahmad Khan's political beliefs, stressing the need for the *ashrāf* to align themselves with the English, while disassociating from practices that were somehow "Indic," or corrupting influences on Islam. Hali's *Majālis*, like his major poem *Mad-o Jazar-e Islām* (the rise and fall of Islam), locate a Muslim future outside of India, unequivocally declaring India as a space of decline and darkness for Islam. Finally, in *Flōrā Flōrindā*, Sharar, a prolific writer of historical novels, revives older Islamic empires as a device through which to move India's Muslims to a passion for Islam and its future. Nazir Ahmad and Hali, in particular, deride the elite practice of courtly Urdu, choosing to develop the colloquial Fort William register that was taught in colonial schools and colleges, thus populating the literary canon of modern, colonial Urdu with new fiction and poetry.

New Tales for Old: Nazir Ahmad's *Mirāt al-'Arūs* and the Invention of a Muslim Domesticity

It is well-known that Nazir Ahmad, a colonial loyalist, wrote his first bestselling work, *Mirāt al-'Arūs*, as a response to a circular that appeared in the Allahabad Government Gazette in August 1868. Authored by William Muir, the circular "with the view of encouraging authorship in the language of the North-Western Provinces" offered "rewards ... for the production of useful works in the vernacular, of approved design and style, in any branch of science and literature."[24] For the work to be considered for the prize, it would ideally have to "subserve some useful purpose, either of instruction, entertainment or mental discipline."[25] And finally, "Books suitable for the women of India will be especially acceptable and well-rewarded."[26] The language and demands of the circular betray the ongoing nature of the vernacularization project that had begun at Fort William at the start of the nineteenth century. The focus of the still youthful literature of modern Urdu now was directed toward women, its purpose, the social and intellectual improvement of the native family. *Mirāt* won the prize and gained substantial recognition, as did Ahmad's third book, *Taubat al-Naṣūḥ*. These are only two of his many works, but I use them here as pioneering examples of how Muslim domesticity would be constructed against what we can think of as an older order, a way of life that reformists such as Khan and Ahmad, echoing colonial ideals, saw as decadent, wasteful, and immoral.

Mirāt is the story of two sisters, Akbari and Asghari, the former, spoiled and lazy, and the latter, diligent, well-read, and rational. The story of Akbari occupies only a small part of the book, for the older sister manages to destroy her marriage and home within just a few chapters. Asghari's story, on the other hand, occupies much of the narrative and takes us from the moment of her marriage to Mohammad Kamil, to her setting right of her marital home, her moral reform of Kamil, and finally, her well-managed relations with other *sharīf* families. Lauded upon its publication by Matthew Kempson, Ahmad's supervisor, as "equal to the recently published letters of . . . Ghalib," and "resembl[ing] the *Alf Lailah*," *Mirāt* was soon translated into English, and recommended to English ladies as a suitable textbook for those inclined to learn Urdu, or "Hindustani," as G. E. Ward, its translator, called the language.[27]

Like that of *Bāgh-o Bahār*, *Mirāt's* falsely modest preface charmed its English translators, readers, and patrons through a quaint narration of its "oriental" origins. It was written by a "Mohammadan gentleman of good family and liberal views for the instruction and amusement of his little daughters. Its fame having soon spread abroad in his Ward (Mohalla), some ladies from neighboring houses would drop in to hear it, read, and others would borrow the manuscript to read to their own families."[28] What has changed from the Fort William days, or even those of Galland and Grub Street, is the proximity of vernacular literary production to prescribed English ideals of literature and its social utility. Mir Amman's main contribution to the new vernacular literature, as inaugurated by Gilchrist, was a colloquial register and a set of stories that authenticated the imagined Mahometan orient for the English. Accordingly, Ahmad's introduction is self-deprecatory; his amateur book, he tells us, owes much of its success to colonial patronage.

Mirāt conveniently fulfilled the various criteria that the government had laid out as part of its program for a suitable native literature in Hindustani or Urdu. For one, Ahmad claims to have searched extensively for a text that was "replete with good morals and sincere advice [*aḵlāq-o naṣāḥ*]." Finding nothing in Urdu, he composed "new type" (*na`ye ṭaur*) of "*qiṣṣā*" to serve his purpose.[29] In accordance with the instructions given by the "rulers" (*sarkār*), the language is "idiomatic, the ideas, pure" (*bā mahāvara, ḵayālāt, pākīzā*) and free from "affectation" (*banāvaṭ*).[30] Continuous, on the one hand, with Gilchrist's plan for Hindustani, yet also echoing Macaulay's Minute, the introductory rationale for *Mirāt* dismisses older Urdu practices as adulterated and immoral, electing to favor the prescribed register and moral code. Ahmad's stories of an ideal Muslim domestic life inaugurate a seemingly "liberal" movement—they advocate teaching women to read and write, for example—that becomes definitive of a distinctly Muslim modernity in the Indian subcontinent. This modernity, I show, positions itself against a past that is imagined in accordance with the orientalist Mahometan chronotope, and propagates a rational, pure Islam as the only means of Muslim progress. There are several well-studied aspects and manifestations of this Muslim modernity in South Asia, but given the scope of this work, I restrict myself mainly to the construct of literature and its relationship to modes of nation-thinking.

Mirāt opens with the story of Akbari Khanum. She is a spoiled, temperamental young woman, with few skills and no wisdom in the way of housekeeping. Occupying a third of the book, the events of Akbari's life are introduced by the narrator as an "entertaining *qiṣṣā*" that illustrates the "pains" caused by "ignorance and lack of talent."[31] Set up to serve more as a dire warning than a source of amusement, Akbari is so spoiled by her grandmother's "idiotic affections" that even marriage failed to improve her bad temper or her clumsiness.[32] Within a few months of getting married, Akbari demands a house of her own, assaults her young sister-in-law, Mehmuda, and eventually, through her own stupidity and carelessness, is robbed by the various lower-class characters she seems to befriend. A *sharīf*-born woman who consorted with the daughter of laborers and working-class families, Akbari has courted the ruin that eventually befalls her. Not entirely an original character, Akbari embodies the particular licentiousness or state of dissolution endemic to women of the Mahometan Orient in both English oriental tales as well as fictions closer to home, including *Bāġh-o Bahār* and *Ṭōṭā Kahānī*.

The first half of the frame story of the *Arabian Nights' Entertainments*, we can recall, is the story of two queens whose infidelities instigate their husbands' agonized moral transformations. Schahriar's first wife's affair, however, is no ordinary case of adultery, for Masoud, her black lover, can almost immediately be assumed to be a slave, or at best, a servant.[33] In the "story of the two sisters who envied their younger Sister," the two elder sisters are represented as gluttonous, materialist, and discontent, while the youngest is blessed with abundant patience and fortitude. In the various tales of *Bāġh-o Bahār*, we encounter women, who if not "bad" or adulterous, like the women of the *Nights*, have wandered out of the enclosed space of the home, making themselves vulnerable to male exploitation and social destruction. An obvious example is the princess in the story of the first dervish whose indiscretions with a pageboy lead her to witness his sexual depravity with his hag-like slave. Similarly, in the story of the third dervish, a European princess converses and sympathizes with lower-order characters, including a beggar woman who almost succeeds in enslaving the princess by capturing her ring. In Syed Buksh Haidari's Fort William *Ṭōṭā Kahānī*, Khojista's physical virtue is controlled by the stories of her husband's parrot, and she is forced to remain within the space of the house, even though by the end, her emotional infidelity is avenged by her husband upon his return.

Akbari, thus, must be read as both archaic and innovative. She is yet another bad, oriental woman who brings grief upon herself by flouting tradition and disrespecting her husband. Her novelty lies in the cautionary role she plays for an emergent class of bourgeois women. The construction of a feminine *sharāfat* through the "acquisition of moral and wifely power for reformed women," Kumkum Sangari has argued, "rested not on othering women from different denominations but on othering women 'below.'"[34] That is to say, the reformed woman had to be constructed against the castes, classes, and spaces of other possible Muslim women—courtesans, domestics, and common labor. This was possible only if, the "ideal," as Lelyveld describes it, was maintained: "to stay at home from marriage to death, visited not visiting, carried in. . . . in a bridal palanquin, carried out in a coffin."[35]

But Akbari violates both conditions of *sharīf* femininity: She is guilty of wandering out of her marital home and instead of distancing herself from lower-class women, she makes them her sole companions. She defies the sanctity of the domestic enclave by going outside of the family home to a house of her own, and through contact with her lower-class and thus more mobile, necessarily compromised friends, Zulfan and Chuniyan. Though Akbari is never shown to be promiscuous or as engaging in sexual dalliances—probably in accordance with the puritan rules that marked colonial patronage for native writing—her general slovenliness and

THE "MUSALMANS" OF INDIA / 97

willfulness perform these attributes, acting as substitutes for the female vices that appear in the earlier corpus. Innovative in terms of her utility for the reformists, Akbari, nevertheless, is associated with an older order of existence—she has been raised by her grandmother who, we can assume, exists at a distance from the colonial space, and thus is illiterate and ignorant of the benefits of Western modernity.

Akbari's propensity to consort with lower-class women becomes her ultimate undoing. Her sister, Asghari, on the other hand, is exemplary for the manner in which she holds both excessively wealthy and lower-class women at bay, thus gaining power and control in her marital home. Akbari's friend Chuniyan's brother robs her new house while she is asleep one afternoon. A second, more serious incident follows when the incorrigible Akbari befriends a "procuress" (*kutnī*), masquerading as a *Hajjan* (literally, a woman who has performed the Haj, but here a deceptive title). This smooth-talking woman manages to cheat Akbari out of all her wedding jewelry as well as a good amount of money by telling her stories of miracles performed by an ascetic (*faqīr*) who resides atop a mountain on the "Island of Blacks" (*kōh-e ḥabshā*). Carefully framed to resemble stories out of the *Arabian Nights*, or *Bāġh-o Bahār*, this deceptive tale fools Akbari who gives all she possesses over to the Hajjan. Doubly didactic, the story illustrates the ills of consorting with common women. The "degenerate condition" of these various maid servants, washerwomen, prostitutes, and here procuresses, is elaborated, literally through their immorality, but also by the threat of the stories they tell to *sharīf* piety and purity.[36] An easy way for the reformists to make tales of miracles, talismans, and fakirs obsolete was to affiliate them with low-born women and common criminals. Wayward women like Akbari, then, could be held up as sorry and unchastised victims.

After telling his readers of Akbari's disastrous marriage, Ahmad turns to the story of Asghari, which is inadvertently framed by the short story of her sister's failures. "But why not write of the state of her younger sister, Asghari," Ahmad begins, "the smallest events of which will be cause for joy for readers and listeners."[37] Asghari, Scheherazade-like in her earnestness to redeem the family she marries into, is treasured in her mother's house "like a rose, or like the eye in the human body," and "there was no skill she did not possess." Her other qualities include "wisdom, sense, manners, etiquette, humility, kindheartedness, sociability, devoutness, dignity, consideration" (*dānā'ī, hōshyārī, adab, q'āidā, ġurbat, nēk dilī, milansārī, ḳudāparastī, ḥayā, liḥāẓ*).[38] Unlike her sister, Asghari, "from childhood, had hated playing games, or laughing and joking."[39] Constructed in opposition to the feminine types of the Mahometan Orient, who were envisioned in oriental tale as unproductive or childlike, Asghari, like Scheherazade, distinguishes herself from other female companions, defined *against* contemporary femininity rather than in conjunction with it.[40]

In complete contrast to Akbari, Asghari embodies Syed Ahmad Khan's desire for "progress," or *taraqqī*, among the Muslims of India. Over the course of *Mirāt*, Asghari sets out to reform, or correct, her husband and in-laws; gets rid of a scheming servant; opens a school for genteel young women from the neighborhood; even inspires a sequel to the book, which details the education of the students at the school. At the heart of all these reforms in the lives of the *sharīf* family and the surrounding neighborhood is a desire to rid this bourgeois class of the degraded, or rather, *Indian* Islam that they practice and instead restore a chaste version of the religion. At the same time, in order to be properly modern, they must also learn from the British whose achievements, particularly those with respect to empire make them a worthy ally. Though Nazir Ahmad would detail his somewhat tormented position with respect to Anglo-Muslim relations in his late work *Ibn-ul Vaqt*, the Son of time (1888), his mentor Syed Ahmad Khan would insist until the end of his life for a Muslim alliance with the colonial government.

In her marital home, where she resides with her husband and in-laws, Asghari becomes a force of change, counseling her mother-in-law against irrational, ritual practices such as "distributing halva at *shab-e bārāt*, sweets at Eid, vows with other wives, offerings to Bibi Fatima, conditional vows, '*arsh*, the decoration of graves, the kite-festival [*basant*]," among others.[41] Declaring these practices, heretical (*bid'at*), Asghari's language aligns with that of Deobandi preachers of the time who advocated a return to the original Islamic moment, with particular emphasis on the hadith.[42] Among these newly prohibited practices are several Shi'ite rituals, which over the course of this period were systematically demarcated as against the spirit of Sunni Islam. When Asghari declares that such practices are not part of the religion (*dīn*), she in essence also separates Islam from India—the aforementioned are rituals wrongfully adopted and invented by Muslims *in India*. Several of these practices centered around communities of women, regardless of religion and sect. Asghari's condemnation of these, thus, also disrupts extant feminine realms, and replaces them with organized units such as family and the colonial school.

A narrow view of Asghari's attempts to purify religious practice in her marital home can easily ascribe blame to the effects of the Deobandi movement, which frequently reverberated across reformist essays and fictions despite the fact that the Deobandi clerics often disagreed with colonial loyalists such as Khan. This delocalization of Islam from India, or the stripping away of "local custom," to borrow from Metcalf, was a central trait of the Deobandis, who saw the entirety of Islam in the Quran and the hadith.[43] A longer historical view asks us to consider the "forceful intervention" of eighteenth-century colonialists that reorganized Islamic law such that the "personal" became "the legitimate modern domain for the religious" in a fashion never known before in Islamic societies, a fact that Shahab Ahmed explicates at some length in his opus, *What is Islam?*[44] Here, by way of Asghari's condemnation of local custom as bid'at, Ahmad participates in what Shahab Ahmed has so unequivocally argued is the making of Islam as law, as opposed to Islam as a broader formation constituted collectively and equally by "theology, philosophy, ethics, poetics, and Sufism."[45] The introduction and enforcement of terms such as bid'at, to limit what was within the prescribed precincts of dīn, was a distinctly modern approach to the Western category of "religion," an approach that until the orientalist effort had little significance in North India.[46] Asghari, like Nasuh from *Taubat*, derives authority from the modern colonial institution of religious law that now governs the individual, and becomes the means through which local beliefs and practice could be dismissed as superstition or fantasy.

Asghari's next target is her husband, Muhammad Kamil. Representing what we can think of as an older Muslim order, Kamil, while attentive to his studies in Persian and Arabic, also spent a good amount of time playing cards, chess, and dice with other boys. Though these were popular recreational pursuits of men from elite Muslim and Hindu backgrounds, Asghari finds such activities frivolous and tells her husband "playing such games was a habit comparable to opium [afyūn]."[47] More important than their addictive potential was the fact that "these games are sinful [gunāh]" and "impede man from attaining higher goals."[48] The reader is told that Kamil eventually heeds Asghari's counsel, leaves his play, and focuses instead on his mathematics. He also shifts his focus from Persian, the centuries-long language of the North Indian elite, to Arabic, the language preferred by reformists. (Persian, the longstanding language of Mughal judicial courts, had in 1837 been replaced by Hindustani in the new legal system being run by Company officials.) The particular word used for what I have crudely translated as counsel is naṣīhat, which, like iṣlāḥ, has its roots in Quranic Arabic and means well-meant or sincere advice. The act of prophets or, in the case of religious India, religious reformers, naṣīhat comes from a position of truth and authority. The reformer, here, Asghari, takes the wasteful, hedonistic Mahometan of the orientalist imagination as her subject with the intent of converting him to a pious Muslim whose newly acquired rationality allowed him to be a proper colonial subject.

Muhammad Kamil successfully finds employment at the *kačehrī*, or local office of the vast network of British courts and administrative offices in India after Asghari unequivocally orders him to search for an "English job."[49] When he complains about the nature of his employment and the meager salary of ten rupees, Asghari admonishes him for ingratitude, reminding him of the days when he was unemployed and using the example of her father who rose to the level of *tehsīldār* (revenue officer) in his service to the English. Eventually, Muhammad Kamil becomes indispensable to James Sahib, who takes him with him at a higher salary when the Sahib is transferred to Sialkot. The episode of Muhammad Kamil's reeducation and subsequent employment unequivocally heralds a moment in which courtly life and attendant pursuits become irrelevant. Prestige and a dignified living are now to be found only in colonial employment. The process of Kamil's embourgeoisement, however, is mediated entirely through a narrowing category of Muslimness and is framed as the *iṣlāḥ* (correction) of a degraded people.

Once the matters of the house—piety, servants, the return of Akbari to the family house—have been managed, Asghari turns her attention to the women and girls of other families by opening a school (*maktab*) in her home. Though everyone in the neighborhood and beyond wants to send their daughters to the school, Asghari handpicks her students, ensuring only girls from reputable, *sharīf* families are enrolled. In her school, girls receive a proper "education" (*t'ālīm*, from the root '*ilm*, or knowledge), which includes reading, writing, and sewing.[50] Informally, the girls are taught much more, including how to run household accounts and how to cook. A female servant is hired to clean the school and fan the girls as they study. At the end of the day, the girls sit together and read stories.

If Asghari's curriculum of choice is essentially the same as that prescribed by the English at native girls' schools, as can be found in colonial reports, then the girls' moral edification, which they gain through stories, also diverges from traditional routes.[51] Departing from the older trend where women were entertained by meaningless "stories of cock- and hen-sparrows," Asghari assigns Nazir Ahmad's own compilation, the *Muntakib ul-Hikāyāt*, Selected stories. In the 1900 edition of the India Office library's catalogue of Hindustani Books, the work is more accurately described as "A Collection of Moral and Entertaining Anecdotes."[52] In the brief preface to this collection of what we can approximately call fables, Ahmad decries the pointlessness or lack of purpose in extant children's stories, thus positioning his stories as providing both entertainment and advice.⁵³ As with *Mirāt*, Ahmad concludes, this set of stories enables its young readers to learn modern Urdu, instead of remaining attached to the older, stylized register.

Bearing a strong resemblance to Gilchrist's own *Oriental Fabulist*, Ahmad's *Hikāyāt* is also made up of page-long stories that are accompanied by a lesson (*ḥāṣil*). In one story, a hungry rooster searching for food comes across a precious stone hidden in the ground. Instead of rejoicing at this newfound wealth, all the rooster can think about is the uselessness of such an object in a time of basic need, a lesson that Ahmad reiterates at the bottom of the page.⁵⁴ In the story of two travelers, readers are told that those who betray trust remain unloved. In another, those true to God and their faith receive, while those who feign belief are punished.⁵⁵ The audience of young female readers, then, are both entertained but also given moral instruction through stories whose lack of complexity or length ensures that only a limited amount of time can be spent reading at all.

Though Asghari allows this collection of "good stories" to "divert" her students, she often stops them mid-story to impart a lesson.⁵⁶ When one student, Fazilat, reads a story beginning with "there was once a king," Asghari interrupts her and asks, "Whom do we call a king?" By sparking a discussion that visits the brutal deposal of the last Mughal king Bahadar Shah by the British, and the establishment of Queen Victoria as queen, "our king [*hamārā bādshāh*] is the Queen Victoria," Asghari rewrites India's history for her young students as it was to be understood in the post-1857 years.⁵⁷ Telling the course of events such that the accession of Victoria as the empress of India followed naturally from the capture and exile of Bahudur Shah, Asghari molds her female pupils into acquiescent subjects of the colony rather than allowing attachment to an older order whose glory was represented by the Mughal throne.

Within a year or so of publication, *Mirāt* officially became part of the curriculum at girls schools that were run by the colonial government. In terms of numbers, however, this was not a grand audience: For example, in 1873, only 1208 girls were studying at the elementary level in the North-West Provinces, it had clearly also gained circulation in homes and private gatherings. This was not all: In 1869, just a year after its publication, the lieutenant-governor, Muir, also recommended *Mirāt* to the "Board of Examiners as a suitable textbook of examination," which he described as "incomparably superior in its contents to the vapid and often objectionable tales of common Oriental writing."⁵⁸ *Mirāt* sets into motion a second wave of canon-making in Urdu that was both continuous with and a break from Fort William literature. Though advocating the simple, colloquial language that the Fort William texts were intended to popularize, reformist literary fiction was posited as a progression from the almost obsolete aesthetic and storytelling tradition whose traces were so evident in the Fort William publications. This deliberate evolution, for lack of a better term, was facilitated with the specific purpose of incorporating bourgeois Muslim women into the reading public. In the works that followed, with *Mirāt* as a prototype, a modern Muslim domesticity takes shape, where men and women come together to form families and the home becomes a place where morality and piety are reformed and protected.

The Repentant Mahometan: *Taubat an-Nasūḥ* and the Invention of a Modern Muslim Literature

Published four years after *Mirāt*, the story of the repentant Nasuh and his quest to reform his errant and wayward family garnered strong praise from the colonial administration and was immediately cited as a worthy example of literature.[59] Focused on the question of piety, more specifically, a *domestic* piety, *Taubat* revolves around the reformation of the errant family and inculcating piety among its members by upholding the book as an object of authority, or in some cases, as a source of moral degeneration. While men are reformed or judged with respect to the various books that the author sacralizes or dismisses over the course of the work, the female members of the family are educated in a curriculum deemed fit by the patriarch.

Lauded by Muir as a book that could only "present itself to the Moslem mind in a country under Christian influences," *Taubat* also won prize money from the government and was soon translated into English by Ahmad's superior, Matthew Kempson. In its early editions, *Taubat* was marketed as the third part of *Mirāt* (the second being the less successful *Banat an-Nash*, or Daughters of the Bier, the story of a spoiled and rich little girl's education at Asghari's school). Ambitious in its reach, *Taubat* announces a program of reform that will extend from the home to the *mohalla* or neighborhood, from thereon to the city and eventually to the entire country.[60] In that vein, Ahmad specifies the purpose of *Taubat*: It is a guide on how to nurture one's offspring (*tarbiyat-e aulād*).[61] Differing from a basic education, which Ahmad says is more easily achieved, *tarbiyat* demands that a Muslim correct his child's morals, temperament, and habits, as well as rectify their thoughts and their beliefs (*aḵlaq kī tehzīb, mizāj kī iṣlāḥ, 'ādāt kī durustī, ḵyālāt aur m'ataqdāt ki taṣīḥ*).[62] Thus framed, the story of *Taubat* follows the attempts of the reformed Nasuh, whose name derives from *naṣīḥat*, or sincerely intended advice, to reclaim his wayward family into the fold of a purified Islam.

The idea of the book looms large in *Taubat*, beginning with Ahmad's preface, which establishes its own authority by citing from the Quran. In the opening quote, readers are reminded that Allah "trusted" (*amānat*) or gave man "wisdom" (*'aql*, this is Ahmad's interpretation) above and beyond the rest of creation, but man failed to utilize this wisdom for good.[63] This degraded moment, Ahmad implies, is the result of an absence of *tarbiyat* in the children of his countrymen (*hum-vatanōñ*). This book is an offering that may help to remedy the situation.[64] If the Quran is the ultimate and eternal book, *Taubat* is a temporal one whose purpose is to act as a "beginner's guide" (*abjād*) to *tarbiyat*, and thus to the eventual progress of the nation as evidenced by English society.[65] The story (*qiṣṣā*) of a Muslim household (*musalmān k̠āndān*) that is contained within the pages of *Taubat* establishes the sole authority of the Quran while discounting that of an entire corpus of Persian and Urdu texts from the thirteenth century all the way to the present moment.[66] *Taubat*, then, is one of the first serious exercises undertaken by native subjects of a simultaneous literary canonization and exculpation of prose fiction in Urdu.

In the opening sequence of *Taubat*, the titular character, Nasuh, undergoes a miraculous reformation from an apathetic Muslim subject to a pious patriarch. While ill with the cholera that has spread over the city, Nasuh has a dream in which he sees himself enter a great *kačehrī*, typically the central administration complex of the colonial government, containing courts and other administrative offices. But this is not the English *kačehrī*, which Nasuh is well-acquainted with given his past employment as an inspector. The dream *kačehrī* is the court of Judgment Day. Nasuh's father appears and shows him the set of charges he faces now that he is dead. Expecting the British Penal Code, Nasuh sees instead a set of rules from the Quran in which his father is charged with infidelity and pride, and, above all, with disloyalty to Islam because of his attachment to worldly pleasures. The *sharīf* Muslim, Nasuh then realizes, must repent while he is still alive.

He resumes life after cholera, a changed man whose gaze is now turned away from the worldliness that previously governed his actions. This opening scene offers what develops into a continuous theme in the text—the removal of the elite Muslim male from the worldliness and materiality that has corrupted him in colonial India. The divine *kačehrī*, then, forces a reevaluation of the relationship this figure has so far held with objects of power in the colony—no more is the British *kačehrī* the omnipotent arbitrator. The reformed Nasuh must look to another center, one that is abstract and intangible. This is not to say that *Taubat* advocates a break or rejection of the British, but rather that it complicates the comparatively simple rhetoric of allegiance in *Mirāt*, invoking a powerful separation between a Muslim's worldly occupations and the subsequently private and spiritual existence he must strive toward as a subject in what is increasingly depicted as a foreign land and empire.

It is with the divine *kačehrī* in mind that Nasuh first converts his compliant wife. The couple then collectively address the failings and potential of their three sons and two daughters. Nasuh's project, it must be noted, is what Muir happily identified as "the effect of our religious teaching in India."[67] Nasuh, in other words, sees his community not as a rooted North Indian *ashrāf*, but as wayward Mahometans. As in the case of *Mirāt*, *Taubat* advocates a return to a pure Islam, unadulterated by "non-koranic, customary forms of celebration" and free of "syncretic and other shared religious practices."[68] Like Asghari, Nasuh's initial tasks involve ridding his family of their attachments to ritual practices and reacquainting them with basic religious tenets such as prayer. His wife, Fehmida, we are told, was taught how to read and write by her husband in the early days of their marriage when the "drive for women's education had just begun."[69] Seeing some sense and no harm in this colonial endeavor, Nasuh had bought some of the new books being published in those days and instructed his wife in their use. A literate woman, Fehmida, though initially befuddled by Nasuh's altered, repentant persona, soon joins him in his project to re-educate his family.

Of their two daughters, the elder, Naima, another Akbari, is a spoiled young woman who, having refused to get along with her in-laws and husband has returned to her parents' house. The younger, Hamida, is easily convinced of the significance of prayer and practice. Nasuh's sons, on the other hand, are a varied lot. The younger two are wise and pliable, while the eldest, Kalim, is a recalcitrant figure, unwilling to abandon his worldly attachments. The youngest son, Salim, has had the good fortune of receiving religious counsel from an observant friend's family, and his second son, Alim, ascribes his conversion entirely to the influence of good books, indirectly attacking the state of religious literature in Urdu.

At the *madrassah* (local school), where Alim studies, the Quran is taught in a language he does not understand (presumably and surprisingly, Arabic). The "tales and stories" (*qiṣṣē, kahānī*) Alim reads at his school "often contain immoral ideas."[70] When he hears of a famous *pādrī*—presumably an English missionary—who gives out beautifully bound books to native children, Alim finds his way to his house and chooses a gold-covered book. In what is the Bible or a derivative work, Alim reads the story of a "god-fearing and chaste man," written in "simple Urdu" (*salīs urdū*).[71] At the madrassah, in the meanwhile, Alim is prescribed Inayatullah's Persian *Bahār-e Dānish*, or the Wisdom of Spring, an entertaining seventeenth-century tract where a parrot comforts a lovesick young prince by telling stories of women's infidelity. After reading the missionary's gold-bound message, he finds *Bahār-e Dānish* repulsive and immoral. Moved by the event of nothing less than what Bhabha deemed the venerable "English book" disguised in the vernacular and its attendant message, Alim realizes the errors of his ways and privately renounces the world around him well before Nasuh's own transformation has even begun.[72]

Mediated entirely through the question of text and canon, Alim's conversion is an exercise in the linking of literary production to the possibility of a reformed, yet pure Islam. Alim becomes a better Muslim by way of a Christian text that is presented to him in *readable and unadorned Urdu*. The native subject's appreciation of the book handed to him by the missionary takes us back to early orientalists, above all, Gilchrist, who favored the "expediency of a Hindostanee and Persian Version of the Holy Bible with the benevolent and pious intention of diffusing the light of the Gospel" among the natives of India.[73] When Kalim, Nasuh's eldest son, finds the book, he tears it to shreds, warning him that were the book not destroyed he, Alim, was at risk of becoming a Christian.[74] To Alim, however, this book represents something much deeper, "if now my thoughts are at all connected with faith and religion, then it is all the influence of this book."[75] Though Nasuh explains to his son that Christianity was an affiliate religion to Islam, the book itself has been destroyed, and the imminent threat of conversion removed. What is being delicately staged in this scene, then, is the urgency of Nazir Ahmad's own attempt to write a book "molded by Islam" (*islām kē sānčē meiñ*) that "is free from any such claims that when read by someone of another religion, prove offensive."[76]

Indirectly, Alim's near escape from conversion is a reminder that Ahmad, like other major reformists, believed that "recourse to the Koran . . . was a way to eliminate those customs and practices of Indian Muslims, which had no basis in the Koran but were a major obstacle in their social, economic, and political progress . . ."[77] This distinctly modern position plays out in Ahmad's carefully crafted engagement with Christianity. While Kalim, the prodigal son, is made out as an intolerant and illiterate young man, Alim and Nasuh carve out a religious position in line with Syed Ahmad Khan's political teachings: There are differences between Islam and Christianity, but ultimately, Muslims should remain amenable and allied with Christians. This construction is followed by the unspoken but apparent sequitur: "against Hinduism." Though never an open declaration in Ahmad's works, the idea that Hindu ritual and practices have infiltrated and degraded a once pure Islam recurs in his other works, *Mirāt, Taubat,* and even *Fasānā-e Mubtalā*.

Alim's encounter with the priest and Nasuh's s intervention offer readers a docile and benevolent version of Islam that can function in accord with the British empire. Kalim, who retains his attachments to an Indo-Persian courtly culture, is cast as a hostile enemy of Christianity and missionary institutions. If Alim is the model son, a Muslim who recognizes the need for a religious literature in the vernacular, Kalim is the reformist appropriation of the Mahometan, that irrational itinerant of the oriental tale. In a *mush'āirā*, or poetry recitation, Kalim's *ghazals* are well received; in a game of chess, the only one who can beat him is the old master Mirza Shahrukh; he plays cards on occasion, but once he sits down, he is never beaten by an ace; there are no rivals to his pigeons in the city; he can fly a kite and cut scores of others with his maneuvers; and he is able to read and write on his own.[78] Unwilling to suddenly change his ways at his father's whim, Kalim ignores repeated entreaties from his brothers and mother to see his father, and henceforth to dedicate himself to a regimen of prayer and austerity.

Kalim occupies separate quarters in his father's house, the opulent nature of which is discovered when Nasuh, having received no answer to his summons, decides to enter on his own. Kalim's two rooms are elaborately titled the "House of Pleasure" (*'ishrat manzil*) and the "Room of Retirement" (*k̲alvat k̲ānā*), the first furnished for "ceremony" (*takalluf*), while the second, comparatively simple, boasts a shelf full of books. In the "House of Pleasure," Nasuh finds a book "elegantly bound in gold" that turns out to be a picture album. Far from containing portraits of "scholars, hafizes or dervishes" (*'ālim, hāfiz̤ aur darvēsh*), the book is replete with images of composers, musicians, singers, and performers, the sixteenth-century Hindu musician Tansen among them. The walls of this room are adorned with "clippings and calligraphies," whose subjects and meanings were "against faith, contrary to religion" (*dīn kē k̲ilāf, mazhab kē bar'aks*).[79] Enraged, Nasuh aims an ornament at these hangings, but his anger knows no bounds when he enters Kalim's bedroom to find a collection of books in Urdu and Persian: "all the same, untrue tales [*jhūtē qiṣṣē*], shameless topics [*bēhūdā bāteiñ*], licentious meanings [*fahash maṭlab*]."[80] Nasuh stares at these books for a few hours, knowing full well that in the beautiful bindings, the purity of script, the whiteness of the paper, and the correctness of style, he beheld a veritable "treasure" of Urdu. But the "injurious" implications of these books for Islam compel Nasuh to burn them.[81]

Joined by Alim who desires revenge for Kalim's earlier tearing up of his book, Nasuh throws title after title into the fire, "*Fasānā-e 'Ajā'ib, Qiṣṣā-e Gul Bakaulī, Ārā'ish-e Mehfil . . . Bahār-e Dānish* and *Daryā-e Laṭāfat*" some of the more prominent ones.[82] Alim brings two volumes of his own to add to the carnage, the collected works of the poet Atish and a volume by the fiction writer Abdul Halim Sharar—ironically a reformer himself—declaring these to be as "dangerous" as the rest.[83] Though Nasuh's hesitation adds some nuance to an otherwise violent act, there is, no doubt, as C. M. Naim has argued, of the scene's unequivocal "rejection of the old poetry (and prose)" by the reformists.[84] "What Lord Macaulay had only hinted at in his famous minute, Nazir Ahmad has Nasuh put into action," Naim astutely argues.[85] The list of books destroyed in the name of Nasuh's pious anger consists largely of works produced at a distance from the colonial ambit, but also includes a volume or so from Fort William College. Collectively, however, these works embody the state of the "literature" of the unreformed Muslim, the range of their themes extending from fantasy to the poetics of the once-elite Urdu register. Echoing colonial critiques of North Indian aesthetics as well as of the early vernacular prose patronized at Fort William, Nasuh collapses the longer, complex history of Urdu and reconstitutes it through the single parameter of religiosity.

When Fehmida, Nasuh's wife, hears of the bonfire of books, she reminds Nasuh of the one volume he had permitted her to read in the early days of their marriage: Saadi's *Gulistān*. Nasuh reminds her that after he had removed offending material, what was left were the words of a man who could be "counted amongst the friends of Allah." In referring to Saadi as a "friend of Allah," whose wisdom is clouded by his dalliances in the "licentious topics" (*faĥash bātōñ*) that seem to pervade so many works of Persian and Urdu, Nasuh offers a hazy notion of an earlier Muslim purity that was slowly obliterated in its opulent North Indian setting. What, then, was the solution for their son Kalim, his wife asks. The solution, Nasuh tells her, is for Kalim to devote himself to "religious and moral books" (*dīn-o aḵlāq kī kitābeiñ*), an effort that will only bear fruit once he tears himself away from the snake-like poison and satanic chants that draw him to more pleasurable and entertaining books.[86] The only readable prose, or even poetry, for that matter, Nasuh can permit must be religiously inclined and morally edifying.

Kalim's story is the story of the old Muslim, the Mahometan destined to wander because of his worldly attachments. He stands in sharp contrast to the rest of his family, reformed Muslims, who recognize their only possible home is in a "kingdom" (*salṭanat*) that is ruled by the "emperor of both the worlds" (*shahanshāh-e dō jahāñ*).[87] Kalim, on the other hand, is a proud subject of the worldly, now ruined kingdoms of unreformed rulers, symbolized by Oudh's Vajid Ali Shah, a celebrated patron of poetry and the arts until his exile in 1857. There is a bitter irony in the realization that for Kalim, a cosmopolitan aesthete, North India *is* a religio-cultural home. For this obsolete subject, whose attachments to Islam are lived experience understood through local ritual and practice, and whose aesthetic inclinations testify to a long-standing, fluid Indo-Persian poetics, this notion of belonging is a fragile one, broken by the increasingly dominant idea of modern and colonial Muslim identity. Ironically enough, it is the reformed Muslim who *actually* conforms with the Mahometan condition, deliberately breaking from the idea of India as a home of many centuries. Instead, a Muslim *qaum*, or nation, begins to form around the sign of the divine *kačehrī*, an abstraction that assumes the form of the holy city of Mecca in later works.

Kalim is cut off by his father, forced to vacate his ravaged quarters, and ends up passing his time wandering from one town to another, meeting one failure, one betrayal after another until he is fatally wounded while serving the local military unit of the small princely town of Daulatabad. Described as a "little Lucknow," Daulatabad comes to stand a last bastion of the old courtly life in North India, and Kalim's refusal to abandon this culture ultimately leads to his death.[88] Kalim's tragic end illustrates the duality with which the Mahometan chronotope plays out in this growing body of reformist prose fictions. Even as Nazir Ahmad marks him out as symbolic, like Kamil from *Mirāt*, of a way of life at odds with colonial modernity, his rootedness in a fast-disappearing landscape is clear. In other words, it is not men of Kamil and even Kalim's order who see India as deleterious to Islam, but rather it is characters such as Nasuh who dislocated from their North Indian home by the force of their modern piety. In *Taubat*, the Mahometan skin of an opulent, pleasure-seeking sultan is shed, but what is even more deeply inscribed upon the Muslim that emerges from this chrysalis is his foreignness in India, his allegiance to a past Islamic or divine empire, and an abstract sense that he must return to a former purity that his presence in India has corrupted.

Mothers for the Muslim *Qaum*: Altaf Hussain Hali's *Majālis un-Nisā*, or the Assemblies of Women

Staunchly loyal to Syed Ahmad Khan and his cause to advance India's Muslims was Khwaja Altaf Hussain, a poet and scholar, born in Panipat in 1837. By taking "Hali" (one who is of the present) as his *takalluṣ* (pen name), Altaf Hussain located himself as a reformer of his moment, a poet whose concerns were with the immediate conditions of North India's Muslims. Celebrated for his innovative poetry, which on the advice of Khan and a few colonial patrons was fashioned in deliberately realist terms, Hali was an active and searing critic of the extant Urdu *ghazal* and its seemingly abstract concerns. His many projects included a number of poems; a conduct book-like work, *Majālis un-Nisā* (1874), which I will discuss presently; biographies of Hali's heroes, Saadi, Ghalib, and finally Syed Ahmad Khan himself; a long poem in the Persian *musaddas* form titled *Mad-o Jazar Islām*, or the ebb and flow of Islam (1879); as well as a critical work on the state of Urdu poetry, *Muqaddamā-e Sh'er-o Shā'irī*, a title we can roughly translate as an introduction to verse and poetry (1890). Hali's literary opus, as well as his trajectory toward and around Syed Ahmad Khan are dense subjects, but for my purposes here, I turn to the *Majālis* and its relationship with *Mad-o Jazar*, which I will henceforth refer to as the *musaddas*.[89]

Hali was not formally educated in the colonial school system but came into close contact with the colonial education department once he was hired by the Government Book Depot, the official textbook printer in India, to correct the Urdu of books translated from English. Though closely mentored by maestros of the ghazal in his earlier years—Mirza Ghalib among them—by the 1870s onward, he came under the powerful influence of Syed Ahmad Khan and Colonel W. R. M. Holroyd, the Director of Public Instruction in Punjab at the time. Holroyd, in particular, pushed the agenda to "develop" what he considered the decadent and wasteful tradition of Urdu poetry, an aesthetic realm that up until then had resisted colonial efforts of vernacularization.[90] Under Holroyd's direction and Khan's concurrent advice, Hali began to write "natural" poetry, "which embodied an aesthetic of realism, whether in its depiction of history or the external world."[91] Going against the elaborate metaphor and lover's persona that so often characterized the ghazal, a form that orientalists found impossible to accommodate and master, Hali's poems unequivocally addressed questions of Muslim identity in colonial North India. His prose writings were as innovative as Nazir Ahmad's with regards to their imitation of women's speech, their progressive themes, and their invention of exemplary individuals who could serve as models for a wasted society.

One of three works by Hali on the question of Muslim women, the *Majālis* is structured as a series of conversations in a *sharīf* gathering, the topics of which range from the ideal education for a woman to the best way to raise a son. Though the *musaddas* followed some five years later, and was, in both scale and intent, a grand endeavor that traced the ascent of a Muslim civilization and its subsequent decline in recent centuries, both works are concerned with the potential of literary reinvention and its ability to affect the increasingly coherent idea of a Muslim *qaum*. Maintaining a powerful continuity with Ahmad's stories, *Majālis* and the *musaddas* retain the Mahometan chronotope of the oriental tale, using it as a point of departure with which to critique the state of the *ashrāf*, while also revisiting certain elements to determine the attainment of a better, corrected present. If in *Majālis*, a tenable future for Muslims is offered in the possibility of a return to the caliphate, in the *musaddas*, the glories of a golden past are simultaneously definitive of what can be achieved should the *ashrāf* heed the call of reformers such as Khan. Return—to a golden past, to the caliphate—is, ironically, a means for North India's Muslims to become properly modern as well as the signifier under which the emergent *qaum* will imagine itself.

In the *Majālis*, three *begums*, upper-class Muslim women—Mahmuda, Bari (or elder), and Mariam Zamani—sit with a governess of sorts, Atuji, and discuss various methods of raising a son. Over the course of some nine of these sittings, the women discuss—with some intervention from Sayyid Abbas, the son of one exemplary mother, Zubaida Khatun—the place of a woman in her in-laws' house, the domestic skills she must possess, and most important, the nature of her education. Though Khan, Hali's mentor, had historically not extended his efforts toward the education of Muslim women, Hali and Nazir Ahmad gave significant attention to this problem, often with the view that a reformed mother or wife could influence an entire household. Much of the initial conversation follows the story of the exceptional Zubaida, an acquaintance of the women, while the second half rests mainly on the story of her son, Syed Abbas, brought up solely by his mother after the premature passing of his father.

Zubaida Khatun, like Asghari from *Mirāt* and Nasuh from *Taubat*, is an exceptional figure. In this sense, *Majālis* is a lesser, but clearly fictional version of Hali's better-known biographies of great men. To that end, a woman like Zubaida and her son, Abbas, constitute figures whose lives must be shared with the *qaum* in order that their apparently unconventional lives become models to be emulated rather than outliers to be forgotten. Outwardly a lesson on the potential of a properly educated mother, the story of Zubaida and Abbas also functions as an exercise in the creation of an insulated Muslim domain within the foreign empire in which Muslims are now resigned to live. It is worth noting that Atuji, the governess, holds Zubaida up as an example of a mother whose education was such that there was little need for her son to attend the English *mak-*

tab (school). Even as the women of *Majālis* are openly conciliatory, at times admiring of the English, the movement of the narrative is inward, retreating from the possibility of a Muslim future in India. The cultivation of women's education in *Majālis* does not easily conform with Partha Chatterjee's now canonical argument of *ghar* and *bāhir* in colonial Bengal, where the women, who represented a spiritual purity unadulterated by the material dealings of the world, became the symbol of a known "inner spiritual self" and a "true identity."[92] Rather, Hali's exhaustive curriculum for the *sharīf* begum reinvents her, quite literally, as the mother of an embryonic nation.

Zubaida is educated at home by her own mother, a wise woman, a veritable "*ṣāhib-e 'ilm*," a master of knowledge, the turn of this masculine phrase extended to accommodate exceptional women. In addition to training her daughter in domestic affairs, Zubaida's mother ensures that her daughter is taught to read and write.[93] This department is overseen by an *ustānī* (teacher), as well as her father. After Zubaida finishes reading the Quran with her teacher in Arabic, her father instructs her to read Shah Abdul Qadir's Urdu translation of the book, and also begins to teach her Persian and mathematics. Following these mandatory lessons, Zubaida is allowed to read *Bāgh-o Bahār* and the *Aklāq-e Muhsinī*, or *The Morals of the Beneficent*, a didactic Persian text with stories that inculcate good morals in kings, which was also translated into Urdu by Mir Amman during his Fort William days.[94] Her mother, though not involved in teaching her how to read, nevertheless encourages her daughter to cultivate a relationship with books. By reading, Zubaida is told she would understand the journeys of the sun; she would be able to travel the world; she would be able to find the whereabouts of her lost uncle; she would be as learned as Queen Victoria who rules over two countries; and that there was no possession in the house as valuable as the "prettily bound" books that her mother had arranged in a little bookshelf for her.[95]

With the book as object, as authority, and as an alternative to the colonial education system, Hali expands the domain of knowledge available to *sharīf* women, making it akin, in fact, to the education received by a *sharīf* man. This becomes increasingly evident as the story of Zubaida continues:

> By the time I was thirteen, I had studied the *Gulistān, Bōstān, Aklāq-e Muhsinī, 'Iyār-e Dānish* in Persian, and in Arabic, the necessary beginning grammar, and in arithmetic the common factors and decimal factors and the two parts of Euclid's geometry. I had also studied the geography and history of India and had

practiced both *naskh* and *nasta'līq* calligraphy and could copy couplets in a good hand. At that point, my father began to teach me two lessons a day. In the morning we read *Kimiya-e Sa'adat* and in the evening *Kalīlā va Dimnā* in Arabic.[96]

Noticeably absent from this curriculum is poetry and training in poetics as would have been an essential part of an elite Muslim man's or courtesan's traditional education. The reformist curricula, despite minor variations between major figures such as Hali and Ahmad, "were meant to do for women what they did for men: promote civilization and Islamization, in short, conversion."[97] Hali's carefully curated list of books is in harmony with the recommendations made in *Taubat*—women and reformed men are restricted to reading morally beneficial *prose* texts, most of which had also gained approval from the colonial administration. By educating *sharīf* women in a fashion similar to *sharīf* men, what the reformists achieved was an increasingly private space, overtly compliant but at a distance from both the colonial government and the greater entity of India itself. The Muslim home and the mosque, in other words, become the sites where a new Muslim public could begin to imagine itself.

Zubaida's education enables her to raise and educate her son, Syed Abbas, within the family home. Much of Abbas's education at the hands of his mother is concentrated on ridding the young Muslim man of any aspirations to the opulence or extravagance that reformists associated with the old, now powerless, aristocracy. He is given plain and useful clothes with the admonition that fine clothes may lead people to mistake him as a woman or eunuch. He is told to eat less bread to keep his body slim. His calligraphy teacher is only allowed to teach him the basic *nastaliq* script for writing Urdu but forbidden to teach him more stylized forms such as *tughra* and *ghubar*. He is trained to shoot a target, wrestle, and ride a horse, but once again, only taught the useful minimum. Zubaida also coaches him in diction and language, such that he remains different from illiterate or common people.[98] He is also told to refrain from using words that are exclusive to the *zenana*—*bēgmātī zubān*, or upper-class women's language—for language, Zubaida tells him, commands authority.

Even though he eventually begins to attend a "government school" where he learns English, Abbas takes private tutorials with a *maulvī* who reads the *Shahnāmā*, the *'Ain-e Akbarī*, and the *Sikandernāmā* with him in Persian, and works of *fiqh*, the *hadith*, and *tafsirs*, or Quranic exegeses in Arabic. As part of his training in "*adab*," Abbas reads the *Alf Laila*, the *Nafhat-ul Yaman*, or Breezes of Yemen, a series of moral stories and poems originally in Arabic, and the *History of Taimur*, or Tamerlane.[99]

The category, *adab*, now equated with the English "literature," no longer appears to hold its original implications of sensibility and taste and appears as an afterthought to all the other works Abbas has read. Relegated to include works of fiction sanctioned by Fort William, and the brightly illustrated telling of the travels of Taimur, *adab* is stripped of its poetic, historical, and religious richness by Hali.

Abbas's education at his mother's hands prepares him for a greater calling than just service in the *kačehrī* or in other colonial offices for natives. As Atuji continues her story of the exemplary mother and son into the ninth sitting, the narrative takes a turn. In his sixteenth year, Abbas is asked to leave school in order to search for Zubaida's long lost uncle, Khwaja Kumail, whose son, Huzail, had been seen in Aurangabad. Though Zubaida faces resistance for this decision from her in-laws and family, she is adamant and thus Abbas, accompanied by two servants, sets off on his journey. At this point in the text, the *Majālis* turns into what can only be described as an oriental tale, albeit written with a cultural politics that is compliant with the orientalist discourses that shaped it, but premised on the claim of having produced a Muslim narrative from *within*.

On arriving in Aurangabad, Abbas discovers that his cousin has left for *hajj*, the major pilgrimage to Mecca. He, too, decides to make the pilgrimage and sets off for Mecca. On the road to Bombay, however, the small group is separated by quicksand, and Abbas is separated from his servants, who end up living as wandering fakirs for almost a year, but the next year chance upon and join a caravan of *hajj* pilgrims. After completing the pilgrimage, the two men travel to Turkey where they are reunited with Abbas, who by this time is a man of means, employed directly by the sultan of the Ottoman empire. Abbas himself has endured several trials during his separation from his companions, but eventually also completed the pilgrimage, found his uncle, and settled in Istanbul at his advice. His education at Zubaida's hands qualified him for a job with the sultan. Eventually, as the *Majālis* concludes, we discover that Zubaida, too, has come to Istanbul where Abbas is happily married to the daughter of a nobleman.

The elements of the Mahometan chronotope—itinerancy, vast geographies of the Mahometan orient, merchants, and sultans—come together at the happy conclusion of *Majālis*, presenting *sharīf* Muslims with an alternate to their subject status in colonial India. Progressing from *Mirāt*, which instructed Muslims to reconcile with the English, and from *Taubat*, which destabilized the reconciliatory stance of the former, *Majālis* invites its readers to return to a Mahometan Orient that continues to be defined in terms of English oriental tales, but is now the revived site of true Muslim belonging, crowned by the holy city of Mecca. The virtuous mother and son are rewarded not just with a home in a Muslim empire, but also with wealth that is earned by service and profession, inaugurating the rise of a new Muslim elite. Abbas's knowledge of English, Persian, and Arabic, supplemented by his efforts to learn Turkish and French, allows him to inhabit the mantle of a modern Muslim whose return, if I may say, to a Muslim empire, augurs a new direction for the emerging *qaum*.

Hali's most influential work, however, was to follow. In the Urdu tradition, the *musaddas*, a style of poem borrowed from Persian, had become associated with *marsiyah*, or elegiac poetry specifically lamenting the death of Hussain, the Prophet Mohammad's grandson, at Karbala. "The Ebb and Flow of Islam," as Hali's *musaddas* is grandly titled, presages an elegiac tone, but the poem mourns, not for Hussain and his family, but for the Muslims of India. The critiques made by the *musaddas* read as continuous with the exemplary characters of the *Majālis*, allowing us to see Hali's grander construction of the Muslim *qaum* as a distinctly modern body that could, in accordance with Enlightenment conceptions of the nation, boast origin, civilization, and a culture. In the reformist imaginary, however, these constitutive categories are rewritten in terms of Islam. Thus, origin becomes Mecca, civilization suggests expansive caliphates, and culture one and the same with orthodox religious observance. The ideal lives of Zubaida and Abbas, viewed through this longer lens, serve as models for a degraded and erring people, whose faults, though partially detailed in the *Majālis*, are expounded in historical depth in the *musaddas*. My concern with regards to this ambitious and influential poem is with the orientalist models of nationhood and colonial edicts on modernity and progress that the poem espouses.

Framed with a verse that disavows the "nightingale," or bulbul, a classic image from the *ghazal*, the *musaddas* begins with the Dantean image of the poet as a man who has strayed from the moral path. Wandering in false fields of wine and lovers—more allusions to the *ghazal*—the poet has falsely come to think that he has "traversed the entire world," but in truth has merely been walking in the same circle for many years.[100] In his fortieth year, the poet comes across a "servant of the Lord, a hero in that plain" (*k͟hudā kā bandā jō is maidān kā mard hai*) making a difficult journey.[101] This man, we know, is Syed Ahmad Khan, whose message of a religiously tinged progress arrested Hali's attention. From thereon, the introduction details the events in the poem, which Hali reminds his readers is not intended to elicit pleasure or applause, as was the case with the ghazal, but to arouse shame and outrage in an apathetic people.

Beginning with a section on the age of *Jahaliya*, or Ignorance (as histories of Islam describe the period in Arabia prior to the birth of Muhammad), the first part of the poem celebrates the coming of Islam and its early achievements. In death, Muhammad leaves behind a "*qaum*"—a people, a following, a community—that in the colonial moment begins to see itself as a modern nation "with few parallels in the world."[102] Traveling from the caliphates to Muslim Spain, Hali lists the glories and achievements of this *qaum*, which range from the sciences, to trade and architecture, to the revival of Greek philosophy. In short, Islam and Muslims until recently were a civilization whose empires spread benevolently from Europe to Asia. Captured as a single movement, a single people (as opposed to diverse communities with distinct local practices and rituals), Hali's idea of a Muslim people borrows from orientalist ideals of golden pasts, a construct also foundational to the maturing Hindu nationalist movement. Though Arabia is the point of origin for the Muslim *qaum*, it is the "pillars of Islam" (*arkān-e islām*) that have continued to stand from the moment of their establishment.[103]

This veritable house of Islam, as Hali's metaphor goes, survives merely in name as the period of decay sets in. In general terms, the downfall of the Muslims is due to their increased worldliness and distance from the spirit of Islam. But more specifically, "the religion of the Hijaz" (*dīn-e ḥijāzī*) that conquered much of the world "sank when it came to the mouth of the Ganges" (*ḍūbā dahānē meiñ gangā kē ā kar*).[104] Disregarding orientalist narratives that repeatedly cast Muslims as conquerors responsible for the decline of Indian civilization, Hali inversely sees India as having defeated or drowned Islam—by corrupting the purity of its pre-Indic practice. Whether we turn to the *Majālis* where page after page is devoted to warnings against those women whose practices diverge from that prescribed in the Quran or *hadith*, or whether we remain in the verses of the *musaddas*, it is clear that Hali sees no sign of true Islam in India other than, perhaps, in the rare and exemplary ranks of the reformed. In India, as Hali elaborates in the *Majālis*, women have strung together "thousands of silly tales" in place of a true Islam.[105] In the *musaddas*, Muslim men, "descendants of kings" (*shāhōñ kī aulād*), are now "beggars from door to door."[106] Their version of Islam—and here Hali, like Nazir Ahmad, excoriates Shi'ite practices, in particular—"exalt the Imams above the Prophet in rank," "make offerings day and night at shrines," and "offer their prayers to the martyrs" (*imāmōñ kā rutbā nabī sē baṛhā'eiñ; mazārōñ pē din rāt nazarēiñ čaṛhā'eiñ; shahīdōñ sē jā jā kē māngēiñ du'ā'eiñ*).[107] Without explicitly naming Hinduism as an influence, Hali writes off those Shi'ites and other Muslim sects as "infidels," or *kāfir*, the Arabic term for those who reject Muhammad's message.

The waywardness of India's Muslims, however, extends beyond just degraded faith. India is also the site where a previously grand culture is now reduced to "the filthy archive of poetry and odes, fouler than a cesspool in its putridity" (*voh sh'ēr-o qaṣā'id kā nāpāk daftar / 'afūnat meiñ san ḍās sē jō hai badtar*). Continuing Ahmad's attack on the *ghazal* form, Hali pushes this grand Indo-Persian poetic tradition to the peripheries of a reformed Muslim culture, leaving it to the *bhānḍs*—folk entertainers—to sing the *ghazals* of "our poets."[108] Though Hali's attacks expand to include the wealthy and their pigeon-flying offspring, his attack on the poetry of his times is by far the harshest, yet credited by many as instrumental in the so-called modernization of Urdu poetry. In these verses, *ghazal* poetry is equated to the newly instituted immorality of musical castes, courtesans, and popular singers who are joined in their practice by Iblis, or the devil.

There is little irony in the fact that Hali refers to his *musaddas* and most other lyric compositions as *naẓm*. Disowning the traditional terms *sh'ēr* (couplet) and *shā'irī* (poetry), Hali privileges the idea of the *naẓm*, a term whose original meaning remains an ordered arrangement, a string of pearls, a deliberate arrangement. In the poetic sense, it often implied a verb, that is, the ordering of verses. Its primary meanings, as colonial dictionaries such as those of John T. Platts record it, are: order, arrangement, regulation. Far removed from the subtlety suggested in the meaning of *sh'ēr*, or the feminine undertones inherent in the meaning of *ghazal*, *nazm* is the diminutive of *niẓām* (system), and *intiẓāmiā* (administrative body), "a complex of meanings that no doubt would have appealed to Colonel Holroyd."[109] Though Hali never entirely abandoned the *ghazal*, he remained intent here, and in other works including his famous treatise, the *Muqaddamāh*, to undertake a project of *iṣlāḥ* with respect to the themes included in a poetic form that had otherwise been written off by colonial administrators as decadent and useless.

Hali's *Majālis* and *musaddas*, when read together, mark a decisive change in the growing Muslim conception of *qaum*, an idea that is only hinted at in Ahmad's *Taubat*. A term that once loosely implied a community or a people is transformed in Hali's works, taking on the idea of a modern nation instead. Unlike the parallel nation emerging under the Hindu revivalist movements that based themselves upon the argument that Hindus were the indigenous people of India, the Muslim *qaum* was formed around a newly adopted foreignness to India, a critical element, as I have repeatedly shown, of the orientalist Mahometan chronotope. The origins of the Muslim *qaum* lie in "Hijaz," the Arabian Peninsula, and its essence can only be recovered once Muslims leave the foreign empire in favor of the Islamic or Ottoman caliphate. Hali's deep appropriation and transformation of the Mahometan chronotope is a powerful one, its enduring influence shaping narratives of Muslim identity in Urdu from this point onward.

Empires for the *Qaum*: Abdul Halim Sharar's Invention of a Popular Muslim Past

Born in Lucknow in 1860, Sharar grew up in a city devastated by the fall of its *nawabs* at the hands of the colonial administration. His family remained close to the exiled ruler, Wajid Ali Shah, to the point of joining his makeshift court in the outskirts of Calcutta where the deposed *nawab* was to live out his remaining days. Educated at home in the traditional *sharīf* style, Sharar later spent some time studying under the *'ulema* of Farangi Mahal in Lucknow, a city that he constantly returned to, both in his writings and his pursuits. Unlike Ahmad and Hali, Sharar had comparatively little contact with colonial institutions and officials, though he did have a chance to visit England in 1891 while serving a Muslim dignitary of Hyderabad. His main occupation and passion, however, remained writing and publishing in what by then had become a burgeoning print industry in India. Over the course of his life, Sharar was able to start three papers or journals: *Māhshar*, the day of judgment; *Muhazzib*, "the refined"; and *Dilgudāz*, or "heart stirrer," the last of which continued as long as Sharar lived despite occasional setbacks.

Sharar's respect and admiration for leading figures of the Aligarh movement, including Syed Ahmad Khan, Hali, and Nazir Ahmad, is evidenced in his essays and editorials, though it is safe to say that these feelings were hardly reciprocated. The petty politics of this elite Muslim polity dismissed Sharar as a crude, even shameless, author, whose novels would surely embarrass the reformed mothers and wives of the *shurafā*. Yet, I would argue that we can credit Sharar with transforming often dry, at times even harsh reformist tracts into popular historical fictions that shaped the wider Muslim imagination in the late nineteenth and early twentieth centuries. Best known for his numerous "novels," many of which were influenced by Walter Scott—a ubiquitous presence in colonial libraries set up for natives—Sharar contributed to Khan's reform movement through his well-circulating magazine, and more lastingly through his sensational, serialized bestsellers. Despite their steamy plots, improbable characters, and romantic titles—*Hasan Angelina, Malik-ul Aziz Virgina* among them—Sharar's novels colored the emergent ideal of a Muslim *qaum*, or nation, with a glorious historical past that mostly alternated between the Crusades and Moorish Spain.

Sharar's deep attachment and vivid engagement with what he often described as "*guzishtā*" (adjectivally past) and "*tarīḵ*" (history) were defining features of his many novels and essays.[110] Though Hali's works identify a golden moment of origin for Islam in Hijaz or Arabia, and a period of stability in the caliphates, Sharar emphasizes the heyday of Islam through the glory of past empires where the enemies of Islam—dark sects, Christians, or Jews—were always vanquished by heroic individuals. The Muslims of India, as Sharar viewed them, were part of a continuous "*ahl-e Islām*" (people of Islam), a formation that extended across time and geographic boundaries.[111] Imagined thus, the *ashrāf* were the rightful claimants of pasts, ancestors, and empires throughout the course of Islam's existence, India just one among them. Like Hali, Sharar's novels, short stories, and even journalistic anecdotes draw on the elements of the oriental tale, casting the now-Muslim protagonist back into various empire-formations, armed with the power of his faith and, at times, an army as well. In *Flōrā Flōrindā*, a novel based in Moorish Spain—a favorite theme—it is the Muslim and not the Mahometan who is protagonist. His empire is a center of learning and benevolence within which we also find Christians and Jews, who ofttimes are depicted as a corrupted people, needful of reform, but on occasion grateful for Muslim rule.

But this evocation of certain pasts cannot be dismissed merely as an imitation of the English historical novel or as a commercial technique. The past in the reformist discourse, as argued earlier, comes to embody a pristine, chaste moment to which the errant Indian Muslim must attempt return. In the case of a novel such as *Flōrā Flōrindā*, which I examine at length directly, Moorish Spain, though overtly an embodiment of a high moment in the history of the grander Muslim nation, also serves as a warning against integration and trust with the native, non-Muslim populations of the empire. More explicitly, the Spain of *Flōrā Flōrindā* illustrates the dangers that Muslim men and women in India may face should they come to imagine themselves at home, or partake of local custom, whether they are rulers or, as is the case in nineteenth-century India, amongst the ruled.

The majority of Sharar's novels are framed by the idea that the "destitute nation" (*maflūk al-ḥāl qaum*) in question must reclaim the past in which it was once considered "progressive" or developed by the world.[112] The "past state" was one where the "entire world was under [their] rule"; the *ahl-e Islam* possessed both "knowledge and wealth" (*'ilm-o daulat*); they excelled in trade as well as the arts.[113] In short, the "jewel of Islam" (*islām kā jauhar*) was the centerpiece of the crown that rested upon the head of the "entire world" (*tamām dunyā kā sar-e tāj*).[114] But in the present, this *qaum* is sunk in a state of "abjection" (*żillat*), "ignorance" (*jahālat*), and "apathy" (*ġhaflat*).[115] Apparent from this briefly excerpted description from Sharar's first *Dilgudāz* editorial in 1887 are the author's distinct terms of reference. Diverging from the modern, forward-looking works of a contemporary such as Nazir Ahmad whose only point of return is an abstract, chaste Islam, Sharar, closer to Hali, actively advocates a progress premised on what he believes is an exemplary and unique history.

Conscious of the literary innovations he and other reformist writers were making, Sharar aligns himself with the form of the novel, actively embracing an English terminology to describe his works. In a *Dilgudāz* essay promoting one of his early novels, Sharar promised his audiences a "modern novel" (*jadīd nāvil*) that merited readership for three reasons.[116] The first, that this particular novel, *Malik-ul Aziz aur Virginia* (1888), a work about Richard I and Saladdin, was located in "*shām*," or Syria, a place Sharar believed was held in great esteem by the entire world. The "fount of all religions," Syria possesses a history so ancient that it makes even "Europe always bend down before it."[117] The second quality that recommends the novel is that unlike other "original novels," it is of "historical" (*tarīḳī*) nature.[118] According to Sharar, comparable works in Urdu have made little attempt to conform with historical events, and thus have made use of typically trite, "obligatory" stories (*farżī qiṣṣē*).[119] As a result, the difference between his novels and other original novels in Urdu is roughly that between truth and falsehood.[120] And finally, the event of history that the book deals with—the Crusades—is one Sharar believes is of universal interest and continues, in particular, to fascinate Muslims and Christians.

Unabashed and bold, Sharar launches himself as a novelist who believes himself to be Western and *modern*. His idea of what it means to be *jadīd* (modern) derives, not surprisingly, from a newfound, Eurocentric consciousness of history. That is to say, the condition of being modern—in this case, aesthetically—was premised primarily on a mimicry, to use Homi Bhabha's term, of the Western prototype. Moreover, for a novel or literary genre of a vernacular such as Urdu to be properly modern it had to possess historical truth, something that Sharar, and ironically enough, the later All-India Progressive Writers' movement, bemoaned as lacking in the entire corpus of Urdu fiction writing. Sharar's stress on history and historical awareness as a way to make fiction modern is both a reaction to repeated colonial critiques of Urdu prose and poetry as unrealistic and immoral, *and* an attempt to produce a classical, evergreen Muslim past through which the present moment—albeit a dark one—can be negotiated and situated.

Much like his Bengali contemporary, Bankimchandra, Sharar too was caught up in the beginnings of a "nationalist consciousness" that sought to "write for itself the account of its own past."[121] Sharar's forays into history—going between fictions such as his novels and essays and accounts in *Dilgudāz*—are derived, as Partha Chatterjee has explained, from criteria established in European historical scholarship. In Chatterjee's incomparable account of Bengali nationalism, "ancient India became for the nationalist the classical age, while the period between ancient and contemporary was the dark age of medievalism."[122] A national history for Muslims, then, could claim either the moment of inception as its classical age or, as Sharar chooses, the various high points of past Islamic empires. There is no irony in the fact that the Mughal empire, dismissed by orientalists and reformists as marking Muslim decline in India, is mostly absent from Sharar's historical forays. The golden age of Islam is instead located in Moorish Spain. Iran, the seat of the Persian empire, becomes home to dark enemy sects of Islam in Sharar's most famous novel, *Firdaus-e Barīn*, or the Paradise of Assassins (1899). The one historical novel Sharar did write about India, *Mansūr Mohnā* (1890), deals with the invasion of Mahmud Ghaznavi into India and his battle against the Hindu raja of Ajmer in the tenth century. In Sharar's rearrangement of the Mahometan chronotope: Muslims, or the "*ahl-e Islam*," reappear as the masters of great empires, sites of a pristine Islam that the Indian *ashrāf* have long forgotten.

As a result, *Flōrā Flōrindā*, one example from Sharar's corpus, is located in tenth-century Spain. The moment or times (*zamānā*) in which the caliph Abdur Rehman II rules are the best of times as evidenced:

> Thousands of mosques and buildings that could be of use to ordinary people were constructed all over the Andalus. Roads were commissioned. Water was brought over specially from the hills of Cordoba and distributed across the city through the use of lead canals. Reservoirs were constructed here and there on major roads so that herds and horses could quench their thirst. Knowledge had reached such a peak that there was no town in which genuine scholars of the *hadith* and *fiqh* were not present . . . [123]

Despite all this, however, the Christians of Spain remain a thorn in the flesh of the benevolent caliph, staging rebellions and violent uprisings in

Toledo and Madrid. Portrayed as following a corrupt version of their religion, the Christian community operates in the dark and is shown as plotting in secret against Muslims and Muslim rule. The novel follows two siblings, Ziad and Flora, born to a Christian mother and Muslim father. Ziad, a devout and well-respected Muslim, is a theologian whose "uprightness" (*diyānatdārī*) and sincerity (*pākbāzī*) have earned him the love and trust of him community.[124] His sister, Flora, on the other hand, chose to be a Christian like her mother, a fact that troubles Ziad who wishes for her to change her ways and convert to Islam. Though Ziad despises the Christian community, Flora is always desirous of learning more and wants to devote herself to the church.

Flora's religious leanings are well-known to the Christians, particularly one priest, Yulajis, who constructs an elaborate plot to bring Flora back into the Christian fold through abduction, an act he believes would lead to Muslim violence against Christians, that would in return inspire a Christian uprising after which "Spain would be free of the harsh tyrannies of the cruel Muslims."[125] Yulajis enlists a nun by the name of Florinda to disguise herself as a Muslim widow, gain the sympathies of Ziad, and from there, access the guarded Flora. Accompanied by another nun, who plays the role of a maidservant, Florinda—now, Hallava—arrives in Ziad's neighborhood and begins her grand deception.

In these early parts of the novel, Flora is described as a model young woman whose only flaw is her attraction to Christianity, even though she is forced to perform and proclaim herself Muslim because of pressure from her brother. Like other "*sharīf*" young women of Andalus, she possesses such wonderful "manners" (*adab*) and "decency" (*shā`istgī*) that Ziad could never find fault with her.[126] Frustrated by his sister's ambivalence toward Islam, Ziad decides she should be married to a Muslim man, but before that can happen he meets the disguised, but beautiful Hallava. Deeply attracted to her beauty and convinced of her pure faith, Ziad decides to marry Hallava, or Florinda, who consequently moves into the brother and sister's home. After a few months of gaining Flora's trust, Hallava finally tells her that she has traveled all the way from Cordoba to undertake the "defense" (*dastgīrī*) of the imprisoned Flora.[127] One evening, when Ziad is away from the house, Flora and Florinda flee to Cordoba, and from thereon to a church hidden away in the mountains.

In this lonely retreat, Flora meets Yulajis, the priest, who gives her the option of marrying a French officer, but all the while also makes untoward advances at the young girl. But Flora rejects his offers, reminding Yulajis that it was not Islam that she wished to renounce, but the world itself. Christianity, as she had understood it, offered her a means to live a life that was not "worldly" (*duniyādārī*), bereft of "luxuries and opulence" (*'aish-o ishrat*), yet it was precisely these things that Yulajis offered her.[128] Eventually, she is joined by Helen, the daughter of a French nobleman named Alphonso. Helen and Flora become friends, only to discover the terrible nature of the Church in Spain. Among the lurid details Sharar includes are the lewd questions Flora is asked when she confesses in front of Yulajis. Over the next few months, any illusions Flora may have had about leading a chaste life as a nun are shattered. Yulajis makes his sexual desire for her abundantly clear, and Flora spends much of her time trying to keep her "honor" (*ābirū*) safe from this insistent perpetrator.

But Flora fails in this endeavor and Yulajis manages to rape her. In this time, she also witnesses the various atrocities that abound in the Church, including the frequent rapes of nuns and the ceremonial killings of any resulting children.[129] After realizing "the true nature of the Christian religion," while also feeling that she was no longer "fit to be Muslim either," Flora attempts, unsuccessfully, to kill Yulajis and then escapes, successfully, from the convent.[130] Pregnant with her rapist's child, Flora wanders alone for some time disguised as a man until she is discovered by the man who employs her, incidentally, Helen's father, Alphonso. Eventually, she delivers her child, "the curse of Yulajis."[131]

After some months, she discovers her rapist is still alive and is determined to seek revenge. In the meanwhile, her brother Ziad, after colluding with Helen, Flora's friend from the convent, has managed to find his sister's kidnappers. In a dramatic final scene, Flora strikes Yulajis a deathblow, but is struck herself as well. Ziad and Helen enter the room to find Flora dying, while her child lies next to her. Just before she takes her final breaths, Flora confesses that she chose to embrace Islam after experiencing the "depravities" (*žillateīñ*) of the Church: "Weeping, I would prostrate and kneel in front of Allah's door every night and ask for forgiveness."[132] Her only regret remains that she came to Islam not through the "wisdom and merit" of her brother, but only after losing her "chastity and honor" (*'izzat aur ābirū*).[133] Her last words, quite obviously, are the core edict (*kalimā*) of Islam: "There is no god but Allah and Muhammad is his prophet."[134]

At a first glance, *Flōrā Flōrindā* appears incongruous, even luridly entertaining when compared to the conciliatory, domesticating, and rational stories told by mainstream reformists such as Ahmad and Hali. Though Sharar's focus clearly is not on questions of ritual, religion, and domesticity, elements that other reformists so seriously elaborated upon, his novels—if we can take that liberty—are the most uninhibited in their elaboration of a Muslim *qaum*. For Sharar's readers, the *qaum*, or nation, is enlivened through the author's identification of an enemy or other who is vanquished by the virtue and might of Muslim heroes. In this case, the enemy is the Christians of Spain, though the same plot would work just as well with the Hindus in India as the antagonists of Islamic rule during Mahmud Ghaznavi's era, for example. Flora, whose religious ambivalence becomes the cause of her tragic life and death, exemplifies the fate of those who are blind to the true Islam. At the end of the novel, Helen, the good Christian of the story, converts to Islam, professing that it is her heart that compels her to believe in the oneness of Allah and the prophet-hood of Muhammad. The truth of Islam, as elaborated in the novel, is inherently known to all mankind, but those who prefer worldly pleasures are the ones who will inevitably meet a terrible end.

As the novel closes, Sharar unites the entire Muslim *qaum*, past and present, Indian and Arab, around the tragic figure of Flora. Her errors are forgiven in death, and she is buried in a grand funeral in Cordoba, which is also attended by the caliph. As the final rites are performed, "all the Muslims raised their hands, tears were streaming down their eyes, and with great tenderness of heart they prayed for the forgiveness [*maġhfirat*] of the departed girl."[135] And thus, Sharar turns to his audience, a group he frequently addresses in his writing: "At this moment, we too raise our hands, and place a bouquet of the *fāteḥā* on Flora's grave. Come readers, join us in strewing flowers."[136] Together, the characters of the novel, Sharar, and his reading audience form a single community, all of whom pray for the re-inclusion of the repentant Flora into the fold of Islam. A tragedy and lesson from Moorish Spain, then, becomes a tragedy for the present times as well. Collective prayer around the grave of a Muslim woman ravaged by the enemy of Islam unites North Indian readers with a past that they may otherwise be at risk of forgetting.

What Sharar also invents through moments such as these—somewhat differently from Hali and Ahmad—is the idea of a Muslim public, or what he refers to as an "*islāmī pablik*" in his *Dilgudāz* writings. As the funeral scene from *Flora Flōrindā* makes apparent and as C. Ryan Perkins shows in his essay on Sharar, the latter's notion of reform was more expansive than that espoused by his contemporaries. If Nazir Ahmad, Hali, and Syed Ahmad Khan propagated a more elite politics of reform where class and caste remained determinants of *sharāfat*, and in fact, posed a hierarchy in the formation of the *qaum*, Sharar embraced the idea of a "public" where individuals from different classes could come together for the benefit of Islam. In one issue of *Dilgudāz*, Perkins argues, Sharar speaks of presenting his work to the "*pablik kā darbār*," or the "court of the public," signifying a movement away from the *darbār* or the court as a place ruled over by *nawābs* or by a colonial administrator and toward a jury consisting of varied individuals.[137] The formation of an "*islāmī* public," as Perkins puts it, "represented the attempt to create both a language and a space for a type of Muslim engagement that would be truly public at its core."[138] Perhaps even unknowingly, it "provided a subtle critique of prevalent elitist models" that Khan and other major reformists remained attached to for most of their lives.[139] In Sharar's work, families do not trace genealogies; the entire Muslim formation does. A hero such as Ziad, though well-respected in his community, does not require the same pedigree as Asghari's father and father-in-law in Ahmad's *Mirāt* to qualify as *sharīf*. Likewise, Sharar incorporated all kinds of women into the Muslim *qaum*, including converts, village girls, even women born out of wedlock.

While Nazir Ahmad has been accorded the honor of writing the first Urdu bestsellers, Sharar, we can say, transformed the colonially patronized didactic fiction in Urdu into a truly *popular* form. In other words, he moves away from the narrower, class and caste-based Muslim communities we find in Hali and Ahmad's work, opening up the idea of the *qaum* to time and space, as well as to people. This is not to say that his divergences from the Aligarh reformists were necessarily antagonistic, or even starkly different. Whereas Hali and Ahmad rely on the image and draw of a pure, Salafi Islam to reform their readers, Sharar offered an extended, at times even sensational, history, replete with heroes and martyrs, through which to eventually direct Muslims to a similar religious ideal.

The extended moment of Muslim reform that begins in the wake of 1857 and continues into the early decades of the twentieth century is arguably a powerful turning point in the history of Urdu prose fiction. While the golden era of the Calcutta orientalists is long over, this moment of colonially mediated literary reform remains anchored in the ideals of the oriental tale and attendant orientalist scholarship. The continuous engagement of reformist fictions with the oriental tale, both English and vernacular, forces the clear emergence of a modern Muslim identity from within the ubiquitous chronotope of the Mahometan. If—to return to my argument of earlier chapters—the English oriental tale thrived on the condition of the Mahometan's itinerancy, despotism, and opulence, then over the course of the nineteenth century, vernacular prose fiction in the now Muslim-associated register, Urdu, initially imitated, and later appropriated, the Mahometan as the sign of a corrupted and false self. In other words, the Mahometan, an invention of orientalist fictions, takes on an actual form for the North Indian reformists—elite men and women of Muslim descent who resist the institutions of colonial modernity. Their task then becomes the conversion of the Mahometan to a modern Muslim, a national subject defined by his religion, language, and origin.

This is not to say that dissident and highly aestheticized texts such as Mirza Hadi Rusva's *Umrā'o Jān Adā* (1899) did not find audience or success, but rather that the dominant, lasting canon of modern Urdu prose (and to some extent, even poetry) is shaped as a response to the orientalist edicts and colonial patronages. By the final decades of the nineteenth century, even a figure like Sharar—who, for the most part, had little contact with imperial institutions when compared with Hali and Nazir Ahmad—imagined Urdu literature as a body of works in need of modernizing, a task that could only be achieved by casting Muslims in much the same political and social molds as Europeans. Despite their differences, all three men contributed much toward the same end: the invention of belated Urdu canon that would allow India's Muslims to see themselves as a nation rather than integrated in a regional or local fabric.

4 / Martyr/*Mujāhid*: Muslim Origins and the Modern Urdu Novel

There are two ways to continue the story of the making of a modern literature in Urdu after the reformist moment of the late nineteenth century. The better-known way is to celebrate a rupture from the reformists by writing a history of the All-India Progressive Writer's Movement (AIPWA), a Bloomsbury-inspired collective that had a tremendous impact on the course of Urdu prose writing. And to be fair, if any single moment in the modern history of Urdu "literature" has been able to claim a global circulation (however limited) or express worldly aspirations, it is the well-known moment of the Progressives from within which the stark, rebel voices of Saadat Hasan Manto and Faiz Ahmad Faiz emerged. Founded in 1935–6, the AIPWA was best known for its near revolutionary goals: the desire to create a "new literature," which stood directly against the "poetical fancies," religious orthodoxies, and "love romances with which our periodicals are flooded."[1] Despite its claim to represent all of India, AIPWA was led by a number of Urdu writers—Sajjad Zaheer, Ahmad Ali, among them—who continued, even in the years following Partition in 1947, to have a "disproportionate influence" on the workings and agenda of the movement.[2]

The historical and aesthetic successes of the movement, particularly with respect to Urdu, have gained significant attention from a variety of scholars, including Carlo Coppola, Neetu Khanna, Aamir Mufti, and Geeta Patel, though admittedly more work remains to be done. Writing as a collective with national aims, the Progressives for a few decades or so managed to demonstrate, to quote Mufti, "that Urdu could be and was the terrain for truly national social imaginings."[3] Abandoning aspirations of religious piety and markers of bourgeois domesticity, the collective wrote stories of prostitutes at the peripheries of the emerging nation, of the desolation and paralyzing poverty of peasants and farmers in the so-called modern colony, of wives at the mercy of husbands with alternative sexual interests and shared streams of consciousness that denied god and nation. Actively positioning themselves against the stylization and separation of Hindi and Urdu established from the Fort William years as well as the nationalist agendas of the Congress and newly founded Muslim League, the Progressives offered the possibility, perhaps for the first time, of a utopic India where peasant and aristocrat could be equal, women liberated, and language secular. At the very least, they forced readers, as Mufti argues, to "confront the paradox that the era of modern Indian history that saw the most decisive bifurcation of national politics along religio-communal lines is perhaps the most secularist period in the history of modern Urdu literature."[4]

The question that remains, however, is one that has gone largely unaddressed by scholars and historians of the Progressive movement: What was it that the Progressives positioned themselves against? That is to say, what kind of literary production did the collective hope to counter, perhaps even reform? In the case of Urdu, a major recruit in the movement, the Progressives railed against what they deemed a fanciful poetic tradition and vacuous prose fictions. In a more direct iteration of these questions we can ask, what were those works, narratives, and writers that commanded the mainstream Muslim imagination? That is to say, if the Progressives aligned themselves with the idea of a secular India, who and what were their literary and political antagonists? This latter set of questions directs us to the other, still unexplored corpus of prose fiction in Urdu, a vast body of novels and stories produced in conformity with the increasingly powerful markers of *qaum* or nation that had emerged during the reformist moment.

My interest in this chapter, thus, is in that which was *not* Progressive and yet managed to claim a lasting, if not universally acknowledged, place in the greater literary canon of Urdu as it advanced into the twentieth century. While the Progressives and their ideology for a new literature are generally (though not necessarily accurately) seen as severing ties with the past, the writers and works I intend to examine, are *continuous* with reformists such as Nazir Ahmad and Hali and extend from the early part of twentieth century until well into its final decades. There is, in other words, no rupture or revolt in this case: Prolific, bestselling, ubiquitous writers such as Rashid ul-Khairi, Nasim Hijazi, and Razia Butt, among others, produced a body of Urdu fiction, mostly in the form of the novel, that allows us to see the moment of Muslim reform as decisive and enduring for Urdu and the particular cultural and political identity the language comes to hold for Muslims in India and, later, Pakistan. Their predilection for the novel form, in fact, complicates Mufti's well-known argument regarding the failure of the novel as a dominant literary form in twentieth-century Urdu. While Progressive and associated Urdu writers such as Manto, Faiz, and Ismat Chugtai garnered well-deserved literary fame both within the subcontinent and beyond by way of their works finding their way into English and gaining scholarly attention in the Euro-American academy, writers such as Khairi, Hijazi, and Butt were household names even before the official creation of Pakistan.

To be clear, I am not making an argument here that dismisses the significance the Progressive group has exercised on Urdu literary writing. I am making a case in this chapter for considering that which aesthetes and scholars have largely ignored when writing histories and critical volumes on Urdu, particularly with respect to the twentieth century. I argue that *in spite* of the parallel rise of a Bloomsbury-inspired movement in Urdu literature, as espoused by the Progressives, the twentieth century remains critical to the maturation of Urdu literature as a body of works that claimed the authority to determine and prescribe ways of being Muslim, and of imagining the pasts and futures of the Muslim *qaum* that had begun to take form in the late nineteenth century. An inadvertent collective of nationalist writers, if we may describe them as such, takes on the helm of fiction writing in Urdu in the early and middle decades of the twentieth century, at much the same time as the AIPWA forms and publishes. Their concerns, expressed through serialized or standalone, often romantic, novels are with narrating the past in terms of Muslim conquests and conquerors, with the correction of an errant society, and with the place of women within the larger workings of the nation, or *qaum*. The perspectives these writers take on religion are largely one dimensional and derive from the notion that a chaste and finished Islam was bequeathed to the world during the lifetime of the Prophet Muhammad. Their relationship with the idea and realization of Pakistan, however, is a more complex one, where the emergent nation-state is both an aspiration and an eventual object of nationalist critique. The Mahometan chronotope, whose evolution and transformation I have traced in earlier chapters, persists in these novels, articulated from a nationalist, at times anticolonial, position.

One explanation for the marked absence of writers such as Hijazi and Butt—and to a lesser extent Khairi—in academic volumes on Urdu literature or the history of Urdu is the overwhelming success the Progressives commanded as the "modernizers" of Urdu prose. To be sure, Manto and Chugtai, as well as the infamous *Angārē* group, dealt with obscenity charges in their time, but their cultural capital extended from a changing literary world to that of All-India Radio and the thriving Bombay film industry.[5] Little stock, however, has been given to the fact that even as the Progressives took up the mantle against religious orthodoxies and fought for literature to represent the peasant, prostitute, and laborer as much as it did the *nawab*, an entire world of fiction, shaped within a series of Urdu journals and serial novels, continued to thrive on account of its unfailing devotion to issues such as *sharīf* morality, the significance of Islam and Islamic history for Muslims living under British rule, and the rights and duties of Muslim women in Indian society.

It is from this world of domestic novels and literary journals such as *'Iṣmat* and *Zamānā*, the latter set founded by Khairi, that a new generation of fiction writers in and *for* Urdu emerges. The purpose of *literature*, for Khairi or Hijazi, is not to uplift and find beauty in the lives of a "struggling humanity," as the Progressives would have it, but rather to improve the declining state of the Muslim *qaum* and restore it to its former moral and political glory.[6] At the same time, it would be simplistic to claim that there was merely contradiction and opposition between the Progressives and this second group. Both, though differently, were consciously writing what can informally be called an *avāmī*, or "people's" literature, a term first used in the contexts of Urdu and India by the Progressive writer Ahmad Ali.[7] The idea of *avāmī* functions indirectly against what is a high or elite literature. The latter was considered difficult to access and too abstruse for the common reader. In much the same vein, Nasim Hijazi located his novels as works whose purpose was to revive the withered glories of Islam, an ambition he acknowledges must arouse the ire of those who "raise the slogan of *adab* for the sake of *adab*," or more approximately translated, art for art's sake.[8] If the Progressives imagined the *avām*, or people, as peasant and subaltern, the writers I examine here imagine this same body as largely constituted of *sharīf*, or middle-class, Muslim men and women, in need of moral guidance and reprieve from the day-to-day oppressions experienced in a state such as Pakistan, founded as it may be in the name of Islam.

This is not simply a case of what Pascale Casanova has casually called "deprived spaces" where writers were, "in effect, condemned to develop a national and popular theme."[9] According to Casanova, literature "becomes national or popular or both, devoted to promoting the nation as an idea and helping it, once the idea has become a reality, to join the ranks of all those nations that enjoy literary existence and recognition."[10]

Her examples, strangely and incoherently diverse—South Korea, Nigeria, Mexico, Spain under Franco—seem to collapse experiences of imperial domination and fascism into a single whole that then yields a semi-historical explanation for the emergence of a "national literature." The truncated histories of the non-European world in Casanova's *World Republic of Letters* suggest that literatures from regions such as the Indian subcontinent or modern-day Turkey first became known to the "world," a code for the West perhaps, in the decades following decolonization. While Casanova's clear disengagement with the worldly or *colonial* origins of literary formations from spaces such as the Indian subcontinent and South Africa is evidenced in the ahistorical approach she takes toward what she terms "small literatures," her description of what constitutes national literatures and their histories remains problematic and limited.[11]

To be sure, the term "national literature" is an important one and relevant in the case of writers such as Hijazi and Butt, who continue to exercise a hold on the Pakistani national imagination many decades after their literary heyday. While they are, undoubtedly, *nationalist* writers in terms of their orientation, literary elites continue to dismiss them precisely on account of their blatant politics. But despite their lack of global fame or international circulation, they occupy a critical place in the longer evolution of a Muslim selfhood in Pakistan, thus demanding that any literary history of Urdu seriously grapple with the question of how and what narratives manage to endure in the national imaginary. Any consideration of how this idea of this national imaginary takes form must turn to Partha Chatterjee's meticulous mapping of the "moment of arrival." This moment of "fullest development," Chatterjee remind us, is marked by its order, by its false consistency, its assimilation of the past into a cohesive history, and finally by its demand to actualize itself in the form of a nation-state.[12] In the case of North India's Muslims, this realization was not merely the work of Muhammad Ali Jinnah, the political founder of Pakistan, or for that matter of orthodox religious theologians, but rather a large-scale, often complex and conflicting effort whose iterations extended from party politics to the domain of popular literature.[13] The latter, of course, is the category I am interested in here and in the chapter to follow.

Any exercise in closely reading and situating these *not*-Progressive, *not*-modernist writers as continuous with not merely the reformists but with the longer presence of the Mahometan chronotope in modern Urdu literature betrays that literary critics and scholars of Urdu prose have invented a canon in accordance with Western literary and political teleologies. Indeed, if we examine any conventional history or edited volume of the evolution and development of the English novel, we move from early renegade versions, such as Daniel Defoe's *Robinson Crusoe* and Laurence Sterne's *Tristam Shandy*, to the domestic novels of Samuel Richardson that are reimagined by women writers such as Frances Burney and Jane Austen; to the historical novels of Walter Scott; then to the dense, almost socialist works by the Victorian, Charles Dickens; to Hardy's return to England's rural past; from thereon, to Bloomsbury and the modernists; followed, of course, by the anti-modernists, led by Kingsley Amis; and conclude, for now, with the postcolonial Anglophone novel.

Twentieth-century critics and literary historians have searched tirelessly for the "first Urdu novel" and arrived at roughly similar conclusions from whereon they are able to trace a development of the form that mimics the English tradition. Others have resigned themselves to the lack thereof, but nevertheless argued in favor of a modern literature whose short stories and themes—usually by the modernist Progressives—are on par with those of writers from other Western and like literary traditions.[14] The erasure or remarkable absence of figures such as Hijazi, Butt, or even the immensely popular A. R. Khatun from what has become a traditional canon of sorts for scholarly historians and critics of Urdu in both South Asia and the Anglophone academy is reflective of a method that until very recently relied on Western modes of criticism and literary evaluation. Thus, the progression of Urdu prose, as recounted in these largely similar accounts of canonization, credits (and occasionally discredits) Fort William with the birth of Urdu prose, the nineteenth-century reformists (and their nemesis, Mirza Hadi Rusva) as the first novelists and literary critics of modern Urdu, the Progressives as the classic leftist, secular firebrands, and finally, Askari's *jadīdiyāt* movement as hearkening a much-needed spiritualism, variously evidenced in the works of Bano Qudsia and Intizar Hussain, for example.[15] But if we reimagine the method through which to constitute a literary canon of Urdu—keeping in mind both Mufti's assertion of Urdu's minor status in India as well as the national ambitions it takes on during the reformist moment—we see a dominance and pervasion of the novel, and a logic, in the fact that Khairi, Hijazi, or Butt remain major writers.[16]

In singling out the novel as its preferred form, this overlooked set of fiction writers privileges the subjectivity of the middle-class, *sharīf* Muslim and the inner workings of his identity with respect to the modern nation-state. Formally modeled on the English novel, but thematically reimagining the English oriental tale, these novels are both domestic and national, or *qaumī*. Their heroes or heroines are, on the one hand, bourgeois subjects with a view of the world that is informed by the totality of Islam, and their aspirations, as characters—exemplary or other—function within the limits of this worldview. This ability or drive—rather, to imagine the world through this lens—is shaped by a distinct perception of modernity as akin to Islam. Women in these novels are subjects whose sexual and spiritual identities coalesce to produce a domesticity proper to the politics and ambitions of North Indian and, subsequently, Pakistani Muslims. When examined as part of the extended transformation of a once-elite literary register into a vernacular for India's Muslims, these now self-identifying "modern" novels testify to how the Mahometan chronotope of the oriental tale becomes a definitive element in the national narrative of an infant Pakistan.[17] Though directly descended from the earlier generation of reformists, novelists such as Hijazi and Butt internalize and redirect specific Western conceptions of Muslims—itinerancy, origin, even despotism—to create a specific didactic history for the Muslim state.

In outlining the political and cultural weight of these works, I borrow from Nancy Armstrong and Edward Said's theorizations of the English novel while privileging the English and later vernacular oriental tales in India as equally influential sources.[18] But in Armstrong's now canonical history of the domestic English novel, it is the form itself that is a political act. A closer estimation to the political histories of these Urdu novels is Said's searing critique of the English novel in *Culture and Imperialism* where he asks us to remember that "novels participate in, are part of, contribute to an extremely slow, infinitesimal politics" that uphold the national image.[19] A clearer understanding of the rise of writers such as Khairi and Hijazi must acknowledge the increasing influence and Islam-centric rhetoric of anti-colonial intellectuals and leaders such as Abul Kalam Azad and Maulana Abul Ala Maududi. Whether we think of the dynamic Azad, who as a young man led the Khilafat or pro-Caliphate movement in India during World War I, or Maududi, the major Islamic political philosopher to emerge from India in the twentieth century, the pervasion of a political Islam—conceived both through and against European terms—into literary outputs and popular discourse is far from passive. Thus, anti-colonial, at times even anti-state, ideologies that remain a constant feature in the novels of the writers I examine in this chapter are not literary coincidences but in fact active engagements with Islam and the political imaginaries it inspired in the late colony.

The fact that the majority of the novels I read in this chapter are historical in theme is not a deliberate choice. History and the attempts to write a narrative specific for the cause and support of a young Pakistan were as much a project of fiction writers as they were of nationally revered religious figures (Maududi chief amongst them); historians such as I. H.

Qureshi and S. M. Ikram; and state actors such as the dethroned and publicly hanged prime minister, Zulfiqar Bhutto, and his nemesis, Zia ul-Haq, the army general and Islamist dictator. But these are no ordinary histories that trace the origins of Pakistan onward from ancient ruins of Mohenjodaro and Harappa. These histories of Pakistan claim Islam as their beginning, and thus are located either outside of the Indian subcontinent in Spain or North Africa or are recountings of the earliest Muslim conquests of India.

I begin by exploring the literary world in which Rashid ul-Khairi, a close relative and acolyte of Nazir Ahmad, rose to fame. Known as much for his novels for women as for his women's journal *'Iṣmat* (quite literally, modesty), Khairi was a decisive figure in the Urdu literary world at a time when women's liberation movements had begun to take hold in India as well. But if Khairi restricted his rather didactic and often tragic novels to the question of women and their place in a fast-changing colony, a writer of Hijazi's ambitions took up the mantle of *qaum* by turning, like Sharar, to the past. Hijazi's version of a golden Islamic past is vividly colored by the idealized lives and brave conquests of Muslim warriors such as Muhammad bin Qasim and Mahmud Ghaznavi. Concurrent with Hijazi but known mainly—and incorrectly—as a writer of romantic novels for women, Razia Butt wrote some fifty-one novels and more than three hundred *afsānās* (short stories), many of which were published serially in literary magazines and weekend literary supplements of national newspapers such as Pakistan's *Navā'e-Vaqt*. *Bānō* (1971), a novel about the experiences of Muslim women during Partition and the early days of Pakistan is a classic example of the tension between the state and the duties of a good Muslim. Her other novel, *Vaṭan kī Bētī*, literally, daughter of the homeland, though overtly a historical novel about the annexure of Golconda by the Mughals, acts also as a metaphor for the immorality that compromises a so-called Muslim state such as Pakistan.

A final note on method as I advance my argument: Given that Khairi, Hijazi, and Butt remain largely unstudied by literary scholars, I establish their significance by considering their publishing histories, the aspirations and agendas of their publishers, their engagement with the language and its literary past, their concern for history and their perception of the present, the afterlives of their works in contemporary Pakistan, as well as occasional interviews with publishers and other writers. Khairi, though one of the most published and reprinted writers of his time, also has commanded comparatively little scholarship, even in area and language studies. In his case, however, the family and public archive remains a vibrant and viable source.

Rashid ul-Khairi, the "Painter of Sorrow": Tragedy, Didacticism, and the Threat of Women's Emancipation

Of much the same class and social milieu as Nazir Ahmad (and a relative by marriage as well), Khairi was prolific—his published works include almost sixty novels and longish short stories, in addition, of course, to the several domestic journals he founded, *'Ismat, Tamadun*, and *Sahelī* among them. The most successful of these was *'Ismat*, which he continued to edit and write for from its inception in 1908 until 1922, when his son Raziq ul-Khairi took the helm. Given that Khairi came from an old family of *'ulema*, or Muslim scholars, as well as the fact that he did not enter government service, he remained, in contrast to Ahmad, distant and even antagonistic at times toward the British. After leaving a low-ranking post in the postal department, Khairi began to pursue a writing career in earnest, benefiting to some extent from Ahmad's patronage. There is little doubt that Khairi took the scale of what constituted "bestselling" to unprecedented highs, with some novels being reprinted every year during the early decades of the twentieth century. His *Ṣubḥ-e Zindagī* (Dawn of life) series alone had gone into their fifteenth editions at the time of his death in 1936.[20] Part of this fame was accorded by his family's own printing press, Ismat Book Depot, which was set up in the later part of his career, but his initial success began with the publication of his stories in *Makzan*, a well-known Urdu literary journal of the time. Other publishers of Khairi's work include Delhi's Hamidiya Press and Mahbub ul-Matabi Press, both carrying lists of largely Islam-related books.

Khairi's entry into what we can think of as a flourishing world of Urdu print came at a time when anti-colonial, Marxist fiction writers such as Munshi Premchand had gained popularity and acclaim on the national front, while more conservative, communally inclined figures such as the Deobandi Maulana Ashraf Ali Thanvi had gained credence within the Muslim community of North India. In the historical context of Urdu prose writing, Khairi is situated between the first generation of reformists and their successors: novelists such as Hijazi, Butt, and Bano Qudsia. His transitory role is clearly visible in his writings, which borrow theme and structure from Nazir Ahmad but tell stories whose tragic endings often involve villainous—non- or unreformed Muslim—others, earning him the title of *"musavir-e ġham,"* or the Painter of Sorrow. In an adulatory essay written in 1932 on his father's achievements, the younger Khairi claimed that "it was through the Painter of Sorrow's literature that women began to improve and develop themselves."[21] Replacing the term *adab* with "literature" entirely, Raziq characterizes his father as a "novelist" (*nāvilist*), a "journalist" (*jurnalist*), "short-story writer" (*afsānā nigār*), "historian" (*moraḵ*), "poet" (*shā'ir*), and "letter-writer" (*inshā pardāz*).²² On the occasion of 'Iṣmat's seventieth year, Quratulain Hyder, the acclaimed novelist and literary grand-dame of Urdu, described Khairi as "one of the greatest national reformers of this century," whose efforts gave birth to a "large assembly" of women writers.²³ 'Iṣmat, Hyder wrote, was a "milestone" in the "social history" of "our country."²⁴ The journal itself ran regular features commemorating its founder's services to women, immortalizing Khairi as a figure in the longer history of women's literature and writing first in Muslim India and then in Pakistan, despite the fact that Khairi passed away a decade or so before Partition.

To fully explore Khairi as a nationalist writer at a critical juncture in the history of colonial India, as well as the lettered world he helped perpetuate, I turn to early issues of 'Iṣmat and to two short novels, *Andalūs kī Shehzādī*, or The Princess of Andalus, and *Bint ul-Vaqt*, the Daughter of Time. Unlike those of his predecessor reformists, Khairi's stories neither received nor reciprocated colonial patronage. Imbuing his didactic stories with elements of tragedy, Khairi cast the *sharīf* Muslim woman as a central figure in the rehabilitation and revival of Islam against Western influence that in his view had become an inevitable evil of the foreign empire that ruled India. Thus, Khairi came to represent a sharp turn from Ahmad and Hali, who had advocated cordial relations with the British and the partial embrace of Western precepts on women's education and the rationalization of religion. While his works mourn the tragedies that befall women in an unreformed Islam—polygamous husbands, the difficulties of remarrying for widows, materialistic husbands and fathers—they nevertheless, in the reformist vein, also offer ideal characters, exemplars like Asghari Khanum whose character and faith serve as models for readers. This construction of a mythic ideal to critique the present remains a cornerstone of women's journals as well.

The founding principles of 'Iṣmat, representative of Khairi's novelistic didacticism, begin foremost with the desire to "uphold the sanctity [*ḥurmat*] of the *ḥaram*."²⁵ I leave the word *ḥaram* untranslated because of the myriad of meanings it takes, the most dominant among them being the central mosque of Mecca, which houses the Ka'abah, or symbolic house of Allah. But the idea of sacred space is hardly limited to Mecca, and thus *ḥaram* comes to assume the meaning of sacred or inviolable property as well, including the home, women's quarters, wives, and concubines. In using *ḥaram* to signify the discursive space, then, Khairi aligns himself with a longer Islamic teleology, which links the present-day home and the domestic lives of Muslim women to the historic center of Muslim belief. Convinced that the world outside the home had seduced Muslim men and women, Khairi intended for *'Iṣmat* to correct and redirect its readers aspirations toward the "living world" of the home. Subsequent aims of *'Iṣmat* included the "advancement of the standards of women" by way of education and both specialized and general knowledge.[26]

In advertisements for the magazine published in other Urdu journals of the time, including *Makzan*, Khairi described *'Iṣmat* as essential for both unmarried and married women, a guide for their conduct and morality both in their parents' and their husband's home. While its task was to be a constant companion for "Urdu-reading [*urdū kvāñ*] ladies," Khairi also advertised it as a product for men who were well-wishers of women's education.[27] Most importantly, the journal would present essays and advice according to the "tastes and duties" of its female readers that were "easy and for the popular perception."[28] Through *'Iṣmat* and its ambitions for reading women and men, Khairi became a central figure in determining the direction and dissemination of ideas first popularized in Ahmad and Hali's works. Wedded to the possibilities offered by modern Western textual forms such as the novel and the monthly digest, Khairi directed these forms into solidifying a national domesticity modeled on Islamic tenets, with reference to a historic past and an eye to the future.

Until the elder Khairi remained in charge, *'Iṣmat* was concerned with issues such as child-rearing, serial excerpts from his novels, the correct clothing for Muslim women, whether women should be able to speak in English, and recipes and tips for housekeeping. Its earliest covers carried no images, slowly moving to covers with palm trees and Quranic verses to more progressive and attractive illustrations of women doing housework or wearing fashionable but religiously appropriate attire. While Khairi was an advocate of women's education, as were the editors of other concurrent, comparatively liberal journals, *Ḵātūn* and *Tehzīb-e Nisvān*, he remained deeply tied to the concept of purdah, and against what Gail Minault in her excellent work *Secluded Scholars* describes as a "slavish imitation of the West."[29] Thus, the discussions on women's attire almost always leaned toward its "Islamic" correctness, the various ways and purposes of wearing a burqa, and the spiritual and symbolic relationship of women's clothing to the Muslim *qaum*. Although there were frequent articles on women from other parts of the world, including China and Denmark, the point of comparison was always the *sharīf* woman. The actual heroines among the various articles in *'Iṣmat* were women from Islam's golden past: Fatima and Zainab, the Prophet Muhammad's daughters, and Rabia Basri, a virtuous eighth-century mystic, among others. In the September 1909 issue, another ideal woman is celebrated: the mother of a son who becomes a *shahīd*, or martyr, fighting in the name of Islam, a trope that reappears in Hijazi's and Butt's novels.[30] Likewise, the entire February 1918 issue was dedicated to the Prophet Muhammad, his life, and significance of his teachings for women.

Though Nazir Ahmad's early works read in part as amiable to English practices, one of his final works, *Ibn ul-Vaqt*, or the Son of time (1888), betrayed a conflicted resentment toward the colonial government for its hypocritical treatment of a loyal but weak Muslim subject. But Khairi's stance on Muslims' relations with the English, or a larger West, is unambiguous and continues to influence successive writers as well. Thus, in his novels and essays, the issue of women's education is negotiated through idealized Islamic history and civilizations rather than the figure of Queen Victoria, as was evident in *Mirāt* and *ajālis*. In addition to *'Ismat*, Khairi ran two other journals for women, *Ban 'āt* (sisters) and *Sahēlī* (a female friend). The latter, though short-lived, was concerned mainly with housekeeping and child-rearing for young women. *Ban'āt*, more so than *'Ismat*, was concerned with giving Muslim girls a religious and moral education, and so, for example, it ran regular columns such as "religious history" (*mažhabī tārīḵ*), "stories from the Quran" (*qurān kē qiṣṣē*), and "prevailing traditions" (*ġhalabā-e rivāj*), the last a column about the corrupt practices Muslims had picked up from Hindus while living in India.[31]

While a discussion on Khairi's women's magazines and his empire—if I may—of women's literature can continue indefinitely, given that *'Ismat* ran until as recently as 2016, what remains central is the profound effect it enacted on *sharīf* cultural and domestic politics. Three generations of the Khairi family continued to represent *'Ismat* as something greater than just a commercial venture or a family business. Of particular note is a story Raziq ul-Khairi tells while recounting his father's legacy. During *'Ismat*'s first ten years or so, its publication was funded by an "Islamic protectorate" (*islāmī riyāsat*), a person or place the younger Khairi leaves unnamed.[32] When the funding is suspended due to Rashid ul-Khairi's disagreement with his patrons on questions related to religion, the younger Khairi berates his father on his indiscretion and the financial loss it has caused the magazine and the family. To this, of course, the elder, much-revered Khairi tells his son that " *'Ismat* will bear the harshest losses, but will never veer out of the bounds of truth."[33] Placed at the beginning of Raziq's coyly titled " *'Ismat kī Kahānī*," or the Story of *'Ismat* (1938), the narration of the event helps style *'Ismat* as something greater than just a women's home journal.[34] Thus, both *'Ismat* and its honorable founder are reinvented as symbols of truth, virtue, and most of all, loyalty to an Islamic center. Essays by the family commemorating Rashid ul-Khairi's character and services to women, as well as ones recounting the struggles 'Iṣmat faced in its early years frequently appeared in the magazine and other publications, canonizing both the man and his writings for decades to come.

Khairi's novels are hardly originals in that they frequently follow the good sister, bad sister theme, occasionally turn to Muslim Spain or admonish readers for digressing from a true Islam. But their narrative structure and plot dynamics also take us back to the oriental tale—a form that is reinvigorated in Hijazi's writings as well, and to a lesser extent in Butt's novels. An excellent example is *Andalūs kī Shehzādī*, a novella-like work based in Spain after the fall of Muslim rule. Though this work is certainly not among Khairi's best-known—better-recognized are the *Ṣubh̄*, *Shām*, and *Shab-e Zindagī*, or Dawn, Evening, and Night of Life stories—it is true to the general caste of themes that repeat themselves across Khairi's corpus. Reading at times like a simple fable and at times like a political drama, *Andalūs* is the story of a Spanish princess who is saved an assassination attempt by a Muslim goatherd. Opening with the fall of Granada when Abdullah XII, also known as Boabdil, hands over the throne to the Castilians, the novella begins by telling readers of a time when "Islam's floundering ship" (*islām kī d̄agmagātī kashtī*) seemed to hit rock-bottom.[35] Ferdinand, who assumes the throne after the Spanish victory, is succeeded by his niece, Elifitia, a kind and beautiful princess. While celebrating her fifth year as queen with her adoring people, Elifitia is bitten by a snake. The castle and her family, believing her to have died of the bite, bury her and begin the process of succession.

Within days of the burial, the princess's body disappears from the grave and a search for the perpetrator begins. In the meanwhile, the narrator takes us to the home of the true hero of the tale, Asim, a poor goatherd who has revived the princess and given her haven in his cottage. Upon hearing the news of the princess's demise, the goatherd, believing that "his holy book, the Quran [*mērī kitāb-e muqaddas y'ānī qurān*], was the remedy for all pain and the cure for all afflictions," had rescued her from her grave, convinced that he would be able to drain the venom from her body.[36] Overcome by the faith of her savior, the princess immediately disavows from Christianity, and converts to Islam, declaring the "prophet who arose from the dusts of Arabia spoke the truth" (*k̄āk-e 'arab sē uthnē vālā paiġhambar ṣādiq tha*).[37]

In the meantime, the royal palace has moved on. A false pretender to the princess's affections, James, has hijacked the throne and threatens the peace of the city. The princess's family, including her brother, Frederick, her rightful successor, have been removed to the peripheries of the city. The search for the princess's kidnapper is ongoing and eventually Asim, the goatherd, is captured and imprisoned, but the princess escapes and finds refuge with a small community of Muslims who welcome their "*kalima*-saying sister," and despite their simple, rural lifestyle amass an army of five thousand men to accompany the princess back to the city.[38]

The story predictably ends with the princess restored to the throne and the evil James deposed. In a rightful correction of the opening—the end of Muslim rule—the princess marries her savior and resumes her duties now as the Muslim queen of Granada. Trite, Khairi's version of Andalusia and Muslim Spain sits between Sharar's tragic, oftentimes didactic, historical novels, and Hijazi's later commemorations of Muslim conquests across Southern Europe, North Africa, and the Indian subcontinent. Though situated in a moment of Muslim decline, the story is inspired by the idea of an eternal Muslim truth, which emerges triumphant despite the evil that surrounds it. Its alternative title, "*taʾid-e ġhaibī*"—quite literally, the affirmation of the divine—thus offers more than just a romance between two disparate individuals. As in Sharar's works, Christianity appears as a degraded version of itself, one that is best absorbed by the uncorruptible Islam. It is also, without any pretenses to irony or satire, an oriental tale in the vernacular, structured and executed in a form and language close to its English and Fort William predecessors. Its closer antecedents are most visible in Sharar's novels, in Nazir Ahmad's short children's stories and Hali's romantic poetic images of Islam's golden past, all of which I have discussed earlier in this volume.

In an overtly different vein from *Andalūs*, Khairi's well-known *Bint-ul Vaqt* is the story of a young woman, Farkhanda, who is born to an old, *sharīf* family. But Farkhanda's penchant for English company and belief in Western doctrines of women's liberation lead her to ruin. At the beginning of this short novel-like work, we are told that Farkhanda and her family have little regard for Islam but instead are impressed by the Christian missionary workers in their town, Mohsinpur. The only and much-indulged daughter of her family, Farkhanda, in the company of the missionaries, begins to roam the town in pursuit of charitable works, thus forsaking her *purdah*, or confinement to women's quarters. Though her father is chided by a family elder for allowing his daughter these liberties, Farkhanda continues to keep company with the English missionaries. In a subplot to her story, we learn that her paternal uncle, Majid, is convicted and hanged for alleged involvement in the events of 1857. While Nazir Ahmad and Hali usually brushed over 1857 and the shame of the treatment meted out to Muslims in its wake, Khairi's engagement with the same event betrays a deep sense of resentment.

Unwilling to ignore the indignity of once "great and royal households being made into beggars, and those who once governed forced to depend on the mercy of others," Khairi's history of the Muslim experience in late colonial India tells of a misjudged community, wronged by its Christian rulers.[39] It is no surprise, then, that the missionaries who seduce Farkhanda into an English agenda of charity also take the small plot of land on which her uncle is buried, demolishing his grave to make way for a building project. Bereaved and stricken, Majid's widow is given no choice by the colonial government but to surrender her husband's grave for purposes of development and progress. Though this event is embedded in the longer narrative of Farkhanda's misspent life, it is a critical indicator of a changing attitude within the Muslim *shurafā* on the politics of allegiance.

Farkhanda joins a branch of the All-India Women's party led by Miss Walker, the missionary, and other Englishwomen, whose main aim was to advocate for native women's education. Deciding that Muslim women were underrepresented in the party's conference, she decides to write to a well-respected community elder, newly returned from Mecca. In her letter to Rabia Sultana, Farkhanda describes Muslim women as "ignorant and sticklers for tradition," who are attached and convinced by nothing other than their "religion" (*mažhab*).[40] She invites Rabia to speak at a women's gathering in her home, instructing her to speak briefly of Islam and then to turn to the real cause: women's education. Though Rabia, a much-revered figure in the small town of Mushinpur, agrees to join the gathering, her sermon is anything but what Farkhanda expects.

Far from extolling the merits of a modern education, as advocated by the colonial government, Rabia declares the ignorance of Muslim women to be a consequence of their estrangement from their religion.[41] The real problem, the scholar claims, is that Muslims are no longer Muslims, for even at a supposedly religious gathering such as this one, there wasn't a single prayer mat to be found. A Muslim home, such as the one she believed herself to be in, should "emanate the glory of Islam from every inch and corner," yet there was no such sign in Farkhanda's house.[42] Thus, Rabia Sultana concludes that "our dress is corrupted, and our society which used to be blessed with imperishable treasures is now plundered and ruined."[43] More importantly, Rabia reminds the "*ummat*," or the faithful: "our vessel [Islam] is in danger, our ship in stormy weather" (*humārā jahāz kaṭrē meiñ humārī kashtī ṭūfān meiñ*).[44]

Exemplars such as Rabia Sultana are stock figures in the reformist imagination that preceded and was concurrent with Khairi's—men and women who returned from the pilgrimage to Mecca commanded a respect bordering on reverence, and religious authority among *sharīf* Muslims. British officers remained suspicious of them, believing that they picked up incendiary and anti-British ideas during the pilgrimage.[45] In Ahmad's *Mirāt*, a procuress masquerading as a Hajjan, a returned female pilgrim, had been the undoing of Akbari, while in *Majālis*, Zubaida Khatun leaves India for Hajj and then assumes residence in Ottoman territories. Here, the figure of the female pilgrim is an agent of change, an alternative to the colonial rhetoric of development and advancement that writers such as Khairi and Thanvi saw as threatening to the sanctity of the Muslim home. "*T'alīm-e nisvāñ*," literally, the education of women, a catchphrase at the turn of the century, thus, was not a task to be left to the colonial government or its Muslim sympathizers. Women such as Rabia Sultana, models of piety and learning, were better-suited to guide the flailing ship of Islam to its true destination.

But Farkhanda, charmed by the missionaries and their rhetoric of women's liberation, remains unchastised. As the story progresses, she becomes increasingly distant from *sharīf* circles, spending much of her time at rallies and conferences. She is unkind to the domestic help at her house and neglectful of her husband, even as he lies ill with typhoid. She alienates her female friends and neighbors by writing unwelcome letters to their husbands urging them to liberate their wives from *purdah* and domestic duties. She becomes obsessed with English food and English ways of eating. She comes to believe that she is ill, and sees only an English "lady-doctor," who in broken Urdu blames her long-suffering husband, Naseer, for Farkhanda's illness. The "hysteria patient," as Khairi describes her, hires a nurse for herself who performs mundane tasks.[46] Farkhanda's domestic life reads in part as an unflattering caricature of English women in India, and in part, of course, as a condemnation of *sharīf* women who try to find a place for themselves outside of Islam and the home.

Some fifteen years after her marriage, Farkhanda is childless; her temper has become intolerable and her husband emaciated.[47] Abandoning any hopes of a better life at home, Naseer disappears one day, leaving a note wishing Farkhanda well. Soon after, her father, a wealthy man who had much to do with his daughter's ruined temperament, also dies. Despite her advocacy for a Western-style women's education, she had no skill with which she could fend for herself, and she is forced to become a low-paid employee at the local mission. Once a rich and pampered woman, she has to work long and difficult hours for a pittance. Her life, the narrator concludes, thus becomes a picture of grief and suffering (*'ibrat*) for passers-by to look at and learn from.[48] Tragic in its ending, but unequivocal in its message, *Bint-ul Vaqt*, like Khairi's similarly themed novel, *Sarāb-e Maghrib*, or the mirage of the West, rejects colonial curricula and models of women's education for what it argues is an already enlightened and just religion. Sullied and obscured in its current state in colonial India, a true Islam, Khairi repeatedly reminds readers, is both viable and rewarding.

Given his prolific and varied career, Khairi merits more than the brief examination I have offered in this chapter. Though most of his works follow similar patterns in terms of plot and characters, Khairi's legacy for Urdu prose lies in his transformation of pure but anti-colonial Islam into an essential part of fast-developing form of the novel, particularly as it lent itself to female readers. At the risk of repeating myself, Khairi's breathes a revitalizing but pugnacious spirit into the concept of *iṣlāḥ* (religious correction) that first took form in Nazir Ahmad's and Hali's works. Taking up many of his predecessors' tropes—the ship, the fable, errant women—Khairi narrows the myth of a chaste Islam as the single redemptive possibility for Muslim women and families that remains distinct from and against the colonial administration. Under Khairi's pen, the novel becomes a distinct means of *iṣlāḥ* for the *shurufā*, upholding in all its totality, the supremacy of Islam as the only path its protagonists can tread.

Kingdom and Conquest:
Nasim Hijazi, the Novel, and Muslim Origins in India

What in Hali's or Khairi's works were figurative tropes and metaphors around Islam—ships, unconverted women, conquest—become literal plot elements in Nasim Hijazi's celebrated historical novels. Born with the commonplace name Muhammad Sharif in 1914 in Gurdaspur, a small town now in Indian Punjab, Hijazi modeled his person in accordance with the heroic myths and stories of origin that he was to propagate in his novels. His pen name, Nasim Hijazi, quite literally, the scented breeze of Hijaz, the site of Islam's origins, though reflective of his familial claim to descent from the Arab Peninsula, is believed to have been given to him by Allama Muhammad Iqbal, the Muslim nationalist-philosopher-poet, a literary hero and model for Hijazi. His name and the unequivocal political meaning it carried reverberate throughout his novels, many of which directly explore Muslim conquest in India, whether it be Andalus, Muhammad bin Qasim and his supposed capture of Sindh, or Mahmud of Ghaznavi and his invasions into Punjab.

At the time of Partition, Hijazi was already in the newly formed Pakistan where he worked as a journalist, later becoming the editor-in-chief of a conservative daily, *Kohistan*. His literary career in Pakistan was hugely successful, gaining renewed impetus during the almost decade-long rule of Zia ul-Haq, the Islamist dictator of the 1980s. This is not to say that Hijazi did not remain prominent with the establishment prior to Zia (there is a photograph of him shaking hands with Jackie Kennedy when the first lady visited Pakistan in 1962). For the Zia government and its Islamist agenda, however, Hijazi's novels were instrumental and were re-issued with state support, an event I expound upon in depth later on.[49] Hijazi was prolific, having completed around twenty-one novels, several *afsānās*, as well as a few non-fictional works, one of which is a travelogue detailing his journey to Mecca from Pakistan. His newspaper, *Kohistan*, had a circulation of at least 80,000 readers in Lahore from 1953 to 1963. Like Sharar and Khairi, Hijazi spent the early days of his career as a journalist at major newspapers and journals, including the literary magazine *Zamana*, which had published the likes of the Progressive writers, Premchand and Firaq Gorakhpuri.

Hijazi's life and times gave rise to a particular kind of nationalist writer. By the late 1930s, the rhetoric of an Islamic *qaum* could be channeled into both the domestic sphere and an increasingly active political domain, which to a major extent was represented by the formation of the Indian Muslim League, but also by the rise of fiery anti-colonial thinkers and organizers and political leaders such as Azad and Maulana Maududi. The latter's ideas on *jihād*, *qaum*, indeed on Islam itself as it was conceptualized by the West and thus its diverse colonial subjects, are critical markers when it comes to understanding the political impetus underlying Hijazi's literary project.

I examine two of his early novels, *Dāstān-e Mujāhid* (1943/44) and *Muhammad Bin Qāsim* (1945). The first is the story of a young Muslim, his family, and his quest to expand Islamic territories during the rule of the Caliph Hajaj bin Yusuf, and the second is a rewriting of the story of the eponymous Muslim hero who is believed to have first brought Islam to India. Hijazi must be read as one of the most enduring figures in what I call an extended moment of colonial influence on Urdu prose. That is to say, Hijazi's novels are sophisticated, re-imagined versions of vernacular oriental tales, written, this time, in the throes of the decolonization movement by the colonized subject. His re-imagined Muslim is, on the one hand, continuous with the Mahometan: itinerant, warring, at times a conqueror, a ruler of foreign people, non-native to territories such as India, or Central Asia, and subject to the ideological authority of the caliphate. The terms of engagement, however, come from the nationalist subject at the cusp of realizing his freedom. Thus, the marauding protagonist of the oriental tale is now a *mujāhid*, or one who undertakes *jihād*; the lack of a national or domestic center is now vested in the figure of Muslim and other women who are compelled to Islam and piety through the figure of the *mujāhid*; and the once-conquered territories are now part of a beholden empire, liberated by Islam from cruel past rulers. In other words, Hijazi's novels mark a moment of arrival—to use Partha Chatterjee's phrase—the coming full-circle of the oriental tale and its attendant forms in the shape of a distinct Muslim nationalism whose allegiances can never align exactly with state or territory, but remain always with the abstract and intangible category of *dīn*, or religion, and whose antagonists are both the English, in their role as colonizers, and the Hindus, in their roles as the natural enemies of Islam.

Developed out of an *afsānā* published in 1938, *Dāstān-e Mujāhid*, quite literally, the story, or *dāstān*, of one who fights in the name of Islam, was well-received at the time of its publication and gained further popularity in the years following the success of *Muhammad bin Qāsim*. Hijazi's stance as a novelist is clear in this preface of this early volume in which he announces that it had taken some time for him to decide "which event in the history of Islam was to be the ornament of my story" (*tārīk̲-e islām kē kis vāq'ē kō apnē afsānē kī zīnat banā'ūñ*), but in searching for that single flower he ended up collecting a bouquet, which he presented to "our youth" with the hope that it would instill in them a "desire" to return their "decayed garden" to its once "blossoming and verdant" state.[50] Aware that those who favor "art for art's sake" (*adab barā'ye adab*), would be angered at the opposition he posed to their agenda, Hijazi denounces their efforts to make "literature" (*adab*) into a source of "wasted time and mental confusion."[51]

Deeply conscious of his adoption of the novel as the form best suited for his ambitions, Hijazi clarifies to his readers that "in contemporary literature, it is the novel and *afsānā* that help in presenting life's important and dense trials in an interesting fashion" (*maujūdā adab meiñ nāvil aur afsānē kī madad sē zindagī kē ahm aur t̲hōs masa'il kō ziyādā dilčasp andāz meiñ pēsh kiyā jā saktā hai*).[52] This work, *Dāstān-e Mujāhid*, is a novel, he reiterates, and given that it is his first attempt at writing one, he cannot guarantee its formal or literary success, though the true guarantor of his success are the colors of Islamic history. Hijazi's deep engagements with history and the novel form in this preface conform, to some extent, with the political conditions that gave rise to the European historical novel, the most famous exponent of which in Gyorg Lukacs's meditative account remains Walter Scott.

If we consider, as Lukacs theorized, that the "appeal to national independence and national character is necessarily connected with a reawakening of national history, with memories of the past, of past greatness, of moments of national dishonor," it becomes infinitely clear that Hijazi's conceptions of nation and history derive, in part, from influences such as Walter Scott and Thomas Carlyle, both of whom commanded a considerable presence in colonial libraries and literature syllabi.[53] Given that Hijazi received his university education at the Islamia College, Lahore, then under the auspices of the Government of Punjab's education department, there is much to suggest that he, like other anti-colonial thinkers and writers, did, in fact, encounter Carlyle's writings. Indeed, Hijazi's attitudes toward a nation and the significance of its great history echo much of what Carlyle had to say in works, such as *Past and Present* and "On History." Far from being concerned with historical or factual accuracy, the purpose of these novels, in Lukacian (and Carlyle-ian) terms, then, is the "poetic awakening of the people who figured in those events" in a manner that makes them "re-experience the social and human motives which led men to think, feel, and act just as they did in historical reality.[54] Though Hijazi imagines the purpose of the historical novel in much the same terms, his ideas of nation and action derive from figures closer to home, Maududi and Azad chief among them. Choosing templates similar to English histories and historical novels, Hijazi makes Islam and the Muslim warrior into the prophetic subjects of his stories.

First published by the Qaumi Kutab Khana, a prestigious but now defunct publishing house in Lahore, *Mujāhid* has been reprinted regularly since—its first publisher re-issued the novel in 1953, 1972 (a 1971 edition came out in Lucknow, India), 1980, and then in 1990, while Jahangir Book Depot, to whom the rights now belong, has reprinted the book at least twice since the year 2000.[55] Both publishing houses have commanded significant influence in the world of Urdu letters; their combined author lists include poets such as Parveen Shakir and Nasir Kazmi, political and religious authorities such as Abdul Kalam Azad and Javed Ghamdi, as well as a range of well-known and bestselling fiction writers. *Mujāhid* follows the life and career of Naim, a young Muslim, who from his boyhood days in Umayyad Iraq wishes to fight in the name of Islam and expand Islamic territories. The reader is introduced to Naim's mother, Sabirah, who is raising two sons by herself after her husband, Abdurrehman, has been martyred while fighting abroad.

Framing the events of the novel is a letter that the latter sends from his deathbed, entreating her to remain aware of her "religious duty" (*farz*), by teaching their children that "life in this world is false and worthless when compared to the death of a *mujāhid*."[56] The soldiers who bring news of Abdurrehman's death to the small settlement outside of Basra where

Sabirah lives return his sword to his family as a symbolic reminder of their father's bravery. A model Muslim mother, Sabirah does not grieve, but delights in her young sons' desire to become soldiers, encouraging them by singing songs that inspire them:

> O lord of the Kaabah, may my darling become a *mujāhid*
> Whose young blood can water the trees planted by your beloved.
>
> *ai rab-e kāʿabā! Mērā yēh lʿāl mujāhid banē*
> *tērē meḣbūb kē lagāʾē huʾē daraḵt*
> *kō javānī kē ḵūn sē sērāb karē.*[57]

The "beloved" in this verse is the Prophet Muhammad, whose trees, Islam, can only continue growing if the blood of its men is shed in its name. Sabirah also takes in a young orphan girl, Azra, whose father, Zahir, has also died in battle and whose Persian mother, Yasmin, we are told, not as resilient as her Arab counterparts, also passes away from grief. One after the other, the brothers go to Basra, where they are trained as fighters, while Azra and Sabirah become companions, the former tending to the latter as she grows older, her sons visiting on their occasional leaves from training and then battle. Sabirah and Azra exemplify the ideal Muslim domesticity of Hijazi's imagination. They, along with the other female characters who enter the narrative, are active members of the Muslim *qaum*, their roles as the mothers and wives of *mujāhids* become a means of incorporating them into a comprehensive national narrative.

The plot follows Naim's career as he travels with the famous general, Muhammad bin Qasim (the hero of Hijazi's next book) to India; his kidnapping on his return journey by Ibn Sadiq, a villain of Jewish descent who seems to move fluidly between Islam, Christianity, and Judaim; and then later adventures among unconverted tribals in Turkey and China. Ibn Sadiq, a learned yet dangerous enemy, is probably modeled on the mysterious seventh-century figure of Ibn Saba (also a character in Sharar's *Firdaus-e Barīñ*), who plotted against the caliphate. Ibn Sadiq tortures and threatens Naim, who eventually manages to escape with the help of another captive, a Christian girl, Zuleikha, who begs him to return her to her family in Damascus. As they set off, Ibn Sadiq's men pursue them. A skirmish follows during which Zuleikha, convinced of her luckless life, commits suicide with Naim's sword. Before she dies, however, she converts to Islam out of love for Naim. Naim buries her and travels back to Basra.

He returns home to find his mother has died, and that his brother is marrying Azra, their adopted sister, whom he himself had wanted to marry and who had wanted to marry him. But Naim stays away from the house until the ceremony is completed and then reunites with his brother and now sister-in-law. After this brief visit, he joins Qutibah ibn Muslim, the commander who led the Arab invasion into what is now modern Central Asia. In Turkistan, Naim reencounters Ibn Sadiq, who this time around is attempting to provoke the locals into a rebellion against the Muslim conquerors. However, the elders in the gathering of locals refuse to revolt, claiming that Muslim rule, though not ideal, is just, and oftentimes, citing the case of Iran, preferable to local rule. Ibn Sadiq is forced to fight the Arab army on his own but Naim's men repel his people, even though their leader is gravely injured in battle.

Thus begins the next chapter in the *mujāhid's* journey: He gains consciousness to find himself under the loving care of a young woman called Nargis, who lives in a small hamlet with her brother, Humaan. During his convalescence, Naim gains the love and respect of the villagers, and in the final days of his stay, gathers them around to tell them about Islam: "A few speeches like this and he drew all the inhabitants of the settlement towards Islam."[58] The first to convert, not surprisingly, are his hosts, Nargis and Humaan. In just a few days, we are told, the mood of the village changed: "Naim's recitation of the *āzān* would reverberate through the verdant meadows, and in place of dancing and singing, prayers would be offered five times a day."[59] Having created an ideal Islamic community in this part of Turkistan, Naim sets out to reconnect with the Arab army, promising Nargis that he will return. Worth noting, as well as in subsequent events, conversion to Islam is never an act of force but a natural option. The *mujāhid* is an *exemplary* figure whose piety—not violence—draws subject people to his faith.

The penultimate leg of Naim's journey takes him through Samarkand, where Qatibah, the Arab commander, strides fearlessly into a temple and destroys the idols of the local people who upon seeing their shattered gods immediately recite the "edict of the oneness of God" (*kalima' tauĥīd*) and convert to Islam.[60] From there, Naim travels to China as an ambassador to the king, where he announces his mission as not one that is interested in riches or power, but one that establishes a law by which the "reach of the strong does not extend beyond that of the weak, there is no culture of master and slave, and the distinction between the king and his subjects is no more."[61] This law, he tells the king, is "Islam." Having completed this task as well, Naim travels back to the hamlet in Turkistan to marry Nargis, the woman who nursed him back to health. After a few blissful weeks, Naim is recalled to Samarkand by Qatibah where he is told that instead of continuing their expansion into China, they must return to Damascus, where the new caliph, Suleman, has assumed power. Depicted in both this novel and *Muhammad bin Qāsim* as antagonistic toward the heroic commanders of Arab forces, Suleman demands the heads of both Qatibah and bin Qasim.

It is Naim who returns to Damascus, however, and faces the caliph, who, the reader learns, is under the influence of Ibn Sadiq, that old enemy of the Muslims. Although Naim is temporarily imprisoned, his name is eventually cleared by his brother, Abdullah, and he is made governor of southern Portugal while the caliph and his men turn on their true enemy, Ibn Sadiq. Naim's battles in Europe take him to Spain, where he meets his brother's son, also a soldier named Naim, and then to Tunis, where he is severely injured but decides nevertheless to journey home to die. The novel ends, finally, with a moment of reunion for the two brothers and their families in the same small house where they grew up; Naim takes his lasts breaths knowing his wife is in safe hands.

Startlingly familiar in its range of geography, the itinerancy of its heroes, and its rewriting of conventional domesticities, Hijazi's "novel" reads like any number of English oriental tales—we can think here of Aboulfouraris or Fadlallah from the *Persian Tales*. The point of difference, however, is the compelling elaboration of a Muslim self as an agent member of greater *qaum*, who travels *deliberately* in the name of Islam. Thus, in the novel, the Muslim is essentially a figure who is not destined to, but, in fact, actively *desires* to roam the earth in the name of Islam. The domestic now consists of Muslim women from distant territories—Zuleikha and Nargis are made vital parts of the *qaum* upon their conversion. The focus on romance, love, and marriage is not a pulp strategy or a move to attract a female readership, but rather a direct inclusion of women in what Hijazi (and others of this milieu) imagined as a model Islamic community. Hijazi's modern oriental tale, if I may ironically refer to it as such, repurposes its English predecessor in the service of an increasingly anti-colonial Muslim nationalism.

Dāstān-e Mujāhid's distinct concern for how to envision a Muslim nationhood at the moment of decolonization articulates a national position concerned not so much with state or local ties, but rather with the intangible, all-empowering idea of Islam. As is evident here (and will become more explicit in my reading of *Muhammad bin Qāsim*), Hijazi's political worldview is a simplistic derivation of Maududi's more complex one. The latter had by this time founded the Jamat-e Islami, today, the single most important religio-political party in contemporary Pakistan. Maududi, unlike other *ulemā* and religious leaders of the time, was also a newspaper man whose career began at the pro-Congress weekly, *Al-Jamiat*. In 1933, he started his own journal, *Tarjumān-ul Qurān*, or the translation of the Quran, which carried both religious and political content. Prolific and authoritative, Maududi became an unparalleled force when it came to defining politics and society in South Asia from an Islamic point of view.[62]

Explicitly defining, for perhaps the first time, what constituted *qaum*, or nation, from an Islamic perspective, Maududi argued that race, language, origin, or ethnicity—all European markers—were neither humanist nor universal. In the September 1933 issue of *Tarjumān*, Maududi wrote that

> every Muslim, whether a resident of China or Morocco, black or white, speaking Hindi or Arabic, Semite or Aryan, subject of one government or the other, is part of the Muslim *qaum*, member of the Islamic society, citizen of the Islamic state, soldier of the Islamic army and protected under Islamic law.[63]

Conceptualizing the Muslim *qaum* for the first time, both through and against Western markers of nationhood and sovereignty, Maududi offered the Muslims of North India an expanded, global affiliative network, anticolonial in its thrust, and paints over localized expressions of Islam. The *qaum*, of which the Muslims of India were part, spanned the globe, indifferent to class and race, and was subservient only to "Islamic" laws and governance structures. The colonial state, or any state modeled on Western ideals of democracy, obviously, was repugnant to Maududi, who advocated rather that India itself be made a "*dār-ul Islām*," an abode or country of Islam.[64]

Even more complex, at times seemingly contradictory, is Maududi's conception of *jihād*, a pivotal theme in almost all of Hijazi's novels. He critiques Western and colonial interpretations of jihad as conjuring up

> the vision of hordes of religious fanatics [*mazhabī dīvānōñ*] bearing naked swords, unruly beards, with bloody eyes, marching forward proclaiming, "Allah is the greatest" [*allāh-o akbar kē n'ārē*]. Wherever one of them sees a man [*kisī fard*], he takes hold of him, and forces him to recite the *kalima* [*lā illāhā illallāh*] at the cost of having his head separated from his body.[65]

Both in this speech, given at the Town Hall in Lahore in April 1939, and in a longer, theoretical volume that draws from both European and Islamic sources, Maududi accuses the West, with its capitalist conquests and its own tradition of violence—he mentions the Roman gladiators, among others—of having obscured and corrupted the image of Islam with its skillful artistry, so much so that Muslims themselves were no longer properly cognizant of its essence and meaning.[66] Islam, Maududi argues, is not a religion, something he dismisses as merely a set of shared beliefs, morals, and prayer and rituals. Islam is that "revolutionary worldview [inqilābī nażrīyā-o maslak] and path which seeks to change the established order of the world [ijtam'āyī nażm] and reconstruct it according to its own ideal and process [apnē nażrīyā-o maslak]."[67] Muslims, Maududi adds, are the "international revolutionary party" responsible for bringing about this change. Jihād, he finally establishes, is the name of that "revolutionary struggle and utter conversion of power" (inqilābī jad-o jahd kā aur initihā'yī ṣarf-e ṭāqat) that is essential in realizing the purpose of Islam.[68] Not war in the European understanding of the word, jihād is to "exert one's utmost endeavor in furthering a cause [maqsad]."[69]

Although much of Maududi's rhetoric of Islam's universality is reflected in the events of Mujāhid, it is in Muhammad bin Qāsim and the later, Ākrī M'arkā, the story of Mahmud Ghazavi's invasions into India, that his second mission—making India into an Islamic territory, or state—is elaborated and celebrated. Though Hijazi remained involved with the Muslim League, a political party Maududi opposed right up until Partition, the former's conception of the qaum borrowed heavily from the latter. Likewise, Maududi sanctioned Hijazi's books as a great "service" (k̲idmat) to the "millat," a term often used by Iqbal, and whose meaning suggested a nation or people bound by religion or faith.[70] Approving of Hijazi's use of "this popularly accepted genre" (is maqbūl-e 'ām ṣinf), Maududi congratulates him for making the novel a form that tries to instill in Muslims "a great attachment to Islam and its values, a warrior's spirit for its [Islam's] glory [sarbulandī kē liy'ē mujāhidānā rūh]."[71] Any reader, Maududi concludes, will find both entertainment and "a lesson" (dars) in Hijazi's works.[72]

Maududi's appreciation for Hijazi's novels appears on the front flap of the 2002 edition of Muhammad bin Qāsim, possibly his most acclaimed and well-known work.[73] Published in 1945, immediately after Mujahid, Hijazi's second novel is known to have been reprinted in 1954, 1970, 1983, 1985, 1989, and 1991 by the Qaumi Kutab Khanah, and in 2005 and 2010 by Jahangir Book Depot, which subsequently bought the rights to the book (and these are only the known, catalogued editions). The basic story Hijazi tells in this novel is hardly original and has constituted a part of Indo-Persia's chronicles since as far back as circa 850 and 1224 C.E., where we find versions written by Al-Baladhuri, an Abbasid courtier, and Ali Kufi, a writer from medieval Uch, Sind. But orientalists such as Henry Myers Elliot and Alexander Dow systematically read these accounts as empirical histories of Muslim "origins" in India, thus recodifying these medieval texts in terms of a European modernity. Thus, Hijazi's novel is one symptom of this colonial reorganization of local forms of knowledge.[74] An everyday hero, bin Qasim reappears as a reference in novels, including Butt's *Bano*, in urban landmarks such as Karachi's Port Qasim, and in sermons by celebrity *maulvis* that are often broadcast on national television.[75] His conquest of Sindh in 712 A.D. is still recognized as the founding date of Pakistan in official accounts, including textbooks.

The many letters he received after the success of *Mujahid*, Hijazi writes in the preface to his second novel, gave truth (*taṣdīq*) to his claim that even in this day and age, the telling of past events is more enchanting for Muslims than stories of "Qais and Farhad," the doomed lovers of the Persian *ghazal* tradition.[76] Echoing earlier reformists' calls to discard the *ghazal* and *dāstān* for more realist and instructive forms of fiction, Hijazi offers the "memory of past springs" as a means to a better future.[77] Alternatively titled "*fatâh-e Hind*," or the "conquest of Hind," the Persian name for India, the novel serves to remind Muslims that their place in India is that of conquerors, not citizens or subjects, as they are in the present moment.

The first half of the novel begins in Serendib, or present-day Sri Lanka, where a small community of Arabs whose ancestors came to the island before the birth of Islam, trade and live peacefully under the Hindu ruler. A young woman of this community, Salma, swims in the ocean, rides wild horses, and roams freely, until the day that a shipload of Arab traders arrive, led by a man named Abul Hassan. After Abul Hassan saves Salma's life, she falls in love with him and under his tutelage abandons her past persona in order to become a modest Muslim woman who prays, dresses modestly, and maintains purdah. As she struggles to inhabit this new persona, Hassan instructs her in how "a Muslim girl's most beautiful ornament is modesty," and in the selflessness with which "Muslim women send their husbands and sons for jihad."[78] After some years, during which Hasan travels for both trade and battle, he and Salma marry and have two children, Khalid, a son, and Nahid, a daughter. Eventually, Hassan decides to travel for Hajj, the major pilgrimage, but his ship disappears, and he is never heard from again.

Salma dies of grief, and the children, deciding that their actual "*qaum*" is the Islamic caliphate, prepare to board a ship that will take them to Basra. They are joined by Zubair, a young companion of Hassan's, other Muslim orphans and widows, as well as by Dilip Singh, the king's emissary, who is piloting a companion ship loaded with elephants, gold, and diamonds for the caliph. Early on into the voyage, they repel the attacks of a pirate ship; take the captain, Gungu, captive; and rescue a young

Rajput prince, Jai Ram, and his sister, Maya Devi, from the pirates. But when the ship stops at Debal, a port city on the Sindhi coast, Jai Ram and Zubair are taken prisoner and the waiting ships are stormed by the soldiers of Raja Dahir, the ruler of Sindh. Fortunately, Khalid and the women on the ship, though wounded, have been saved by Gungo, who offered them refuge in an old abandoned fort near Brahminabad, a town further inland. Eventually, Zubair and Jai Ram escape and reunite with their friends at the fort; Jai Ram, Maya, and Gungu convert to Islam and take the names of Nasir, Zehra, and Saad. Knowing that they cannot take the Raja on themselves, the group sends Zubair out in the dead of the night to seek help from the caliphate.

The second part of the novel begins in Basra, where the reader is introduced to Hajjaj bin Yousaf, the governor of Iraq, a man whom "nature chose for the purpose of ensuring that the flags of the Muslims' power [*musalmānoñ kī sitvat kē jhandē*] waved over Sindh, Turkistan, and Spain."[79] He is also the paternal uncle and father-in-law of Muhammad bin Qasim, the youthful hero of the novel. When Zubair finally arrives in Basra after escaping from Raja Dahir and his men, he presents Hajjaj with a handkerchief on which Naheed has written a plea for help with her own blood. Convinced, Hajjaj tells his audience that he is ready to declare jihad against Sindh.[80] An army, led by Muhammad bin Qasim is prepared and the entire city of Basra participates in the efforts to free the prisoners in Sindh.

Part of this effort is distinctly feminine—a critical feature in many of Hijazi's novels. It is Naheed's choice of ink that convinces Hajjaj. In Basra, bin Qasim's wife, Zubaida, sells all her jewelry to finance the buying of horses and weapons, convincing all the women of the city that "Naheed's ordeal was the ordeal of every daughter and daughter-in-law of the *qaum*."[81] Bin Qasim's mother, though elderly and in poor health, travels from neighborhood to neighborhood with a small group of women, preaching the importance of *jihād* and gathering support. Inspired by the women of Basra, women across Iraq donate money and jewelry, gathering hundreds of thousands of rupees for the cause.[82] We are reminded of a lesson that Abul Hassan had taught the domesticated Salma earlier in the story: "What men cannot do on the battlefield, women can accomplish whilst staying within the four walls of their homes."[83] The domestication of *jihād*, then, enables the Muslim woman to imagine herself as part of a greater *qaum*, even as she remains in purdah, confined to the women's quarters of her husband or father's home. Likewise, the *qaum* itself, as Hijazi constructs it, appears inclusive, accommodating, even dependent on efforts of its tamed and compliant women.

Bin Qasim, the seventeen-year-old warrior who leads the mission has a face that is "strong and serious" and his beautiful black eyes betray "innocence" rather than "bravado."[84] Upon reaching Sindh, bin Qasim and his men take city after city: Nirun (present-day Hyderabad), Sewan, Debal, and Arore, where they find Abul Hassan in one of the king's prisons. Raja Dahir, the evil king, keeps retreating inland, accompanied by an army that defends its precincts by day and rapes local women by night. Dahir is killed in battle in Brahminabad, and it is his young queen and son who are left with the task of resisting the Muslim army.[85] Both relent under the might of bin Qasim's army and the promise that unlike Alexander, bin Qasim's mission is not to enslave, but rather to "make those who until yesterday were his enemies [*dushman*] into his new companions [*sāthī*], for his victory is not his; it is the victory of Islam's truth [*islām kī ṣadaqat kī fatāḥ hai*]."[86] During the battles, bin Qasim also officiates the marriages of the Khalid and the converted Maya or Zehra, and Naheed and Zubair, whose romances have colored the captivity and battle narratives.

In the time he spends in Sindh after his victory, bin Qasim educates the locals, many of whom then convert to Islam. But soon he receives news of his uncle Hajjaj's passing, followed by the caliph Waleed's demise. Waleed is replaced by Suleman—the same cruel caliph we encountered in *Mujāhid*—who has reason to believe bin Qasim is a traitor because of his relationship with Hajjaj, and thus has ordered him to return to Damascus where he will be put to death. Though several concerned members of the community try to intervene and the caliph relents, incidents are timed in such a fashion that bin Qasim does indeed die. In the last scene of the novel, as bin Qasim is being lowered into the earth, a mob of young men attacks Salih bin Abdur Rehman, the government official responsible for carrying out the caliph's orders.

Muhammad bin Qāsim is about the origins of Islam in India. The origins of the novel, however, are betrayed by its simultaneous appropriation and renewal of orientalist histories and tropes surrounding the Muslim presence in India. Bin Qasim and Naeem, exemplary Muslim men from Hijazi's larger oeuvre, are infused with the spirit of the Mahometan. They are loyal to the caliphate, if not the caliph himself; they are itinerants who wander the earth, and the conquerors who fight in the name of Islamic empires. Even as the modern North Indian Muslim defines himself and his nation against historic figures such as Raja Dahir, he does so by inhabiting the terms of the Mahometan chronotope. Hijazi's particular role in the longer history of modern Urdu is his marriage of the Western constituents of nation—origin, language, history, and territory—to Islam, a self-declared universal category, through the fecund form of the novel. To dismiss Hijazi as popular or pulp, then, is to dismiss his powerful influence on the fashion in which a properly national imagination for North Indian, and soon Pakistani, Muslims materializes in the literary and popular fiction in Urdu.

The (Nation-) State of Sin: Razia Butt and the Feminine Martyr

Roughly of the same generation and political moment as Hijazi, Razia Butt was even more prolific, leaving some fifty or so novels and three hundred *afsānās* behind at the time of her death in 2012. Dismissed by many a critic as a romantic women's novelist with little profundity or depth in her novels, Butt nevertheless commanded a serious presence in just about every middle-class household in Pakistan from the 1950s onward. Her novels continue to be reprinted and, in recent years, adapted for hugely successful television serials. There is little point in declaring Butt to be a writer of high aesthetic merit, but there is much to be lost in writing her out of Urdu's literary history, an act that surely betrays the deliberate nature of canon-making in a language whose modern presence is largely the result of its colonial past. Hardly cut of the same cloth as the searing oppositional and feminist writer, Ismat Chugtai, or even the historically contemplative, modernist Quratulain Hyder, Butt and her contemporaries, the equally popular though less prolific A. R. Khatun and Salma Kanval, made *sharīf* women into their heroines, telling often tragic stories of national failures whose consequences were borne by these heroines.

Despite being mostly house-bound, Butt's trajectory as a writer was not terribly different from the male authors I have already spoken about. Of Kashmiri descent, born in 1924 in Wazirabad, Punjab, Butt spent part of her childhood and adolescence in Peshawar, publishing her first short story, "Naila," at around the age of twelve or so, in *Hūr*, a popular women's digest. During this time, she also became an active participant in the women's wing of the Muslim League, campaigning and attending rallies for the creation of a separate Muslim state with her maternal aunts and sisters. Married and based in Ambala at the time of Partition, Butt migrated to the newly made Pakistan at the height of the riots and violence, later basing parts of her bestselling novel, *Bānō* (1971), on her own experiences. In Pakistan, Butt embraced the role of a writer, her novels appearing as serialized stories in literary digests such as *Zebunnissā*, *Urdū*, and *Sayyārā*, many of them eventually being picked up for television or film adaptation as far back as 1961. By the 1990s, Butt published several serialized and standalone stories in the Friday literary supplement of the well-known conservative daily *Navā'e Vaqt*, a clear indication of her popularity across Pakistan.

Her novel *Sā'iqā* (1967) met with much acclaim and was made into a hit film, running for twenty-nine weeks in Peshawar alone. Other novels, including a re-worked *Nā'ilā* and *Norīnā* (1972), were adapted for both television and film soon after their publication. The plot lines of these early but bestselling novels were roughly similar, focusing on the evils and selfishness of the upper classes of Pakistan. The heroines of these works were usually reformed and repentant wealthy women, or sincere and long-suffering young women from middle- or lower-income backgrounds. In a novel such as *Sā'iqā*, for example, the arrogance of a wealthy feudal family meets its comeuppance when the son marries a village girl, an event whose consequences unravel over the course of two generations. In addition to its adaptation for film, *Sā''iqā* was recently also televised in serial form, a reminder, perhaps, that the story remains relevant in Pakistano today. Over the course of her long career, Butt's novels acquired more thematic sophistication: *Bānō* and *Vaṭan kī Bēṭī* (1990) both move away from themes of inter-class romance and take up the questions of nationhood and religion, positing virtuous, believing heroines as the guardians of the nation-state and the representatives of a modern Islam.

Though she maintained a public narrative about being a housewife whose chief preoccupation was raising her five daughters, Butt commanded commercial success. The print-runs of her constantly reprinted novels usually approached 5,000, a significant number, somewhat engineered by the fact that most would run as serial stories in women's digests and only the novel would carry the final installment.[87] In later television appearances, she is a demure, grey-haired lady who modestly admits that she wrote in the mornings while her husband was away, while also stitching, knitting, and cooking for her family. Other than her first novel, which Butt dismisses as a youthful folly, her works, she tells her audiences, have always borne the weight of trial and purpose.[88] The morals in her stories, she claims, are the morals that were given to mankind "fourteen hundred years ago," with the revelation of Islam.[89] There is nothing overtly revolutionary or progressive about Butt, whether in her stories or in the biographical details she and family members narrate. Her avid participation in the Pakistan movement, her one meeting with Muhammad Ali Jinnah, and her relationship with his sister, Fatima Jinnah, emerge as defining moments of her youth, and many of her works from the 1960s onward can be read as reflections on the social and cultural politics of the new nation-state.

In this section, I turn to Butt's novel *Bānō*, the story of a *sharīf* Muslim girl's struggles during Partition and her eventually tragic and violent fate in the much dreamt of Pakistan. Whereas in Hijazi's novels, the threat of sexual violence to believing women was often a central element in the movement of the plot, in *Bānō*, the tortured body of the Muslim woman *is* the tragic elaboration of a social and religious failure on the part of the Muslim *qaum*, an idea that the eponymous heroine struggles to defend with her last breaths. But if Hijazi's novels rewrote the marauder of the oriental tale as a *mujāhid*, here the Muslim woman is forcefully displaced, her itinerancy the crime of a wayward nation.

Published in 1971, as the tensions between West and East Pakistan (soon to be Bangladesh) simmered, *Bānō* was dedicated to the "modesties ['*iṣmatōñ*] that were ravaged in the riots of 1947, whose bodies continue to whimper today," and was read to great acclaim.[90] In 2010, the novel took on renewed importance when it was made into a highly rated television serial, aired under the name of *Dāstān*. Beginning in Ludhiana, now a part of Indian Punjab, the novel is the story of a young woman from a well-to-do Muslim family, Bano, and her sacrifices in the name of Pakistan. Though her father, Naseerudin, is not wealthy, his family and that of his short-lived brother, Haji Mairajuddin, command great respect in local circles. The brothers and their families live in a seemingly diverse neighborhood; friends and neighbors are Hindus and Sikhs in a united India. Initially, Mairajuddin's daughter is engaged to Naseerudin's son, and soon Bano becomes engaged to her cousin, Mairaj's son, Hasan, a young man who aspires to become an engineer.

But this idyllic situation soon takes a turn. It is not as if, Butt tells us, "Hindu animosity for Muslims was a new thing. This enmity had been born in Hindus' hearts at the moment when Muhammad Bin Qasim's *āzān* had resounded through temples of idolatry [*but kadē*]."[91] Leading up to the present moment where Bano's story begins, Butt presents an entire history of the Muslim presence in the subcontinent, beginning, not surprisingly, with the aforementioned Muhammad bin Qasim and the conquest of Sindh, followed by the invasions of Mahmud Ghaznavi and Mughal rule. The Hindus of India, sensing opportunity in the arrival of the English, schemed against the Muslims with the new rulers of India, resulting in the formation of the Indian National Congress, a body Butt declares was loyal to the English. Though great Muslim leaders such as Syed Ahmad Khan tried their best to rehabilitate their people and gain representation for them in the evolving system, they were unsuccessful. It was, thus, not until Iqbal and Jinnah that Muslim consciousness was truly revived, and that, too, in a moment when,

Urdu had been replaced with Hindi and those who prostrated themselves before the pure God were being forced to bend to the likenesses [*mōrtī*] of Mahatma Gandhi. The Vidya Mandir scheme was imposed upon those dutiful ones who believed in the oneness of Allah. The educational programs for daughters of the *millat* included the ritual dances of the idol worshippers. Those who used to read poems praising Allah and Arab Prophet were now taught Bande-Mataram.[92]

Rehearsing tropes already offered by Hijazi, Butt writes the demand for Muslim separation from India entirely in terms of the threat that continued unity posed to Islam. The rallying voice for this version of events is Hasan, Bano's selfless young fiancé, who has become involved with the Muslim League while studying in Lahore.

There is opposition to Pakistan even within Muslims, and when Hasan visits Ludhiana for a family wedding, he spends much of his time convincing reluctant elders that "the English are our enemies. The Hindus are our adversaries."[93] In the debates that ensue, his cousins question Hassan as to why Islam has transformed into a passion when it is a religion, best left out of political causes. The pro-Pakistan movement members unequivocally answer this rather rational query through various markers of identity, including the clarification, "We are not Hindustani, we are Muslim, only Muslims."[94] At other times, Bano's anti-Pakistan brother, Saleem, is told, "We are first Muslims, then something other."[95] It is by listening to these debates among the men in her family and, of course, by way of her romantic association with Hasan that Bano thus becomes an active member of the Muslim League women's wing, attending various rallies and women's gatherings to spread support for Pakistan.

Nineteen forty-seven dawns in India, and daily life becomes more difficult for Muslims, with violence reported from Allahabad to Bombay. Though Hasan is in Lahore after passing his exams and becoming a successful engineer, much of the family, including Bano, her parents, and her brother, Saleem—anti-League Muslims—decide to stay in India, convinced that their Hindu and Sikh neighbors will protect them in the case of a threat. But when the violence finally reaches their neighborhood, their neighbors do nothing to stop the looters and killers. Bano's father, brother, and his pregnant wife are killed, but the mother and daughter manage to escape by feigning death, even as the rioters seek them out to rape and then kill. They find their way to a refugee camp where they begin the journey to Pakistan on foot. But the "*qāfilā*," the Arabic word for caravan, is soon attacked by other roaming looters. The young man under whose protection the refugees were traveling is killed, and Bano and her mother are taken captive by the looters, who take them to a small thicket where Bano's mother is made to watch her daughter being raped.

When Bano finally gains consciousness after being abandoned by the gang of rapists, she finds her mother is dead, and she is alone in her journey to Pakistan. She is saved by a kindly Sikh man, Sardar Goband Singh, who takes her to his home in a village nearby, where she is tended to by his mother and sister. But the villagers threaten the family for safeguarding a Muslim girl, and in the dead of the night, Goband takes Bano to Jalandhar, where he is able to put her on a refugee train going to the new Pakistan. The train, too, is derailed by attackers, and this time Bano is taken by another Sikh, Basanta, a man Butt describes as having "played *hōlī* with Muslim blood."[96] Obsessed with Bano, Basanta keeps her captive while his mother, Bebe, tries to convert her to the Sikh faith so that she can marry her captor. But Bano resists, despite the torture she has to endure, reminding her tormentors:

> You do not know the *qaum* whose honor I represent. I am that sister on whose plea the halls of Damascus trembled with rage. Muhammad bin Qasim traveled hundreds of thousands of miles to come to his sister's aid ... The Muhammad bin Qasims of my Pakistan are not that far away. Do not test me to the point where my screams reach their ears.[97]

But a hero such as bin Qasim is nothing more than a driving myth in this novel. Basanta rapes Bano regularly. She exists in a feverish, almost mad state; eventually she bears a child, living under captivity until one day Basanta dies in an accident and she, aided by another kindly Sikh who has recently returned to the village, is once again set on a train to Pakistan, this one carrying abducted women who were being returned to their families.

By now, Bano is barely rational, and upon being told she is in Pakistan, she falls to the ground, kissing the earth. She is placed in a women's shelter—one of the many that were set up in both India and Pakistan in the years following 1947. Hasan is located, and Bano finally goes to her rightful home. But in the five years that have passed, Hassan has become engaged to another cousin, Rabia, and in fact, is about to marry when news of Bano's return reaches him. Hasan brings Bano home, only to discover a broken and often delirious version of the girl he had been engaged to. Eventually, Bano realizes that she does not have a future with Hasan and runs away from his house, expecting that the new Pakistan will welcome her with open arms, that every home will have a space for her as their sister, mother, or daughter. At some point in her senseless wanderings, she is found on the steps of a mosque by a humble retired schoolmaster, Ramzan Ali, who takes her to his home and adopts her as a third daughter.

Slowly realizing that the new Pakistan is not a utopia, or even a place where there is justice for the good and the poor, Bano decides to work for a living. She finds a job as a nanny for a wealthy, young family, only to have her dreams dashed even further. The children call their mother "mummy" and their father "daddy," instead of "*ammī*" and "*abū*," their Urdu titles. She teaches them the *kalimā*, weans them from the English poems they normally recited, making them memorize Iqbal's poem, "A child's prayer [*bačōñ kī d'uā*]," instead.[98] She would return to Ramzan Ali's house in the evenings, bemoaning the fact that "These children have been entrusted to the *qaum*, they are the *qaum*'s future. While they should surely study English, they should treat it as another language . . . Our national language [*qaumī zubān*] is Urdu. What a sweet, wonderful language it is."[99] When she discovers that her employer does not breastfeed her baby, letting him feed from his Christian ayah instead, Bano admonishes her as well:

> Begum, if you do not give them your own milk how will they know the maternal bond? How can a Christian ayah nurture [*tarbiyat*] them the way they deserve? How will they become Tariq or Khalid?[100] How will they become Muhammad bin Qasim? You don't know, but there are still scores of our daughters and sisters in Hindustan.[101]

But her employers don't take kindly to such advice, and Bano is dismissed from her post. Her next employment is as a Quran teacher to the children of a woman named Hameeda, well-known to Ramzan Ali and his family. Though Hameeda is a good woman, her husband is a man of loose morals. Two months into Bano's employment, she comes to the house only to find the man alone at home. He tricks her into entering the empty house and rapes her, an act during which she keeps begging "Basanta," her Sikh ravisher, to leave her alone. This time, of course, her rapist is a Muslim and a fellow Pakistani. Utterly broken, Bano runs first to Ramzan Ali's house where she strangles her child, declaring that she has finally killed "Basanta," and from there, makes her way to Hasan's house. She finds Hasan at the verge of getting married to Rabia, but Bano's only concern is to accost him for having deceived her into believing that Pakistan was safe and pure. Surrounded by family and friends, she finally breathes her last, destroyed by the dream that she knows she sacrificed so much for.

Overcome by what the body before them represents, the men in the room, including Hameed, a cousin and a soldier in the Pakistan army, salute her and swear "that they will take revenge for you and prove that your brothers are still alive. The Muhammad bin Qasims of your homeland [dēs] are still alive."[102]

In an afterword penned for the thirtieth year anniversary of the novel, Butt wrote of a *qaum* that has stepped away from the path that had been determined for it fourteen hundred years ago (*jis kī rāheiñ čaudāh sau sāl pehle muta'aiyin kar dī ga'ī thī*).[103] There is little doubt that *Bānō*, the novel, was authored very much in the spirit of *iṣlāḥ*, the desire to correct and restore the citizens of a twentieth-century, postcolonial nation-state to their once chaste and preserved origins: Islam at the moment of its revelation. The construction of Bano as a heroine gives reference to Hijazi's novels, but also elaborates on the trials of a believing Muslim woman at a moment when the enemy is not merely a Hindu or Sikh, but a Muslim who has strayed from Islam. In engaging with Partition and the violence done to women both by the other and by their own, Butt takes up a question that until very recently was discarded or deliberately ignored by scholars and even writers of literary fiction.[104] But in doing so, she makes the Muslim woman into a symbol of Islam itself. Partition is necessitated not in the moment of the late colony, but from the moment that Muhammad bin Qasim invaded India. It is necessary in order to save Urdu, a language Butt equates with Islam; the Muslim woman, whose honor and purdah are threatened by a unified India; and Islam itself, the religion whose practice is impeded and interrupted by the nationalist bent of the Congress.

It is in her engagement with the new Pakistan, the supposedly sacred state whose foundations had been laid with the advent of Islam, that Butt unforgivingly holds up the female body as a final and merciless symbol of Muslim degradation. Bano is descended from earlier reformist characters such as Asghari Khanum, and her journey is the story of women living at a time when Muslim heroes are far and few. That is to say, if in Hijazi's works the *mujāhid* in the form of Muhammad bin Qasim saved the Muslim woman's honor, at the time of Partition and later, there are no such saviors. In fact, the *qaum* is so removed from its original morality that it requires the raped and dishonored body of Bano to hold up the mirror of its sins. The national narrative that Butt reinforces in this novel is an enduring one: The ravaged body of the Muslim woman has in the past, and should in the present and future, inspired the rise of warriors and conquerors such as bin Qasim, or Khalid bin Waleed. Even in Pakistan, the novel explicitly suggests, there is a need for Muslim heroes and Muslim reform for the nation-state, despite being made in the name of Islam, has utterly failed to honor and uphold its foundations.

In a similar vein is Butt's longer and multi-faceted historical novel, *Vaṭan kī Bētī*, the title an allusion to the young heroine, Mahrukh, who chooses to die in the name of her homeland's sovereignty. What Butt sets into motion through novels such as these is a dynamic participation of women in the continuous narrative of the Muslim *qaum*. Forced out of the protection of the home, these Muslim women offer themselves and their virtue as sacrifices in the name of Islam and its people. Set in sixteenth-century Golconda during the Qutub sultanate, the novel tells the story of an opulent and wasteful dynasty, whose enemies, the Mughals and the Marhattas, are actively plotting against it. Despite being a "Muslim" state, Golconda, under the rule of Tana Shah, is in a state of decline. Evoking the Mahometan of the oriental tale and the unreformed Muslim of reformist novel, Butt describes the palace as a "pleasure stop" and the sultan or Shah as usually to be found "in a wine-induced stupor, pouring a rain of gifts and accolades over courtesans."[105] His evil Hindu prime minister, Madna, a secret spy for the Marhattas, recognizing the possibility of a Hindu takeover, further encourages the ruler's habits, ensuring that soon "women and wine had become the purpose of the Shah's existence."

Given the Shah's lifestyle, most of the Muslims of Golconda, three quarters of the population, were poor and downtrodden, but the Hindus, thanks to Madna's power, lived in luxury, so much so that they "flattered the oppressed Muslims with offers of wealth and luxuries in a plot to make them change their religion [*mažhab*] and become Hindus instead."[106] Its other enemies, the Mughals, though Muslim in terms of the official religious affiliations of the rulers, threaten Golconda because of the kind of Islam that they represent. A fluid empire during a period known as the high point for multiple Indo-Persian aesthetic exchanges including Quranic calligraphy, music, and dance, the Mughal empire was blamed for the demise of Islam in India by the reformists (a narrative learned from colonial tracts on India, of course), and largely written out of historical novels by Sharar, Hijazi, and Butt.

Madna's ambitions, however, are kept in check by the Shah's other minister, a Muslim named Mir Haider, an honest man intent on ensuring that the government of Golconda continues to function. Haider has two children, a son named Shuja and a daughter named Mahrukh. Though both children are upstanding examples of courtly beauty, Mahrukh is an unusually talented young woman, skilled at the bow and arrow, as well as in "music and other graceful accomplishments," and who, in spite of her beauty, prefers a simple, almost masculine attire over the jewels and rich fabrics that other women of the court espouse.[107] Mahrukh's distinguishing quality, however, is her deep commitment to her "*vaṭan*," or homeland. When other women of the court speak of their desires or their romantic aspirations, Mahrukh speaks of her love for Golconda. There are no handsome princes or suitors in Mahrukh's dreams, for she "breathes the scent of her soil" and her "life's purpose and true ambition is her love for her homeland's [*vaṭan*] soil."[108] But Mahrukh's chaste dreams are soon interrupted: Her brother is in love with a palace courtesan called Nori, a woman who Tana Shah, the ruler, also desires and, in fact, goes on to rape one night. When the Shah later discovers that Shuja and Nori are in love with one another, he has Shuja put to death.

From this moment on, Mahrukh's father, Mir Haider, once so loyal to the throne and Golconda, now wants nothing more than to destroy the kingdom, and he decides to conspire with the Mughals, who have already captured the neighboring state of Vijyanagar and are now looking toward Golconda. Unbeknownst to his daughter, Mir Haider forms alliances with two Mughal spies, Adil and Murad, who become regulars at the court. Mahrukh falls in love with Adil, but when she discovers his actual identity, she chooses to expose him to the court, knowing that her love for her country is greater than any other. When Mahrukh eventually becomes aware of her father's changed loyalties, she attempts to dissuade him, pleading with him not to "sacrifice the state's benefit on the altar of his personal enmities."[109] "Golconda," she tells him, "is your own state, your own homeland, your own free, independent state, father. Freedom is a blessing."[110] But Mahrukh's warnings that the "snake-like" Mughals will only bring destruction to Golconda as they had done in Vijyanagar, fall on deaf ears.[111] Declaring herself to be a "daughter of the homeland" (*vaṭan kī bētī*) before she is her father's daughter, Mahrukh proceeds to travel to Hyderabad where she finds Argu Khan, the leader of Tana Shah's armed forces, and makes him aware of the plot against the state.

Through Mahrukh's intervention, the army is able to arrest Adil and Murad as well as Mir Haider. As she leaves Adil, the man she loves, in the hands of the Shah's army officers, she tells him, "Living without you will not be living, but my homeland [*vaṭan*], my nation-state [*riyāsat*] needed the blood of my love."[112] Finally, in the dramatic concluding chapter, Mir Haider comes face to face with his daughter in Shah's court, and upon discovering that she is the spy who has exposed and destroyed his plans to bring down the state of Golconda, he lashes out at her with a poison-laced sword before any of the army officials surrounding him can stop him. Mahrukh dies almost immediately from the wounds and the poison, and Mir Haider is led away in handcuffs. Even as the women in the room raise their voices in sorrow, the state's army steps forward and "salutes that life-sacrificing, devoted daughter who died for her homeland's honor [vaṭan kī ḥurmat]."[113]

The emphasis on the tentative formation that is *vaṭan*—as opposed to *ummāh, qaum, mulk*, even *riyāsat*—reads as a direct reference to Pakistan itself, the state that was founded as a "homeland" for India's Muslims. Whether we look at the impassioned speeches of M. A. Jinnah or the poetry of Iqbal, Pakistan (or the idea) is consistently iterated as a *vaṭan*, an implication, of course, that India was not and could not be a homeland. The nation-state, homeland, or *vaṭan*, to use Butt's term, is raised to the level of the sacred, to an entity that is above critique, and whose protection is the duty of every citizen. Golconda, threatened by Hindus from one end and bad Muslims—the Mughals and its own ruler, Tana Shah—from the other, is another Pakistan, the state that must protect itself from India and from its own, corrupt citizens. Butt's commitment to the idea of *vatan*, however, is merely a symptom within the longer evolution of Muslim nationalism in the subcontinent, a movement that I show in the concluding chapter, continues to see itself above and outside of its geographic location.

The true extent of Butt's hypernationalism lies in the privileging of the state military in both novels. *Vaṭan kī Bētī* first ran as a serial in the weekend supplement of the conservative, hawkish, yet much-revered daily, *Navā'e Vaqt*, in 1990—the same year, incidentally, when Pakistan's populist prime minister, Benzair Bhutto, promised a thousand-year war in Kashmir—leaving little doubt as to the metaphor that Golconda and the martyred Mahrukh represent.[114] Where democratic or monarchical governments fail, Butt seems to suggest, the military remains true in the service of the state and its citizens, saluting and pledging vengeance for the sufferings of Mahrukh and Bano. Likewise, Hijazi's novels upheld the *mujāhidīn* as an ethical body while the caliphate, or government, was depicted as an erring body in need of moral guidance—something it incidentally received from the exemplary *mujāhids* themselves. Whether in the role of an avenger for the Muslim woman as in *Bānō* and *Muhammad bin Qāsim*, or as a stable sign of state sovereignty, as in *Vaṭan kī Bētī* and *Dāstān-e Mujāhid*, the idea of an eternal Islamic army—warriors who fight in the name of Islam—is canonized in the Pakistani domestic imagination through the form of the novel.

Part of my task in this chapter has been to make a case for considering domestic, historically inclined novelists such as Khairi, Hijazi, and Butt as canonical, in fact, inseparable from the longer story of Urdu and

Pakistani literary development, which to a large extent has included only literary elites such as Intizar Hussain and Quratulain Hyder. To ignore the sheer command that this group exercised over both the popular and elite Muslim imagination leading up to Partition and in the decades that followed in Pakistan is to write a deliberately curated and inaccurate literary history of twentieth-century Urdu prose fiction. Their historical engagements, in particular, develop the Urdu novel as a form within which centuries of lived Muslim experience in the broader Indo-Persian complex are overwritten by a Muslim identity that has its origins in Mecca and the Umayyad caliphate. Premised in what is now nothing less than a sacred past, these narratives remain continuously relevant in the new Pakistan, whether in the case of Hijazi's novels that became essential texts for Zia-ul Haq's Islamization project, or *Bānō*, which is frequently reprinted or re-aired (as the serial *Dāstān*) at times of heightened political tensions with India. This, then, is the established canon of Urdu prose fiction by the end of the twentieth century.

5 / Modern/Mecca: Populist Piety in the Contemporary Urdu Novel

> Literature [*adab*] and the people related to it have done us a great service by expelling us from their ranks. We have become closer to the common people. Allow me to say that today when the common person reads works written by myself and other such writers, he or she is able to relate to our characters. They learn from our works; our works change them; the visible smile on their lips owes itself to popular fiction writers [*pāpular fikshun likhnē vālōñ*]; our works are the reason behind the fleeting tears in their eyes.
>
> The writings of popular fiction writers are just as useful or useless as those of established authors.
>
> ... Allow me also to say, that if it is true that literature has been proven the guiding torch during the tenuous and difficult times of a nation's history, then in twenty first-century Pakistan, this role will be realized by the writings [*tehrīreiñ*] of "popular fiction writers," and not the literary inventions [*takḷīqāt*] of elite artists [*adīb*].[1]
>
> —UMERA AHMAD

Though denounced as cheap bestsellers by literary scholars, critics, and aesthetes, the most influential Urdu novels written in the past two decades or so (post-9/11 years) remain those of popular writers such as Umera Ahmad, Farhat Ishtiaq, Hashim Nadeem, and Nimra Ahmad. In the face of the cultural capital commanded by these popular novelists, the *adībs*, characterized in the preceding epigraph by Umera Ahmad as the elite guardians of high literary culture, appear irrelevant. Little more than a footnote in the history of the present, the writers of high literature seem to exist at the margins of society. It is the domestically oriented novels of popular writers that now command the national character, Ahmad argues. A revolutionary writer, anointed by the average Pakistani reader, Ahmad recognizes her detractors' attempts to exclude her from the domain of literature (*adab*). Her novels and *afsanās*, however, have come to redefine the accepted norms of literariness in Urdu, and despite the odds, have carved an essential place for themselves in the longer history of the beleaguered nation-state that is Pakistan.

The remarkable, unprecedented success that Ahmad and writers of her ilk enjoy in present-day Pakistan—the same success that allows her to dismiss critics and artists associated with the category of *adab*, or high literature—marks the coming-of-age of a literary religio-populism in Urdu. The origins of this moment, this book has argued, lie in the orientalist endeavors and institutions of eighteenth-century England. In other words, Urdu novel writing in twenty-first-century Pakistan is distinguished and dominated *not* by the experimental, philosophical novels of Mirza Athar Baig, the deeply unsettling stories of rural Punjab by the internationally acclaimed Ali Akbar Natiq, the ironies of Nilofer Iqbal's short stories, or for that matter, by magisterial authors of the twentieth century, including Intizar Hussain, or the feminist poets Parveen Shakir, Kishvar Naheed, and Fehmida Riaz, but by a set of writers whose concerns are unabashedly religio-populist. Given the literary genealogies I trace in this book and the historical present within which these novels exist, I use the term "religio-populist" to mark a radical domestic order, defined its majoritarian evangelism, its exclusion and vilification of religious minorities, and its heightened anti-class/West consciousness, all of which take anchor from modern Salafi thought.[2]

These Urdu novelists are anti-elite; they position themselves against what they describe as a corrupt, "Westernized" establishment; their views on minorities and non-Sunni sects of Islam in Pakistan are nothing short of hostile; and most importantly, their moral claim to authority is always premised on the existence of a pure Islam, which in practice takes on an increasingly Salafi bent, and is both superior to the modern institution of the state, and yet is also advocated as a means by which the state can be saved. The rise and popularity of these populist writers is no accident of history. We cannot simply dismiss them as the children of the Pakistani dictator, Zia-ul-Haq's Islamization era, as many are wont to do. They are the immediate heirs of writers such as Razia Butt and Naseem Hijazi, but they are the longer descendants of a systematic categorization and organization of the Muslim subject in the colony and in the postcolonial nation-state, historical processes that have culminated in a powerful religio-populist impulse whose cultural manifestations are predominantly textual and visual. The historical continuity that these novels forge with reformist and nationalist writers force us to rethink their exclusion from the Urdu literary canon, and therefore, rethink the canon itself.

As I have argued earlier, literary and cultural histories of Urdu have largely ignored writers who failed to conform with Western teleologies of literary development and canon-making. Major writers such as Hijazi and Butt remain unaccounted for in the scholarship on twentieth-century Urdu literature, much in the same way that today, criticism and reviews in major Urdu journals such as *Dunyāzād, Sayyārā*, and *Urdu Digest*, literary supplements in the major (and politically liberal) English daily *Dawn* attend only to a fast-shrinking set of writers whose novels and *afsānās* represent a "progression" or "development" in tune with Anglophone or Western novel and story writing. The word "popular," when currently used in English criticism or scholarly work on Pakistani or Indian literatures and cultures is a positive term, signaling indigenous folktales in Punjabi, Sindhi, or Pashto, among other regional languages. "Popular" usually implies those oral forms that are increasingly sidelined in a state where Urdu is the single national language, but make occasional secular appearances in the Anglophone novel, independent theatre, poetry and some Urdu fictions.

But there is nothing as *popular* in present-day Pakistan as the seemingly non-literary, often low-brow set of writers who command deep influence in the triple nexus of the Urdu domestic digest, cheap weekly or monthly magazines descended from publications like Khairi's *'Iṣmat* and other women's journals that began flourishing at the start of the twentieth century. This "nexus," as I call it, begins usually in well-established digests such as *Shu'ā* or *Ḵavātīn* where writers first gain recognition and fame by way of well-appreciated stories and serialized novels. From thereon, these serialized or standalone fictions are published as novels with the last chapter available only in the published novel, a practice already mentioned in the previous chapter. Finally, a popular story or a bestselling novel is bought by a television channel and produced as a serial, a narrative form patronized by almost every class of Pakistani society, and though associated largely with women, is inevitably consumed by all members of a family. It is the contemporary equivalent, in more ways than one, of the nineteenth-century English domestic novel, or the America sitcom of the 1980s and 90s, consumed across social classes, multi-generational, even socially aspirational, but its legitimacy and popularity is underwritten by its attachment to Salafi Islam. The dismissal of this dense, self-affirming nexus of fictional forms as inconsequential or unworthy of close study by critics and academics alike has led to the writing of a skewed and positivist literary-cultural history of a state formed in the name of an intertwined language and religion.

It is worth noting that in recent years, the circulation of Pakistani fiction in English has gained some impetus with writers such as Mohsin Hamid, Kamila Shamsie, and Muhammad Hanif making regular appearances on the world literature scene in the United States, the United Kingdom, and Europe. Reading this suddenly bustling Anglophone scene in Pakistan as hopeful, perhaps even indicative of a "distinctly Pakistani literature," Aamir Mufti ventures whether "this new generation of writers [is] collectively producing in English, the epos of the nation?"[3] Mufti offers a genealogy of the Pakistani Anglophone novel that itself is culled from Orientalist-Anglicist tensions of the colonial moment, acknowledging the largely minor, mostly bourgeois and upper-class constituency of English readers in Pakistan today. And while it is true that several of these novels either challenge the national narrative through satire or even historical forays into centuries past, their claim to authentic representation of the "distinctness and scope of 'Pakistani' historical experience" is viable and imaginable only for their Western readers and critics.[4] It would be more accurate to say, then, that Pakistani Anglophone novelists, particularly Hanif, Bilal Tanweer, and to some extent, Shamsie in her later works, adopt an ironic, disenchanted attitude toward the idea of both nation and nation-state.

The populist Urdu novel *also* exhibits a disenchantment with the state and with the domestic affairs of what its predecessor versions—works by nineteenth-century reformists and twentieth-century nationalist writers—envisioned as the *qaum*, or the Muslim nation. The state, as most of these domestically oriented novels elaborate, is made up largely of a struggling middle class and an affluent but Westernized upper class that has entirely forgotten Islam in the pursuit of material and worldly pleasures. Institutions such as government and law have little role in these novels, though the Pakistan Army—as an instrument of Islam—makes an occasional appearance. The absent or struggling government and its attendant institutions are replicated on the level of the domestic where we encounter either impotent or dictatorial fathers, weak mothers, scheming mothers-in-law, and wealthy, bored young men. The heroines of these novels are young women who are inevitably described as "liberal" or "modern"—both words appropriated by popular writers to denote someone who is too Western, affluent, and thus out of touch with Islam's true teachings.[5] Alternatively, the heroine emerges out of the middle or lower middle class and arrives in an upper-class home as a prophet or reformer.

But this is not the comparatively benign reform of Nazir Ahmad or Hali, or the golden figures of Islam's history held up by Hijazi or Butt, all of which were offered in the service of the modern Muslim *qaum* (nation). In the religio-populist novels of Isthiaq, Ahmad, and Nimra Ahmad, the *qaum* fails as a viable or even relevant body and Pakistan, the revered *vaṭan* of Butt's novels, becomes secondary when posited against the sacred city of Mecca. Religious reform or a revival of past glories can no longer offer salvation from the menace of the West and enemies of Islam. The urgency of the present moment and its stark distance from the life and times of Muhammad, as these novels see it, call for the single, subversive act of *conversion*—a conscious and deliberate acceptance of Islam and its prescribed way of life. All of this takes place within the broad parameters of what broadly appears as domestic fiction, a terrain that is repurposed for radical ends.

My use of the term "conversion" shifts somewhat from conventional ideas of disavowing from one religion to another. I suggest that the religio-populist novel asks its readers to become Muslim on an entirely new set of terms and through processes that demand an *abandonment* or *death* of a past self. On a literary level, this is a departure from the general mode of domestic fictions where, for example, in a novel such as Samuel Richardson's *Pamela*, the hero is morally reformed and reconciled with the Anglican Church. We can consider, as Saba Mahmood has done, using the more historical situated term "Islamic revival," which "refers not only to activities of state-oriented political groups but more broadly to a religious ethos or sensibility that has developed within contemporary Muslim societies."[6] Mahmood's elaboration of the term, premised on a study of revivalist movements in Egypt, the aforementioned sensibility manifests itself through the "proliferations of neighborhood mosques and other institutions of Islamic learning and social welfare, in a dramatic increase in attendance at mosques by both men and women, and in marked displays of religious sociability."[7] The idea of "revival," however, gestures to a return, the re-enlivening and re-establishing of an accessible past order, better-suited, in the case of the Indian subcontinent, to describe the Muslim reform movement of the nineteenth century.

What I refer to as *conversion*, then, is the suspension of everyday belief, a phenomenon Gauri Viswanathan has described as "as a reference not to doctrinal authority but to the aspirations, understandings, expectations, needs, imagination, and goals that constitute the self-definition of people," and the subsequent isolation and reinvention of the self in a mode that is both "transgressive and assimilative."[8] In the act of conversion, the convert must sever ties with the past, and exist "at variance with the cultural meanings sanctioned" by his or her society.[9] Viswanathan's excellent study of conversion, though premised largely on the experience of colonial modernity, makes the case for "historicizing conversion not only as a spiritual but also as a political activity," an acknowledged reality even in revivalist movements.[10] Here, I make the case that in contemporary religio-populist novels in Urdu, the demand is not for the revival of a better and past Muslim practice, but for radical action. Given the failures of the Muslim nation, *qaum*, and the Muslim homeland, *vaṭan*, to uphold the Islamic values that once defined them, these novels place the onus of discovering and pledging oneself to Islam upon the individual, who upon doing so must abandon the worldly and material institutions that those around him or her continue to inhabit. The domestic itself, therefore, has to be reestablished; the marriage-plot is not merely about the reform of individuals, but the redefinition of marriage and family in entirely orthodox Islamic terms.

This Islam is promulgated as the pure Islam that the Prophet Muhammad preached and the Islam that was followed by his early companions, the first converts.[11] The language and emotive discourse which surrounds the conversion impulse that these religio-populist novels propagate is best exemplified by Muhammad Asad, né Leopold Weiss, the Austrian-Jewish convert, whose early career included a stint as the young Pakistan's minister of religious affairs. *Road to Mecca*, his autobiography of conversion, a much-celebrated work in the Muslim world, is the story of a young man embittered at a Europe in "upheaval and convulsion," who finds peace in his travels in the Arab world[12]—Palestine, Jordan, and present-day Saudi Arabia—by way of a people he saw as "spiritually so different from Europeans."[13] Whether Asad was a twentieth-century William Jones or Richard Burton is a longer question that demands a separate historical examination, but the rhetoric of his moment of conversion to Islam is worth some remarks.

Toward the end of his autobiography—told mostly through his travels in the Middle East—Asad arrives at Mecca, the center of the Muslim world: "Mecca had always been my goal. It called me long before my mind became aware of it with a powerful voice."[14] Islam, for this European Jew is "the brotherhood" he had been "waiting for ever since I was born."[15] The idea of Islam as a destiny or as a latent impulse within *all* mankind that needs only to be discovered through experience and self-recognition recalibrates Islam as a singular phenomenon, superior to other possible religious or secular moral experiences. Asad's terms are hardly original, clearly descended from Calcutta orientalists such as Jones, and German philosophers such as Herder. Present-day Muslims, Asad argues, have fallen into "the idolatry of progress," that is the result of "Western cultural influences," and hence are at risk of falling into the same abyss as Western civilization.[16] Asad's arguments regarding Islam and the West, which appear with some frequency in his volume, are in part reiterations of the Islamist ideas of the poet Muhammad Iqbal, considered a founding father of Pakistan, and in part, strident calls for a separation between a Muslim East and a Euro-American West. Asad's false distinction, the idea that "one could not really follow the call of Muhammad and still maintain one's inner links with a society that was ruled by diametrically opposed concepts," re-establishes for the purposes of the contemporary moment the constructs of Islam and Euro-America as fundamentally and eternally at war with one another.[17] In other words, an essential part of Asad's *individual* conversion is the re-inscription of the classical orientalist idea of the Muslim as incompatible with a Western modernity.

If the Urdu novels in question do not advocate a *literal* return to the pristine, peaceful deserts of Arabia, which played so essential a part in Asad's conversion, they take an unequivocal position against what they imagine as signs of Western modernity: women's clothing, professions, certain kinds of knowledge, technology (though often the plot is premised on cell phones and the Internet), class (where the upper-class is automatically seen as Western), "liberal" or unorthodox practice of Islam, as well as against minorities, particularly non-Sunni sects such as Ahmadiyya, who are, with full state support, deemed threats to Islam and pious Muslims. In several of the novels I examine, Mecca and Ka'abah appear either in the dreams or in reality to the converted protagonists, signifying their arrival at a single true destination, a symbolic spiritual marriage of sorts. This religiously underwritten, literary populism, if I may call it that, is at once subversive, in that it sees the true followers of Islam as rare and few in a country whose complete title is the Islamic Republic of Pakistan, but also mainstream, in that it is premised on Salafi Islamic tenets, and masquerades as non-discriminatory and universal.

These novels, as any novel in the history of the genre, do not exist in a historical or cultural vacuum—this much I have shown in my earlier examination of nineteenth-century reformist fictions and the twentieth-century nationalist novels in Urdu. On the one hand, the literary-historical contexts of novelists such as Farhat Ishtiaq, Umera Ahmad, and Nimra Ahmad are part of the long, unfolding shadow that orientalism and its attendant institutions cast in the colony two centuries ago. The legacy of the oriental tale and the orientalist scholarship that came in its wake—as traced over the course of this book—is overtly visible in the formal and plot elements of novels, such as Nimra's *Jannat kē Patē*, Leaves of paradise, and Umera's *Shehr-e Zāt*, City of the self, but also shapes Ishtiaq's *Humsafar*, Fellow traveler. In present-day Pakistan, however, these novels are an essential part of a dominant state and privately sponsored religious populism—perhaps the only applicable term—that has in recent years manifested itself in the form of discriminatory laws against the

Ahmadiyya; murderous mobs against Christian, Hindu, or even intellectual "blasphemers"; deeply conservative religious "academies" for women such as Al-Huda and Zainab Academy; pop-up and often military-supported political riots; and now formal parties such as the Tehrik-e Labaik Pakistan (TLP), who have begun to gain ground in local elections on the single-point agenda of labeling the Ahmadiyya as an internal threat to Islam.[18] The modes of thinking that inform these religio-populist acts and movements are inseparable from these novels, and must be considered contemporary iterations of colonial mechanisms, which instituted religion to exist and conform within the domain of the modern state.

This chapter offers a tentative conclusion to the gradual transformations of the oriental tale and the simultaneous metamorphoses of the Mahometan, that itinerant, marauding, shape-shifting libertine who defied Enlightenment ideals of nation and origin. We are well past the "moment of arrival," to borrow Partha Chatterjee's term for the moment in which a colonized people enunciate their desire for a modern nation-state.[19] The present moment—the accumulation of two and half centuries of orientalist influence—is beyond the pale of mere nationalism. In its most recent reincarnation, the oriental tale—once a versatile, politically resistant genre—is the vessel of a religious populism that obscures both national canons and secular aesthetic efforts. If in the contemporary Western imagination, the wandering Mahometan of the oriental tale reappears in the threatening guise of the abject Muslim migrant, then what of the so-called orient, the original stomping grounds of the Islamic potentate? In these utterly transformed territories and vernaculars—here, North India, Pakistan, and Urdu—the Muslim appears first as a reflection of his orientalist identity, the Mahometan, and subsequently as an entity needful of puritan reform that accords with the bourgeois morality of an emergent *qaum*. In the moment of arrival, the apparent climax of nationalist thought, the Muslim is reconfigured as a martyr, the sign of a virtuous and victorious past reclaimed by the nation-state. The present moment, terrifyingly alien, eerily comparable to a fascism the Western world believed was a thing of the past, is the natural child of nationalist thought, an exposure of the rupture that has always been contained in the idea of "nation-state," which as Hannah Arendt so presciently argued, is inherently a tenuous category, fraught by the tensions between nation and law.[20]

Conversion in the novelistic worlds of Umera Ahmad or Farhat Ishtiaq figures as a conscious act of allegiance, not to the state, but to the increasingly narrow and exclusive ideal of an Islamic collective or nation that now exists above and outside of political boundaries and civil institutions such as law and government. The novels and stories I examine often read as realist performances of Mahmood's ethnographic subjects of the Egyptian *da'awah* movement, oftentimes bearing extended theses on Quranic interpretation. That is to say, on a literal level these novels offer an alternative notion of agency, one in which the telos is not a Western version liberation or resistance but rather a slowly learned closeness to the Prophet Muhammad and to his nature of being. Mahmood, in her work both on the *da'wah* movement and elsewhere, questions the "secular-liberal inquisition," which she argues has intellectually marginalized piety movements in the postcolonial Islamic world by deeming them fundamentalist, conservative, or oppressive.[21]

While this may well be true from Mahmood's perspective as an anthropologist—one I am not in disagreement with—she evades grappling with the broader ramifications of how such movements unfold *within* the societies they criticize as "secular" or not Islamic enough. These questions are of urgent concern, one that should be taken up by humanists and social scientists with intellectual stakes in these societies. If we examine the histories of piety movements whether in Egypt or Pakistan, a task Mahmood evades, we know (as much of this book has tried to show) that the various organized versions of Islam we encounter in the present are themselves symptoms of the colonial experience, Deobandi, Barelvi, and Wahabbi being just a few examples. By eschewing a historical interrogation of these movements, Mahmood inadvertently ends up condoning the colonial legacies for religion and religiosity in colonized Islamic societies. Likewise, in Mahmood's quest to define her female subjects as agent individuals, albeit within a non-Western tradition, she elides a confrontation with the broader practices and beliefs of such piety movements, including the invention of antagonist others: liberals, Jews, queers, and minoritized sects, to name a few. Unlike veiling, these other elements of piety movements enable physical and social penalties for a wide variety of citizens in Islamic societies—intellectuals, queers, Christians, Hindus or Ba'hais and non-Sunni Muslim sects—many of which the law itself punishes with death or stoning.

I ask, therefore, that we consider present-day piety or revivalist movements in postcolonial Islamic societies in terms of their historical contexts as well as their far-reaching and expansive political implications. Thus, the claim that these movements—whether in their literal or performative forms—address themselves to the individual or emerge in the wake of a secular or liberal governance, is naïve at best, for it forecloses any critical examination of the newly created pious self. The rise of this new piety, I argue, is an indispensable element in the rise of a religio-centric populism in the post-colonial Islamic world that is anchored in various colonial pasts. The *performative piety* of the contemporary Urdu novel, therefore, cannot be treated, to use Abbas's phrase, as merely the "sympathetic novelistic portrayal" of religion, but very much as symptomatic of a coming-of-age of the totalizing colonial reorganization of Islam within the modern imaginaries of nation and religion.[22]

I begin my argument with the religio-class politics that undergird Farhat Ishtiaq's *Humsafar*, a serial novel—televised to record-breaking audiences in 2012—about a pious young woman, Khirad, and the trials of her marriage to her wealthy cousin, Ashar. The call to conversion, I subsequently argue, is accompanied by the invention of multiple "others," enemies of the convert and Islam. In the case of Umera Ahmad's *Shehr-e Zāt*, the conversion tale of a wealthy, westernized young woman, and Nimra Ahmad's *Jannat kē Patē* (2013), a novel about the heroine's journey to the *niqāb*, or veil, her previous life and those associated with it are characterized as the original enemies and naysayers of the Prophet Muhammad himself. In their most virulent form, these novels imagine religious minorities as active enemies of Islam and of the true Pakistani Muslim. Umera Ahmad's bestselling serial novel, *Pīr-e Kāmil* (2004), tells the story of a young Ahmadiyya woman's "conversion" to Sunni Islam, while Bushra Rehman's *Pārsā* (2011) rehearses the dangers that the Christian community of Pakistan poses to the country's Muslim daughters.

Pious Poverty: *Humsafar* and the Religio-Class Politics of Post-9/11 Pakistan

Humsafar, fellow traveler, first appeared in *Ḳavātīn Digest* from 2007 to 2008. It may have remained a popular serial story, published in a novel form after its completion, well-sold and reprinted within reasonable limits, were it not for its television adaptation in 2012. The production marked a momentous turn in the fortunes of its writer, Farhat Ishtiaq, who has since then rocketed from a middle-class pilot's daughter with a degree in engineering to the "queen of love" in Pakistan.[23] Overtly harmless, even trite, *Humsafar*, the romantic story of an orphaned young woman, Khirad, and her wealthy cousin, Ashar, captured the national imagination, and brought in its wake a new wave of serial plays that established the ideal Pakistani woman as pious, modest, and subservient. This is a far cry, of course, from the independent serials of the 1980s that often circumvented the restrictions placed on women's television appearances during Zia's Islamist dictatorship.

To briefly digress, the television serial had, since the late 1970s, at least—when middle-class Pakistanis gained widespread access to television—been an integral genre in the national imagination, known for its often-bold social critiques and comparatively risqué outfits and themes. At times conservatively nationalist, other times socially liberal, encouraging a progressive modernization of Pakistan's middle class by way of heroines who were working women, or through a critique of the feudal class and its treatment of peasants and women, the television serial up until the late 1990s exhibited a diversity of attitudes toward the work of its own genre. Its sense of purpose included but also extended far beyond the task of just imagining a national domesticity.

The golden period of the television serial, extending from the mid-1970s to the early 1990s, was remarkable and innovative precisely because television serial writers such as Haseena Moin and Noor-ul Huda Shah wrote screenplays exclusively for broadcast, as opposed to the practice of adaptation from digests and novels. The decline of the serial and of the industry had much to do with the fact that by the early 1990s, Pakistan still had only two channels—both state-run—while India's burgeoning television industry claimed many of its viewers in Pakistan thanks to satellite transmission.[24] It was only in the early 2000s under Pervez Musharraf, the military dictator to follow Zia, that Pakistan saw an apparent liberalization of media laws, and a sudden proliferation of local television channels. By 2010, the serial was well on the way to recovery with Hum TV's adaptation of Razia Butt's *Bānō* as a serial by the name of *Dāstān*. In 2012, *Humsafar* brought old and new viewers back to the television screen in record-breaking numbers.

Unlike these serials of yore, *Humsafar* marked a revival of the televization of popular novels. Writers such as Ishtiaq and Ahmad entered a mainstream that extends beyond digest readers to include the vast, at times overlapping breadth of television viewers as well. Given the almost literal adaptation of Ishtiaq's novel for the screen—only a couple of scenes were included for effect—I will in my reading turn occasionally to the television serial. To read *Humsafar* as a *rupture* from what some see as the once progressive, near feminist serial of the 1980s is a prescriptive solution.[25] I argue against a number of liberal critiques of *Humsafar* that despite the revitalizing role it has played for the digest-novel-serial cultural nexus as a fictional narrative it is neither innovative nor regressive. Likewise, it does not, as Jennifer Dubrow has suggested, mark a "resurgence of the Urdu cosmopolis in the digital and visual realms."[26] It inherits and perpetuates the politics of women novelists such as Razia Butt, albeit in a post-9/11 Pakistan. Given the expansive possibilities available to popular fiction due to television and now social media, a work such as *Humsafar*, or for that matter, earlier novels such as those by Butt and Nasim Hijazi, are ubiquitous. The significance of a work such as *Humsafar* lies in the transitioning of the Urdu novel from a position of reformative nationalism to one of rising populism. That is to say, the domestic and social politics of *Humsafar*—embodied in the symbols of the dutiful, pious wife, and her upper-class antagonists—conflate wealth with westernization, poverty with piety, domesticity with subservience, and modernization with loss of tradition. The encounter of a globe-trotting, areligious and heartless elite with the virtuous and faithful denizens of small-town Pakistan, does not conclude in reform or forgiveness, but rather in the death or utter destruction of those who refuse conversion.

Humsafar begins in the present with the scene of a simple young woman staring up at the heartless high-rise from where her wealthy but estranged husband, Asher, runs his corporate empire. The building she has come to stands "arrogant and proud," reminding her of her own lowly status in comparison to the "supremely expensive glass and concrete" that is before her.[27] Likewise, its inhabitants, are "showpieces of modernity," female secretaries dressed in western clothing (*maġhribī libās*), who exude pride and self-importance.[28] Dowdy in comparison, the young woman asks for Ashar Hussain, identifying herself as "Umm-e Hareem," the Arabic equivalent of "the mother of Hareem."[29] From there on, the plot of the novel unfolds. Khirad, the same young woman, had grown up in the small town of Nawabshah, far from the material comforts of the big city and the wealth commanded by her uncle, Asher's father. After her father's early passing, Khirad and her mother find support and comfort in their neighbors, a family with whom their connections went back to pre-partition India and the migration to Pakistan. When her mother, Maimuna, falls ill with cancer, the two women are summoned to Karachi by Khirad's maternal uncle, Baseerat, a man who until then had little time for his impoverished sister. Baseerat arranges for the best treatments but Maimuna knows she will die. Before passing, she asks her brother to promise that his son, Asher, will marry Khirad. Though the match is initially opposed by both Baseerat's wife, Fareeda, and Asher, an emotional Baseerat forces them to relent and Khirad, orphaned and alone, is married to her handsome, Yale-educated cousin.

Ideally, this would conclude a good romance, but the mystery of Khirad's visit to the man who is now her estranged husband occupies much of the novel. What is clear from the opening sequence is the nature of the trials that Khirad, the heroine of the novel, will face. She is not merely positioned against the simple schemes of a jealous rival, but against the cold capital and power that the embrace of a Western modernity has brought to Pakistan. The early days of her marriage to Ashar are surprisingly happy. Used to the "modern" (*māḍurn*) women of his own class, who openly flirted with him, Ashar discovers that "he had never seen such simplicity, such innocence, and such honesty" as he found in Khirad.[30] In the television serial, Khirad, whose name means wisdom, is played by the fair, wide-eyed Mahira Khan, and is dressed in long flowing *kamīzes*, which are further always covered by a dupatta or scarf.[31] For Ashar, she is "so pure [*ḵāliṣ*], so rare, and so precious," as to make him question all that he believes in.[32] He loves Khirad not for her intelligence or her beauty, categories he was previously attached to, but because he comes to believe that she had been made exclusively for him. "No matter how liberal [*libral*] or modern a man is," the narrator tells us, "a woman's modesty [*ḥayā*] always appeals to him."[33] In sharp contrast to Khirad is Sara, Ashar's rather westernized cousin, a fashion designer by profession. Sara, we are told, was desperate to marry Ashar only to be foiled by a girl she considers well beneath herself. On screen, Sara is played by the tall and dark-complexioned Naveen Waqar, who dresses in black jeans and black blouses in every episode of the serial. Among Sara and Ashar's other friends, "high society's [*hā'ī sōsā'itī*] extremely modern women," Khirad is made uncomfortably aware of her "lower-middle class" origins.[34]

But trouble soon begins brewing. Baseerat, her father-in-law, also passes away, and though Fareeda, his wife, has never openly shown her disgust for Khirad, we learn that she had been angrily forced by her husband into accepting the match. A professional woman who runs an NGO, Fareeda's concern for the poor is portrayed as largely cosmetic, in accordance with state and popular propaganda against charitable organizations and their work in Pakistan.[35] She is described to us as a "feminist," who tries to ruin Khirad's innocence by teaching her lessons of "freedom and equality."[36] But her attempts to alter Khirad's subservience to Ashar through both material pleasures and ideas fail and she is forced to more desperate measures.

Fareeda; her sister, Zareena; and Sara join hands against Khirad, who in the meanwhile has enrolled in a math master's program at a local university. Knowing Ashar's jealous temperament, they bribe a distant relative, Khizar, who is also enrolled in Khirad's program, to trick her into coming to his apartment one afternoon. Believing herself to be chaperoned by Sara's mother, Khirad, who, by now, unbeknownst to Ashar, is a couple of months pregnant, busies herself in the apartment with some light kitchen work. But when Ashar, just returned from a trip to Dubai, is manipulated into entering the apartment with Fareeda, he finds Khirad alone with Khizar, who performs his role perfectly by declaring that he and Khirad have been having an affair. Fareeda who has been waiting for this moment all along—and has knowledge of Khirad's pregnancy—loudly bewails Khirad's infidelity and lack of gratitude to her son, while Ashar, swallowed by jealousy leaves the apartment without hearing out the weeping Khirad. When Khirad makes her way home, she finds only Fareeda, who gives her an hour or so to pack her things and leave. Pushed out of this mansion, Khirad finds herself alone in a neighborhood where the narrator tells us, "When someone died, the neighbors would not find out for days. Ensconced within these grand palaces, who would hear the weak pleas of a single girl sitting on the edge of the street?"[37]

Noorafza, one of the housemaids, finally comes to Khirad's rescue, for despite being "poor and illiterate, and never having heard of MIT and Yale," she "was more able and sensitive to human nature than these educated people."[38] Knowing Khirad to be innocent, she arranges a lift for her to travel to Nawabshah and take refuge in the home of her old neighbors. These small-town people with their simple morality and daily piety allow Khirad to live in their home, where she gives birth to her daughter, Hareem, and finds employment that allows her to support the child. But Hareem is soon discovered to be suffering from congenital heart disease and Khirad's modest salary cannot afford any treatment. It is in these circumstances that she returns to Karachi and finds herself at Ashar's office building—the opening scene of the novel. When Ashar accepts that Hareem is indeed his daughter, and takes charge of her treatment, Khirad discovers the "power of money" for "the fact of the matter is," the narrator reminds her readers, "that no matter how much the rulers of this country tell us about progress and development, basic resources along with access to healthcare are inaccessible to ordinary people."[39] Ashar secures an apartment where he begins to secretly live with his daughter and estranged wife, managing hospital visits and medical appointments. Khirad's role, naturally so, is reduced to domestic tasks, as well as repeated acts of prayer, and frequent recitation of Quranic verses in an attempt to secure Allah's mercy for her ailing child. Her power, the narrator constantly emphasizes, lies in her selfless role of a mother, above all.

Khirad's chaste and empowering maternity is in sharp contrast to that of Fareeda—a woman who seems to care nothing for her son's happiness, unwilling to accept his marriage to a wife of humble origins despite the apparent care and public largesse her vaguely described NGO stands for. Ashar's dramatic confrontation with his mother upon his eventual discovery of her duplicity is told by the narrator as a public spectacle where it is the narrator's voice that issues the final judgment upon Fareeda:

> With what wisdom [ḥikmat] did god ensure that this little girl's illness remained hidden. Allah's knowledge of what is best [maṣleḥat] was surely behind Ashar's decision to keep her away from everyone. But from you, Fareeda, Allah took away your life's reward [ḥāṣil], He snatched your son from you, and Allah's grip is a hard one. When He takes revenge for the weak, He ensures that there is no place between earth and sky where sinners [gunāhgār] like yourself can find refuge [panāh].⁴⁰

It is worthwhile to closely read this passage to understand the politics that inform Fareeda's fate and actions in the novel. For one, Hareem, Khirad and Ashar's child, is named to signify the inner sanctum of the Ka'abah, the symbolic center of the Muslim world. In guarding Hareem from his mother, Ashar becomes the unknowing guardian of purity as well. He is guided not by a rational consciousness, but by Allah's ḥikmat, literally wisdom and reason, but also medicinal and curative sciences. Fareeda is punished not for a private act, but for her arrogance and for the misuse of her power against Khirad and Noorafza, the poor but God-fearing and pious characters of the novel. Fareeda is destined to wander alone as punishment for her sins, while Ashar begs forgiveness from Khirad. The encounter between Fareeda and Khirad is staged as a battle where Khirad emerges victorious because of her piety and chastity, while Fareeda is stripped of the object she held most dear: her son. The true hero of the novel, however, is Allah himself. The way the die falls is not, as in the realist novel, human or chance-driven. Divinity is the *only* driver of the plot.

Along with Fareeda, other villainous characters meet various unsavory ends. Sara, Ashar's glamourous cousin, who is literally "ill with the West," or "west-stricken" (maġhribzadā), commits the unforgivable sin of suicide upon discovering that Ashar has reunited with his wife and child.⁴¹ Khizar, Sara's cousin who had helped frame Khirad, earns enough money from his crime to escape to the United States. But Khirad and Ashar, the narrator finally concludes, were two "travelers" (musāfir) who had "traversed difficult terrains" to find each other, and who now live with the promise and future of the sacred "Hareem," a simultaneous gesture to both their daughter and the inner sanctum of Mecca.⁴²

Though the liberal critiques of *Humsafar* (and similar works) have rightly focused on gender and the celebration of the subservient chaste woman, their points of reference have extended no further back than the television serials of the 1980s. But *Humsafar* has a much larger sphere of influence and a more powerful claim than merely that of reform. Women and their bodies are, no doubt, indispensable instruments of the new populism, but they are subsumed under a more compelling and popular politics of religiosity, which employs class and its attendant attitudes to invoke ending, and breaks with the old self, here signified by the "modern" Fareeda and Sara. It is Khirad, sustained by her piety, wisdom, and her willing subordination to her husband, who survives the trials that wealth and westernization throw at her. Saved from the sins of the upper class and their worship of Western modernity, Ashar finds both spiritual and material "refuge" (*panāh*) in the pious Khirad.[43] Through Ashar and *his* redemption, the novel advocates conversion or the recognition of a holy presence within oneself. Thus, *humsafar*, though formally used to indicate a life partner, refers as much to an earthly companion as it does to god or Allah, the only beloved.

Overcoming *Jahiliyyā*: Conversion in Umera Ahmad's *Shehr-e Zāt* and Nimra Ahmad's *Jannat kē Patē*

The reviled modern woman of *Humsafar* returns in the novels and short stories of Umera Ahmad and Nimra Ahmad (the two are not related), this time as the protagonist and subject of conversion. Currently two of the highest selling writers in Pakistan, celebrated figures in the world of women's digests and television serials, Umera and Nimra's works revolve around the trials faced by the rare, truly Muslim women of Pakistani society. Mecca, a symbol in *Humsafar*, gains renewed significance in works such as *Shehr-e Zāt* and *Jannat kē Patē*, which liken the present moment to *jahiliyyā*, the pre-Islamic period in Arabia. Mired in a society that is as ignorant, illiterate, and pagan as pre-Islam Arabs have historically been dismissed by modern Muslims, the protagonists of these novels become contemporary avatars of early Muslims. Their enemies and detractors who perform the historic role of the recalcitrant Meccan tribe, the Quraish, are now liberal, modern, wealthy Pakistanis, who in place of Allah, worship the West. The domestic predicament is rewritten in these novels as historically equivalent to seventh-century Mecca, but spatially it is located in twenty-first-century urban Pakistan and derives its values from a virulent pan-Salafism. Though the works I discuss in this section ostensibly trace the journeys of their female protagonists from a state of *jahiliyyā* to piety, the attainment of piety is a condemnation of certain class practices as well as of fluid and lived expressions of Islam that do not conform with Salafi doctrines.

Umera, the author of some twenty or so novels in addition to a number of short stories, is a household name in Pakistan. Born in 1976 in the industrial city of Sialkot, which was once known as the birthplace of Muhammad Iqbal, the nationalist poet, Umera has brought Sialkot a second wave of fame. After completing a master's degree in English literature from the once-missionary Murray College, Umera worked briefly as a schoolteacher at an army school until finally giving this up to work full-time as a writer. Her earliest serial novel, *Zindagī Gulzār Hai*—literally, life is a flower garden—was published in *K̲avātīn Digest* in 1998, and was picked up for the screen in 2012, becoming the next big hit after *Humsafar*, bringing Umera into the spotlight of Pakistan's now booming television industry.[44] Today, Umera is an almost corporate brand; she runs Pakistan's first "digital publishing platform," Alif Kitab, in addition to a team of writers who now work on a number of digest stories and television projects under her name. The television adaptation of her latest serial story, *Alif*, signifying Allah, is a mega-budget production shot in Istanbul and Karachi, and boasts the biggest names of the local industry.

One of Umera's early works, "Shehr-e Zāt" (City of the self), was published in the "novel section" of *Shu'ā Digest* in 2002, and made into a television serial in 2012, starring Mahira Khan who rocketed into fame after *Humsafar*. The notion of the self, alluded to in the title of the story, is not a material or literal one, but rather an allusion to the core meanings of the Arabic word *zāt*, the essence or substance of an individual. The city of self, then, is a gesture toward a spiritual construction, the human body as the self-sufficient structure of Allah, a lesson the heroine, Falak, learns after her forays in the material city.

Falak Sher Afghan is the beautiful, college-going daughter of wealthy but misguided parents, Sher Afghan and his wife, Maimuna (renamed Mehrunissa in the television serial). At the onset of the story, Falak is described to us as "liberal," a flaw that is attributed to the fact that her parents failed to give her the right "*tarbiyat*," that is, the right moral and spiritual education.[45] We are told that

> She had read the Quran once in her childhood, and since then had not felt the need to turn to this sacred book. Like her mother, she was unacquainted with the concepts of prayer and fasting. She believed that in this day and age to be religious [*mazhabī*] was a rather antiquated [*daqyānūs*] thing.[46]

Though the idea of "*tarbiyat*" takes us back to the initial moment of Muslim reform, in particular, Nazir Ahmad's *Taubat an-Nasuh* where North Indian Muslims are instructed on the importance of imparting a spiritual education to their children, Falak's problem is more urgent.[47] A child of her moment, the narrator suggests, Falak thinks of religion, in this case, Islam, as something temporal that has little relevance in the twenty-first century. It is worth noting that Ahmad uses the word "*daqyānūs*" when pointing out Falak's perception of Islam as antiquated—literally, the word refers to the Roman emperor, Decius, who persecuted the seven believing Christian youths for their beliefs, but himself became irrelevant with the passing of time. Faith, however, lived on and the story of the seven sleepers, also found its way to the Quran, where the believing young men are the ones who survive their persecutors. There is prescient irony in Falak's dismissal of religion: It is she who is *daqyānūs*, the narrator hints.

When Falak sees a man by the name of Salman Ansar at a party, she decides to pursue him, despite the fact that she has enough men and proposals to her name. Her brief pursuit is successful, Salman agrees to marry her, but the terms of the marriage are hardly equal. Falak

> molded herself according to Salman's tastes. She could not imagine doing anything against Salman's wishes, and she started wearing only those colors that Salman liked ... Things Salman liked to eat suddenly became her favorite foods and that which Salman seemed to avoid, she began to hate. All this would happen without Salman having to say anything. He had never asked her to do anything, but she wanted to keep him happy.[48]

Overcome by her love for Salman, a man who does not seem to reciprocate, Falak worships a false god. In the television serial adaptation of the story where Falak's artistic skills are fleshed out in some depth, a good part of her relationship with Salman plays out with Falak as a modern-day Pygmalion, reverently gazing at a male bust she has created herself. The implications of this passage are clear enough: Falak's absolute subservience toward Salman is the subservience one should have toward Allah. She is akin to the idol worshipping Quraish tribe that Muhammad was sent to reform. But unlike Allah, Salman does not return the love he receives, instead he is unmoved by it.

Things take a strange turn after Falak insults a poor beggar who happens to cross her path one day while she picnics by the river Ravi. The beggar, a mystic in disguise, warns her against her ways, but Falak and Salman, both arrogant in their dismissal of such people remain unchastised. In a matter of a few months or so, Falak begins to notice a change in the otherwise pleasant Salman. He has little to say to her and avoids coming home. After several attempts on her part to understand this atypical behavior, he finally reveals that he is in love with another woman and wishes to marry her immediately. Falak is shocked; she wonders whether her rival's beauty surpasses hers, only to discover that this woman is a plain-looking secretary at Salman's factory. She tells Salman he has her permission to marry a second time—as is his shariah-given right in Pakistan. In a hysterical frenzy she calls her mother and levels a single accusation at her: "Mummy! You did not teach me how to love Allah. You did not teach me how to find Allah."[49]

Falak suffers a "nervous breakdown" after this realization—a favorite event in popular novels—and her recovery is marked by her conscious journey toward the Allah that Maimuna, her mother, had denied her. But the new Falak who prays, speaks of "Allah, god, possessor [*rab*], master ['*āqā*], deity [*m'abūd*]," and roams around in wrinkled clothes, her face unadorned by makeup is only a source of fear and "dread" for Maimuna, who is convinced that her daughter has gone mad.[50] After hearing the story of the famous Abou Ben Adhem from her housemaid's daughter, Falak understands that she must actively find Allah, a task that she fulfills through prayer and by becoming a kinder person, generous toward the poor and abject. She begins draping her body in a shawl, reading the Quran in English translation, and when the month of Ramadan comes around, she fasts and spends time at a local mosque. When her mother dismisses this as "*junūn*," or madness, Falak reminds her that it is she, with her expensive cars and palace-like home who is mad.[51]

At the right moment—that is, when Falak is assured in her knowledge and love for Allah—a repentant Salman arrives at her parents' home, desirous of taking Falak back to his home. His second wife had left him after taking much of his money and he had realized that it was Falak whom he really loved. Though Falak agrees to return home with him (they have never divorced!), she warns him that she is not the woman he was once married to:

> I will come with you, but I want to tell you that the Falak you married four years ago is now dead. The woman you wish to take with you today is someone else. For that Falak, you were everything. For me, Allah is everything. Everything about the old Falak was in appearances. Everything I have is within [*bāṭin*]. She used to enjoy seeing a show, even being one. I don't like either of these things. She spent her life in society. I want to spend my life in my home. She didn't know how to hide her faults or her body. I want to conceal both. If you want to take me home despite these things, I can come with you. If not, you don't have to destroy my life and yours, you can just leave.[52]

Barely comprehending what Falak has said, Salman agrees, and the story concludes with them on their way home. Salman is playing an "English cassette" and humming along to the song, while Falak wonders how it is possible for one to love another human after they have learned to love Allah.[53] Noticeable in Falak's speech to Salman is the totality of her conversion. Characterized as the death of a prior self, conversion, in Falak's context, is a subversive act. In converting to a Muslim who seeks and loves only Allah, Falak leaves behind the material pleasures of wealth to which her family and husband remain attached. Through conversion, Falak sees escape from a rootless and capitalist patriarchy which makes her a victim of her husband's actions or her parents' worldly pursuits. In devoting herself to Allah only, the story argues, she is liberating herself from the trials that non-believers suffer in this world.

As in *Humsafar*, the villains and the subsequent have-nots of the story are members of an upper-class who are inevitably liberal and westernized. That is to say, wealth is automatically conflated with a lack of piety and a love for all things Western. The old, unconverted Falak frequently breaks into English and sprays herself with Chanel 5, while Salman listens to English music. The pious, on the other hand, appear in the form of beggars and servants, and it is only through a spiritually driven kindness to the abject that the errant wealthy can eventually find redemption. The oppositions offered in the story are contemporary Pakistani renditions of oppositions so frequently found in English and vernacular oriental tales: princesses encountering *faqirs* or dervishes in disguise; royal arrogance reformed through harsh lessons. A supposed end where the princess reunites or finds a princess, however, is rewritten with the princess's discovery of Allah. Although the narrative advocates a rejection of the evils of a westernized patriarchy, it only offers an alternative, albeit divine, patriarchy as an alternative. The converted Falak, though liberated from any hurt Salman may inflict in the future, now subordinates herself to a system that requires her to cover her body, disavow past pleasures such as makeup and perfume, stay within the home, and presumably influence the eventual conversion of her husband as well. In the television serial, the final scene shows Falak as a mother, asking her young daughter whether she has offered her prayers and then praising her for having done so. A new domestic order is born here, where the family unit is not father, mother, and child, but, in fact, believing Muslims and Allah, the latter protecting the former from their unbelieving family members.

All of this is blown up to large-scale geographical and spiritual proportions in Nimra Ahmad's opus, *Jannat kē Patē*, a novel that spans from Islamabad to Istanbul, the site of the final Islamic caliphate. Nimra is the author of almost twenty novels, the best known of which are usually concerned with the conversion of a female protagonist, followed, inevitably, by a romantic resolution with a fellow Muslim. Unlike Ishtiaq and Umera Ahmad, Nimra remains a shadowy figure, hesitant to appear in public or to sell her novels for television adaptation. On occasion, she has offered written interviews and engaged with readers' letters in women's digests such as *Shu'ā* and *Ḵavātīn*, both instrumental to her writing career. Little is known about her personal life, other than small facts such as her devotion to Islam and her commitments to female gatherings of Quran readings and *dars* (religious lectures).

Her bestselling novels include *Mushaf*, the story of an orphan, Mehmal, and the strength she gains from her reading of the Quran; and *Namal*, the story of an intelligence officer, Faris Ghazi, his false conviction of murder, and the efforts of his pious, believing relatives to find justice. The latter is named for the Quranic surah Namal, or The ants, which tells the stories of Solomon, Moses, and Lot. *Jannat kē Patē* (literally, the leaves of paradise) was serialized in *Shu'ā Digest* 2012–13 and appeared as a novel in May 2013. A reference to the Quranic "leaves of paradise" that Adam and Eve used to cover themselves upon discovering their nakedness, the novel is the story of a young woman from a bourgeois family and her journey toward taking the *niqab*, the facial veil, in a society that has otherwise forgotten the tenets of Islam.[54] The site of her conversion is not Pakistan, but Istanbul, a city she visits as an exchange student also in search of her first cousin and husband, Jehan Sikander, a spy for the Pakistan Army who operates under the alias of a Subway franchise on Istaklal Street in Istanbul. Described by its author as a "*farzī dāstān*," or a *dāstān* about religious obligations, *Jannat* is at once a thriller, a romance, and a conversion novel, replete with lessons and verses from the Quran.[55]

A work such as this one, then, offers some finality to the longer journey of the oriental tale into the orient, and subsequently into the postcolonial nation-state. According to Nimra's introduction, the novel is a *dāstān* about adherence to certain "sharia laws," a task that a wayward society often makes difficult for the believers.[56] Although ideally readers of the novel should also observe these laws—principal amongst them the order for women to cover their hair and faces—they should at the least "refrain from becoming the Banu Qurayza during the Battle of Ahzab."[57] In referencing the betrayal of Muhammad and his early band of Muslims by a Jewish tribe that they considered an ally during the historic battle against the Quraish of Mecca in 627 A.D., Nimra asks her readers to consider the believing converts of their own time, the present, as none other than the earliest Muslims, a beleaguered minority surrounded by enemies of their faith. In doing so, she recreates the present as a decisive moment in the history of Islam. Finally, her use of the term "*dāstān*" (a term I have situated in some detail in Chapter 2) to describe a novel about religious obligations for women is itself a crude paradox, a gauche appropriation of a fiction form that persistently defies hegemonies of all kinds.

The winding and tortuous plot of the novel begins in the capital city of Islamabad, where we are introduced to Haya, the college-going daughter of a well-to-do businessman. Haya, we are told, has just been selected for an exchange program at Sabanci University in Istanbul, an opportunity that she is doubly excited for. In her naïve mind, Istanbul is a Western city, a place where she will be free of the strictures placed upon her by her father and elder uncle, who lives next-door to her family. Istanbul is also home to her mysterious cousin, Jehan Sikander. As children, the two cousins had been wedded to each other by their parents through a *nikkah*, or Islamic wedding ceremony, and Haya still considers Jehan her legal husband. But Haya's father, Suleman, it seems, has long given up on Jehan or the viability of the unconsummated child-marriage and has in recent weeks begun entertaining other proposals for Haya, a prospect his daughter is unwilling to entertain. Haya's resolution is further affirmed when one potential candidate, Waleed, the son of her father's business partner, tries to molest her after engineering to be alone with her in his car. She is mysteriously saved from serious assault by Dolly, a *khvajah-sirrah*, a local term for the cross-dressing transgender community of Pakistan, who after saving Haya, reminds her that her predicament was caused by her *bē-ḥayā'i*, or immodesty.[58]

The series of tumultuous events that occur in the first twenty or so pages of the novel direct the reader to contemplate the heroine's name and its implications for the rest of the novel. *Ḥayā*, an Arabic word for chastity and modesty, takes the same meaning in Urdu as well. Rooted in the Arabic h-y-a, *ḥayā* extends into *aḥiyyat*, the life-giving part of a woman, and from there in Urdu, into life. It is the same term used by Mahmood's Egyptian subjects with regards to veiling and reappears in Ishtiaq's *Humsafar* as well. Also close to "*havvā*," the Hebraic title for Eve, the original life-giver and the first woman to know the feeling of shame, the name Haya, then, carries an inevitable fate. Thus, when Haya's mysterious savior accuses her of transgressing the bounds of modesty, we know that in some sense Haya has suffered Eve's fate and must now redeem herself by arriving at the knowledge of her sin, that is to say, by converting and reclaiming her *ḥayā*, or modesty.

Predictably, this does not happen immediately. Prior to her departure, Haya finds out that a video of herself and her cousin, Irum, dancing at her brother's wedding is circulating on the Internet under the title of "*sharīfoñ kā mujrā*," or a public dance by *sharīf* women.[59] *Mujrās*, usually performed at weddings by transgender dancers or prostitutes in South Asia are associated with indecency. Haya manages to find a short-term solution to her predicament by reporting the video to the national cybercrime cell, where a man by the name of Major Ahmad assures her that the video will be removed, and her reputation will remain untarnished. But the two events do not convince Haya that the free and easy life she lives is sinful. She persuades her father to let her go to Istanbul for the semester so she can meet Jehan and decide the fate of the marriage she is committed to. For Western and even some readers within Pakistan, Haya and Jehan's child marriage may appear otherworldly and anachronistic, but for the purposes of the novel it is one of the several re-enactments of early Islamic society. The reference here is to the commonly held perception that the Prophet Muhammad wed his best-loved wife, Aisha, when she was nine years old.

At Sabanci University, Haya meets her roommate, Khadija, a high-spirited girl from Pakistan, who becomes a constant companion. She also has her first somewhat confusing encounter with Jehan, though on subsequent visits to her aunt's house she discovers more about her elusive husband and his mannerisms. For one, she finds out that her aunt, Sabeen, her father's sister, lives in Turkey, not out of choice but because her husband, once a member of the Pakistan Army, had been accused of being a traitor and defector. As a result, Jehan, his mother, and his now mentally and physically ailing father, are exiles in Istanbul where Jehan manages a Subway outlet. Though Jehan is often moody, hot and cold in his interactions with Haya, we know of his ultimate virtue soon enough, for when he prays, his offering is "deliberate and overwhelmingly calm."[60] In these early days of her Istanbul adventure, Haya, however, does not pray or pay attention to the tenets of Islam.

Despite Turkey's secular and Europeanized exterior, it soon becomes apparent to Haya that all is not as it seems. On a visit to Buyukada, the largest of the Princes' Islands near Istanbul, Haya's purse is stolen and when she runs after the little urchin who has taken it, like a "princess who has lost her way," she finds herself in front of a "sultan's palace."[61] She enters the building only to be welcomed by a woman who seems to know everything about her, including her past in Pakistan. She is told that a smuggler by the name of Abdurrehman Pasha owns the palace and that he had seen her once at a hotel in Islamabad and has been desirous of marrying her since. Later on, we find out that Pasha is, in fact, Jehan, who also masquerades as Major Ahmad of the cybercrime unit, as well as the eunuch, Dolly—all roles designed to learn about Haya, test her, and perfect her as his wife. Jehan's extended project to make Haya into a "*marih jamīlā*," Arabic for a "beautiful, chaste woman," begins in Pakistan with the incidents such as the dance video and goes deep into Turkey where both her experiences and her company persuade her to change her ways.[62]

After the purse-snatching incident, Haya experiences a personal tragedy—her roommate Khadija dies suddenly of a brain aneurism. Haya has to grow up overnight and take on the responsibility of transporting Khadija's dead body back to Islamabad. Jehan decides to accompany her back to Pakistan, where he meets his extended family after many years, though he mostly keeps to himself, brooding or going off by himself for work. Terrified by Khadija's death, Haya's father suddenly announces that Haya will not be returning to Sabanci to complete her semester, a decision is that nothing less than a prison-sentence for his daughter. Jehan steps in and convinces his uncle to allow Haya to return, promising that Haya will now live with her aunt and uncle, instead of in the university hostels. Upon returning to Istanbul, Haya spends a couple of weeks with Jehan and his family, and then returns to the hostels. But within a day or so of returning, she is suddenly kidnapped by a Russian gang who keeps her captive for a couple of days, during which she is mostly kept sedated, only waking with pain when a new name, "Natasha," is branded onto her arm. She realizes that she is the prisoner of one of the prostitution rings she has heard about. When she screams for help, "the Russian," as her captor is identified, tortures her to a point that she passes out with pain.[63]

Upon waking, Haya finds herself in a pleasant room, a beautiful young woman attending to her. Ayeshe, her caretaker, tells her that she had been picked up by one of the many Russians, Moldovians, and Ukrainians who frequently kidnapped young female tourists and sold them as "call girls," and that Natasha is a common moniker for prostitutes in Turkey. After being saved by a police raid (clearly engineered by Jehan), Haya had been deposited with Ayeshe, and her little sister, Bahare Gul, who identify themselves to Haya as Pasha, the smuggler's nieces. Half Iranian, half Turkish, Ayeshe and Bahare Gul live in a cottage on Buyukada, where they spend most of their day crafting boxes and knick-knacks to sell to tourists. Bahare is just a child, but Ayeshe is a mature and practicing Muslim woman who soon becomes a major influence on Haya.

Advised to stay away from Istanbul for a few days, coincidentally also her spring break, Haya soon settles into Ayeshe and Bahare's simple life, an experience that begins to transform her. It begins with conversations on head-covering, during which Haya reveals to Ayeshe that though she often thinks about covering her hair, she is discouraged by what people around her would say. "I cover myself," Ayeshe tells Haya, "because Allah likes me this way."⁶⁴ Women, she further explains, are akin to the sand on a beach. If the sand remains on the beach, it is stepped on or becomes muddy when taken into the ocean. "But that bit of sand which decides to cover itself in a strong shell becomes a pearl."⁶⁵ Likewise, these pearl-like women must refrain from using perfumes or other seductive materials, lest they become "muddied" by the world.⁶⁶ By the end of the break, Haya has started covering her head. Though the headscarf is banned at Turkish universities, Haya returns defiant to Sabanci, telling those who admonish her on breaking the law that she is a guest in the country and thus is outside the purview of the law. When relating her success, she tells Ayeshe, "I have defeated Sabanci, I have defeated Ataturk."⁶⁷

Haya, in other words, sees herself as having "defeated" the imposed secularism that Mahmood has argued revivalist movements are a reaction to. At another point in the novel, Haya recalls how when her father and uncle tried to convince her to cover herself, they only tried "force to impose their decision upon her."⁶⁸ The mistake these men made was they never told Haya "about Allah." Instead of deciding for her, "they should just have tried telling her about Allah, and then they would have realized that every Muslim girl, young or old, a soft branch or a hardened clay, has the same heart. A heart that after hearing about Allah prostrates immediately."⁶⁹ We can read Haya's reasoning as one iteration of Mahmood's argument, which thinks of agency as "not simply a synonym for resistance to social norms, but as a modality of action," through which "action does not issue forth from natural feelings, but creates them."⁷⁰ For Mahmood's subjects, the realization and practice of *al- ḥayā* through veiling is a means of teaching the body to actively desire it.⁷¹ The mosque participants of Egypt's Da'wah movement are "strongly critical of the nationalist-identitarian interpretations of religiosity because these views treat the body primarily as a sign of the self rather than as a means to its formation."⁷²

Before moving further into *Jannat ke Patē*, it is worth noting that this novel, like others in this chapter, actively enacts and explicates the notion that veiling is an act of agency in the terms that Mahmood designates. Mahmood's carefully theorized argument works well within the bounds of theory and has served as an important intermediary for Muslim practices to Western audiences, liberal and conservative alike. But the *claim* that is made by Mahmood's subjects in Egypt corresponds to that made by women novelists such as Umera and Nimra Ahmad. Ayeshe's metaphor of the woman as sand functions as a metaphor of the body, largely on the lines elaborated by Mahmood's subjects. If we read Mahmood *in the light of* works such as these ones—novels that I argue are religio-populist in nature and argument—the question of context becomes increasingly urgent. A close reading of Haya's reflections shows Haya as reinforcing an undesired earthly patriarchy with a spiritual one in which Allah is the ultimate patriarch. Even as she or Ayeshe discipline their bodies as instruments for the realization of a pious self, they do so under the sign of a patriarchal system that is culled from modern religious laws that have themselves been fashioned as part of the colonial project. What Mahmood has failed to appreciate in her study is that women's Islamic revival movements, or in this case, *conversion movements*, are themselves part of the extended influence that orientalism exercised over the question of who a Mahometan or Muslim even was. That is to say, the subjects of her study, or the characters of the novels I examine here, are directly descended from, and in conversation with, colonial institutions—schools, curricula, literature, among other—that shaped the *political* fashion in which Islam came to be perceived by Muslims in the nineteenth and twentieth centuries.

Disguised as journeys that seek an authentic and chaste Islam unadulterated by Western or Indian ideas, novels such as *Jannat kē Pattē* actively create a new national subject that imagines itself as disenfranchised on account of its piety. The young convert's most vehement opponents and critics come from the "liberal," upper-class to which he or she often belongs. While this class is inevitably morally and financially corrupt, the convert disrupts this order with a set of moral attitudes toward Pakistan and the world that derive directly from the life of the Prophet Muhammad and the perceived Islam that he preached in his lifetime. This preference for Salafist Islam is, in fact, the search for origins that orientalist scholarship claimed Muslims lacked, a claim that I have shown acquires deep importance in Urdu literary writing from the late nineteenth century onward. After her conversion, Haya's naysayers become enemies, infidels who threaten Islam and its teachings. In Haya's case, covering her hair is not enough, and she seeks further guidance upon return to Istanbul from Buyukada. She begins attending seminars on the Asian side of the city, incidentally also the site of the first mosque in Turkey and, inspired, also starts to veil her face.

Haya's conversion and second life extend beyond the personal. Like the mythologized women of Muhammad's time, she becomes involved in the greater battles of Islam. When the Gaza Freedom Flotilla is captured by the Israeli Navy, days after Haya's conversion, her response is not "to change the channel after expressing sadness at the news," as it would have been had she been in Pakistan. Here in Turkey, she was "a part of the pain and trouble" that was afflicting the Muslim world.[73] The students of Sabanci, we are told, don shirts and carry posters bearing slogan such as "Hitler used to say, had I wanted to kill all the Jews I could have, but I let a few hundred go so that the world could understand why I had killed their other folk."[74] They walk toward the Israeli embassy chanting "Down with Israel," and until June 6, 2010, when the captives are finally freed, Sabanci and Istanbul remain cloaked in grief and anger. Through her involvement with Freedom Flotilla, and that too in Istanbul, a city that is forcibly imagined as a political capital for twenty-first-century Islam, Haya actively defends her globally threatened faith. Her enemies, thus, are not merely those who oppose her conversion, but also those who oppress her religion and its people, i.e. Jews and the West. The reductive politics and the violent rhetoric that accompany a rightful protest are celebrated in the novel as the actions of a believing Muslim subject.[75]

Meanwhile, Haya's romantic life has improved. Jehan has accepted her as his wife and wants to marry her afresh. His father's health, however, is declining. As the summer holidays come around, he passes away. Jehan is missing at the time and Haya accompanies her aunt to Pakistan for the funeral rites, not knowing that Jehan's absence means he is away on a secret mission. Jehan misses his father's funeral but arrives in Islamabad late one night, deciding to stay for a few months while his mother settles into widowhood in Pakistan. Even as things look bright for the young couple, Haya's father, Suleman, suddenly suffers a massive heart attack, which renders him hospitalized and bedridden for several months. Given that Haya's brother, Rohail, is in the United States, it falls on her to take her father's position at his company, a task that comes with its own set of obstacles.

For one, Haya's immediate family, including her mother, have not been supportive of her decision to take the *niqāb*, or face veil. When Fatima reminds her daughter that she used to be "modern" once, Haya equates her past to the "*zamānā-e jahilliyā*," or period of ignorance, much in the same way that Umera Ahmad's Falak imagined her pre-conversion, "liberal" past.[76] In the workplace, she encounters her old nemesis, Waleed. Her uncle, Furqan, once an ally, now sees her as a threat, declaring himself alienated by his niece's facial veil. Meanwhile, Jehan has once again disappeared, following a fight with Haya who had mistakenly come to believe that he, too, opposed her decision to veil. Later, we discover that it was Jehan who, in fact, had engineered the events in Haya's life that led her to cover her hair and face. In Jehan's and her father's absence, the "strength" (*maźbūtī*) that Haya had recruited to take the *niqāb* and face naysayers has to be directed toward the office where Waleed and her uncle try—unsuccessfully—to ambush her.[77] She withstands their enmity, running the business profitably from her father's CEO desk until he is well enough to return to work.

When her father returns to the office, now purged of enemies such as Waleed, Haya decides it is time to go search for Jehan. She returns to Turkey, where she reunites with Ayeshe and Bahare, and finds Jehan, who is in the middle of mission. This time around, Jehan tells Haya about his actual line of work. Much of the second volume of the novel engages with his perspective. We discover that his purpose stems not from a simple patriotism, but for a desire to give his life to "Allah's path" (*allāh kī rāh*).[78] That is to say, as a spy for the Pakistan Army his allegiance is to the state of Islam, not Pakistan necessarily. His three identities, Major Ahmad in Pakistan; Jehan, a Subway franchisee; and Pasha, the smuggler in Turkey, have emerged over the course of his career, the last after being taken as a prisoner by the Indian army during one of his spy assignments. Having suffered terrible torture in India, he is in need of a surgery for which he and Haya travel to Ankara. Haya nurses Jehan in the days following, and their mutual love and trust grow as they prepare to return to Pakistan to celebrate the marriage that was solemnized in their childhood.

In the last part of the novel, a few loose strands are tied up. Waleed is given his just desserts by Jehan. Haya's brother, Rohail, it is discovered, has decided to marry an American girl, ironically also named Natasha. Haya and Jehan's marriage is celebrated alongside that of Rohail and Natasha's. When Haya goes to the salon before her wedding, she is able to dress as a proper Muslim bride: hair arranged to allow for prayer, no nail color so as to perform ablutions, no false eyelashes because Allah does not like them, and no threaded eyebrows because Allah dislikes those even more. Instead of showing her face to the wedding guests, she decides to keep it entirely covered in the traditional "*ghūngat*" style.[79] When the beautician asks her if she is from Al-Huda, a major Wahabbi women's movement and institution in Pakistan, Haya replies that she is "just a Muslim girl," finally identifying herself as the single, chaste exemplar of a pure religion.[80]

A final chapter is a flash forward to several years later where Jehan and Haya are now parents to a little girl but are debating taking on a mission in Cairo, Egypt. The novel ends without resolution to this question, but the draw of Cairo as a site of Islam's early glories is obvious. To save

Pakistan's wayward Muslims, converts such as Haya and Jehan must journey to other parts of the Islamic world, seeking knowledge through which to return their people to Islam. The politics that accompany such organized conversion movements, then, advocate a worldview that, as seen earlier, is violently antagonistic to those perceived as Islam's enemies, but imagines sites of Islam's imperial pasts as regenerative and affirmative, whether they be Istanbul, Cairo, or even Palestine. It is this Islam-centric orientation that compels us to think of these novels in the terms that I offer here, rather than as merely common domestic novels.

It is thus impossible to ignore the intertwined nature of these organized religious movements—textual or practical—with a nationalist sentiment that is not necessarily directed at the nation-state. In *Jannat kē Patē* or *Shehr-e Zāt*, the *ummah*, or global community of Muslims, is imagined as a series of rigid, sometimes historical abstractions, obliterating what Mufti calls "the myriad of forms and lived experiences of Islam."[81] These novels unabashedly condemn the various ways of imagining and practicing Islam, including those local to South Asia, or those that do not visibly perform piety. They elaborate, on the other hand, Mahmood's notion of certain "socially authorized forms of performance" as the "potentialities" or "the ground" "through which the self is realized."[82] These socially authorized practices, then, come to signify the pure Islam through which contemporary piety movements claim legitimacy as a condition for enabling this self-realization. Falak and Haya perform their newfound piety, through verbal elaboration, the disciplining of their bodies, altering their attitudes toward the world outside of their faith, and practicing obedience toward their husbands. In Falak's case, conversion ensures she stays with an unfaithful partner. In the television serial, she receives guidance from the added character of her grandmother, who repeatedly tells Falak and her mother how divorce is disliked by Allah and Muhammad. Haya, on the other hand, finds religious instruction through the series of "accidents" that Jehan engineers, and only once she gains spiritual *"maźbūtī,"* or strength, can she claim her role as his wife.

For many Pakistani women, these novels exemplify self-realization or even a legitimate form of social empowerment that is premised on the relinquishing of physical and legal freedoms, including the right to divorce. More properly, they are symptomatic of the "conjuring trick" of the "new anthropology of Islam," by which the historic complexities of Islamic societies "disappear from view altogether."[83] In the place of this teeming variety, Mufti argues, comes a "configuration of contemporary political Islam" that is "Salafi-revivalist in its constitutive gestures."[84] The "elaboration of these religio-cultural practices," he continues, is undertaken by "an intelligentsia consisting largely of middle-class professionals with (very often) a scientific or technical education."[85] There is no better example than the writers of these novels, engineers, English teachers, and housewives, who in their adopted occupations are sensational preachers, first, and romance novelists, second. In the context of a postcolonial state such as Pakistan, the appropriation and re-elaboration of this Sunni-orthodoxy by novelists writers such as Nimra and Umera Ahmad is an essential part of a growing, state-sanctioned religious populism that defines itself as much through class lines as it does through a political theology.[86]

The Hypocrites: Minority in Umera Ahmad's *Pīr-e Kāmil* and Bushra Rehman's *Pārsā*

The greatest sinner in the stories and teachings of the Quran is the *munāfiq* or hypocrite, a figure who masquerades as a Muslim but inwardly poses a threat to Islam and the Muslim community. In various revelations, Muhammad is repeatedly warned against a particular set of people who would come to him, claiming to be Muslim, but whose behavior and allegiances would suggest otherwise. The hypocrites, the Quran tells believing Muslims, breed evil, abandon virtuous behavior, do not spend in Allah's name, and above all, are rebellious.[87] A designated and anonymous figure in Quranic contexts, who Muhammad was instructed to quietly accept as a member of the community, the hypocrite is a common antagonist in the popular Urdu novel. While the liberal or modern Pakistani can be redeemed through his or her conscious conversion to Islam, the hypocrite is an internal enemy and insidious presence in any Muslim community. For a number of reasons, including the ease of identification and the peril that such a figure's purported economic mobility may pose to Sunni believers, the hypocrite, in these religious novels, is conflated with minority Muslim sects and minor communities such as Christians, the majority of whom live in abject poverty in urbans slums across the country.

For the most part, minorities—whether Shi'ite Muslim, impoverished Hindus, or ethnic minorities such as the Baloch—have simply been written out of mainstream Pakistani narratives. Naturally, then, the Pakistani protagonist is assumed to be a Sunni Muslim, whose life unfolds in or as a journey toward one of the major urban centers, Karachi, Lahore, or Islamabad. Historically, exceptions to this narrative were present in the nostalgic, oft-times devastated novels of the renowned writer Intizar Hussain, and more recently, are visible in the nuances of Ali Akbar Natiq and the stories of Punjabi writer Nain Sukh. But in popular contemporary novels, the same novels that Umera Ahmad has claimed are beacons of light in the darkness of Pakistan's present, the minority is reintroduced to the mainstream as a dangerous and disloyal citizen whose presence inevitably augurs destruction.

The question of minority is important given that Pakistan itself was carved out of the greater Indian subcontinent as an autonomous haven for Muslims. Likewise, liberal narratives of the state history are quick to cite Muhammad Ali Jinnah's first address to the constituent assembly of Pakistan, which famously enjoined citizens to go to their temples, mosques, or any other places of worship they may choose. Jinnah died soon after the creation of Pakistan, and his questionably secular creed increasingly seems like an obscure moment in the country's seventy-three-year existence. The category of minority in a state that within a couple of years of its existence declared itself as an Islamic Republic, furthermore, was principally negotiated in religious rather than ethnic terms. That is to say "non-Muslims," the state's official term for Christians, Hindus, and later the Ahmadiyya, constituted minor groups, were ostensibly to be given the same rights as the state's majority Sunni population.[88] Constitutional mismatches between a mostly colonial bequeathed parliamentary style law book, a parallel shariah legal system, and frequent bouts of martial law have effectively dealt a death-blow to any aspirations to equality on the part of these groups.

Mainstream fiction, such as the novels this chapter examines, takes a more specific target: upper-class, bourgeois minority figures whose economic and perceived social capital enables them to circulate amongst middle- and upper-class Muslims. One of the most widely read and reprinted of these works is Umera Ahmad's *Pīr-e Kāmil*, a novel about the conversion of Imama, an Ahmadiyya woman, to Sunni Islam, while parts of its sequel, *Āb-e Ḥayāt*, take on the question of what fates await unrepentant Ahmadiyyas. A staple item at booksellers ranging from the elite, mostly English-selling Liberty Books, to makeshift stands at train stations and airports, *Pīr-e Kāmil* reiterates with no uncertainty who is Muslim and what constitutes Islam in twenty-first-century Pakistan. The novel's title, "the perfect mentor," has a double function, at once signifying those who live their life like the Prophet Muhammad as well as Muhammad himself.

If we read *Pīr-e Kāmil* in the contexts of the moment in which it is written, read, and celebrated, there will be little doubt as to the politics it espouses. The epigraph in place of a dedication is a Quranic verse in which Allah addresses Muhammad, reminding him that he has been raised in the eyes of mankind through dedicated acts of *žikr*, or remembrance.[89] Thus, the novel positions itself as more than just a romance: It is a religious act, the praise of the Prophet Muhammad, and a work of fiction, which re-establishes his status as the ultimate messenger of Allah. But this is not an innocent act of faith or a prescriptive fiction in which good reigns and evil is destroyed. Ahmad both responds to and participates in what over the past few decades has been a systematic effort on the part of the Pakistani state to mark the country's Ahmadiyya as internal enemies, threats to the establishment and to Islam itself.

The history of the Ahmadiyya sect in Pakistan is a long one, the details of which are beyond the scope of this discussion, but a brief contextualization is important. Founded roughly in 1880 by Mirza Ghulam Ahmad, a resident of the city of Qadian in colonial Punjab, the Ahmadiyya movement was initially seen as a reformist effort that positioned itself against the activities of colonial Christian missionaries. Ghulam Ahmad's claims soon changed from declaring himself a *mujadid*, or renewer of faith, to identifying as the Mahdi, an apocalyptic figure whose appearance is foretold in the Quran. But it was his reinterpretation of the principle of "*Ḵatam-e nabūvat*," or the finality of Muhammad's prophet-hood, that led to a series of condemnatory *fatvahs* against him from the North Indian *'ulema*. Despite some support from the colonial government, Ahmad was seen as a false prophet, one of several who were predicted to threaten the sanctity of Islam after the death of the Prophet Muhammad. The colonial government continued to recognize and count the Ahmadiyya, or Ahmad's followers, as Muslim, and *fatwahs* by one set of *'ulemas* against another were a common practice in the larger North Indian Muslim community post-1857. The most significant pre-independence blow to Ahmadi Muslims came from the poet Allama Muhammad Iqbal, who declared the sect non-Muslim in a series of newspaper articles, a political move through which he extricated himself from accusations of familial ties to Ghulam Ahmad.

Though opposition to the Ahmadiyya claim had begun in earnest by the mid-1930s, spearheaded by the religio-political Kashmiri party Majlis-e Ahrar-e Islam-e Hind, it gained new confidence with the creation of Pakistan as a Muslim homeland. The 1953 Ahrar-led effort against the state's seemingly conciliatory attitude toward Ahmadis turned violent, leading to the first imposition of martial law in the infant country. From thereon, the issue remained a flashpoint in Pakistani politics, gaining stronger ground in 1974 when the democratically elected, cosmetically secular People's Party prime minister, Zulfiqar Ali Bhutto, declared the minority sect non-Muslim, an edict that is now enshrined in Pakistan's constitution as the Second Amendment. Bhutto's own end came at the hands of the Islamist dictator, Zia ul-Haq, who further forbade the Ahmadiyya from proselytizing or affixing Islamic symbols atop places of worship. This brief history of the Ahmadiyya minority in Pakistan, of course, does not include continuous small-scale events such as assassinations of community leaders, extortion of known members, daily discrimination in schools and workplaces that in recent years have spread to shopping arcades and other urban sites.

In the novel, we are introduced to Imama, the protagonist whose name signifies a female leader, or *imam*, a term with diverse valences across various Islamic sects. The daughter of a wealthy Ahmadiyya businessman, Hashim Mobeen, Imama is made to question her beliefs by friends at school and college. She learns early on that Sunni Muslims consider her and her family to be heretics, a charge she innocently defends by asserting that the Ahmadiyyas believe in Muhammad's prophet-hood, but also in another prophet who is as "worthy of reverence" as Muhammad.[90] This crude summarization of what is a more complex set of beliefs sets up the Ahmadiyya faith from the beginning of the novel as one that is incompatible and heretical to pure Islam, here embodied by a set of Sunni characters. Imama's first antagonist, or guide, her school friend, Tehreem, thus tells her that her sect is worse than Hindus or Christians, for the latter do not make false claims to Islam. In other words, the Ahmadiyya sect is a sect of *munāfiqīn*, or hypocrites.

Imama's family, her friend, Tehreem, goes on to tell her, was not originally wealthy or Ahmadiyya. Her grandfather was a poor farmer who happened to live near Rabwah, the designated administrative center of the Ahmadiyya sect after the creation of Pakistan. Seduced by a friend, Imama's uncle begins to travel to Rabwah and "converts" (*mažhab iḵtiyār*) from Islam to the Ahmadiyya sect, and subsequently becomes incredibly rich, a change that inspires the rest of the family to convert as well.[91] Imama's family, Tehreem tells her, is not the only one to benefit from conversion; the majority of converts (*yēh kām karnē vālē*) were convinced by monetary bribes, not belief. When Imama accosts her father after hearing Tehreem's version of events, he ascribes her accusations to a conspiracy on the part of Sunni *maulvis*, but the damage has been done and Imama begins to view her community's practices with suspicion.

Imama's conversion to Sunni Islam, though initiated by Tehreem, is realized during her medical school days, away from the influence of her family. Sabiha, a fellow medical student in Lahore, invites her for *dars*, or religious lectures at her home. Taught by Sabiha, the lessons revolve around the perfection and finality of the Prophet Muhammad. Imama is increasingly attracted to what Sabiha tells her about the Quran, and to the fact that Muhammad's perfection concluded mankind's need for another prophet. This logic, of course, belies the flat presentation of Ahmadiyya belief in the novel. Fearful of the persecution she will face from her community should she convert, Imama lays her case bare to Sabiha, who has become a spiritual guide for her. Sabiha urges her to convert to Islam, telling her that "the answer to every question is inside you. You know, all you have to do is to pledge your belief [*iqrār*]."[92] Imama finally converts—the moment is wrought with uncontrollable tears and emotion as she repeats the *kalima* after Sabiha.[93]

To her family, Imama has to be silent about her conversion, for Hashim, her father, had in the meanwhile arranged a marriage for her. When she finds out in the days following her conversion that the wedding is imminent, she tries to convince Hashim to end the engagement. Failing to do so, she then asks one of her classmate's brothers, Jalal, to marry her. But Jalal's parents, hypocrites of another kind, refuse, more concerned about what people would say if their son married a girl of Ahmadiyya descent than about helping Imama as their "religious obligation" (*mažhabī farīža*).[94] The young convert's trials appear endless until she settles into a strange arrangement with one of her brother's friends, Salar, a rich and spoiled young man who, despite having an IQ of 150, spends most of his days reading Western philosophers such as Nietzsche, visiting prostitutes, and performing acts of self-harm. It has so happened that the medically trained Imama had earlier helped save Salar from an attempt to kill himself. Indebted, Salar initially tries to convince Jalal to marry Imama and, failing that, offers to file a paper marriage with her, saving her from having to marry back into the Ahmadiyya sect whose beliefs she now reviles.

Salar and Imama—through various secretive efforts, including a smuggled cellphone—enter into a *nikkah* or marriage with each other. When Hashim finds out that Imama can no longer marry Asjad, the Ahmadiyya man he desired her to marry, he resorts to physical violence and to keeping Imama captive in the house. She eventually escapes in the middle of the night with Salar, who drives her to Lahore, where she finds refuge with Sabiha's extended family. After reaching safety, Imama asks Salar to divorce her and set her free, but Salar, taking perverse pleasure in Imama's situation, does not relent. In the meanwhile, however, his own journey to Islam has just begun. Despite having spent most of his youth drinking, visiting red light areas, and wasting his parents' money, Salar manages to get admitted to a number of Ivy League schools and decides to attend Yale Business School as a graduate student. Though his first year is spent reveling in his old habits, his second year is marked by a series of alarming incidents. He becomes seriously ill for the first time in his life and begins to contemplate death and his purposeless existence. Shortly after, he returns to Pakistan for a holiday, but he is attacked by a gang of young men during an evening jog who take all his possessions and leave him bound and trussed with no means of calling for help. The moment is transformative, for the captive Salar realizes how little his life is worth and prays to Allah to give him one last chance. He gets this chance and from thereon, embraces Islam wholeheartedly.

He returns to New Haven after the holidays and begins his "new journey" (*nayā safar*) as a Muslim.[95] He starts Arabic classes at the Islamic Center close to campus under the tutelage of an Arab named Khalid bin Abdurrehman. He decides to dedicate his exceptional mind to memorizing the Quran, believing that the act will cleanse him of his past sins. When he is close to finishing this pledge, his teacher, Khalid, informs him that he dreamed of him performing the Haj and urges him to perform the major pilgrimage. Salar is convinced, and in the brief scene of his first visit to Mecca, we are told that as he stood among Muslims he understood his own insignificance and "rid himself of any remaining traces of arrogance, self-centeredness, desire, egotism, and pride."[96]

After graduating from Yale, Salar visits Pakistan where his conversion is further tested and consolidated. Though his liberal parents accuse him of extremism and embarrassing them with his newfound piety, his friend, Furqan, takes him to meet Dr. Sibte Ali, a religious scholar and mentor. Unlike other religious scholars, who the narrator tells us are divisive and sectarian, Dr. Sibte is humble, even self-critical.[97] An inspiring speaker who lectures Muslims in cities such as London and New York, Dr. Sibte is a learned author and university professor who has taken it upon himself to bring change to Pakistan by guiding young Muslims such as Salar, Furqan, and we discover later, Imama as well. Salar has taken a job at the United Nations in New York after graduating, but his meeting with Sibte makes him consider returning to Pakistan to serve his country through Islam. Within a year or so, he acts on his religious conscience and returns to Islamabad where he begins working at a bank, all the while also attending university seminars on "economics and development," two fields he has severe reservations about. During this time, Salar sets up a school in a village between Lahore and Islamabad, having realized that the "poverty of the country had conveniently been hidden in its villages."[98] In his private life, he has realized that he is no longer like his family. He sees himself as a "*mōmin*" (true believer), the opposite of the "sybaritic" (*'ayāsh*) class that he has been born into.[99]

Imama has begun to invade his thoughts after his conversion. He even sees her in a dream where he is, once again, in Mecca, and Imama is alongside him, but in reality, there seems to be no trace of her despite a couple of false leads, including a letter in which it appears that she believes him to be dead. Salar spends his days working and his evenings with Dr. Sibte who continues to mentor him, until one day he happens to give an elderly lady a ride home. Though Salar pays little attention to the old woman's ramblings about her daughter, Amna, events are forced to a point where one day, Dr. Sibte himself, who also happens to know the lady, Saeeda, asks Salar to consider marrying the mysterious Amna. Salar tries to muster up the courage to tell Dr. Sibte that he is married already, but Dr. Sibte approaches him with prior knowledge of the fact. Salar confesses his earlier *nikkāh*, but Dr. Sibte's only response is to assure him of Amna's suitability and to congratulate him on being "*ṣāliĥ*," or virtuous, a quality that one only attains after overcoming one's personal "*zamānā-e jahāliat*," or "era of ignorance," a term that specifically denotes pre-Islamic Arabia.[100] Salar's journey, Dr. Sibte tells him, is almost complete for now that he has attained the particular state of being properly "*ṣāliĥ*," Allah will demand his service.

But when the day of the *nikkāh* draws close and Salar arrives at Saeeda's house to meet his bride, he discovers that Amna is none other than Imama, who since cutting ties with her parents had, through her Sunni Muslim friends, found help in the form of Dr. Sibte and his family. We find out that the elderly lady Salar had helped is Dr. Sibte's widowed cousin, who had willingly adopted the hapless Imama when she discovered the girl's predicament. Imama returns to the novel's narrative as Amna, the convert, who is embraced by a community of true Muslims, the leader or "perfect mentor" of which is Dr. Sibte. Imama's own story from the moments after Salar dropped her off in Lahore is finally revealed to readers. Dr. Sibte, whose daughter was also a friend from medical school, not only arranged for Imama's adoption, but also had her personal documents altered, helped admit her to a program in pharmacology in the southern city of Multan, and paid the fees for her continued education. The early days of her new life were a "difficult and painful time," but as time goes by she acquires more "*ṣabr*," the Quranic term for "endurance," at times "resignation," a state from which the Quran historically always promises some kind of deliverance.[101] Eventually, she finishes her degree, returns to Saeeda's home, and begins to support herself through small-scale employment. She runs into her old love-interest, Jalal Ansar, a successful doctor and divorced father of one. She asks him once again to marry her, but this time is turned down because she is reminded that her conversion and new identity had become a scandal that a doctor, no matter how religious, ought to disassociate himself from. When Dr. Sibte persuades her to meet a suitable match, she is amenable, but upon discovering it is Salar, she rejects the proposal, believing Salar to be the same boy she knew eight years ago.

Like Salar, Imama/Amna had also dreamt of Mecca and performing pilgrimage with him by her side. After Dr. Sibte convinces her of Salar's transformation and conversion, she decides to re-marry him, this time as Amna, a Sunni Muslim. "If Allah has chosen him for me," she reasons to Dr. Sibte, "I cannot dare defy Allah's arrangements."[102] After a second *nikkāh* ceremony is performed, she leaves for her new home with Salar. Their second wedding ceremony takes place in the holy month of Ramadan, and soon after, the once star-crossed, now blessed, couple leave for Mecca where they finally perform the pilgrimage together in reality. The novel ends with Salar gazing at the door of the Ka'abah and coming to the realization that he had been "blessed with one of the best and most *ṣāliḥ* women to have been sent to the world."[103] In marrying her, "he had undertaken a heavy responsibility of becoming the guardian [*kafīl*] of a woman who was far ahead of him when it came to goodness and chastity."[104]

While *Pīr-e Kāmil* ends on a note of attainment, first spiritual and then romantic, its sequel, *Āb-e Ḥayāt*, takes on a markedly virulent note toward those the author believes are responsible for the destruction of Islam. It is a conduct book for Muslims wives such as Imama, reminding them of their domestic duties and the kind of morality they must espouse. With respect to men, *Āb-e Ḥayāt* diverges, painting an international order that schemes against Muslims. The World Bank and the United Nations are accused of conspiring to keep the third world enslaved. It is men like Salar and his children who must rise to the occasion and save Muslims from the financial traps that these corrupt organizations have laid. The Ahmadi question is resolved through a series of violent events: First, Imama's father attempts to kill Salar when he sees the couple in a restaurant one day. Next, a bomb blast on an Ahmadi mosque kills both of Imama's brothers, leaving her father alone. Humbled, Hashim Mobeen finally converts to Sunni Islam and is then taken in by Imama and Salar, who remind the readers that Hashim's troubles are Allah's judgment for challenging the sanctity of Muhammad's prophet-hood. Concluding somewhere around 2030, this sequel explodes the original *bildung* of the convert into a Muslim quest to rescue a collapsing world order from Western control.

Less vindictive is the treatment meted out to Pakistani Christians in Bushra Rehman's *Pārsā*, a novel in which the eponymous heroine rebels against her upbringing and decides to marry her best friend, a Christian named David. Though Christians remain a less socially mobile group than the Ahmadiyya are perceived to be, the novel reads as a warning against those that have climbed the socio-economic ladder. Rehman, in addition to authoring around a dozen novels, several of which have been produced for television, has also served as a member of Pakistan's National Assembly and Punjab's Provincial Assembly. *Pārsā*, the title meaning a virtuous woman, was published as a novel in June 2010 and picked up for television almost immediately, the production changing minor details such as time and setting, while adding a major qualifier at the end.

Parsa is a carefree, young woman who has grown up in a traditionally conservative household, where religion was emphasized. As the younger daughter, she is spoiled by her father who, seeing her excellent scores on school exams, allows her to go to medical school in Multan, a city south of her hometown, Lahore. Unlike her acquiescent older sister, Naik, Parsa is a bit of a rebel, who describes herself in an internal monologue as honest, the opposite of a "hypocrite" (*munāfiq*).[105] She prides herself in not taking the dupatta or scarf, that is, not covering herself, when she does not wish to, and wearing jeans when she wishes to wear jeans. No matter what relatives may say, Parsa tells herself she is better than "ordinary girls" who immediately dress conservatively and behave traditionally in the presence of elders.[106]

Parsa meets David when his parents move into the house next to that of her parents. Incidentally, the two couples are old friends from the days when both fathers served in the Pakistan Army. David's parents, a harmless Christian couple, speak a broken, pidgin version of Urdu, dispelling any claim that they or others like them may make for properly belonging to Pakistan. Parsa and David, both free and easy in their temperaments, strike up a heady friendship. Though neither set of parents finds it problematic, Parsa's parents soon decide to marry their younger daughter to her cousin, Ghazali (renamed as Salman in the television serial). Described as "wonderful, a mild and obedient boy," Ghazali is the son of Parsa's widowed aunt, a woman who is keen on making her niece her daughter-in-law.[107] Parsa agrees to the engagement, but her friendship with David continues, reaching a head at his New Year's Eve party when the two, while dancing with each other, end up kissing. Realizing that she has feelings for David, Parsa stumbles out of the party and back to her house, only to discover that her aunt, Ghazali's mother, is seriously ill.

Ghazali is soon orphaned and Parsa returns to medical school in Multan, without speaking to David or admitting the truth to her formal fiancé. David begins to make visits to Multan and confesses his love for

Parsa. He proposes to her, the violence of his feelings apparent in his threat that should she refuse, he would kill her and then himself. When Parsa brings up the obstacle of religion—Muslim women are not allowed to marry out of the religion—David tells her,

> "Let it go, Pari! We are the products of a progressive moment [*tarraqī pasand daur*]. What kind of ignorant ideas are these? We are educated. We are all part of the same human brotherhood. Our only religion [*mažhab*] should be our humanity."[108]

Convinced by these rather compelling, secular ideas, Parsa decides to run away with David, but on the condition that he accept Islam, one he acquiesces to immediately. Their children, they agree, will be free to choose their own religion. Parsa has received the shocking news that she will be wed to Ghazali sooner than she expected, prompting David and her (or Daoud, his Islamic name) to find a mosque where the *nikkāh*, or formal marriage, is solemnized with a few of David's friends as witnesses. They spend the next few days in a hotel, their marriage a secret from their families. Once back in Multan, Parsa receives a surprise visit from Ghazali, who has brought her a ring, believing them still engaged. It is then that Parsa breaks the news to him, and charges him—knowing his love for her—to tell David's and her parents.

The honorable Ghazali does as he is told, but the news has devastating effects on both families. David's parents are convinced that their son has "destroyed their reputation" and "deceived" Parsa into marriage.[109] For Parsa's parents, the marriage is a tragedy. Parsa's father disowns her immediately, and within a few days suffers cardiac arrest and dies. Her mother continues to act on her husband's instructions and honors his decision to never see their daughter again. The onus to accept the rebellious young couple falls on David's parents, who help them get a small apartment close to the medical school. Parsa graduates and begins the next stage of her medical training but just as she is settling into her new job, David finds out that they have won the Canadian green-card lottery. Parsa, more than anything, "wanted to bury all her bittersweet memories in Pakistan and begin life anew in Canada. She wanted to run away, and once again become the princess that she used to be."[110]

But once Parsa and David arrive in Canada, life is the complete opposite. They are dependent on their hosts in Toronto, David's cousin, Coco, and her Hindu husband, Gopal, who decide to use their penniless, young guests as labor in their bakery business. Parsa is made to work like a "captive" (*qaidī*) in the kitchen while David labors at the store with Gopal.[111] Matters take a turn for the worse when Parsa discovers she is pregnant. Although Coco tries to convince her to abort the child, Parsa refuses to do so and instead is faced with a diatribe from Coco decrying "Muslim girls" and their "refusal to come out of the shell of their religion, no matter how educated they may be."[112] After a few months with their cruel hosts, David and Parsa finally manage to escape to a small apartment of their own in Mississauga, a predominantly immigrant area of greater Toronto.

Things seem to look up as Parsa also finds a job managing a pharmacy owned by a kindly Sikh couple, Iqbal and his wife, Soni. Their new landlady, Robin, is kind and generous. On the personal front, however, David exhibits a different side of himself to Parsa when he declares that she cannot give their unborn child a Muslim name. When she reminds him of their marital vows, he responds, "I said all that when we lived in Pakistan. That was for there. Here, my child will be called by a Christian name, no one will have a Muslim name."[113] Parsa is shocked, and though David apologizes later, their relationship only deteriorates further. A few days later, Parsa comes home with what she calls a "Pakistani calendar," a calendar with both Roman and Islamic months on it, decorated with images of the Ka'abah in Mecca. David's displeasure is immediately visible as he vehemently declares: "You still haven't got Pakistan out of your system!"[114]

It is clear to the reader by this time that David, a Christian by birth, has little interest in Islam or Pakistan, categories that are signified as inseparable on the calendar. He assimilates willingly in Canada, a country he happily sees as Christian and for Christians. His conversion, likewise, is exposed, discarded like a skin that is no longer required. A different kind of hypocrite from the Ahmadis we encountered in *Pīr-e Kāmil*, David is a false convert, among those who change their religion for convenience. That is to say, despite finding a place in the Muslim community, David threatens its balance, rather than enriching it as a true convert would.

Parsa gives birth to a baby girl, and while still in the hospital, requests her friends, Iqbal and Soni, to arrange for a *maulvi* to recite the *āzān*, or call to prayer, in the baby's ear, a familiar Pakistani ritual. Upon hearing the maulvi's recitation, Parsa bursts into tears, moved anew by a sound that was once so familiar to her. When David finds out about the performance of the ritual, he reacts angrily, telling Parsa, "My daughter has not been born a Muslim, she is Christian!"[115] In what Parsa sees as an act of revenge, he takes her and the baby girl, whom he calls Mary and Parsa calls Maryam, to church for baptism. A strange sense envelopes Parsa inside the church, "The painted scenes she beheld seemed lifeless, but a living, eternal feeling was beating inside her heart, *dhug... dhug... Allah... Allah... Allah!* An unseen god [*andēkha kudā*], an untouched deity [*ančhu`ā rab*] ..."¹¹⁶ She runs out of the church, leaving David and Maryam inside, overcome by the palpable presence of Allah.

Having a child makes Parsa all the more aware of her identity as a Muslim. With Maryam in her life, she "who was once utterly divorced from the Quran and prayer, now had Allah and his Prophet forever in her thoughts."¹¹⁷ She begins to regret her marriage to David as an error made out of ignorance and absence of religious passion. In the meanwhile, her mother has also passed away, and Parsa spends most of her day working, preparing to take the Candian medical exam, and in prayer. She passes the exam with flying colors, and her career takes off as she receives offers from the country's top hospitals. She is able to move her family to a new apartment, and within a few years, to a grand house in the suburbs of the city.

In the second part of the novel, Maryam is grown up, and the center of her parents' existence. Parsa and David have little to say and do with each other. Parsa believes herself to be living in sin as a Muslim woman married to a Christian man. Blaming Parsa for her lack of sexual intimacy, David has taken up with a Canadian woman named Roslyn. Parsa has now begun covering her body and hair with voluminous scarves, a further testament to her piety. She sends a generous amount from the millions she makes as a famous pediatric surgeon to the Islamic Center in Toronto, and also tries to celebrate the religious occasions in her Islamic calendar, both sources of tension between her and David. Given her work schedule, she has hired a Pakistani immigrant, Ghulam Rasul, as a housekeeper, who, given their common religion, becomes a close confidant.

Maryam, on the other hand, has enrolled in a South Asian Studies graduate program and decides to travel for research to Pakistan. Though David discourages her, believing she will become like her mother should she travel to Pakistan, Maryam persists, eventually announcing to David that she has chosen to become a Muslim, having listened to lectures on Islam on the Internet. David gives up, and Maryam travels to Pakistan, where she meets her aunt and Parsa's ex-fiancé, Ghazali. While Maryam is away, Parsa is diagnosed with cancer and finds out she only has a few months to live. Knowing that Maryam is happy in Pakistan, Parsa keeps her illness a secret, telling only Ghulam Rasul about her condition.

But Maryam sends startling news from Pakistan: She has decided to marry Ghazali, a man who is her father's age and her mother's ex-fiancé. Telling her parents that argument is futile, Maryam describes herself as wanting to enter Ghazali's life like a "*m'aujzā*," a miracle performed by prophets.[118] The event marks yet another reference to the marriage of the Prophet Muhammad and Aisha in the popular novel.[119] Given Maryam's name is one and the same with Mary whose body housed the "miracle" of Christ's birth, her marriage to Ghazali *is* a miracle of the prophets, played out this time in the present. Maryam or Mary remains the most frequently referenced woman in the Quran, and in her conversion, Rehman quite literally claims Mary's chastity as a testimony to Islam's supremacy over Christianity. Parsa gives her blessings to her daughter, soon after which she dies in a car accident. In the television serial, however, her death is a long-drawn event where Parsa's slow decline from cancer is shown over the course of several episodes. Right before she takes her final breath, she pleads with guilty David to divorce her and thus allow her a chance for forgiveness while still on earth. In a dramatic penultimate scene, David is shown weeping while holding the drooping Parsa as he divorces her in accordance with traditional Islam, declaring his decision three times. As soon as he finishes, Parsa dies. Audiences are told that David finally realizes the error of his ways and becomes a true Muslim. In the final scene, David is shown prostrating on a prayer mat, now devoting himself entirely to the praise and worship of Allah.

A novel of multiple conversions and converts, *Pārsā* offers various routes to finding the Islam and Allah that the narrative suggests exist within all mankind. Whether the convert is Parsa, who truly becomes Muslim after encountering David's false conversion as well as enduring exile to the West; Maryam, whose faith is awakened by Internet preachers and love for Ghazali; or David (from the television serial), who understands the value of Islam after beholding Parsa's steadfast faith, Islam beckons all who behold it, whether at home or in exile, abroad. The Muslim with no sins, Ghazali, who patiently endures Parsa's loss, is rewarded with her reincarnation, Maryam. Enemies of Islam and Muslims, including Coco, David's cousin, are punished in various fashions, trial by their children's disobedience among these punishments. The solutions of the novel, far from hinting at tolerance or acknowledging the status of minorities, indict the Christian as a traitorous figure, whose societal freedoms in Pakistan result in the undoing of Muslim women and subsequent Muslim families. As converts, such individuals are unreliable, their conversions usually only for material or worldly benefit. When the state's concept of minority as a socio-political entity that exists alongside the majority is undercut by the popular narrative, which casts minority groups as the internal enemies of Islam, the idea of minorities as a natural consequence of nationalism is replaced by minorities as the inevitable victims of populism and its violence.

While the plot elements, strictures, even commonplace language of this wide selection of contemporary Urdu novels may appear prescriptive or pedestrian, as scholars and critics we must treat their demand for inclusion and participation in the category of literature in an ethical fashion. That is to say, we need to come to terms with the manner in which Muslims are imagined in influential textual and visual forms, such as the Urdu novel and television serial, and in doing so confront the particular histories that forged the category of literature to take on the implications that it holds in a postcolonial state such as Pakistan. To dismiss populist imaginaries, as has long been our customary position both in the Euro-American world and in the postcolonial state, is to deny the urgency of the present moment and the violence that our cultural forms endorse.

Present-day iterations of Islam in the novels that I have examined in this chapter persist in mirroring the binaries that we imagine have been dispelled by the rise and widespread acclaim that works such as Said's *Orientalism* have received. These binaries, once simplistically contained in phrases such as "Islam and the West," now operate through various hegemonies, the most dominant and unforgiving of which remains Salafi Islam and its local variants. While we must not and cannot reject point-blank the valuable insights of works such as Mahmood's *Politics of Piety*, revivalist and conversion movements, Egyptian or Pakistani, are consequences of tortuous colonial histories and neo-nationalisms that anchor themselves in religion. Whether we think with respect to form (the oriental tale) or geographies (the Orient and the West or Euro-America) or even journeys (spiritual and physical), we keep encountering the indelible mark of orientalism and its idea of Islam and the Muslim in the postcolonial vernacular novel.

Epilogue: Us, People / People Like Us

Fehmida Riaz and a Secular Subjectivity in Urdu

I treat this epilogue as a simultaneous act of contemplation, mourning, celebration, and speculation of what the late Fahmida Riaz might have meant when she titled her 2013 prose trilogy *hum lōg*. Translating variously to "us," "us people," or even "people like us," the title remains fluid, encompassing, and generous in its possibilities, yet possessed with capacity to limit. Even as *hum lōg* could mean "us" or "us, people," in a twist and a turn, it could become insular, and imply "people like us."

But this is precisely what Riaz suggests in her prose opus, which consists of three novella-like works: *Zindā Bahār*, *Gōdāvarī*, and *Karāčī*. Taking place in the 1980s and 1990s, in Dhaka, Mumbai (and Maharashtra), and finally in Karachi, the trilogy offers an extended treatment of modern nationhood in the Indian subcontinent in the years following independence from British rule. In its deliberate contemplations upon the secession of East Pakistan into Bangladesh in 1971, the repression of the Warli tribe in northern Maharashtra, or urban violence in Karachi of the 1990s, the trilogy asks its readers to occupy uncertain positions, to live with the discomfort of doubt, and therefore, exercise a careful opposition to state narratives of identity and nation-thinking.

As one of Urdu's (and Pakistan's) most outspoken, deeply expressive female poets, Riaz, who recently passed away in Lahore, needs little introduction. Yet the events of her life, reflections on *hum lōg*, on us, people, or perhaps, people like us, demand a brief reconsideration. Born in Meerut (now a part of India) in 1946, Riaz ended up spending most of her childhood in Hyderabad, Sindh (that fell to Pakistan in 1947), and thus inadvertently became a Pakistani. Her failed first marriage took her to

London, where she worked as a broadcaster for BBC Urdu. She returned to Karachi after her divorce, eventually remarrying Zafar Ali Ujan, a Sindhi leftist worker. Riaz's haunting collection of poems around the female body, *Badan Darīdā*, or "the lacerated body," was published in 1974, but disparaged by many as obscene and shameless. During this time, the couple also started publishing a leftist journal, *Āvāz*. But Zia ul-Haq, the Islamist military dictator, began his decade of rule in 1978, and Ujan was soon imprisoned on charges of sedition. Riaz was forced to flee to Delhi, taking up a position of poet-in-residence at Jamia Millia University. After a decade in exile, Riaz returned to Pakistan, where despite a change in government, she was considered suspect: a "bloody Indian bitch," she reveals as she reminiscences about anonymous, threatening phone calls.[1] She spent the rest of her life in Pakistan, celebrated in leftist and literary circles, but viewed with some suspicion by an establishment that occasionally had to recognize her artistic achievements. Yet her work, poems about the female body—"yes, the flavor of those kisses remains in my mind, ones that the heart had declined to even taste," she writes—or lyric and prose about rising authoritarianism, remains persistently relevant in our darkening present, but ever-hopeful for the capacities of human beings, men and women, *hum lōg*, to rewrite the moment.[2]

This book has largely been concerned with prose writing in Urdu and its foundations in a moment of high orientalism. At this final juncture, I turn to Riaz's work in an attempt to understand what a *secular* history or experience of Urdu, Muslimness, and even national identity might look like in prose writing. Riaz's trilogy moves between fact and fiction, past and present, the various persons of a single narrator, Mumbai, Karachi, and Dhaka, Urdu and its others, lyric and prose. If, for the most part, as this book shows, Urdu prose fiction imagines its protagonists as conquerors of foreign lands and later, as non-national subjects whose true home is Mecca itself, Riaz, in this work and others, transforms her exile, indeed her itinerancy, into a powerful critique of the orthodoxies that undergird this totalizing system of thought. Though I focus on *Zindā Bahār*, the story of Riaz's travels to Dhaka, any account of one of the novellas directs the reader to contemplate the others as well.

In *Zindā Bahār*—the name of a street in old Dhaka, literally translating to a "living spring"—perhaps, more so than in the other novellas, Riaz lays bare the experience of exile and the fecund renditions of both history and geography that the minority position can produce. The title, however, is an uncertain construction, for what the reader takes as *bahār*, or spring, can, through the addition of a single diacritic (usually unused though an essential part of Urdu orthography) be read as *zindā bihār*, or living Bihar, a reference to the minority population of Bihari Muslims, who after the creation of the new nation-state in 1971, were permanently exiled to live in refugee camps in Dhaka, not Bangladeshi and no longer Pakistani. Emerging out of Riaz's travels to Dhaka in December 1989, just eighteen years after East Pakistan seceded to become Bangladesh, is a narrative whose title slips between the age-old joys of spring and the modern trauma of statelessness. Spilling across the boundaries of literary forms, it disrupts established accounts of national history, destabilizing through its slowly learned doubt, the notion that the ethical subject can ever truly be *at home* in a postcolonial nation-state such as Pakistan or India.

1971: A History from the Peripheries

The novella, as I approximately call it, begins with Riaz recounting the moment of her arrival at Dhaka airport, marked by her shock at the "human whirlpool" that greets her in the immigration area, her own bewilderment at having lost her travel documents, the incredible wave of loneliness that overtakes her as she listens to the hum of Bangla, a language she cannot speak or understand.[3] Reacting instinctively, she wonders whether to turn to the ground staff of Pakistan's national airline, which carried her to Dhaka, for "they were Pakistani, they spoke Urdu, and thus would not kill her."[4] Ultimately, she rejects the national and turns to the only community she knows to be true—that of other women—and in doing so, finds assistance, her initial consternation giving way to joy and relief. All of this is expressed variously, the narrator clarifying to readers that she will refer to her subject by her name, Fahmida Riaz, at times, as her, an unnamed feminine subject (*vōh*), while also retaining the first person I (*meiñ*), at other junctures.[5] Her three feminine personas reveal the crisis of the postcolonial subject who is ravaged at once by the calls of the nation, a humanist impulse, fear of disbelonging, and the charms of nostalgia. The confrontation between I, Fahmida Riaz, and her is, at its core, a destabilizing exercise that wrests authority from any single voice through the critical and interrogative presence of the other voices, other selves.

The beginning, then, is rife with markers that carry through the narrative: the uncertainty of the ethical subject in a subcontinent that is now defined by the certainties of its boundaries—national, religious, and ethnic. Many of the categories of national, even populist, thought that this book has traced resurface in Riaz's story, but this time in terms of their tenuousness, the dangers and violence of their possible power always exposed and imminent. *Zindā Bahār/Bihār*, on the one hand, exemplifies the placelessness of the exile, whether that is Riaz herself or the Bihari population of

Dhaka, but also their deep attachments to all that is deployed against them, to the same categories that are used to strip them of the dignities of citizenship and belonging. Thus, notions of Muslimness, religio-nationalist affiliations with Urdu, forms of storytelling, belief in the state and the battle for its creation, even itinerancy are told to us through the historical experience of minority. Riaz, both in terms of biography and in her writing, appears as a feminine Erich Auerbach for our place and times, creating from her "loss and displacement" an "ethical imperative" of how to live as a critical and secular citizen in modern South Asia.[6]

Riaz and her personas of narrator and character arrive in Dhaka a day or so before the eighteenth anniversary of Bangladesh's independence from Pakistan, an event that was preceded by a bloody genocide of a number of intellectuals, journalists, artists, and political workers by the West Pakistani armed forces and satellite groups within Dhaka, Al-Shams and Al-Badr, the best known. Her hosts, the organizers of a literary conference on South Asian writers, are professors at Dhaka University, eager to tell her the history of their young country and to show her around a city that is at once novel and familiar. Bearing uncertain memories from a school trip that never took place, as well as a burning curiosity to find a mysterious "Zinda Bahar Lane," Riaz slowly begins to reconcile the romantic with the real.

As the anniversary of the West Pakistani surrender of Dhaka approaches, Riaz attempts to comprehend the atmosphere around her, watching television commemorations of the Liberation War with her hosts, reliving a history of events that she knows only from a distance. While listening to the testimonies of the families of massacred intellectuals, she takes on the definitive first-person voice, telling her readers: "My mind was not ready to suddenly come face to face with 1971 again. I had felt and contemplated upon the events from a distance. And then suddenly . . . where had I suddenly landed up?"[7] The moment progresses and the narrator returns, watching herself now as a character who attempts to ask dispassionate questions of her hosts, but "cannot stop the tears from falling in her mind," or hold down the nausea that this encounter with the past causes.[8]

During these initial nights in Dhaka, Riaz, alone and fearful in her hotel room, is haunted by two "*hayulā*," monsters of unformed matter—conceived as pre-human forms of life in medieval Islamic philosophers—who assail her thoughts and question her convictions. Tossing and turning, Riaz goes between one *hayulā*, who celebrates her growing respect and warmth for Dhaka and its inhabitants, egging her on with whispers of "*joye banglā*" or "Victory to Bengal," a common cry during the Liberation War of 1971. The other, mostly stony and silent, coldly reminds her to reign in her desire to be one with the Bangladeshis. Did she wish, once again, to suffer the threatening phone calls and the slurs accusing her of treason that she suffered upon her return from India? Could she, the second monster asks, survive the condition of exile and the violence of exclusion all over again? Better, it seems, to advise her to stay loyal to Pakistan by containing the love that she seems to feel for her traitorous hosts and their city.[9]

But Riaz resists the lures of the nationalism and the stability of a single identity. She forces herself, instead, to revisit her own past as a Pakistani (or at the time, West Pakistani) subject in order to understand Bangladesh as a site of belonging, both in terms of the state narrative but also as a site of unbounded human agency, expressed through hospitality, generosity, empathy, language, and humor. Islam, its histories, and its practices in the region are regular references, whether at an early moment when Riaz almost bursts into laughter at hearing the *āzān*, or call to prayer, in Bangla-accented Arabic for the first time, or in more somber discussions, during which Riaz, conscious of the irony of the situation, finds herself arguing in favor of Islam as a communal bond between Bengalis and Biharis. The hegemonic, totalizing authority that Sunni Islam had taken on in Pakistan, however, is never absent, an implicit condition whenever Riaz recalls her exile. Her scrutiny, most often directed toward herself and the instruments of affiliation—staged by the persistent *hayulās*—exposes the *proximity*, really, of the secular with the orthodoxies that it opposes. What this gesture allows us as readers to visualize, then, is, as Said suggests, the "moment" at which a critical, secular conscious slides into "organized dogma."[10]

As Riaz, the visitor from Karachi, traverses the city, encountering historic sites such as the Ramna Racecourse, she recalls her own thoughts and conversations during the 1971 war, an event she experienced from London. One phone call, in particular, stands out in which she speaks to a Pakistani friend on December 14, 1971. He shouts, "Dhaka will not be taken. We will make Dhaka into our final fort. Our *ākrī chattān!*"[11] His last phrase is, of course, a reference to Nasim Hijazi's eponymous novel, *Ākrī Chattān*, quite literally, the final rock, a work recounting Genghis Khan's conquest of the Khwarazam Sultanate, told as a tribute to a Muslim soldier who tries to resist the Mongol invasions. Just a few months before, Riaz recalls, this friend had been distraught at reports of violence and killings taking place in Dhaka, but the "hysteria of war" had "transformed him into the hero of a Nasim Hijazi novel."[12] Dhaka had become Granada, and her friend was not in London, but, in fact, on the battlefield. She recalls herself at the time, a girl-woman of no more than twenty-six years, just a year older than Pakistan, a country that hadn't even turned twenty-five. She wonders, but does not ask out loud, where was it that all the university professors were lined up and shot by the Pakistan Army? And then, a frequent phrase of the time crosses into her mind, "All these sister-fuckers are Hindu, anyway . . ."[13]

Referring to herself as "she" and "her" throughout this narrative stream, Riaz offers her past self as a passive bystander who silently absorbs the hyper-nationalist rhetoric of West Pakistan against East Pakistan's struggle for autonomy. At the same time, this painful reverie, replete with ethno-religious slurs, allows her, as author and narrator, to expose the violence of the moment to readers of Urdu, readers, we can assume, who are largely based in contemporary Pakistan. It is worth clarifying that although much of the world is aware of the atrocities committed by the state apparatus during the Bangladesh liberation struggle, the discussion is largely muted within Pakistan where even liberal history textbooks brush over the event, and only a few writers, Intezar Hussain prominent among them, have produced work that grapples with the war, its human, and humanist, casualties. Above all, what Riaz achieves through this extended confrontation with the past—her own and that of Pakistan—is a secular critique of her own subjectivity, one that she is only able to conceptualize from a place of exile, or from the fragile peripheries of the state of which she is citizen.

A number of other strange, perhaps even unchronicled, events, revisit Riaz as she travels deeper into Dhaka, the city and the historical place. She reads the diary of a woman by the name of Jahan Ara, whose sons and husband are disappeared and tortured by the West Pakistani armed and paramilitary forces at the height of the liberation struggle. She recalls herself sitting in the BBC cafeteria when the first images from Dhaka emerge. In her mind, she studies one image of bodies strewn here and there on a street, reexamining the exact postures of the dead, recalling the sexual and physical torture marks that were so apparent on them. Fragmented, often brought on through seemingly unrelated happenings in the present, Riaz's memories offer both an alternative history of 1971, Pakistan's forgotten second Partition, but also hint at the alternative forms of narrative that are required to produce this history. That is to say, her account—neither a novel, nor a travelogue—is defiant, or perhaps, unaware of formal narrative structures and genre, foregoing the national claims of the novel, or the authoritative wonder of the travel writer who describes foreign lands to his or her readers. Her prose—split between three personas—is unassured; the narrative itself shifts between reluctance and blind enthusiasm, often reversing its own advances; and her language, Urdu, is interspersed with phrases of Bangla she has practiced and learned; moments of Punjabi sacred lyric; cliched, colonial English; and memories of Hindi. There are no convictions—formal or narrative—in the text that permit ordinary literary affiliations between reader and text.

Zindā Bihār: Nationalisms of the Stateless

Riaz's strange and growing attachment to Dhaka and its citizens—borne out of an instinctive familiarity and a shared past—appears at times as the involuntary and naive sentiment of an exile, eager to belong in a place that will have him or her. Yet, as she finds herself at the camps within which Dhaka's Bihari population are mostly confined, the living spring, or *zindā bahār*, of discovery and affinity soon morphs into its darker other, *zindā bihār*, or living Bihar. The presence of Biharis in Dhaka goes back to the Partition of 1947 when almost two million Muslims from West Bengal and Bihar migrated to East Pakistan. Urdu-speaking, the Bihari migrants, though relocated to the Bangla-speaking East Pakistan, continued to imagine and affiliate themselves politically and culturally with the West Pakistani national narrative.

As the East Pakistani struggle to create an independent Bangladesh became a pulsing reality in March 1971, the Bihari population aligned itself with West Pakistan, organizing—in addition to its political activity—paramilitary groups such as Al-Shams and Al-Badr, both of which are considered as central to the large-scale killings of Bengali intellectuals and activists that occurred during the war. But after the Pakistan Army laid down its arms and conceded defeat, Biharis found themselves abandoned in the new Bangladesh, no longer Pakistani in this new country, and unable to go to Pakistan, a country some two thousand kilometers away that many had never even seen. Effectively stateless since 1972, the Biharis have been confined to urban camps that have over the years expanded into large slums. Despite political agreements between India, Pakistan, and Bangladesh in 1974, the repatriation of war prisoners and other Biharis was limited, with neither Pakistan nor the new Bangladesh offering citizenship to this sizeable minority. In 2008, the Bangladesh government decided to award citizenship to the generation of Biharis born after 1971, and although a number of young people have embraced the opportunity, others remain recalcitrant, insistent that Pakistan is their true home. In the novella, the Biharis inadvertently become a perverse counterpart of sorts to Riaz herself. That is to say, if Riaz serves as a figure in the narrative who is able to transform the ongoing condition of exile into a contemplation on the orthodoxies of ethnic, linguistic, and religio-nationalisms, the Bihari population of Dhaka allow us to understand, in human terms, what it means to be victim to these selfsame nationalisms.

The shadowy reference to a certain Zinda Bahar lane in the older part of Dhaka becomes a synecdoche for the larger Bihari presence in the city. On her way to finding Zinda Bahar lane, an address that haunts and calls to her, Riaz passes through one of Dhaka's largest Bihari camps, the Geneva camp in Muhammadpur, a place she initially believes could not be home to human beings, and yet "everywhere, people were milling and buzzing around like flies."[14] The camp, both a ghetto and a site of a misplaced nationalism, takes on myriad significations, charming Riaz through filiative offerings of language, while simultaneously repulsing her with the crudeness of its political attachments. In other words, the non-citizen Biharis of Dhaka are a placeless people, the once-citizens of a state that has ceased to exist, whose performance of certain nationalist affiliations—Urdu and Islam, in particular—is, paradoxically, a reification of the same state that continues to elude them.

As a guest from Pakistan, Riaz is initially taken to an office belonging to the president of the Bihari collective. When she enters the shabby room, she beholds a portrait of Muhammad Ali Jinnah, the founding father of Pakistan, and next to that, some three times larger, a portrait of Zia-ul Haq, the Islamist dictator who had died just a year earlier in mysterious plane crash. Riaz is stunned to behold the man who had arrested her husband, and whose draconian laws had forced her into an eleven-year-long exile in Delhi. This nationalist gesture—exercised in the bounded non-place that is the Geneva camp—renders her silent, but "in her mind, the entire period of her exile [*jilāvaṭanī*] replayed in a circle like film, a curse to this open devotion of the Biharis."[15] She recalls—speaking of herself in the third person—"the shudders of fear in her stomach . . . the tanks that would wait silently outside her lane, her waning hopes . . ."[16] She sees herself as a mother, carrying two small children to safety in India, far from the place they knew as home. The distant sound of the *āzān* breaks her reverie, coming as a distraction to Riaz, as if a "glass of a closed room had been broken and a wave of fresh air had entered."[17] In this moment, the *āzān*, read in Bangla-accented Arabic, is a release, an at-once communal yet secular sound that unlike in Pakistan does not here function as imperative.

Upon hearing that a Pakistani was visiting the camp, a number of excited, young Biharis make their way to the office, some going off in search of the camp leader. Riaz notices a picture of this man on the wall, as well as a few appropriate couplets, or *ash'ār*, written here and there. The presence of these couplets—whose quality Riaz does not remark upon—has the opposite effect from that of Zia's portrait. Riaz laughs, lightened by the familiar culture of an Urdu-speaking population. "They'll fall in a pit of mud, but it'll take them a second to compose a few couplets describing their situation," she thinks, suddenly feeling an affinity to these people in this sometimes-foreign country.[18] Despite the squalid nature of the camp, the fact that it had become a source for cheap prostitutes and a hub of violent crime, the presence of poetry moves her, reminding her that amidst all this, there remained a human urge within the Biharis to cling to that which they saw as their "*tehzīb*," or tradition.

Abject and abandoned, deemed enemies of the state that rose from the ashes of what was once East Pakistan, the Biharis of Dhaka inhabit a more complex identity than that of simply refugee or traitor. The final scene of an angry, young man who declares, "my grandfather died creating Pakistan, my father died defending Pakistan. And I ... I will die saying Pakistan's name," encapsulates their near ridiculous commitment to the national ideal.[19] And yet, even as this man speaks, others around him chastise him for what they see as a melodramatic performance, reminding him that no one is watching his theatrics. The country he so blindly pines for, his companions remind him, has little care for his "blood and tears," his "fear and his slowly deepening disappointments."[20] As Riaz finally prepares to leave the camp, a couple of Biharis inform her that their leaders have announced that they will depart for Karachi in a ship by the coming year. Here, the section ends. Riaz and her personas offer no response to the naïve confidence of these homeless nationalists, but the experience of the camp indelibly colors her initially romantic perceptions of Bangladesh.

Zindā Bahār Lane: Other Stories, Other Histories

This brief foray into the broader, yet intimately described, historical experiences of the postcolonial subject in and out of the South Asian nation-state is a basic attempt at trying to capture Riaz's effort in *Zindā Bahār/Bihār*. Yet this novella-like work is more than a retelling of the 1971 war fought by Pakistan, India, and the emergent Bangladesh, or an exposé on the past and present of Dhaka's Bihari population. It is, as I have suggested, an attempt to write a secular account of postcolonial subjectivity in South Asia, an effort that is profoundly informed by Riaz's extended experience of exile, but also by her intimate attachments to Urdu, a language that is constantly present in the text, but this time at a distance from the religio-nationalist orientations that this book has detailed for the most part. In this text, Urdu appears not as a vehicle for a national Muslim identity, but as a means through which the hegemonies of the nation-state—India, Pakistan, and Bangladesh—are disrupted, and a language through which the individual subject (here, Riaz) negotiates the assumptions of belief and identity. That is to say, far from affirming the ideal Muslim subject and marking out the bounds of the nation, *Zindā Bahār/Bihār* forces the reader, through the figure of Riaz, to inhabit the discomfort of doubt.

For most of her time in Dhaka, Riaz desires to visit Zinda Bahar Lane, an address she knows only vaguely and that comes to function as a lodestone of sorts for the ways in which she imagines and experiences the city. Where she learned of this place, and what it exactly it means to her, remains a mystery for the most part, though within Riaz's circle of poet and writer friends, there is a vague sense that the address she searches for was once home to Afzal Ahmad Syed, the Urdu poet and translator, who witnessed the events and was forced to leave Dhaka for Karachi immediately afterwards.[21] The indeterminate, conflicting meanings that are coded into this site point to a greater gesture on Riaz's part, an effort to read the past not necessarily as a chronological history, but as a series of events within which she, a postcolonial subject, is implicated. In other words, Riaz's arrival at the address she has sought to find for much of her time in Dhaka, far from a moment of confirmation or historical rehabilitation, is a moment in which the impossibility of ever being at home becomes a reality for her. Moving from her past sense of exile as merely a political condition imposed by the state to exile as an ethical position, a conscious way of *knowing* the postcolonial histories and geographies of a region that was once the Indo-Persian subcontinent, Riaz asks readers to reimagine the religio-national identities that mainstream Urdu prose forms, state narratives, and conventional histories have propagated.

After a number of detours through Dhaka's sites and homes, Riaz reaches Zinda Bahar Lane in the older part of the city, bearing an address whose significance she is loath to explain to the rickshaw driver and professor who accompany her. As she examines the house she has been searching for, her companions ask her questions about its past residents, all of which Riaz answers with some vagueness. The house belonged to an Urdu-speaking family who left eighteen years ago as the war broke out but until then had spent their whole lives in Dhaka, living, marrying, and burying their dead in the city they knew as home. She has no knowledge of the circumstances in which these people left, which camps they were interred in, or how they finally escaped. She envisions the night of their escape through stories she has heard. Once again, Riaz begins to narrate herself in the third person, a woman in a waking dream, standing in a street, wanting to make a home there for the rest of her times, conscious of the impossibility of her desires. Paralyzed in this dream-state, moving in and out of the violence that this place had seen, Riaz echoes a verse from the fifteenth-century founder of the Sikh faith, Guru Nanak's poetic scriptures: "*mērē ādjugād*," this is the beginning of my time.[22] But if Guru Nanak, his lyric opus, and his time, in her mind, signify the love humans can bear each other, offerings affection and kindness, then *her* time, the present, is marked by violence, torture, and abuse.

The reverie before the abandoned house in Zinda Bahar Lane and the possibility that its once-residents may have been part of the paramilitary groups, spirals into an extended contemplation on the violence of the Indian subcontinent's ongoing partitions, events of communal violence and alienation. Struggling to understand this as part of a tradition that has included figures such as Guru Nanak and Siddharta Gautama, the Buddha, Riaz turns to her hosts and answers their queries about the Urdu-speaking family by declaring that their possible actions during the Liberation War must be understood as "*ġhair haqīqī*," or non-real.[23] In her mind, she replays the abduction and killing of the famous Bengali novelist, Shahidullah Kaiser, imagining the part these once-residents may have played in it, and then moves to the anti-Muslim riots in Bhiwandi, Maharashtra in 1970, the Hindu-Muslim clashes in Muradabad during the 1980s, and the terrible massacre of Bihari and other Urdu-speaking migrants by Pashtun migrants in Karachi in 1986, all the while integrating herself as a violent subject, a mother who beats her children, believing the act to be better for them. These events, too, she tells her hosts, were *ġhair haqīqī*, events that do not mark the reality of the human, but, in fact, are "*dakal*," or intrusions upon human nature.[24]

Naively romantic, on the one hand, but at the same time an essential offering to the present and future of this and other places, Riaz's illogical yet instinctive confrontation with the immediate and distant pasts is a gesture of reconciliation and, above all, hope. Old Dhaka, Zinda Bahar lane, the Buriganga River—once an extension of the Ganges—appear to her as if outside of the nation-state and national histories. In this part of the city, which otherwise is marked with signs of political struggle or violent nationalism, Riaz finds other imaginaries. Centuries ago, she recalls, Urdu was one of the many languages that thrived in this area during the fifteenth-century Hussain Shahi dynasty, a period known for its linguistic diversity and fluid forms of faith and practice. But in the present, the "monopoly" (*ajārahdārī*) of Urdu had become the "foremost sign of the Bengali struggle."[25] She wonders where this other past had been banished to. Perhaps one day, she thinks, the "haze will clear on its own." Bangla was the language of Bengal, but Urdu too, she remembers, once had a place here.[26]

In the realms of empirical knowledge and chronological histories, Riaz's hopeful meanderings may appear as irrational and fanciful. Likewise, her narrative as a whole, uncertain in form, shifting from character to consciousness, profoundly attached to the Indian subcontinent offers no grand conclusions, no reformative counsel or political solutions, and no conclusive end. Riaz leaves Dhaka desirous as ever of making a home in the city, her mind invaded by the image of a young child on a roof in Zinda Bahar lane, summoning her by waving a flag of Bangladesh. But she thinks of her own children, the difficulties of a different language, and then finally, of her own incessant wanderings, her exile, and her life in Karachi. She looks at her watch. She had forgotten to change the time zone upon arriving at Dhaka and is reminded, as she boards her return flight, "the old time was still ongoing."[27]

The disruption of her subliminal yearning to find a home by her watch, an object marking linear time and bounded space, forces Riaz into the precarity of her present. To acknowledge and to persist within this precarity, Riaz suggests—in this work and the two novellas that follow it—is the task of the secular subject. Alone, except for her small community of fellow women poets and political activists, Riaz tirelessly grapples with the looming specters of nationalism and the violence it breeds. Her concerns are never national or bordered, evident from *Godāvarī*, the second novella of the trilogy, in which a young mother becomes witness to state-sponsored violence against Adivasis in Maharashtra, or in her poem *"Tum bilkul hum jaisē niklē"* (You have turned out just like us), which decries the rise of the Hindu right in India.

Although this concluding exercise hardly does Riaz and her profound opus justice, it does permit an explication of the forms a possibly secular literary practice in Urdu may take. Riaz's notions of history are non-linear, her linguistic sensibilities are unbounded and non-religious, and her possible attachments to place and people are tempered by her femininity, which in turn, is expressed outside of conventional form, language, and narrative structures. Her work, steeped in the crisis of Urdu's nationalist affiliations and possibilities of ethical existence, persists outside of the orientalist and later nationalist-led development of Urdu prose fiction that this book has argued has become central to Pakistani state-sponsored narratives of origin and identity.

Acknowledgments

This book, for which I am so very indebted to my teacher, mentor, and friend Aamir Mufti, is an effort to remain true to the kind of ethical scholarship and personhood that he tried so hard to teach me during my years in graduate school. Many of the lessons Aamir emphasized make sense years later now that I am a teacher myself. Others have become clear during our wonderful conversations and heady meals in Los Angeles, Lahore, and in the misty green fields of the Kartarpur Gurdvara at the edge of Pakistan. I hope in the years to come that there are many more such joyful moments, that Aamir's lessons on work, family, friendship, and cooking continue to shape me, and above all, that we are able to find better, more hopeful ways to imagine our shared country.

I remain beholden to a number of teachers. At the UCLA department of Comparative Literature, I must thank Ali Behdad and Jenny Sharpe for their constancy and presence. Felicity Nussbaum, a generous teacher and reader, took me on as a student at the last minute and taught me everything I know today about eighteenth-century English literature. Efrain Kristal taught me how to teach, giving me Dante as a guide. During my informal visits to Columbia, Fran Pritchett warmly adopted and directed me toward several of the works that are so critical to this book. At Princeton University, where I discovered comparative literature as an undergraduate, Ben Conisbee Baer, always pushing me to do better, patiently taught me to read texts and traditions that I was often blind to. Eileen Reeves, despite her "haste," opened the doors of the discipline for me in ways I cannot count here. Finally, the late Ted Rabb, who passed away last year, never knew that his lesson in my first undergraduate class,

"*What is this text telling us about a people?*" continues to inform every text I read.

In my six years in the department of Humanities and Social Sciences, I have learned to simultaneously inhabit the position of teacher and student. Ali Raza and Bilal Tanweer have been my best partners-in-crime. Ali Raza's indescribable presence and friendship—personal and intellectual—have been miraculously steady since the day we met. Ghulam Moeenudin Nizami and Zahid Hussain have helped me navigate difficult corners of the Persio-Urdu world with immense kindness. Ali Khan and Hasan Karrar eased me into work life through their unflagging support. Kamran Asdar Ali, an exemplary dean and colleague, encouraged and backed this project in numerous ways. My outstanding undergraduates over the years, Noor Habib, Sara Saleem Khan, Mariam Nadeem, Anam Fatima Khan, and Hamad Abdullah Nazar have made me a better teacher. The ladies and sole gentleman in my Jane Austen seminar of Spring 2018 have been critical interlocuters for the second half of this book. Muhammad Umar Habib deserves special mention for his passionate research skills. The department's support staff, Usman Amin, Salman Amin, Hinna Zahid, Mehreen and Maleeha Jamil, Naseer-udin, Aroosa Subhani, and Aurangzaib Awan from the Dean's office, have always made the impossible happen. Danish Iqbal greets me every morning at work with a cup of tea made just right.

I am incredibly grateful to a number of institutions and people indirectly involved in this book. Marshall Brown, the indomitable editor of *MLQ: Modern Language Quarterly*, made the second chapter a stronger piece. I must also thank Jennifer Dubrow, who has been a critical and supportive reader of this manuscript, and of its earlier excerpted appearance in *MLQ*. Simon Gikandi, another transformative teacher, helped me bring my arguments to the pages of *PMLA*. Parts of this book were presented at Princeton and University of Texas, Austin. I owe much to Gyan Prakash, Syed Akbar Hyder, Nasia Anam, Mary Rader, and Ben and Eileen (again and always) for attending and engaging so closely with my work. I must also gratefully acknowledge the staff at the British Library, the administrators of the Mushfiq Khwaja Library in Karachi, as well as the excellent librarians, particularly Imran Siddique, at LUMS. I must also thank Syed Babar Ali, Saima A. Khawaja and the Gurmani Foundation, and Osman K. Waheed for facilitating research in the humanities at LUMS. At Fordham University Press, Tom Lay has backed this project from the beginning. I look forward to a continued relationship with Tom and his team, including Will Cerbone, John Garza, and Eric Newman. Nancy Rapoport's immaculate copy edits have been an education unto themselves. I am deeply grateful to Bibi Hajra for her generous permission to use the infinitely nuanced "Ramzan Transmission" on the cover. Both my reviewers, Jennifer Dubrow and Michael Allan, have exhibited a rare scholarly generosity that I hope I am able to replicate. Their comments and suggestions have made me a better scholar and writer.

I cannot count or properly thank the many friends from many places who sustain me. Anisa Heravian, my Persian sister, and Julia Liu, my Asian one, made once-strange cities into home for me. Shad Naved has always doubled as a friend *and* a teacher, be it Los Angeles or Delhi. In Los Angeles and Princeton, Michelle Lee, Dana Linda, and Cindy Hong have been sororal pillars. In Lahore (and London), Ammara Maqsood has remained a constant and patient ear since she found me in tenth grade. In Lahore, I am always among generous friends: Spenta Kakalia, Zehra Mujtaba Zaidi, Aamna Khalid, Sophia Anjum, Sanval Nasim, Anum Malkani, H. Emad Ansari, Zahra Lakdawala, Umair Javed, Fizzah Sajjad, Zebunnisa Hamid, Gwen Kirk, Fatima Fayyaz, Urooj Masud, Nida Qureshi, Meher Tiwana, and Amina Samiuddin among them.

I have been blessed with homes and families that have enabled me to write. Shad Bibi's uncomplaining presence in my apartment during the early days of this book project allowed me to shut myself in my office without a care. Waqar Hafeez, Abdul Jabbar, Liaqat Ali, Ejaz Ahmad, and John Emmanuel cheerfully attended to all the urgent tasks that I otherwise dreaded. My in-laws—the Shamsis and the Barkat Alis—the two branches of this large new family, have embraced me with immense warmth and affection, especially Rashda Tanweer, my ever-loving, all-forgiving mother-in-law, Zain Alam Shamsi, Farah Amna, Rabia Ali, Ahsan Ahmad, Ajju Khala, Shaista Khala, Javed, and Nadeem Barkat Ali. My brother, Sulmaan W Khan, and sister-in-law, Anna Beth Keim, have collected countless packages for me these past few years. Seemin Rehman, my Chachi, warms every visit to Karachi with her magical smile and infectious laugh. Salika Aziz, my Lalo, and my cousin, Mo Burhanuddin, bring love, laughter, and delightful English edibles into my life, brightening it in countless ways. Saboohi Aziz, my Lala, fed me through much of the writing process. My grandparents, Soheila Khalid, Shaukat Mumtaz, and Mumtaz Ahmad Khan, have raised and cared for me since I was a child. It is the knowledge that they are (or have been) there that has made me who I am today. Wasif M. Khan, my Abu, and Zeba Aziz, my Amma, are my best friends, my fiercest allies, and my favorite companions. My father makes me brave and free. My mother has given me her spirit, her discipline, and her image. I am never without her.

For what Bilal Tanweer has brought to my life, I do not know how to give thanks. He is my *sakūn*, my *sahārā*, my sanctuary, the companion of my heart and my mind, whose capacity for forgiveness and love fills me with an inexpressible and endless gratitude. May our little Khayyam, my tent-maker *bābā*, always be a source of love, joy, and shelter in the world that he inherits.

Notes

Introduction / Who Is a Muslim?

1. Shahab Ahmed, *What Is Islam? The Importance of being Islamic* (Princeton: Princeton University Press, 2016), 81.
2. Edward Said, *Orientalism* (New York: Vintage Books, 1979), 25.
3. Ibid.
4. Suzanne Marchand, *German Orientalism in an Age of Empire: Religion, Race and Scholarship* (Oxford: Oxford University Press, 2009), xx.
5. Aamir Mufti, *Forget English! Orientalisms and World Literatures* (Cambridge: Harvard University Press, 2016), 4.
6. Said, *Orientalism*, 27.
7. Mufti, *Forget English!*, 22.
8. Srinivas Aravamudan, *Enlightenment Orientalism: Resisting the Rise of the Novel* (Chicago: University of Chicago Press, 2012), 3. See also, Felicity Nussbaum, *Torrid Zones: Maternity, Sexuality, and Empire in Eighteenth-Century English Narratives* (Baltimore, Md.: Johns Hopkins University Press, 1995).
9. I have argued this in an earlier essay, "The Oriental Tale and the Transformation of North-Indian Prose Fiction," *Modern Language Quarterly* 78, no. 1 (March 2017): 27–50. In this project, of course, this moment of literary invention is part of a longer literary history of Urdu.
10. Edward Said, *The World, the Text, and the Critic* (Cambridge: Harvard University Press, 1983), 6.
11. Ibid., 29.
12. Ibid.
13. See, for example, Terry Eagleton, *Literary Theory: An Introduction* (Minneapolis: University of Minnesota Press, 1983); Gauri Viswanathan, *Masks of Conquest: Literary Study and British Rule in India* (New York: Columbia University Press, 1989); and John Guillory, *Cultural Capital: The Problem of Literary Canon Formation* (Chicago: University of Chicago Press, 1993).

14. Vinay Dharwadker, "Orientalism and the Study of Indian Literatures," in *Orientalism and the Postcolonial Predicament: Perspectives on South Asia*, ed. Carol Breckenridge and Peter van der Veer (Philadelphia: University of Pennsylvania Press, 1993), 167–68.

15. Rene Wellek, "Literature and Its Cognates," in *Dictionary of the History of Ideas*, ed. Philip P. Wiener (New York: Charles Scribner, 1974), 81.

16. M. H. Abrams, *The Mirror and the Lamp: Romantic Theory and the Critical Tradition* (Oxford: Oxford University Press, 1971), 87.

17. Michael Allen, *In the Shadow of World Literature: Sites of Reading in Colonial Egypt* (Princeton: Princeton University Press, 2016), 6.

18. Allen's excellent work shows how Arabic aesthetics in premodern Egypt were slowly transformed during colonial rule. In particular, Allen traces how *adab*, once signifying cultivation, conduct, and manners, comes to mean literariness in a Western sense of the word in modern Egypt.

19. A similar exploration of the invention of literature in North India can be found in Aamir Mufti's *Forget English*, in which he argues that "In order to comprehend the structure of literary relations that is not a planet-wide reality, we need to grasp the role that philological Orientalism played in producing and establishing a method and a system for classifying diverse forms of textuality now all processed and codified uniformly as *literature* . . . The (now universal) category of literature itself, with its particularly Latinate etymology and genealogy, marks this process of assimilation of diverse cultures of writing, a process only partially concealed by the use of such vernacular terms as *adab* (in Arabic, Persian, Urdu, and Turkish, among others) and *sāhitya* (in Hindi and a number of Indian vernaculars) to signify the new literariness." See *Forget English: Orientalisms and World Literatures* (Cambridge: Harvard University Press, 2016), 80.

20. Mrityunjay Tripathi, *The Hindi Canon: Intellectuals, Processes, Critics*, translated by Shad Naved (New Delhi: Tulika Books, 2018), 8.

21. Alternatively, the *jadīdiyat* or modernism movement of the 1950s and 60s celebrates itself as marking a true revival or return to an Indo-Islamic tradition. See Chapter 4, "Martyr/*Mujāhid*: The Invention of Origins in the Modern Urdu Novel."

22. See, for example, David Damrosch's *What Is World Literature* (Princeton: Princeton University Press, 2003); Pascal Casanova's *The World Republic of Letters* (Cambridge: Harvard University Press, 1999); Franco Moretti's *Distant Reading* (New York: Verso, 2013).

23. Alexander Beecroft suggests that a "national literature is one that reads and interprets texts through the lens of the nation-state, whether as that state's embodiment, as the dissent tolerated within its public sphere, as its legitimating precursors, or as its future aspirations. Issues of the constitution of the literary language, of course, provide a cultural nexus between literary and political debates." This is, indeed, a comprehensive conception of the works, ideas, and language behind a national literature, but the inclusion of participatory texts and authors as constitutive members of this literature is a more troubled, often evasive, process. In the case of modern Urdu, the condition of Urdu as a national language with a national literature exists prior to the creation of the nation-state, and as this book argues, in its present populist form seems to bypass the idea of the nation-state all together. Beecroft has rightly argued that when national literatures emerge from vernacular literatures, a cosmopolitan source literature is often "obscured," and

those texts in the vernacular that "cannot be assimilated to the narrative of national literary history are marginalized." In the case of languages such as Urdu and Hindi, this process has worked both ways. On the one hand, thanks to literary histories being written in a fashion that emulates Europe, progressive and modernist writers feature prominently in many a literary history in both Urdu and the Euro-American academy. On the other hand, the question worth asking is whether literary histories actually alter the national consumption of certain kinds of narrative texts. Thus, while Manto and Faiz are counted as great Urdu writers from Pakistan by both the state and non-state—critics, scholars, media—their works and ideas remain marginal when compared to writers who are not necessarily celebrated as canonical or exemplar. See Alexander Beecroft. *An Ecology of World Literature: From Antiquity to the Present Day* (New York: Verso, 2015), 197.

24. Saba Mahmood, *The Politics of Piety: The Islamic Revival and the Feminist Subject* (Princeton: Princeton University Press, 2005), 15.

25. Ibid.

26. Saba Mahmood, "Secularism, Hermeneutics, and Empire: The Politics of Islamic Reformation," *Public Culture* 18, no. 2 (Spring 2006): 328.

27. When I say "postcolonial Muslim world," rather than restrict myself to Egypt, I read, as Sadia Abbas has done, into Mahmood's own shifts in the epilogue, where the case of the Egyptian women can be used to read that of Afghan women living under the Taliban. In other words, despite Mahmood's constant assertions to specificity, she herself, both in her introduction and epilogue, utilizes her fieldwork toward making a broader argument regarding Muslim women and the West.

28. See Talal Asad, "The idea of an anthropology of Islam," *Qui Parle* 17, no. 2 (2009): 1–30.

29. Mahmood, *Politics of Piety*, 115.

30. Ibid., 31.

31. Mufti, "Why I Am Not a Post-Secularist," 16.

32. Mahmood, "Secularism, Hermeneutics, and Empire," 346.

33. Mufti, "Why I Am Not a Post-Secularist," 12.

34. Mahmood, *Politics of Piety*, 37.

35. Mikhail Bakhtin. *The Dialogic Imagination: Four Essays*, ed. Michael Holquist, trans. Caryl Emerson and Michael Holquist (Austin: University of Texas Press, 1981), 250.

36. Mufti, *Forget English!*, 37.

37. Bakhtin, *Dialogic Imagination*, 254.

1 / Mahometan/Muslim: The Chronotope of the Oriental Tale

1. Martha Pike Conant, *The Oriental Tale in England in the Eighteenth Century* (New York: Columbia University Press, 1908), xv.

2. Ibid., xv–xvi.

3. Ibid., xvi.

4. Ibid.

5. James Beattie, "On Fable and Romance," in *Dissertations Moral and Critical* (London: W. Strahan, 1780), 510.

6. Jayne Elizabeth Lewis, *The English Fable: Aesop and Literary Culture 1651–1740* (New York: Cambridge University Press, 1996), 3.

7. Petis La Croix, Preface to *Turkish Tales; consisting of several extraordinary adventures*, trans. Anonymous (London: J. Tonson, 1708), ii.

8. Paolo Lemos Horta, *Marvellous Thieves: Secret Authors of the Arabian Nights* (Cambridge: Harvard University Press, 2017), 7.

9. John Richetti, Introduction to *The Cambridge History of English Literature*, ed. John Richetti (Cambridge: Cambridge University Press, 2005), 2.

10. See Srinivas Aravamudan, *Tropicopolitans: Colonialism and Agency, 1688–1804* (Durham, N.C.: Duke University Press, 1999), and *Enlightenment Orientalism: Resisting the Rise of the Novel* (Chicago: University of Chicago Press, 2011).

11. See Ros Ballaster, *Fabulous Orients: Fictions of the East 1662–1785* (London: Oxford University Press, 2005).

12. Srinivas Aravamudan, "In the Wake of the Novel: The Oriental Tale as National Allegory," *Novel: A Forum on Fiction* 33, no. 1 (1999), 10.

13. Ibid.

14. Ibid.

15. Ibid.

16. Aamir Mufti, *Forget English: Orientalisms and World Literatures* (Cambridge: Harvard University Press, 2016), 17.

17. Aravamudan, *Enlightenment Orientalism*, 8.

18. The Mahometan as chronotope in the oriental tale is an important quality that sets this particular strain of Islam-centered orientalism apart from more scientific, linguistically oriented orientalisms, such as Semitic Orientalism, which focused, as Maurice Olender argues, on the origins of language as well as the racialization of language and religion. Olender's ultimate focus, of course, is on the invention of the Aryan and his nemesis, the Semite. For more details of the philological invention of the Jew, see *Languages of Paradise: Race, Religion and Philology in the Nineteenth Century*, trans. Arthur Goldman (Cambridge: Harvard University Press, 2009).

19. In other discussions and articles, I have used Marshall Hodgson's term "Islamicate" to describe the space or territories in question. Edward Said uses the name "Islamic Orient." Shahab Ahmed's groundbreaking work *What is Islam? The Importance of Being Islamic* (Princeton: Princeton University Press, 2016) has since made me rethink the use of this term. Ahmed's longer argument is a compelling and complex one, but Ahmed rejects Hogdson's idea that "Islam = religion" and "Islamicate = culture = secular" on the grounds that "the vocabularies and meanings of the discourses and practices of literature, art, politics, wine-drinking, *etcetera*, appear anything except distinct and separable from vocabularies and meanings of the revelation to Muhammad—rather as we have seen, they are perfused with, implicated in, and constructed of the same working elements, so that it is not at all clear how 'culture' is to be filtered out of 'religion' or 'religion' distilled out of 'culture.'" *What is Islam* makes us rethink the place and discourse around Islam in the modern world entirely, rendering terms such as Islamicate or Islamdom rather superficial (see pages 164–65).

20. Lori H. Newcomb, *Reading the Popular Romance in Early Modern England* (New York: Columbia University Press, 2002), 8.

21. Edward Said, *Orientalism* (New York: Penguin, 1991), 24.

22. See Humphrey Prideaux, *The Life of Mahomet* (London: Curll, Hooke, and Caldecott, 1716). Though Prideaux's version of events was criticized by George Sale in

the preface to his translation of the Quran in 1734, Sale himself believed Muhammad to be an imposter who could not be compared to Moses or Jesus.

23. Ros Ballaster, *Fabulous Orients: Fictions of the East in England 1662–1785* (New York: Oxford University Press, 2005), 267.

24. "Santons" seems to be a corruption of the Sanskrit term *"santan."* *Santan* is both a term for Vishnu, a major Hindu deity, and, in orthodox revivalist usage from the nineteenth century onward, the preferred term for devotees of Hinduism because unlike "Hindu," a Persian term, *santan* is Sanskritic.

25. Raymond Schwab, *The Oriental Renaissance: Europe's Rediscovery of India and the East 1680–1880*, trans. Gene Patterson-Black (New York: Columbia University Press, 1987), 7.

26. Aamir Mufti, *Forget English: Orientalism and World Literatures* (Cambridge: Harvard University Press, 2016) 129.

27. Antoine Galland, *The Arabian Nights' Entertainments: consisting of one thousand and one stories*, Vol. 1, trans. Anonymous (London: Andrew Bell, 1713), vi.

28. Francois Petis La Croix, *The Thousand and One Days: Persian Tales*, Vol. 1., trans. Ambrose Philips (London: J. and R. Tonson, 1714), xi.

29. Saree Makdisi and Felicity Nussbaum, Introduction to *The Arabian Nights in Historical Context*, ed. Makdisi and Nussbaum (New York: Oxford University Press, 2008), 12.

30. Ibid.

31. Worth noting here are two invaluable, now largely obscure, studies that Said mentions in the section he devotes to European perceptions of Islam up until the nineteenth century. Both studies, Samuel C. Chew's study of representations of Muslims and Islam in Renaissance and Tudor England, and R. W. Southern's *Western Views of Islam in the Middle Ages* (Cambridge: Harvard University Press, 1961) acknowledge that Western conceptions and subsequent representations of Islam and Muslims for many centuries were largely the result of ignorance and an inability to "comprehend" this formation through the same frames and meters as itself. To quote Southern, "in understanding Islam, the West could get no help from antiquity, and no comfort from the present." See Southern, 4.

32. Samuel L. Chew, *The Crescent and the Rose: Islam and England During the Renaissance* (New York: Oxford University Press, 1937), 104.

33. Ibid.

34. The case of the Mahometan, though parallel perhaps, is quite different from that of the Jew in early modern and modern English fictions. The physical presence of Jewish communities in England and proximate territories such as France and the Netherlands, merited a more stringent treatment of the Jew, who presented a threat to English Christianity, both through the possibility of a false conversion or by luring Christians toward Judaism. Given that Jews were recognized, albeit through crude markers, as racially distinct, they also presented the constant threat of miscegenation. Thus, the Jew was almost always a criminal, that too, one of insidious tendencies that had to be overcome by the heroics, wit, and open-mindedness of the Christian Englishman. For more specific literary studies, see, for example, James Shapiro's *Shakespeare and the Jews* (New York: Columbia University Press 1996), and Frank Felsenstein's *Anti-Semitic Stereotypes: A Paradigm of Otherness in English Popular Culture 1660–1830* (Baltimore: Johns Hopkins University Press, 1995).

35. See Muhsin Mahdi, *The Thousand and One Nights* (Leiden: E. J. Brill, 1995), 23.

36. See Aravamudan, "The Adventure Chronotope and the Oriental Xenotrope: Galland, Sheridan, and Joyce Domesticate *The Arabian Nights*"; Madeleine Dobie, "Translation in the Contact Zone: Antoine Galland's *Mille et une nuits: contes arabs*," in *The Arabian Nights in Historical Context*. Also see Marina Warner, *Stranger Magic: Charmed States and the Arabian Nights* (Cambridge: Belknap Press, 2012).
37. Ibid., 33.
38. Galland, *Arabian Nights' Entertainments*, Vol.1, vi.
39. For the purposes of this project, I work largely with the phenomenon of the *Arabian Nights Entertainments* in England, and thus refer mostly to the Grub Street translation, i.e., volumes that circulated in England. Where needed, I turn to the French text to corroborate or mark difference.
40. Galland, *Arabian Nights' Entertainments*, vi.
41. Ibid.
42. Ibid., iv.
43. Ibid., vi.
44. Ibid., 17.
45. Ibid., 18.
46. Ibid., 19.
47. Ibid.
48. Ibid., 20.
49. Scheherazade's education would have been rather familiar to the typical bourgeois or aristocratic English or Frenchman. In Philip Sydney's "Apology for Poetry" (1583), philosophy, history, physic or medicine, and the liberal arts are seen as essential elements of "human skill." In France, Renaissance scholars, including Michel de Montaigne and Pierre Ronsard, were schooled in the *studia humanitatis*, which included history, moral philosophy, and poetry among other disciplines. Recent scholarly works detailing Renaissance education in France and England include Michael Pincombe's *Elizabethan Humanism: Literature and Learning in the Later Sixteenth Century* (London: Routledge 2001), and Jonathan Patterson's *Representing Avarice in Late Renaissance France* (London: Oxford 2015).
50. Antoine Galland, *Les Milles et Une Nuits: Contes Arabes* (Chez Pierre Husson, 1704), 40.
51. Though Schahriar is not identified explicitly as Mahometan, his religious practices are in line with Islam.
52. Ambrose Philips, "Epistle Dedicatory," in La Croix, *Persian Tales*, vii.
53. Ibid., x.
54. Ambrose Philips, *The Poetical Works of Ambrose Philips: With the Life of the Author* (London: G. Hawthorn, 1799), xxiv.
55. La Croix, *Persian Tales*, 6.
56. La Croix, Preface to *Turkish Tales; consisting of several extraordinary adventures*, trans. Anonymous (London: J. Tonson, 1708), iii.
57. Ibid., iv.
58. Ibid., 1.
59. Ibid., 2.
60. Beattie, "On Fable and Romance," 509.
61. Lance Bertelsen, "Popular entertainment and instruction, literary and dramatic: chapbooks, advice books, almanacs, ballads, farces, pantomimes, prints and shows" in the *Cambridge History of English Literature*, 65.

62. Ibid.
63. Galland, *Arabian Nights' Entertainments*, 112.
64. Galland, *Arabian Nights' Entertainments*, 116, 118, 128.
65. Gerald Maclean, *Britain and the Islamic World 1558–1713* (New York: Oxford University Press, 2011), 234.
66. Ibid.
67. Galland, *Arabian Nights' Entertainments*, 127.
68. Ibid.
69. La Croix, *Persian Tales*, Vol. 3, 54.
70. Ibid., 70.
71. Ibid., 81.
72. Ibid., 123.
73. Ibid., 135.
74. Ibid., 151.
75. Ibid., 162–84.
76. Ballaster, *Fabulous Orients*, 262.
77. Ibid., 263.
78. Galland, *Arabian Nights' Entertainments*, 57.
79. Ibid., 405.
80. Ibid., 415.
81. Frances Sheridan, *The History of Nourjahad*, in *Three Oriental Tales*, ed. Alan Richardson (London: Houghton Mifflin, 2002), 46.
82. Ibid.
83. Ibid., 55.
84. Ibid., 58.
85. Ibid., 74.
86. For more on early orientalists such as Guillaume Postel, Matteo Ricci, and Jaoa Rodgrigues, see Urs App's fascinating volume, *The Birth of Orientalism* (Philadelphia: University of Pennsylvania Press, 2011), particularly Chapter 1.
87. Ballaster, *Fabulous Orients*, 274
88. Francois Bernier, *Travels in the Mogul Empire*, trans. Irving Brock (London: W. Pickering, 1826), 209.
89. Urs App, *The Birth of Orientalism* (Philadelphia: University of Pennsylvania Press, 2011), 30.
90. Schwab, *Oriental Renaissance*, 22.
91. La Croix, *Persian Tales*, 298.
92. Ibid., 329.
93. Ibid., 331.
94. Ibid.
95. Ballaster, *Fabulous Orients*, 27.
96. Barthelemy d'Herbelot, *Bibliothèque orientale, ou Dictionnaire universale*, Vol. 3 (J. Neaulme & N. Van Daalen Librairies, 1777), 575.
97. William Beckford, *Vathek*, in *Three Oriental Tales*, ed. Alan Richardson, 159.
98. Ibid., 82.
99. Ibid.
100. Ibid., 83.
101. Ibid., 84.
102. Ibid., 89.

103. Ibid., 85.
104. Ibid., 95.

2 / Hindustani/Urdu: The Oriental Tale in the Colony

1. Aamir Mufti, *Forget English! Orientalisms and World Literatures* (Cambridge: Harvard University Press, 2016), 129.

2. This process of forcing past practices and inventing new works to populate the umbrella of "literature" has best been conceptualized by Aamir Mufti in his searing examination of the effects of Orientalism on the formation of world literature. In "Orientalism and the Institution of World Literatures," Mufti writes, "The (now universal) category of literature with its particular Latinate etymology and genealogy, marks this process of assimilation of diverse cultures of writing, a process only partially concealed by the use of such vernacular terms as *adab* (Arabic, Persian, Urdu) and *sāhitya* (Hindi and a number of the Indian vernaculars) to signify the new literariness." See "Orientalism and the Institution of World Literatures," *Critical Inquiry* 36, no. 3 (Spring 2010): 458–93.

3. John Gilchrist, *The Oriental Fabulist; or, Polyglot Translations of Esop's and Other Ancient Fables from the English Language, into Hindoostanee, Persian, Arabic, Brij B[hak]ha, Bongla, and Sun[s]krit, in the Roman Character* (Calcutta: 1803), ii.

4. John Gilchrist, "Appendix to Letters," in *Origins of Modern Hindustani Literature source material: Gilchrist Letters*, compiled by M. Atique Siddiqi (Aligarh: Naya Kitab Ghar, 1963), 153.

5. Ibid.

6. The *munshī* was a cleric or scribe of varying status in the courts of South Asian rulers. Described in eighteenth- and nineteenth-century contexts by Sanjay Subrahmanyam and Muzaffar Alam (2004, 24: 61–72) in "The Making of a Munshī," the *munshī* of Fort William College was hardly a passive figure. The article argues that "the pragmatic realities of political economy that had to be dealt with could not be comprehended within the *adab* of the aristocrat, and the representatives of Company Bahadur were, in any event, scarcely qualified themselves to claim such an unambiguous status. The real interlocutor for the Company official thus was the *munshī*, who was mediator and spokesman (*vakil*), but also a key personage who could both read and draft materials in Persian, and who had a grasp over the realities of politics that men such as Warren Hastings, Antoine Polier, and Claude Martin found altogether indispensable."

7. Srinivas Aravamudan, *Enlightenment Orientalism: Resisting the Rise of the Novel* (Chicago: University of Chicago Press, 2011), 17.

8. See, for example, Garland H. Cannon's fawning biography of Jones, *The Life and Mind of Oriental Jones: William Jones, the Father of Modern Linguistics* (Cambridge: Cambridge University Press, 1990), and Jawaharlal Nehru's well-known *The Discovery of India* (Calcutta: Signet Press, 1946). The latter has gone through several reprints and translations.

9. William Jones, "Discourse I" in *Discourses delivered before the Asiatic Society and Miscellaneous Papers on the Religion, Poetry, Literature Etc. of the Nations of India* (London: Charles Arnold, 1824), 2.

10. Despite the fact that for these later orientalists, the Semite was both Arab and Jew, their focus homed in progressively on inventing Judaism as the static, redundant religion

from which Christianity and the European Aryans self-liberated. Renan, not very differently from Jones, continued to see Muslims as part of a false religious universe.

11. Garland Canon, "Sir William Jones' Persian Linguistics" in *Journal of the American Oriental Society* 78, no. 4 (1958): 263.

12. The consequences of the colonial obsession with translating and reinterpreting the Hastings's administration believed to be religious laws irrevocably transformed notions of society and community in India. In particular, the work of Bernard Cohn, Nicholas Dirks, and, most recently, Shahab Ahmad, traces how entire legal systems were transposed upon people and communities, forcing their fluid notions of self into specific religious identities.

13. Aamir Mufti, "Orientalism and the Institution of World Literature," *Critical Inquiry* 36, no. 4 (Spring, 2010), 471.

14. Joseph White, "Comparison Between Christianity and Mahometanism," *Whitehall Evening Post*, February 10, 1785.

15. Ibid.

16. Ibid., 8–10.

17. M. H. Abrams, *The Mirror and the Lamp: Romantic Theory and the Critical Tradition* (New York: Oxford University Press, 1953), 87–88.

18. Jones, "On the Poetry of the Eastern Nations," in *Poems, Consisting chiefly of Translations from the Asiatick Languages* (London: Bowyer and Nicholes, 1776), 172.

19. Ibid., 170.

20. Ibid., 173.

21. Ibid., 176.

22. Ibid., 170.

23. Ibid., 176.

24. Jones, it is worth noting, actually does not connect the Arab to the Hebrew people in his theory of five Asiatic nations. The orientalist coding of the Muslim as a Semitic, a fanatical counterpart of the Jew, becomes most prominent in the work of Renan in the late nineteenth century.

25. Ibid.

26. Jones, "Discourse III," in *Discourses*, 23.

27. Ibid., 24.

28. Ibid., 27.

29. Mufti, *Forget English!*, 109.

30. Jones, "Discourse IV," in *Discourses*, 47.

31. Ibid., 50.

32. Michael J, Franklin, *Orientalist Jones: Sir William Jones, Poet, Lawyer, and Linguist 1746–94* (London: Oxford University Press, 2011), 259.

33. Raymond Schwab, *The Oriental Renaissance: Europe's rediscovery of India and the East, 1680–1880*, trans. Gene Patterson-King (New York: Columbia University Press, 1987), 5.

34. Michael J. Franklin, ed., Introduction to *Representing India: Indian Culture and Imperial Control in Eighteenth-Century British Orientalist Discourse* (London: Routledge, 2000), xi.

35. A number of works attest to precolonial India as a site where identity and the self were not defined by religious affiliation. It is worth noting that Gilchrist himself speaks of the indistinguishable identities of Hindus and Muslims in his introduction to the *Oriental Linguist*. See, for example, Cynthia Talbot, *Precolonial*

India in Practice: Society, Region, and Identity in Medieval Andhara (New York: Oxford University Press, 2001), and Nicholas Dirks, *Castes of the Mind: Colonialism and the Making of Modern India* (Princeton: Princeton University Press, 2001).

36. Richard Colley Wellesley, "Minute in Council at Fort William: by his Excellency The Most Noble Marquis Wellesley" in *The Annals of Fort William College*, ed. Thomas Roebuck (Calcutta: Philip Pereira, 1819), ii.

37. David Kopf, *British Orientalism and the Bengal Renaissance: The Dynamics of Indian Modernization 1773–1835* (Berkeley: University of California Press, 1969), 96.

38. Shamsur Rehman Faruqi points out that the name Hindustani was rarely if ever used prior to eighteenth-century English encounters in India. Hindustani, according to the English, was the language of Hindustan, or India, just as English was the language of England. Locally, the term "Hindi" was preferred. See Shamsur Rahman Faruqi, *Early Urdu Literary Culture and History* (Delhi: Oxford University Press, 2001).

39. Gilchrist, *The Oriental Fabulist*, ii.

40. See, for example, Nathaniel Brassey Halhed, Preface to *A Code of Gentoo Laws or Ordinations from the Pundits* (London: 1778) ii, or John Borthwick Gilchrist, *The Oriental Linguist: An Easy and Familiar Introduction to the Popular Language of Hindoostan* (Calcutta: Ferris and Greenway, 1798), i.

41. John Borthwick Gilchrist, *The Oriental Linguist: An Easy and Familiar Introduction to the Popular Language of Hindoostan* (Calcutta: Ferris and Greenway, 1798), iii.

42. Ibid., ii.

43. Gilchrist, "Letter to the College Council, 25th January 1802," in *Origins of Modern Hindustani Literature*, 112.

44. Alok Rai, *Hindi Nationalism* (New Delhi: Sangam Books, 2001), 24.

45. A few examples include: Fazal Ali Fazli's *Karbal Katha*, the sacred story of Karbala (1732–33), a dramatic telling of the events at Karbala translated from the sixteenth-century Persian writer Hussain Waiz Kashifi's *Rozat-ul Shuhada*, or the Telling of martyrdom; Mirza Muhammad Rafi Sauda, one of the great poets of the time, also dabbled in prose, leaving behind a biography and purportedly also a prose rendition of Mir Taqi Mir's "*Sho'la e Ishq*" (Flame of love); and Mehar Chand Khatri's *Nau Ain-e Hindi* or *Qissa-e Mahmood-o Geti Afroz* (1788).

46. For a detailed discussion of "Urdu" and the various other names used for the north-Indian language in the eighteenth and early nineteenth centuries, see Shamsur Rehman Faruqi's article "A Long History of Urdu Literary Culture, Part I: Naming and Placing a Literary Culture," in *Literary Cultures in History: Reconstructions from South Asia* (Berkeley: University of California Press, 2003). Rashmi Bhatnagar's contention that the "genealogy of modern Hindi in Enlightenment philology requires that we reopen the historical moment in the long eighteenth century known as the Fort William moment" applies to modern Urdu as well. See Rashmi Bhatnagar, "*Premsagar* (1810) and Orientalist Narratives of the 'Invention' of Modern Hindi," *boundary 2*, 39, no. 2 (2012): 75–110.

47. See, for example, K. Krishnamoorthy, "The Meaning of *Sahitya*: A Study in Semantics," *Indian Literature* 28, no. 5 (1985): 65–70, and Barbara Metcalf, *Moral Conduct and Authority: The Place of Adab in South Asian Islam* (Berkeley: University of California Press, 1984).

48. John Gilchrist, "Letter to the College Council, Calcutta, 20th June 1803," in *Origins of Modern Hindustani Literature source material: Gilchrist Letters*, compiled by M. Atique Siddiqi (Aligarh: Naya Kitab Ghar, 1963), 126.

49. Aravamudan, *Enlightenment Orientalism*, 155.

50. John Gilchrist, Preface to *The Oriental Fabulist or Polyglot Translations of Esop's and other Ancient Fables* (Calcutta: Harkaru Office, 1803), xxxv.

51. Ibid.

52. Gilchrist, *Oriental Fabulist*, 10.

53. Ibid., 96.

54. Ibid., 74.

55. Hugh Blair, *Lectures on Rhetoric and Belles Lettres*, Vol. 1 (London: A. Strathan, 1796), 376.

56. Ibid.

57. Mir Amman, *Bāġh-o Bahār*, ed. Rashid Hassan Khan (Delhi: Anjuman-e Tarraqi-e Urdu, 2009), 3.

58. For a detailed chronology and account of the metamorphoses of the term "Urdu," see Shamsur Rahman Faruqi's comprehensive study *Early Urdu Literary Culture and History* (2001). In addition to tracking the use of the term over the course of the eighteenth century, Faruqi also closely examines the early stages of the linguistic usages that evolve into this term, challenging Orientalist assertions—Hobson-Jobson, Halhed, and Gilchrist, to name a few—that Urdu was a Muslim import, born out of the conqueror's practice, rather than an organically evolved, upper-class register largely reserved for poetic composition.

59. Inshallah Khan Insha, *Daryā-e Laṭāfat* (Delhi: Anjumman-e Taraqqi-e Urdu, 1988), 27.

60. Shamsur Rehman Faruqi, *Sāhirī, Shāhī, Ṣāḥib Qirānī: Dāstān-e-Amīr Ḥamza Kā Mutāl'ah* (New Delhi: Qaumi Kaunsul Barai Farogh Urdu Zuban, 1999), 23.

61. Amman, *Bāġh-o Bahār*, 66.

62. Ibid., 217.

63. Mufti, "Orientalism," 484.

64. Christina Oesterheld, "*Qiṣṣa-e Mehrafrōz-o-Dilbar*," *Annual of Urdu Studies*, no. 14 (1999): 103–17.

65. Pritchett, *Marvelous Encounters: Folk Romance in Urdu and Hindi* (New York: Riverdale Company, 1985), 7.

66. Rashmi Bhatnagar, "*Prēmsāgar* and the Orientalist Narratives of the 'Invention' of Modern Hindi," in *boundary 2*, 39, no. 2 (2012): 85.

67. See, for example, *Report of the General Committee of Public Instruction of the Presidency of Fort William in Bengal for the Year 1835* (Bengal Military Orphan Press, 1836), or *The General Report on Public Instruction in the North Western Provinces of the Bengal Presidency 1844–1845* (Agra: Secundra Press, 1845).

68. Rajab Ali Beg Surur, *Fasānā-e 'Ajā'ib*, ed. Rashid Hassan Khan (Delhi: Anjumman-e Taraqqi- Hind, 2001), 24.

69. Ibid., 30.

70. Ibid.

71. Ibid.

72. Mufti, "Orientalism," 487.

73. Naiyer Masud, *Rajab Ali Beg Surur* (Allahabad: Department of Urdu, Allahabad University 1967), 162.

74. Ibid.

75. Henry Stewart Reid, *General Report on Public Instruction in the North West Provinces, 1854–55* (Agra: Secundra Orphan Press, 1856), 61.

76. Matthew Kempson, *Report on the Progress of Education in the North West Provinces, 1863–64* (Allahabad: Government Press, 1864), 6.

77. For an excellent and detailed history of the Persio-Urdu dāstān and its eventual decline in North India, see Pasha Mohammad Khan's *The Broken Spell: Indian Storytelling and the Romance Genre in Urdu and Persian* (Detroit: Wayne State University Press, 2019).

78. Khalil Ali Khan Ashk, *Dāstān-e Amīr Ḥamzā* (Calcutta: Janab Qazi Ibrahim Sahib), 2.

79. Ibid., 18.

80. Faruqi, *Sāhirī, Shāhī, Ṣāhib Qirānī*, 67–68.

81. Ibid., 64.

82. By the 1860s, Naval Kishore, the entrepreneurial publishing magnate in colonial India, had reprinted Ashk's version of the Amir Hamza cycle, replacing it later with Abdullah Bilgrami's, extending the text to fit several volumes rather than confining it to the original single volume.

83. John Borthwick Gilchrist, *The Hindee Story Teller, or Entertaining Expositor of the Roman Persian, and Nagree Characters*, Vol. 2 (Calcutta: Hindoostanee Press, 1802), iii.

84. Ibid.

85. Though Hamza, the hero of the *dāstān*, is the uncle of the Prophet Muhammad, nevertheless, it remained free from the more rigid structures of nation, religion, dynasty, or country. As Shamsur Rehman Faruqi points out, the *dāstān* takes place in an alternative universe and its concerns are removed from reality or the present, allowing it to operate outside of the rigid structures that often constitute culture.

86. See, for example, Farina Mir, *The Social Space of Language: Vernacular Culture in British Colonial Punjab* (Berkeley: University of California Press, 2010), 58.

87. Abdul Halim Sharar, *Guzistha Lucknow* (Lahore: Sang-e Meel, 2006), 126.

88. Maulvi Ikram Ali, *Ikhvān-us Safā* (Delhi: Anjumman-e Taraqqi-e Urdu, 1939), 7.

89. Bhatnagar, "*Prēmsāgar*," 78.

90. Ibid.

91. Ibid., 79.

92. I quote here from Sir Henry Newbolt's famous 1921 report, *The Teaching of English in England*, p. 44 (London: His Majesty's Stationary Office, 1921), commissioned by the Board of Education to examine the state of English language and literature in England's schools and to advise on its further development as an academic discipline.

93. Gauri Viswanathan, *Masks of Conquest: Literary Study and British Rule in India* (New York: Columbia University Press, 1989), 10.

94. "East India Company Charter Act of 1813, section 43" in *The Great Indian Education Debate*, ed. Lynn Zastoupil and Martin Moir (London: Curzon Press, 1999), 91.

95. Viswanathan, *Masks of Conquest*, 7.

96. H. H. Wilson, "Education of the Natives of India," *Asiatic Journal and Monthly Miscellany* (London: Parbury, Allen, and Co., 1831), 15.

97. Ibid., 13
98. Ibid.
99. "Letter from J. C. C. Sutherland Esq. Sec General of the Committee for Public Instruction, to H. J. Prinsep, Secretary to Government in the General Department, Fort William, Jan 21, 1835," Board's Collection V. 1846, India Office Records and Private Papers.
Ibid.
100. Ibid.
101. Ibid.
102. *The General Report on Public Instruction in the North Western Provinces of the Bengal Presidency 1882-84* (Bengal Secretariat Press, 1884).
103. "Appendix M" in *The General Report on Public Instruction in the North Western Provinces of the Bengal Presidency 1845-1846* (Agra: Secundra Orphan Press), xxxvii.
104. Ibid.
105. *General Report on the Public Instruction in the North West Provinces of the Bengal Presidency 1846-47* (Agra: Secundra Orphan Press, 1849), 39.
106. Ibid., 33.
107. Ibid.
108. *General Report on Public Instruction in the North Western Provinces of the Bengal Presidency 1848-49*, 15.
109. *General Report on Public Instruction in the North Western Provinces of the Bengal Presidency 1862-63* (Allahabad: Government Press, 1864), 56.
110. Ibid.
111. "Letter from J. M. Duncan, Secretary of the College to the Committee of Public Education, January, 1831" in *Report of the General Examination of the Agra College 1831*.
112. Mir Amman, *Bāġh-o Bahār*, ed. Duncan Forbes (London: W. H. Allen, 1860), iv.
113. Ibid., v.
114. Mir Amman and Lewis Ferdinand Smith, *The tale of the four durwesh* (Lucknow: Nawal Kishore Press, 1895), i.
115. Ibid.
116. Ibid., ii.
117. Ibid., iv.
118. Ibid., iv.
119. Ibid., 180.
120. Lalluji Lal, *Prēmsāgar, or the Ocean of Love*, trans. Edward B. Eastwick (London: James Madden, 1831), i.
121. Mir Amman, *Bāġh-o Bahār*, ed. Forbes, ii.
122. Mir Amman, *Bāġh-o Bahār*, ed. Khan, 58.
123. Smith, *A tale for four durwesh*, 79.
124. Mir Amman, *Bāġh-o Bahār*, ed. Forbes, 59.
125. Ibid., 90.
126. Forbes's added distress is visible in his translation, interestingly an example of an increasingly Victorian puritanism with regards to oriental literatures.

3 / Nation/*Qaum*: The "Musalmans" of India

1. William Muir, preface to *The Repentance of Nussooh* by Nazir Ahmad, trans. Matthew Kempson (London: W. H. Allen, 1884), viii.
2. William Wilson Hunter, *The Indian Musalmans: Are they bound in Conscience to Rebel against the Queen?* (London: Trübner and Company, 1876), 11.
3. Ibid.
4. Ibid.
5. Matthew Kempson, *Report on the Progress of Education in the North West Provinces 1869–70* (Allahabad: Government Press, 1870), 112.
6. Aamir Mufti, *Enlightenment in the Colony: The Jewish Question and the Crisis of Postcolonial Culture* (Princeton: Princeton University Press, 2007), 112.
7. Abdus Shakur Shaida, *Bayāz-e Sukhan* (Hyderabad: Zinda Tilismat-e Mishan Press, 1936), 116.
8. The *ashrāf*, at times also called the *shurufā*, was a class whose cultural and social makeup can be traced to the Mughal ruler, Akbar's court, which David Lelyveld describes as an "increasingly distinct variant of the international Islamic culture. In fact, the culture could hardly be called "Islamic" . . . Centered on the Persian language and taking inspiration from courtly styles of Saffavid Iran, it was a culture that had no religious prerequisites for membership . . . The class of people who moved in this cultural milieu were sometimes called *sharīf*, a word of unmistakable religious connotation in the rest of the Islamic world, but in Mughal India indicating respectability in terms of cosmopolitan Mughal criteria . . . One usually acquired *sharāfat* by birth, however; if acquired in some other way, one's identity was quickly redefined in the vocabulary of honorable descent, which implied new bonds of kinship. *Sharāfat* also defined character: a *sharīf* man was one of dignified temperament, self-confident but not overly aggressive, appreciative of good literature, music, and art, but not flamboyant, familiar with mystical experience, but hardly immersed in it. *Sharīf* social relations involved a post of deference, but were, above all, a matter of virtuosity within highly restricted bounds of etiquette." See Lelyveld, *Aligarh's First Generation: Muslim Solidarity in British India* (Princeton: Princeton University Press, 1978), 30.
9. The meteoric rise of these religious schools in the high colony is contrary to eighteenth-century trends in the Muslim world. The latter period, Ahmad S. Dallal argues in his recent book *Islam Without Europe: Traditions of Reform in Eighteenth-Century Islamic Thought* (Durham: University of North Carolina Press, 2018), is a period of grand innovation and expansion in the theological and participatory aspects of Islam, marked by leaders such as Shah Waliullah from India, Muhammad Ibn Ali Shawkani from Yemen, and Umar al-Fulani of the Nigerian Sokoto Caliphate, among others. The eighteenth century, Dallal argues, is the last time Islam is able to see itself "without Europe." From the nineteenth century onward, Islamic thinkers from the colonial world see themselves always against, with, or in relation to Europe.
10. Faisal Devji, "The Equivocal History of a Muslim Reformation," in *Islamic Reform in South Asia*, ed. Caroline Osella and Fillippo Osella (Cambridge: Cambridge University Press, 2013), 3–25.
11. The word *tehzīb* simultaneously also means *iṣlāḥ*, or correction, to make something pure again. In its noun form, it thus implies an original civilization. As

mentioned previously, in Khan's usage it expands to accommodate the idea of a culture, a Muslim culture that must advance (and correct itself) given the decayed state it is in.

12. See, for example, Khan's essay "The Reasons for *Tehzīb-Ul Akhlāq*," where he argues for the need for a monthly journal in Urdu as instrumental for Muslim progress. *Mazāmīn-e Sir Syed: Muntakhibāt Tehzīb ul-Akhlāq*, ed. Ghulam Hussain Zulfiqar (Lahore: Sang-e Meel 1993), 5.

13. A somewhat different version of events is put forth by Jennifer Dubrow in her recent work, *Cosmopolitan Dreams: The Making of Modern Urdu Literary Culture in South Asia* (Honolulu: University of Hawaii Press, 2018). Dubrow argues, not incorrectly, that the last few decades of the nineteenth century also marked a moment of cosmopolitanism for Urdu and allowed for a community bound by language rather than religion. Using the example of the Hindu journalist-cum-novelist Rathan Nath Sarshar, Dubrow suggests that at this point Urdu was not actually marked by communal lines. But going forward, she also acknowledges that within just a few more years, this was no longer the case. My argument in this chapter focuses on the increasingly influential, colonially patronized set of writers and thinkers to show why figures such as Sarshar and his print experiments no longer command cultural relevance in the contemporary Urdu imagination.

14. Barbara Metcalf, Introduction to *Moral Conduct and Authority: The Place of Adab in South Asian Islam*, ed. Barbara Metcalf (Berkeley: University of California Press, 1984), 2.

15. Ibid., 3.

16. C. M. Naim, "Prize-Winning *Adab*: A Study of Five Books Written in Response to the Allahabad Government Gazette Notification," in *Moral Conduct and Authority*, 292.

17. As David Lelyveld elaborates in his still unmatched work on the Aligarh Movement, "Sayyid Ahmad redefined the meaning of '*qaum*.' The word has been a loose one for any group defined by a concept of common ancestry—'tribe,' 'caste,' 'lineage,' 'family.' Now it referred to the Muslims of British India, not just north India but places as far flung as eastern Bengal and the town of Trichinopoly in Tamil Nad." Syed Ahmad's usage of the term obviously was not consistent, going between regionalism and geographies at will. But the most cited and celebrated of his speeches remains one in which he refers to Hindus and Muslims as constituting two distinct *qaums*. See Lelyveld, *Aligarh's First Generation*, 143.

18. Enlightenment ideals that linked the nation to language and ancient civilization did not remain restricted to Europe but, in fact, traveled to the colony as early as the late eighteenth century, and took hold in the nineteenth, by way of the educational system where curricula in history and literature, both English and vernacular, emphasized the importance of nation. An excellent example is a staple exam question on the literature curriculum at Delhi College, where students were asked to translate parts of Thomas Carlyle's essay, "The State of German Literature" (1827) into Hindustani and Hindi. A frequent excerpt is the sentence, "A country which has no National Literature, or a Literature too insignificant to force its way abroad, must always be to its neighbors, at least in every important spiritual respect, an unknown and misestimated country." See "Scholarship Questions: Vernacular Translation" in *Annual Report from Delhi College, 1854–55*, National Archives, New Delhi India, xxv.

19. Chatterjee, "The Nationalist Resolution of the Women's Question" in *Recasting Women: Essays in Colonial History*, ed. Kumkum Sangari and Sudesh Vaid (Delhi: Kali for Women, 1989), 233–53.

20. "Short Notices," in *The Calcutta Review* 47 (Calcutta: Barham, Hill and Co., 1868), 209.

21. Faisal Devji, "Gender and the Politics of Space: The Movement for Women's Reform in Muslim India, 1857–1900," *South Asia: Journal of South Asian Studies* 1, no. 14 (May 2007), 141–53.

22. Ibid.

23. Ibid.

24. As quoted in C. M. Naim, "Prize-Winning *Adab*: Five Urdu Books Written in Response to the Gazette Notification No. 791A (1868)," in *Urdu Texts and Contexts: The Selected Essays of C. M. Naim* (Delhi: Permanent Black, 2004), 123.

25. Ibid.

26. Ibid.

27. Matthew Kempson, "Recommendation" for *The Bride's Mirror* by Nazir Ahmad, trans. G. E. Ward, ed. Frances Pritchett (Delhi: Permanent Black), 200.

28. *Imperial and Asiatic Quarterly Review and Oriental and Colonial Record*, Vol. 9 (Woking: Oriental University Institute, 1900), 410.

29. Nazir Ahmad, *Mirāt al-'Arūs* (Lahore: Ferozesons, 1988), 5.

30. Ibid., 6.

31. Ibid., 23.

32. Ibid., 810.

33. See Felicity Nussbaum, "Slavery, Blackness, and Islam: *The Arabian Nights* in the Eighteenth Century," in *Slavery and the Cultures of Abolition: Essays marking the bicentennial of the British Abolition Act of 1807*, ed. Brycchan Carey and Peter J. Kitson (Cambridge: D. S. Brewer, 2007), 150–72.

34. Kumkum Sangari, *Politics of the Possible: Essays on Gender, History, Narratives and Colonial English* (Delhi: Anthem Press, 1999), 209.

35. David Lelyveld, *Aligarh's First Generation*: Muslim Solidarity in British India (Princeton: Princeton University Press, 1978), 37.

36. Chatterjee, "Nationalist Resolution," in *Recasting Women*, 245.

37. Ibid., 837.

38. Ibid.

39. Ibid., 838.

40. For a more sympathetic reading of *Mirāt al-'Arūs*, see Ruby Lal's *Coming of Age in Nineteenth-Century India: The Girl Child and the Art of Playfulness* (Cambridge: Cambridge University Press, 2012).

41. Ahmad, *Mirāt*, 85.

42. Ibid. In her excellent history of the Deobandi movement in India, Barbara Metcalf mentions how one founder of the movement "dreamed of seeing the Ka'abah located in Deoband's garden; of Hazrat Ali founding a school whose pupils he later realized as Deobands; and of the Prophet himself giving milk to students there." The Ka'bah, Mecca, and the Prophet Muhammad, then, are rewritten by such movements as the actual origins, or lodestones for Indian Muslims. See Metcalf, *Islamic Revival in British India 1860–1900: Deoband* (Princeton: Princeton University Press, 1982), 92.

43. Barbara Metcalf, *Islamic Revival in British India: Deoband 1860–1900* (Princeton: Princeton University Press, 1982), 149.

44. Shahab Ahmad, *What is Islam?*, 191.

45. Ibid., 125.

46. Here I rely on Shahab Ahmad's eviscerating critique of modern, law/state-based interpretations of Islam: "In the cases of the numerous societies of Muslims under colonial rule, the conceptual, discursive, social, political, and institutional reconstitution of 'Islam' into the terms of the modern European binary of religious/secular was effected by the forceful intervention in the societies of Muslim colonial subjects by European colonial regimes, not just in measures such as the confining of the jurisdiction of Islamic law to the domain of the 'personal status law' of marriage, inheritance, and so on (the personal being the legitimate modern domain for the religious), but also in actions with more insidious consequences, such as the severing of the historical relationships of various intellectual discourses through the radical reorganization and reconstitution of educational institutions and curricular content—that is to say, by a prescriptive reconstitution of the discourses and institutions of concept-formation, including the compartmentalizing concepts of 'religious' and 'secular.'" See Ahmad, *What is Islam* 190–91.

47. Ahmad, *Mirāt*, 106.

48. Ibid.

49. Ahmad, *Mirāt*, 132.

50. Ibid., 114.

51. In his report on colonial education for the year 1869–70, Matthew Kempson wrote of the female students in colonial government schools: "They display a very pleasing intelligence and besides being able to read, write, and cypher, learn needle and beadwork." See *General Report on the Progress of Education in the North-West Provinces 1869–70* (Allahabad: Government Press, 1870), 50.

52. J. F. Blumhardt, Catalogue of the Library of the India Office, Volume II (London: Eyre and Spottiswood), 145.

53. Nazir Ahmad, *Muntaḳib ul-Hikāyāt* (Karachi: Urdu Academy Sindh, 1979), 7.

54. Ibid., 9

55. Ibid., 57.

56. Ahmad, *Mirāt*, 122.

57. Ahmad, *Mirāt*, 123–4.

58. *Selections from the Records of Government, North-West Provinces* (Allahabad: Government Press, 1870), 43.

59. The title of this work is perhaps borrowed from one of the tales in Jalaluddin Rumi's thirteenth-century *Masnavi*. A man named Nasuh disguises himself as a woman and gains employment as an attendant in the royal baths. Eventually, Nasuh sees the error of his ways and asks the advice of a wise Sufi who prays for his forgiveness. Nasuh, nevertheless, returns to his work at the bathhouse, until one day when a lady loses her jewelry and all attendants are to be searched. Knowing he could be put to death if discovered, Nasuh faints out of fear. When he comes to, the jewels have been found and he has not been stripped and discovered. From then on, Nasuh stays away from the bathhouse, having learned his lesson that on the day of judgment, his own bodily members will give testimony against him.

60. Nazir Ahmad, *Taubat al-Naṣūḥ* (Lucknow: Shams ul-Matlaba, 1873), 3. This preface disappears from later versions and citations from the main text are from the contemporary Sang-e-Meel edition.

61. Ibid.

62. Ibid.

63. Ibid. Ahmad cites from the thirty-third Surah, *Āhzāb*, or "Calamity" here. The original Quranic verse, according to the Muhammad Asad translation reads: "Verily, we did offer the trust [of reason and volition] to the heavens, and the earth, and the mountains: but they refused to bear it because they were afraid of it. Yet man took it up for, verily, he has always been prone to be most wicked, most foolish."

64. Ibid.

65. Ibid., 7

66. Ibid., 5.

67. William Muir, Preface to *The Repentance of Nussooh: The Tale of a Muslim Family a Hundred Years Ago*, by Nazir Ahmad, trans. M. Kempson, ed. C. M. Naim (Delhi: Permanent Black, 2004), xiii.

68. Sangari, *Politics of the Possible*, 235.

69. Ahmad, *Taubat al-Naṣūḥ* (Lahore: Sang-e Meel, 2004), 292.

70. Ahmad, *Taubat*, 339.

71. Ahmad, *Taubat*, 341.

72. Bhabha, *The Location of Culture* (New York: Routledge, 2004), 102.

73. John Gilchrist, *The Oriental Fabulist* (Calcutta: Hurkaru Office, 1803), xxv.

74. Ahmad, *Taubat*, 342.

75. Ibid.

76. Ahmad, *Lekčaroñ kā majmū'ā*, Vol. 2 (Agra: Mufid-e 'Am Press, 1914), 440.

77. Christina Oesterheld, "Deputy Nazir Ahmad and Delhi College," in *The Delhi College: Traditional Elites, the Colonial State, and Education before 1857*, ed. Margrit Pernau (Delhi: Oxford University Press, 2006), 322.

78. Ahmad, *Taubat*, 365.

79. Ibid., 405.

80. Ibid.

81. Ibid., 406.

82. Ibid., 406-7

83. Ibid., 407.

84. Frances Pritchett, *Nets of Awareness: Urdu Poetry and its Critics* (Berkeley: University of California Press, 1994), 186.

85. Naim, "Prize-Winning Adab," 145.

86. Ahmad, *Taubat*, 411.

87. Ibid., 372.

88. Ibid., 439.

89. An excellent example of the fluid nature of Indo-Persian poetics, the *musaddas*, formally a poem with stanzas of six half verses, traveled to Urdu from Persian in the sixteenth and seventeenth centuries.

90. For more on Colonel Holroyd, see Frances W. Pritchett, *Nets of Awareness: Urdu Poetry and Its Critics*.

91. Christopher Shackle and Javed Majid, Introduction to *Hali's Musaddas: The Ebb and Flow of Islam* by Altaf Hussain Hali, trans. Shackle and Majid (Delhi: Oxford University Press, 1997), 2.

92. Chatterjee, "Nationalist Resolution," in *Recasting Women*, 237.

93. Altaf Hussain Hali, *Majālis-un Nisā*, Part I (Panipat: Hali Press, 1924), 24.

94. Ibid., 38

95. Ibid., 46.

96. Altaf Hussain Hali, "Voices of Silence," trans. Gail Minault (Delhi: Chanakya Publications, 1986), 81.

97. Devji, "Gender and the Politics of Space," 142.
98. Hali, *Majālis-un Nisā*, Part 2 (Panipat: Hali Press, 1924), 33–43.
99. Ibid., 87–88.
100. Altaf Hussain Hali, *Hali's Musaddas*, ed. Shackle and Majid, 90.
101. Ibid.
102. Ibid., 129.
103. Ibid., 141.
104. Ibid., 144.
105. Hali, *Majālis*, Part 1, 54.
106. Hali, *Hali's Musaddas*, 156
107. Ibid., 172.
108. Ibid., 192
109. Nauman Naqvi, "Mourning Indo-Muslim Modernity: Moments in Post-Colonial Urdu Literary Culture" (PhD dissertation: Columbia University, 2008), 44.
110. "Dilgudaz," *Dilgudāz*, January 1887, 4
111. Ibid.
112. Ibid.
113. Ibid.
114. Ibid.
115. Ibid.
116. *Dilgudāz*, January 1888, 15
117. Ibid., 16
118. Ibid.
119. Ibid., 15.
120. Ibid.
121. Partha Chatterjee, *The Nation and Its Fragments: Colonial and Postcolonial Histories* (Princeton: Princeton University Press, 1994), 77.
122. Ibid., 98.
123. Abdul Halim Sharar, *Florā Florindā* (Lahore: Maktab Al-Quraish, 1986), 25.
124. Ibid.
125. Ibid., 35.
126. Ibid., 42.
127. Ibid., 97.
128. Ibid., 149.
129. Ibid., 272.
130. Ibid., 275.
131. Ibid., 349.
132. Ibid., 350.
133. Ibid.
134. Ibid.
135. Ibid., 352.
136. Ibid.
137. Perkins, C. Ryan, "A New *Pablik*: Abdul Halim Sharar, volunteerism, and the Anjuman-e Dar-us-Salam in late nineteenth-century India," *Modern Asian Studies* 49, no. 4 (2015): 1049–90.
138. Ibid.
139. Ibid.

4 / Martyr/*Mujāhid*: Muslim Origins and the Modern Urdu Novel

1. Firaq Gorakhpuri, "The Nature and Purpose of Literature," in *The Marxist Cultural Movement in India: Chronicles and Documents, 1936–47*, Vol. 3, ed. Sudhi Pradhan (Delhi: National Book Agency, 1985), 40.

2. Aamir Mufti, *Enlightenment in the Colony: The Jewish Question and the Crisis of Postcolonial Culture* (Princeton: Princeton University Press, 2007), 180.

3. Ibid., 181.

4. Ibid.

5. While we, in the academy and other progressive social formations, believe that Manto's condemnation is a thing of a dated past, he continues to be labeled as "*fahash*" (obscene) and anti-Islamic by religious groups, Internet warriors, and conservative literary journals. See, for example, the virulent rhetoric directed toward Anwar Maqsood, a well-known actor and producer, for reading out Manto's letters in a performance, and against the University of Sargodha for including a Manto story in a literature textbook at: https://defence.pk/pdf/threads/indecent-writing-included-in-urdu-literature-book-sargodha-university.551112/.

6. At the same time, it must be noted that both schools seem to oppose the idea of *l'art pour l'art*, or art for the sake of art. Within Progressive writings, there is clarity that art and literature must be aligned with the day-to-day concerns of people; it should not be exclusive or abstract, but accessible and realist.

7. Ahmad Ali, "Progressive Views of Art," in *The Marxist Cultural Movement*, 64.

8. Nasim Hijazi, *Dāstān-e Mujāhid* (Lahore: Qaumi Qutub Khana, 1954), 1.

9. Pascale Casanova, *The World Republic of Letters*, trans. M. B. Devoise (Cambridge: Harvard University Press, 2004), 19.

10. Ibid.

11. Closer, perhaps, is Alexander Beecroft's conception of national literatures as emerged from vernacular literature. See Beecroft, *An Ecology of World Literature* (New York: Verso, 2014), 195.

12. Partha Chatterjee, *Nationalist Thought and the Colonial World: A Derivative Discourse* (Minneapolis: University of Minnesota Press), 51.

13. Recent historical accounts of the 1947 creation of Pakistan out of colonial India seem either to credit Muhammad Ali Jinnah as the "sole spokesman," to use Ayesha Jalal's phrase, of the independence effort, or in a bizarre move, as is Venkat Dhulipala's *Creating a New Medina*, to cast Pakistan as the effort of a religious orthodoxy. See, for example, Ayesha Jalal, *The Sole Spokesman: Jinnah, the Muslim League and the Demand for Pakistan* (Cambridge: Cambridge University Press, 1985); Faisal Devji, *Muslim Zion: Pakistan as a Political Idea* (Cambridge: Harvard University Press, 2013); and Venkat Dhulipala, *Creating a New Medina: State Power, Islam, and the Quest for Pakistan in Late Colonial North India* (Cambridge: Cambridge University Press, 2015).

14. See M. Asaduddin's much-cited article, "First Urdu Novel: Contesting Claims and Disclaimers," *Annual of Urdu Studies* 16 (2003): 76–97. See also, Meenakshi Mukherjee's *Early Novels in India* (Delhi: Sahitya Academy, 2002).

15. See, for example: Yusuf Sarmast, *Bīsvīn Sadī Meiñ Urdū Nāvil* (Hyderabad: National Book Depot, 1973); Asif Farrkuhi, "*Hairatī hai yeh 'ā'inā: Urdū nāvil kī dāstān*," literally, This mirror is astonishing: the *dastan* of the Urdu novel (1993); Jamil Jalibi, *Tārīkh-e Urdū Adab*, Vol. 4 (Lahore: Majlis-e Taraqqi-e Adab, 2012);

Shaista Bano Suhrawardy, *A Critical Survey of the Development of the Urdu Novel and Short Story* (London: Longman's, 1945). The exception to all these, perhaps, is *Mīzān*, a slim volume of essays written by Faiz Ahmad Faiz in 1960.

16. In particular, I am concerned with Mufti's assertion that the 1930s and 1940s see the "near-disappearance of what is widely held to be the national form, par excellence, namely, the novel, and sees, instead, the appearance of a new and self-confident short story in the work of a new generation of writers . . ." See *Enlightenment in the Colony*, 183.

17. It is worth noting that this chronotope persists only in Urdu literary and popular writing despite the fact that the Muslim League, the political party that eventually took up the cause of a separate state for India's Muslims was born in Bengal, the province that incidentally had the largest population of Muslims even at the time of Partition. The concerns of Muslim writers writing in Bangla during the first half of the twentieth century are markedly different from those writing in Urdu. Notable figures include Abujafar Shamsudin, Akhteruzzaman Elias, Shawkat Ali, and Abu Ishaque, among others. Their novels and stories have little interest in origin, the practice of Islam, or even the improvement of language. Instead, they explore Partition and other historic events through the construction of social classes, the disparities between feudal landlords and the poor peasantry, urbanization, and local folklore. While this book cannot explore these writers in depth, I am grateful to Nasia Anam for bringing up the systematic erasure of Bengali Muslims in histories of Pakistan written by academics of North Indian/Pakistani descent.

18. See Edward Said, *Culture and Imperialism* (New York: Vintage Books, 1994), and Nancy Armstrong, *Desire and Domestic Fiction: A Political History of the Novel* (New York: Oxford University Press, 1987).

19. Edward Said, *Culture and Imperialism*, 75.

20. Raziq ul-Khairi, "Musavir-e Gham" in *Majmu'ā Rashid-ul Khairī* (Lahore: Sang-e Meel Publishers, 1998), 9.

21. Ibid., 10.

22. Ibid.

23. Quratulain Hyder, "*Adab aur Khavatin*," *'Işmat*, Platinum Jubilee Issue, 1978.

24. Ibid.

25. Sheikh Muhammad Ikram, "'Işmat," *'Işmat*, June 1908.

26. Ibid.

27. Rashid ul-Khairi, "'Işmat," *Makhzan*, June 1909.

28. Ibid.

29. Gail Minault, *Secluded Scholars: Women's Education and Muslim Social Reform in Colonial India* (Delhi: Oxford University Press, 1998), 139.

30. Rashid ul-Khairi, "*Ēk shahīd turk kī mā kā khat*," *'Işmat*, September 1909.

31. *Ban'āt*, Vol. 1, Issue 1, December 1927.

32. Raziq ul-Khairi, *'Işmat kī Kahānī* (Delhi: Işmat Book Depot, 1939), 29.

33. Ibid.

34. A closer investigation into the matter reveals that the unnamed Muslim precinct is Bhopal, at the time ruled by Sultan Jahan Begum, one of the four queens of the small princely state. Rashid ul-Khairi's disagreement with the Begum took place because of her support for the movement against polygamy allowed to Muslim men in Islam. Despite the fact that Khairi had spoken of the social ills resulting from one man marrying multiple wives in his novel *Saukan kā Jalāpā*, he nevertheless

slammed the party in charge of furthering the motion in *'Işmat*, deeming it un-Islamic and a political move to impress the English. More details of this event can be found in Siobhan Lambert-Hurley's *Muslim Women, Reform, and Princely Patronage: Nawab Sultan Jahan Begum of Bhopal* (New York: Routledge, 2007).

35. Rashid ul-Khairi, *Andalus ki Shehzadi ya Tai'd- Ghaibi* (Delhi: Hamidiya Press, 1933), 6.

36. Ibid., 20.

37. Ibid., 23.

38. Ibid., 44.

39. Rashid ul-Khairi, *Bint ul-Vaqt* (Delhi: Mahbub ul-Mataba Burqi Press, 1933), 8.

40. Ibid., 67.

41. Ibid., 29.

42. Ibid., 30.

43. Ibid., 32.

44. Ibid.

45. For a more nuanced and historical view, see John Slight, *The British Empire and the Hajj: 1865–1956* (Cambridge: Harvard University Press, 2015).

46. Khairi, *Bint ul-Vaqt*, 51.

47. Ibid., 62.

48. Ibid., 63.

49. Not only did Zia re-issue a number of Hijazi's novels through the government education board, but he also sanctioned their production as televised serials on the national channel, PTV. Among his televised novels are *Ākhrī Chatān*, about the events of the Abbasid caliphate, and *Khāk aur Khūn*, detailing the events of the 1947 Partition, with particular attention to Kashmir.

50. Hijazi, *Dāstān-e Mujāhid*, 1.

51. Ibid.

52. Ibid.

53. Gyorg Lukacs, *The Historical Novel*, trans. Hannah and Stanley Mitchell (London: Merlin Press, 1989), 25.

54. Ibid., 42.

55. Pakistani publishers are loath to give exact information on sales, but representatives at Jahangir Book Depot confirm that at least 10,000 copies of novels such as *Dāstān-e Mujāhid* and *Muhammad bin Qāsim* are issued in every print run today. Qaumi Kutab Khana, the original publishing house, released 2,000 copies in each print run of *Mujāhid* as attested in the copyright information of their editions.

56. Hijazi, *Dastan*, 14.

57. Ibid., 10.

58. Ibid., 153.

59. Ibid.

60. Ibid., 173.

61. Ibid., 178.

62. I owe much of the explication of Maulana Maududi's work and ideas to Ali Usman Qasmi's excellent chapter, "Differentiating Between Pakistan and Napakistan: Maulana Abdul Ala Maududi's critique of the Muslim League and Muhammad Ali Jinnah," in his volume *Muslims Against the Muslim League: Critiques of the Idea of Pakistan* (Cambridge: Cambridge University Press, 2017).

63. *Tarjuman-ul Quran*, September 1933, 37–40. I borrow Qasmi's translation here.

64. Ali Usman Qasmi, "Differentiating Between Pakistan and Napakistan: Maulana Abdul Ala Maududi's critique of the Muslim League and Muhammad Ali Jinnah," in *Muslims Against the Muslim League: Critiques of the Idea of Pakistan*, ed. Ali Usman Qasmi and Meghan Robb (Cambridge: Cambridge University Press, 2017), 118.

65. Abil A'la Maududi, Transcript of *"Jihad fi Sabilillah,"* Speech at Town Hall, Lahore, April 1939.

66. It is almost shocking to see how much of Maududi's language and terminology is borrowed from thinkers such as Lenin and even Marx. His critique of European colonialism is essentially a critique of capitalism and its attendant violence. Islam, in this speech as well as in his volume on *jihad*, is constructed against Western conceptions of religion, state, and economy.

67. Ibid.

68. Ibid.

69. Ibid.

70. Nasim Hijazi, *Muhammad bin Qāsim* (Lahore: Jahangir Book Depot, 2002), second cover.

71. Ibid.

72. Ibid.

73. The other book flap of the same edition carries an adulatory blurb from Dr. Abdul Qadeer Khan, celebrated in Pakistan as the "father" of the atomic bomb. Despite having been placed under house arrest for selling state technologies to other countries, Khan remains a popular national hero in Pakistan.

74. Hijazi seems to derive much of the basis of his story from Ali Kufi's *Chachnama*, a thirteenth-century Persian text, which became the basis for Orientalist histories of the subcontinent. Manan Ahmad's brilliant monograph *A Book of Conquest: The "Chachnama" and Muslim Origins in South Asia* (Cambridge: Harvard University Press, 2016) exposes the colonial readings through which the *Chachnama* becomes synonymous with history, rather than, as he argues, with "political theory" from "the politically heterogeneous world of thirteenth-century Sind."

75. See, for example, the wildly popular Maulana Tariq Jameel's sermon on Muhammad bin Qasim where he tells his exclusively male audience how bin Qasim visited his hometown, Multan, converting 100,000 people to Islam on his journey from Multan to Makran. Living, breathing, almost palpable in a sermon such as this one, bin Qasim's presence in Pakistan is perpetuated through everyday personal stories (https://www.youtube.com/watch?v=dahuBYn9BmU). More alarming, obviously, is the letter a young man, called Faisal Shahzad, wrote to a group of friends and family in February 2006, after the Danish cartoon controversy: "17 year old Muhammad bin Qasim attacked the sub-continent Pak-o-Hind and defeated an infidel Raja Dahir because there came to him news of a Muslim woman who was raped!! and today our beloved Prophet (Katim Nabieen Mohammad al-Ameen) PBUH has been disrespected and disgraced in the whole world and we sit and watch with shame and sorrow and most of us don't even care." In 2010, Faisal Shahzad was arrested for having planned the failed Times Square bombing in New York City.

76. Hijazi, *Muhammad bin Qāsim* (Lahore: Jahangir Book Depot, 1945), 7.

77. Ibid.

78. Ibid., 25–26.

79. Ibid., 200.

80. Ibid., 226.
81. Ibid., 262.
82. Ibid., 263.
83. Ibid., 40.
84. Ibid., 250.
85. In a footnote, Hijazi dismisses the version of events offered by Ali Kufi in his famous *Chachnama* in which bin Qasim is put to death for allegedly violating one of Raja Dahir's daughters as he carries them to the caliph Walid. Later, Walid discovers this allegation to be an attempt at revenge by one of Dahir's daughters, and he puts both girls to death.
86. Ibid., 352.
87. Over the course of her literary career, Butt changed publishers several times. She was first published by Ehsan Brothers of Lahore, and subsequently, by Maqbool Academy, a well-known literary publishing house established in 1954; Ferozsons, a leading Lahore bookseller set up in 1894; and Mavra Book Depot, a younger literary publishing house set up by the poet Khalid Sharif in the 1970s. Today, the rights to Butt's works have been bought by Sang-e Meel, a major publishing house based in Lahore, whose authors list includes literary bigwigs such as Ashfaq Ahmad, Bano Qudsia, Ahmad Nadeem Qasmi, and Abdullah Hussain, among others.
88. Razia Butt, "*Meri Kitab Dunya*," YouTube Video, 30:51, posted November 2012, https://www.youtube.com/watch?v=uG2S9QEkxV4.
89. Ibid.
90. Razia Butt, *Bano* (Lahore: Sang-e Meel, 2014), i.
91. Ibid.
92. Ibid., 97.
93. Ibid., 113.
94. Ibid., 110.
95. Ibid., 112.
96. Ibid., 229.
97. Ibid., 251.
98. Ibid., 368.
99. Ibid.
100. Here Butt refers to Khalid bin Valid, the Prophet Muhammad's companion, under whose political leadership the caliph of Islam became the leader of a unified Arabia, and to Tariq bin Ziyad, whose eighth-century invasion into Spain via Gibraltar earned him lasting fame.
101. Ibid., 379.
102. Ibid., 421.
103. Ibid., 423.
104. Perhaps the most important scholarly and personal work on this question is Urvashi Butalia's. Though best elaborated in her book *The Other Side of Silence: Voices from the Partition of India*, Butalia has also written a number of essays on the question. Here I borrow a succinct but comprehensive elaboration from her essay "Community, State and Gender: On Women's Agency During Partition" in the *Economic and Political Weekly*: "Thousands of women on both sides of the newly formed borders (estimates range from 25,000 to 29,00 Hindu and Sikh women and 12,000 to 15,000 Muslim women) were abducted, raped, forced to convert, forced into marriage, forced back into what the two states defined as 'their proper homes,' torn

apart from their families once during Partition by those who abducted them, and again, after Partition, by the state which tried to 'recover' and 'rehabilitate' them. Untold numbers of women, particularly in Sikh families, were killed ('martyred' is the term that is used) by their kinsmen in order to 'protect' them from being converted, perhaps equal numbers of them killed themselves. The violence women experienced took particular forms: there are accounts of innumerable rapes, of women being stripped naked and paraded down streets, of their breasts being cut off, of their bodies being carved with religious symbols of the other community. And then there are other, less obvious traumas: for many, particularly middle class women, the dislocation meant that the option of marriage, supposedly a part of 'normal' everyday society, was closed off, and they had to live alone, or as 'spinsters' with their families; others were widowed, along with losing their homes and possessions, and were left to build lives on their own, something that many of them were ill-equipped for. Several had to spend their lives in women's homes, permanent refugees, and many are still alive today, their stories still untold."

105. Razia Butt, *Vatan kī Bētī* (Lahore: Sang-e Meel, 2013), 15.
106. Ibid., 370.
107. Ibid., 29.
108. Ibid., 104.
109. Ibid., 549.
110. Ibid.
111. Ibid., 430.
112. Ibid., 571.
113. Ibid., 581.
114. Headed by Majid Nizami, the paper published in Urdu as *Nava'e Vaqt* and in English as *The Nation* was, until Nizami's death in 2015, known for its anti-India, pro-Islam views in a manner unusual for a national newspaper. Though Nizami was critical of Pakistan's martial law regimes, he remained on friendly terms with figures such as Ayub Khan and Zia-ul Haq.

5 / Modern/Mecca: Populist Piety in the Contemporary Urdu Novel

1. Umera Ahmad, Introduction to *Mein nē Khvābōñ Kā Shajar Dēkhā* (Lahore: Ilm-o Irfan Publishers, 2016), 9.
2. I owe much of my basic conceptualization of right-wing populism to Jan Werner-Muller's recent book, *What Is Populism?* (Philadelphia: University of Pennsylvania Press, 2016). Also, worth perusing is Ayesha Jalal's chapter on South Asian populism of the 1970s in her book *Democracy and Authoritarianism in South Asia: A Comparative and Historical Perspective* (Cambridge: Cambridge University Press, 1995). Though bearing many of the markers Werner-Muller highlights, the populist movements of the 1970s in India and Pakistan did not take religion as the central point of departure.
3. Aamir Mufti, *Forget English: Orientalisms and World Literatures* (Cambridge: Harvard University Press, 2016), 177.
4. Ibid.
5. Once again, Abbas's study of Lela Aboulela's novels is helpful. Also helpful is revisiting Edward Said's *Culture and Imperialism* (New York: Random House, 1994), the first two chapters of which offer a powerful historical elaboration of the novel

form and its inseparability from the national project. While many of the markers and historical functions that Said outlines echo powerfully in this context as well, I am hesitant to appropriate and apply one context to another one.

6. Saba Mahmood, *Politics of Piety: Islamic Revival and the Feminist Subject* (Princeton: Princeton University Press, 2011), 3.

7. Ibid.

8. Gauri Viswanathan, *Outside the Fold: Conversion, Modernity and Belief* (Princeton: Princeton University Press, 1998), 52–53.

9. Ibid., 87.

10. Ibid., xvii.

11. I am aware of Talal Asad's formulation of Islam as a "discursive tradition" in his essay "The Idea of an Anthropology of Islam." Asad describes this discursive tradition as one where past and present go hand in hand in determining a path for the future. Mahmood also turns to Asad's formulation in *Politics of Piety*, where she describes the subjects of her study as understanding their religious activities as reviving and reclaiming Islam's exemplary past. Given the broader contexts of the novels I examine, I find Asad's and Mahmood's understanding insufficient. In particular, neither admits to the invention of the non-Muslim as a deliberate "other" that conversion necessarily causes. Likewise, Asad's abstraction and Mahmood's insistence on the subject as an individual eludes the historic, particularly imperially mediated, processes and structures through which a claim to the past is made. See Asad, "The Idea of an Anthropology of Islam," *Qui Parle* 17, no. 2 (Spring/Summer 2009): 1–30, and Mahmood, *Politics of Piety*.

12. Muhammad Asad, *Road to Mecca* (Kuala Lumpur: Islamic Book Trust, 1996), 141.

13. Ibid.

14. Ibid., 346.

15. Ibid.

16. Ibid., 347.

17. Ibid., 308.

18. Most of these events go unnoticed by Western media and consumers of news on Pakistan because they do not take the shape of bombings or offer sensationalism. To find out more about the question of the Ahmadis in Pakistan, see Ali Usman Qasmi, *The Ahmadis and the Politics of Religious Exclusion in Pakistan* (Delhi: Anthem Press, 2014), and Sadia Saeed, *Politics of Desecularization: Law and the Minority Question in Pakistan* (New York: Cambridge University Press, 2016). Little has been written on the scholarly front about the *culture* surrounding Islamic radicalism in Pakistan, but to understand its quotidian nature, see op-eds and essays by the novelist Muhammed Hanif, including "How to Commit Blasphemy in Pakistan," *Guardian*, September 5, 2012, and "Pakistan's Unnecessary Martyrs," *The New York Times*, January 22, 2016. For more on the religious education of women, see Sadaf Ahmad, *Transforming Faith: The Story of Al-Huda and Islamic Revivalism among Urban Pakistani Women* (Syracuse: Syracuse University Press, 2009), and Ammara Maqsood, *The New Pakistani Middle Class* (Cambridge: Harvard University Press, 2017).

19. See Partha Chatterjee, *Nationalist Thought and the Colonial World: A Derivative Discourse* (Minneapolis: University of Minnesota Press, 2008).

20. Arendt argues that the state and the nation are essentially at odds with one another, the former derived from "centuries of monarchy and enlightened despotism," but open to "all inhabitants in its territory," while the latter demands

that the state "recognize only 'nationals' as citizens," and "grant full civil and political rights only to those who belonged to the national community by right of origin." See Hannah Arendt, *The Origins of Totalitarianism* (New York: Schocken Books, 2004), 296.

21. Mahmood, *Politics of Piety*, 189.

22. Sadia Abbas, *At Freedom's Limit: Islam and the Postcolonial Predicament* (New York: Fordham University Press, 2014), 93.

23. Maleeha Hamid Siddiqui, "Profile of Farhat Ishtiaq: The Queen of Love," *Dawn*, July 7, 2012 (https://www.dawn.com/news/1023018).

24. For more detail on the politics of television programming in 1990s Pakistan, see Steven Barraclough, "Pakistani Television Politics in the 1990s," *Gazette* Vol. 63 (2002): 225–39.

25. See, for example, Sabahat Zakariya, "Drama Serials: Golden Age?" *Dawn*, March 3, 2012 (https://www.dawn.com/news/699862); and Amna Yaqeen, "Pakistan's Love Affair with *Humsafar*," January 22, 2017 (http://www.dailypioneer.com/sunday-edition/agenda/cover-story/pakistans-love-affair-with-humsafar.html).

26. Jennifer Dubrow, *Cosmopolitan Dreams: The Making of Modern Urdu Literary Culture in South Asia* (Honolulu: University of Hawaii Press, 2018).

27. Farhat Ishtiaq, *Humsafar* (Lahore: Ilm-o Irfan Publishers, 2012), 9.

28. Ibid., 11.

29. Ibid., 12.

30. Ibid., 49.

31. On a basic plot level, *Humsafar* resonates with English novels such as Samuel Richardson's *Pamela* or Charlotte Bronte's *Jane Eyre*: The poor, genteel heroine charms her wealthy master (or in this case, cousin), whose character is utterly reformed by the romantic encounter. But as I suggest, the *politics* of this novel, like others of its generation, are in many ways beyond the pale of the national.

32. Ishtiaq, *Humsafar*, 49.

33. Ibid., 50.

34. Ibid., 221.

35. Non-profit organizations are viewed with great suspicion in Pakistan for advocating measures such as contraception, vaccinations, and women's education. Under the current PTI government, a right-wing populist regime, a number of well-reputed NGOs have been expelled from the country.

36. Ishtiaq, *Humsafar*, 232.

37. Ibid., 280.

38. Ibid., 285.

39. Ibid., 80.

40. Ibid., 317.

41. Ibid., 221.

42. Ibid., 320.

43. Ibid.

44. An excellent critique of *Zindagi Gulzar Hai* can be found on the well-known South Asia blog Chapatti Mystery.

45. Ahmad, "Shehr-e Zāt," in *Mein nē Khvābōñ Kā Shajar Dēkhā*, 46.

46. Ibid.

47. Nazir Ahmad, as Faisal Devji points out, gave new meaning to the idea of *tarbiyat* in *Taubat an-Nasūh*. Once mostly to do with the shaping of temperament

and morals through parental nurturing, the word takes on religious weight in the nineteenth century and begins to imply a parental duty to improve the morals, reform the characters, and guide the religious beliefs of their children. See Faisal Devji, "The Equivocal History of a Muslim Reformation," in *Islamic Reform in South Asia*, ed. Filipo Ossella and Caroline Ossella (Cambridge: Cambridge University Press, 2014), 16.

48. Ahmad, "Shehr-e Zāt," 45.
49. Ibid., 59.
50. Ibid., 65.
51. Ibid., 71.
52. Ibid., 78.
53. Ibid.
54. The Quran 7:22
55. Nimra Ahmad, *Jannat kē Patē*, Vol. 1 (Lahore: 'Ilm-o Irfan Publishers, 2013), 5.
56. Ibid.
57. Ibid.
58. Ibid., 24.
59. Ibid., 26.
60. Ibid., 112.
61. Ibid., 115.
62. Ibid., 65.
63. Ibid., 179.
64. Ibid., 220.
65. Ibid., 221.
66. Ibid.
67. Ibid., 245.
68. Ibid., 267.
69. Ibid.
70. Mahmood, *Politics of Piety*, 157.
71. Ibid., 156.
72. Ibid., 166.
73. Nimra Ahmad, *Jannat kē Patē*, Vol. 1, 269.
74. Ibid.
75. This rhetoric is not new, of course. Scholars such as Abul 'Ala Maududi have characterized Jews as a wayward people who are destined to be punished by Allah. Jews and their various sins against Islam and Muslims make frequent appearances in the religious speeches of popular figures such as Maulana Tariq Jameel, Farhat Hashmi, and Zakir Naik. It is worth noting that even in Mahmood's conversations with women of the Da'awah movement, Christians and Westerners are marked as bad influences on Muslims.
76. Nimra Ahmad, *Jannat kē Patē*, Vol. 2, 26.
77. Ibid., 151.
78. Ibid., 64.
79. Ibid., 281.
80. Ibid., 280.
81. Aamir Mufti, "Why I Am Not a Postsecularist," *boundary 2*, 40, no. 2 (2013): 11.
82. Mahmood, *Politics of Piety*, 31.
83. Aamir Mufti, "Why I Am Not a Postsecularist," 11.

84. Ibid.
85. Ibid.
86. Ibid.
87. The hypocrites, for political reasons, were accepted as co-religionists in early Islam, as explained in the *Princeton Encyclopedia of Islamic Political Thought*. The onus to identify them was not put on Muhammad, but rather taken on by Allah in his role as an all-knowing body. Since then, the term has taken on a variety of meanings, and also commands particular significance in Shi'ite history. I am not here conflating the Quranic verses on actual historical beings with present-day practice, but rather, arguing that the historic term has been appropriated to designate a new enemy in Pakistan. See *The Princeton Encyclopedia of Islamic Thought* (Princeton: Princeton University Press, 2013), 228–29.
88. This hollow and publicly emphasized attachment to religious categories downplayed questions of linguistic and ethnic diversity in Pakistan from the moment of its creation, leading to massive fissures within a few decades of the new nation's founding. The 1971 creation of Bangladesh is a glaring historic example. More recent examples include the Pakistan military's brutal treatment of the Baloch people and the widespread Pashtun population. The rise of the Pashtun Tahafuz Movement in 2018 has highlighted the state-based violence and discrimination that Pashtun people have had to endure on a daily basis since 9/11.
89. The Quran 94:4.
90. Umera Ahmad, *Pīr-e Kāmil* (Lahore: Ferozsons Limited, 2005), 76.
91. Ibid., 77.
92. Ibid., 93.
93. The *kalima*, the essential tenet of belief in Islam, translates to "There is no god but Allah and Muhammad, his prophet."
94. Ahmad, *Pīr-e Kāmil*, 145.
95. Ibid., 302.
96. Ibid., 312.
97. Ibid., 330.
98. Ibid., 366.
99. Ibid., 371.
100. Ibid., 447.
101. Ibid., 488.
102. Ibid., 517.
103. Ibid., 565.
104. Ibid.
105. Bushra Rehman, *Parsa* (Lahore: Khazina 'Ilm-o Adab), 77.
106. Ibid.
107. Ibid., 76.
108. Ibid., 124.
109. Ibid., 178.
110. Ibid., 207.
111. Ibid., 222.
112. Ibid., 232.
113. Ibid., 280.
114. Ibid., 283.
115. Ibid., 294.

116. Ibid., 314.
117. Ibid., 302.
118. Ibid., 409.
119. In the television serial, Salman (or Ghazali) puts up some resistance, at one moment even slapping Maryam for suggesting the match. Maryam tells him she has checked for the legality of the match in terms of Islamic law. Eventually, he acquiesces and the two are shown getting married.

Epilogue / Us, People / People Like Us: Fehmida Riaz and a Secular Subjectivity in Urdu

1. Fahmida Riaz, *Zindā Bahār*, in *Hum Lōg* (Karachi: Oxford University Press, 2013), 20.
2. Fahmida Riaz, "Badan Darīdā," in *Badan Darīdā* (Lucknow: Shahi Press, 1978), 57.
3. Riaz, *Zindā Bahār*, 5.
4. Ibid., 6.
5. Ibid., 5.
6. Mufti, "Auerbach in Istanbul: Edward Said, Secular Criticism and the Question of Minority Culture," *Critical Inquiry* 25, no. 1, 105.
7. Riaz, *Zindā Bahār*, 8.
8. Ibid.
9. Ibid., 20.
10. Said, "Secular Criticism," in *The World, the Text, and the Critic* (Cambridge: Harvard University Press, 1983), 29.
11. Riaz, *Zindā Bahār*, 22.
12. Ibid.
13. Ibid.
14. Ibid., 37.
15. Ibid., 39.
16. Ibid.
17. Ibid., 40.
18. Ibid., 41.
19. Ibid., 47.
20. Ibid., 48.
21. In a personal conversation with the author, Syed mentions telling Riaz how much he loved the name of the street, as well as of a famous shrine in the area.
22. Ibid., 60.
23. Ibid., 62.
24. Ibid., 63.
25. Ibid., 112.
26. Ibid.
27. Ibid., 131.

Index

adab, 9, 91, 121, 129, 144; as a practice, 19, 97, 112, 232n6; transformation into literature, 64, 113, 134–35, 165–66, 226nn18,19, 232n2
Agra College, 80–2, 237n111
Ahmad, Nazir (Deputy), 8, 13, 19, 90–91, 93, 98, 100, 105, 107–10, 115, 117, 119, 123–25, 127, 133–34, 137, 139, 141–42, 168, 181, 251n47. See also *Mirāt al-'Arūs*
Ahmad, Nimra, 15, 20, 165, 168, 171, 174, 180, 184–85, 190, 194. See also *Jannat kē Patē*
Ahmad, Umera, 8, 13, 15, 20, 165, 171–72, 174, 180–81, 185, 190–91, 194–95; idea of Pakistani literature, 165, 181, 195. See also *Pīr-e Kāmil*; *Shehr-e Zāt*
Ahmed, Shahab, 1–2, 15, 99, 228n19, 233n12, 241n46; on modern Islam, 15; *What is Islam?*, 1–2, 99, 228n19, 241n46
Allen, Michael, 9–10, 226n18
Amman, Mir, 13, 65–73, 76–77, 83–84, 94, 111; *munshī* in Fort William College, 13, 65–67, 111. See also *Bāġh-o Bahār*
Arabian Nights' Entertainments, 18, 21, 23, 26, 31–35, 39, 41, 43, 46, 48, 66, 68–69, 83–84, 96, 230n39; frame tale in, 31, 34–36, 95, 97; Haroun al-Rashid in, 31, 38–39, 41, 43–44, 46–47, 49; Scheherazade's role in, 27, 35–38, 97–98; Sindbad stories, 31, 38–41, 43–44, 46, 49, 52; translator's preface, 34
Aravamudan, Srinivas, 5, 23–25, 32–33, 45, 65
Asad, Muhammad, 170–71, 242n63
Asiatick Society, 54, 61

Bāġh-o Bahār (Mir Amman): as adaptation or translation, 65, 81, 83, 85; history of, 67, 69, 71–72, 75–77, 80, 85–86, 94; as oriental tale, 8, 56, 66–70, 83, 95–97; as textbook, 67, 69, 81–84, 87, 111
Ballaster, Ros, 5, 23–24, 28–29, 32, 42, 46
Bernier, Francois, 46–47, 51

Colebrooke, Henry, 56, 63, 77
Conant, Martha Pike, 21–22, 24–25

Daryā-e Laṭāfat (Insha, Inshallah Khan), 68, 107
dāstān: characteristics of, 10, 57, 70, 73–76, 85, 144, 151, 185–86, 236nn77,85; at Fort William College, 71–76. See also *qiṣṣā*
Dāstān-e Amīr Ḥamzā (Ashk, Khalil Khan), 70–71, 73–76, 236n85
Delhi College, 81, 239n18, 242n77
Dharwadker, Vinay, 8
Discourses delivered before the Asiatic Society and Miscellaneous Papers on the Religion, Poetry, Literature Etc. of the Nations of India (Jones), 55, 61

education (colonial), 54, 56, 63, 66, 76–80, 82, 86–87, 91–92, 109, 111, 140, 236n92, 239n18, 241n51; Ballantyne, James, 81; Charter Act of 1813, 78; Forbes, Duncan, 77, 84–85, 237n126; Hunter, William W., 87; Muir, William, 81, 87, 93, 101–2, 104; Prinsep, James, 80; Smith, Lewis Ferdinand, 83–88; Sutherland, J. C., 80. *See also* Agra College; Delhi College

INDEX

Faruqi, Shamsur Rehman, 12, 67, 75, 234nn38,46, 235n58, 236n85
Fasānā-e 'Ajā'ib (Surur), 71–73, 80, 107
Flōrā Flōrindā (Sharar), 92–93, 118, 120–23
Fort William College, 2, 5, 8–9, 13, 19, 54–58, 63–65, 67, 70–82, 85–87, 91, 93–94, 96, 101–2, 107, 111, 113, 127, 131, 139, 232n6, 234n46, 237n99

Galland, Antoine, 4, 18, 21–22, 31, 33, 94; as author of the *Arabian Nights' Entertainments*, 33–35, 38. See also *Arabian Nights' Entertainments*
Gilchrist, John, 9–10, 19, 54–58, 62–69, 73–80, 83–87, 94–95, 101, 105, 233n35, 235n58. See also Fort William College; Hindustani

Hali, Altaf Hussain, 13, 18–19, 90–91, 93, 108–19, 122–25, 127, 135–36, 139, 142, 168
Hastings, Warren, 51, 54–55, 58, 62–63, 65, 232n6, 233n12
Hindustani, 19, 56–57, 63–68, 71, 73, 76–84, 94–95, 99, 234n38, 239n18
History of Nourjahad, The (Sheridan, Frances), 18, 26, 31, 36, 38, 44–46
Humsafar: novel, 171, 174–76, 179, 180, 186; television serial, 175, 181, 184

Ishtiaq, Farhat, 13, 20, 165, 171–75, 185–86. See also *Humsafar*

Jannat kē Patē, 171, 174, 180, 184–85, 189–90, 193
Jones, William, 9, 29, 42, 51, 54, 56–62, 65–66, 86, 170, 233nn10,24; *Discourses delivered before the Asiatic Society and Miscellaneous Papers on the Religion, Poetry, Literature Etc. of the Nations of India*, 55, 61; ideas on Islam, 4, 19, 58, 60, 62; *Poems, Consisting Mainly of Translations from Asiatick Languages*, 55, 59–60; relationship to Sanskrit, 9, 18, 30, 55–56, 58, 61–63

Khan, Syed Ahmad, 88, 90–91, 93–94, 98–99, 105, 108–10, 114, 117, 123–24, 156, 239n17; Aligarh movement, 13, 89, 92–93, 117, 124, 239n17; *Tehzīb-ul Akhlāq*, 90, 239n12

Lal, Lalluji, 77, 84
literature, 129–31, 137, 165, 168, 190, 207, 226–27n23, 232n2, 244n6; in Hindustani, 6, 8–12, 17, 19, 54, 56–57, 65, 67, 76, 78–80, 83–84, 87, 90, 94–95, 101, 104, 106, 125–29, 135, 144, 165, 167, 238n8, 239n18; history of term, 3, 5, 8–9, 13, 55, 57, 86; orientalist invention of, 2, 5, 7, 8–10, 20, 24, 53–56, 63–64, 66, 71, 77–79, 82, 90–91, 102, 113, 135, 226n19. See also *adab*

Mahmood, Saba, 14–16, 169, 173, 186, 189–90, 193, 207, 227n27, 250n11, 252n75
Mahometan, as orientalist invention, 2, 6–7, 10, 18–20, 26–62, 64, 67, 69, 71, 76–78, 82–89, 91–92, 94–95, 97, 99, 106–8, 110, 113, 117–18, 120, 124–25, 128, 130, 132, 143, 153, 161, 172, 190, 228n18, 229n34, 230n51
Majālis un-Nissā (Hali), 92–93, 108–16, 141
Mirāt al-'Arūs (Ahmad, Nazir), 8, 91, 93–95, 98, 101–2, 104, 106, 108, 110, 113, 124, 137, 141
Mufti, Aamir, 3–5, 16, 30, 54, 58, 70, 72, 88, 126–28, 131, 168, 193, 226n19, 232n2, 245n16
Musaddas or *Mad-o Jazar Islām* (Hali), 93, 109–10, 114–16, 242n89

Nussbaum, Felicity, 5, 28, 32, 45

Oriental Fabulist, The (Gilchrist), 65, 67, 101
oriental tale, 6, 13, 18–19, 22–26, 28, 31–32, 34, 37, 39, 43, 45–46, 52–53, 55, 57, 61, 65–67, 71, 73, 75–77, 83–86, 91–92, 98, 106, 113–14, 124, 131, 138–39, 143, 148, 156, 171, 184–85, 207; the chronotope of, 26, 28–29, 35, 46, 59, 70, 82, 91, 110, 132, 228n18; definition of, 21–22, 25–26; in eighteenth-century studies, 3, 5, 10, 17–18, 23–24, 28, 30, 52–53, 56, 67; the Indic orient in, 30, 42, 47–49, 51, 61; the Mahometan or Muslim in, 7, 10, 18–19, 26, 28–29, 31–33, 35–36, 38, 40, 44, 46–47, 51, 54, 59, 82, 84, 86, 91, 92, 110, 118, 132, 143–44, 148, 156, 161, 172, 228n18; the Mahometan orient in, 26–31, 33, 69, 83, 95
orientalism, 2–3, 5–7, 16, 24, 26, 29, 30, 33, 52–53, 171, 190, 207, 210, 226n19, 228n18, 232n2; in Calcutta, 6, 10, 54–55, 58, 61–63, 84, 124, 170; definition of, 4–5; and Islam, 5, 29, 228n18. See also Fort William College; oriental tale

Pakistani television serials. See *Humsafar*; *Pārsā*; *Shehr-e Zāt*
Pārsā (novel), 174, 194, 201–6
Persian Tales (de la Croix), 18, 26–32, 40, 48, 69, 148; frame tale, 31, 35–36, 40; story of Aboulfouaris, 31, 38, 40–42, 46, 49, 51;

story of Fadlallah and Zemroude, 31, 48–49, 51, 148
Pīr-e Kāmil, 8, 174, 194–95, 201, 204
Poems, Consisting Mainly of Translations from Asiatick Languages (Jones), 55, 59
Pritchett, Frances, 67, 70–74, 81, 95, 103

qiṣṣā, 57, 67–68, 70

Rehman, Bushra, 174, 194, 201, 202, 206. See also *Pārsā*
Royal Asiatic Society, 5, 54
Rusva, Mirza Hadi, 12, 88, 125, 131

Said, Edward, 1–6, 24, 26, 28–29, 132, 207, 213, 228n19, 229n31, 249–50n5; *Culture and Imperialism*, 132, 249–50n5; *Orientalism*, 1–4, 6, 26, 28–29, 52, 207. See also orientalism
Sharar, Abdul Halim, 19, 76, 90, 92, 107, 117–20, 122–25; historical novel in Urdu, 90, 93, 118–20, 122, 125. See also *Flōrā Flōrindā*

Shehr-e Zāt, 171, 174, 180–81, 193
Surur, Rajab Ali Beg, 71–73

Taubat al-Naṣūḥ (Ahmad, Nazir), 91, 93–94, 99, 102–4, 106, 108, 110, 112–13, 116, 181, 251–52n47
Turkish Tales (de la Croix), 18, 26, 30, 32, 34, 49; frame tale, 28, 31, 36–37

Urdu: evolution of the term, 2, 56–57, 66–68, 71–72, 77, 80; *faṣāhat* as a feature of, 68, 72; Urdu novel, 15, 131–32, 164–66, 168, 171, 174, 176, 194, 207; women's digests, 154–55, 167, 174–75, 180–81, 185

Vathek (Beckford, William), 22, 37–38, 40, 48–49, 50–51
Viswanathan, Gauri, 8, 78, 169

Wellseley, Lord, 63

Zafar II, Bahadur Shah, 88

MARYAM WASIF KHAN is Associate Professor of Comparative Literary and Cultural Studies at the Mushtaq Gurmani School of Humanities and Social Sciences, LUMS University, Lahore.

www.ingramcontent.com/pod-product-compliance
Lightning Source LLC
Chambersburg PA
CBHW020106020526
44112CB00033B/1047